DEEPENING DEMOCRACY

The volume offers a glimpse of the Licence-Permit-Raid *Raj*, critiques India's farm and economic policies, highlights the new divides being created by the country's language policy, and discusses the causes and possible remedies for ethnic conflicts in India.

A common thread running through all the essays is how most of India's contemporary problems arise out of mal-governance, a choice of inappropriate policies, and a lack of accountability in government. This leads Kishwar to argue that the poor need economic freedom far more urgently than the rich, and builds up a case for a bottom-up agenda of economic reforms.

While acknowledging that the current trade regime is biased in favour of powerful industrialized nations, Kishwar points out that if India participates actively and intelligently in the WTO, this will open far-reaching opportunities for her agricultural and industrial sectors.

Dedicated to the memory of my mother and father who gave me unconditional love, respect and support in all my quests, even when I went against some of their cherished values and even when I did not have the time to show through actions how deeply I cared for them.

DEEPENING DEMOCRACY
Challenges of Governance
and Globalization in India

Madhu Purnima Kishwar

OXFORD
UNIVERSITY PRESS

OXFORD
UNIVERSITY PRESS

YMCA Library Building, Jai Singh Road, New Delhi 110 001

Oxford University Press is a department of the University of Oxford. It furthers the
University's objective of excellence in research, scholarship, and education
by publishing worldwide in

Oxford New York
Auckland Cape Town Dar es Salaam Hong Kong Karachi Kuala Lumpur
Madrid Melbourne Mexico City Nairobi New Delhi Shanghai Taipei Toronto

With offices in
Argentina Austria Brazil Chile Czech Republic France Greece Guatemala
Hungary Italy Japan Poland Portugal Singapore South Korea Switzerland
Thailand Turkey Ukraine Vietnam

Oxford is a registered trademark of Oxford University Press
in the UK and in certain other countries

Published in India by Oxford University Press, New Delhi

ISBN-13: 978-0-19-568352-3
ISBN-10: 0-19-568352-8

Typeset in AGaramond by Laser Print Craft, Delhi 110 051
Printed in India by Sai Printopack Pvt. Ltd., New Delhi 110 020
Published by Oxford University Press
YMCA Library Building, Jai Singh Road, New Delhi 110 001

Contents

Acknowledgements

This book has been made possible thanks in part to the support provided by the C.R. Parekh Fellowship for the year 2000–1.

I am thankful to my colleagues at the Centre for the Study of Developing Societies (CSDS)—especially to Dhirubhai Sheth, Ashis Nandy, Rajni Kothari and Giri Deshingkar (who is unfortunately no more)—for having invited me to join CSDS. They have provided invaluable institutional and intellectual support for my work on issues of economic and political reforms. It has been a great privilege and honour to have them as colleagues. Dhirubhai and Giri were extremely generous in providing valuable feedback on some of these essays.

My friend and colleague Berny Horowitz has been one of my toughest critics as well as among my most enduring sources of support. He helped me sharpen my focus and deal more adequately with rigorous criticism.

I owe very special thanks to the readers, friends, and supporters of *Manushi*, where most of these articles first appeared. They have nurtured *Manushi* with enormous love and care, engaged with the various issues we have raised, stood by *Manushi* even when we took stands that were not very popular, kept our morale high through years of struggle, and helped *Manushi* stay alive without any external funding or support. Writing does not come easily to me. I could not have sustained the effort that resulted in this as well as other books but for the affection and warm support of Manushi readers over the last 26 years.

I owe my biggest debt of gratitude to my parents, brothers, cousins, nephews, aunts, uncles and the rest of my family as well as numerous friends who have showered me with enormous love without making demands—except that I occasionally give them a little time to pamper me. It is their love and affection that has enabled me to go on for the last 26 years without burning out.

Last but not least I wish to convey my sincere appreciation to my editors at OUP who nagged me ever so affectionately to finish this book while I procrastinated endlessly. I feel honoured by their enthusiasm for helping see to it that my writings become more widely available.

Madhu Purnima Kishwar
March 2004

Introduction

CRISIS OF GOVERNANCE AND CHALLENGES OF GLOBALIZATION

The chapters in this volume grapple with two major themes:

1. What are the factors responsible for keeping the vast majority of Indian citizens trapped in poverty even after five-and-a-half decades of Independence? Not too long ago in history, India was known for its legendary wealth, a prosperity that incited repeated invasions. Europeans were the last wave of invaders to undertake hazardous journeys, this time across the oceans, attracted by India's exquisite luxury products and exotic spices. Yet India of the twenty-first century is lagging behind many Asian economies that were much poorer than India at the time of our Independence. Poverty in India cannot be a 'natural' condition. India has an abundance of natural resources and our people, even those who are illiterate, are innovative and industrious when they can perceive even small opportunities to earn a better living. The poor in India are neither social dropouts nor drug addicts. They are overwhelmingly self-employed, engaged in a whole range of innovative economic activities requiring extremely hard work and yet they make a poor living.

2. Why is it that our society continually witnesses deadly outbursts of ethnic conflicts and violence, despite our people having evolved fairly sophisticated norms of co-living over centuries on the strength of their traditional bonds and locally worked out consensual arrangements? Despite the fact that Jinnah's Muslim League engineered the breakaway of the Muslim majority areas in 1947 and thereafter established a theocratic regime in Pakistan, the leaders of India's freedom movement

stayed steadfast in their resolve to establish a secular, democratic Republic in India. With such an inspiring legacy, why do we continue witnessing communal polarization, riots and pogroms and increasing mistrust between the Hindus and Muslims in India?

FEELING OF COMMON DESTINY

One of the outstanding achievements of our freedom movement under the leadership of Gandhi was that people of different strata, castes, communities, regions, and economic sectors came together on a common platform with a sense of a shared mission and shared destiny to achieve certain common purposes. The rich and poor, city elite and impoverished villagers, farmers and artisans, 'upper castes' and 'lower castes' as well as people of different religious denominations and linguistic identities were brought together by Gandhi to form an effective coalition on the common platform provided by the refurbished Congress Party, whereby they could put forward their legitimate grievances and get a measure of support from each other. This sense of shared destiny could inspire millions of people only because Gandhi and many others among his colleagues made an attempt to create a broad-based consensus on important social, economic, cultural, and political issues, while ensuring that the problems of the poor and the marginalized received careful attention and historically disadvantaged groups got a special hearing.

Gandhi tried to create an atmosphere whereby a significant section of the wealthy and the relatively powerful groups began to use their clout not just for their own narrow self-interest but in favour of marginalized groups. Large sections of our people were thus able to draw strength from their traditional group identities while rising above various 'us' and 'they' divides and experience a sense of 'we' cutting across class, caste, religious and other divides. The collective energy thus generated was directed at bringing about political freedom for India without needless violence and other destructive modes of expressing people's political aspirations that have been common in many other freedom movements across the globe. Not surprisingly, many of the outstanding political leaders and statesmen and women of the twentieth century—from Nelson Mandela to Martin Luther King, to Vaclav Havel, to Aung San Suu Kyi—acknowledge that they drew inspiration from Mahatma Gandhi's leadership of the Indian freedom struggle.

In today's India that sense of shared destiny has been seriously eroded. For example, it is very common to hear upper class urbanites refer to the poor with utter contempt as though they belong to a lower species. Expressions such as, *yeh log baat se nahin samajhte, laat se hi mante hain*' (These people do not respond to verbal persuasion. They only respond to kicks), to justify all kinds of high handed actions against the poor are being given open expression in respectable circles without any embarassment. The poor are seen as a drag on our society, an embarrassment to be gotten rid of or wished out of sight. When people from impoverished farm families are forced off the land and come in search of meagre livelihoods in cities, compelled to live on footpaths and slums, the urban educated elite see them as a menace and source of urban squalor. When there is a slum clearance operation in the cities, the urban elite applauds the administration for taking a tough posture against the 'illegal encroachers' on public land. They forget that the domestic help, gardeners, chauffeurs they hire and the tailors, plumbers, electricians, auto and cycle rickshaw pullers whose services they use on a regular basis at abysmally low wage rates, all reside in these slums. They do not recognize their dependence on them despite requiring their labour in their homes and business establishments every day.

The increasing emotional gap between the urban elite and the rural population is even more glaring. It is fairly common for a national newspaper to report untimely rains in mid-April with the headline: 'Welcome showers in North India bring down temperatures'—without realizing that the mid-April showers that the urbanites welcome signify destruction of the ready to harvest crops and great economic distress for our already impoverished farmers. The urban elite often use the word *dehati* (literal meaning, 'one who resides in a village') to derisively refer to someone who is ignorant, stupid, and uncouth.

This 'us' and 'they' divide and the mindset to treat the basic survival needs of the poor with callous disregard is reflected in every aspect of our national life. City planners forget to allocate space for street vendors in their eagerness to provide fashionable malls and upmarket shopping complexes, even though street vendors are no less, if not more vital to the health of our city economy. Our planners leave no space on the city roads and on our national highways for non-motorized vehicles while spending all their energies on making high speed motorways and flyovers even though tens of crores of people have to use cycles, *rehdis*, hand carts, cycle rickshaws and other slow moving vehicles for commuting as well as carrying goods.

When middle and upper middle class families, rightly or wrongly suspect their domestic servants of having stolen something, they want the police to forget all due process and simply thrash the suspect to help them recover their goods. They would cry foul if the same treatment is meted out to one of their tribe who indulges in a big financial fraud. This growing disregard for equality before the law is the theme of several essays in this volume to show how this emotional and cultural divide is coming in the way of India's ability to move out of the poverty trap; how the growing economic divide in our country is reflected in the growing gap between rural and urban incomes and increasing disparity in the quality of life of the rich and poor in our urban areas as well.

PROMOTING DIVIDES, NOT BRIDGING THEM

Unfortunately, most of those who champion the rights of the poor and vulnerable sections are not working to bridge this divide but for further widening it. Too many of our social movement leaders and non-governmental organizations (NGOs) who work hard to bring to focus the plight of the impoverished and marginalized groups of our society seem to act out of the belief that they can safeguard the interests of poorer sections of society only by negating or undermining the legitimate interests of others.

The tendency to see all social iniquities and poverty related problems only through the prism of class struggle and to project the interests of various economic strata, as being permanently mutually hostile has remained preponderant among intellectuals and activists in India despite India's social reality being far more complex. For example, many of those attacked as rich farmers or *kulaks* earn less than a Class IV employee in a government office. A large number of them are heavily indebted farmers who can keep their farms running only by sending off one or more of their sons for extremely low paid occupations to earn cash. And yet those who organize the landless poor tend to seek all the answers to the poverty of farm labourers by whipping up sentiments against the landowning farmers leading to a zero sum game for both, rather than understand the causes of poverty of the entire farm sector which makes it impossible for impoverished farmers to pay decent wages. Similarly, many of our Left leaders have articulated the rights of industrial workers in ways that forced the closure of those industries, not realizing that ensuring economic viability and vibrancy of industries is in the long-term interests of workers that gives them relatively better bargaining power than a sick enterprise or a loss making industry.

The mutual complementarity of people in varied sectors of our economy is altogether ignored by the Leftists in their obsession to highlight their conflicts. On the other hand, those who are enamoured with the recent successes of Indian entrepreneurs in the global arena forget that 'the feel good factor' is limited to a tiny stratum at the top, and the vast majority in India are feeling excluded and bypassed because doors of opportunity are not opening up for them as well. Thus very few attempts are being made to make a more equitable distribution of resources and the provision of basic social security a social goal rather than a sectional demand.

The political parties who came to power after India achieved Independence played an active role in fragmenting our society by pitching various groups against each other, and pushed narrow, partisan and often dangerous agendas. In the process they built walls of suspicion and hostility between castes, communities, and classes while claiming that they could stand above such divisions and serve as the only viable and legitimate protectors of the rights of vulnerable groups. The adversarial relationships of labour vs capital, 'upper castes' vs 'lower castes', Hindus vs Muslims, peasants vs farm labourers insisted on the simplified rhetoric of our contesting political parties produces results that are detrimental for all. This is not to deny that there are areas of serious conflict of interests between various castes, classes, and communities that cannot be redressed without determined struggle. All I wish to emphasize is that we need to wage these struggles in ways that lead to meaningful resolution of conflicts while keeping the legitimate interests of each group in view, rather than have a vested interest in permanent simmering of hostilities.

The results are there for all to see—food producers have for long been denied remunerative prices in the name of poor consumers. They are debt-ridden and impoverished while food prices remain high enough to keep a large proportion of our population chronically malnourished. Agriculturists are put in an adversarial relationship with industries dependent on agro-produce. Farmers are projected as the primary enemies of farm labourers, just as industrial workers have been trained to see owners of industries merely as blood sucking exploiters, with the *sarkar* pretending to be the one refuge and protector of all. For example, the permanently embattled relationship between the sugar cane growers, the sugar industry and the consumers have led to increasing economic distress for farmers, distortions in the sugar manufacturing industry, high prices of sugar and regular resort to sugar imports. Similarly, instead of recognizing the inter-relatedness and complementarity of interests of cotton farmers, handloom weavers, powerloom weavers and the textile mill industry, government policies have tended to play one against the other, leading to major losses for all. On the one hand, we have for years witnessed a spate of suicides by cotton farmers due to rising debts because they could not cover the cost of production. On the other hand, the cotton yarn dependent handloom weavers are forced to abandon their occupations because they find the cost of inputs prohibitive and the prices they get for their products unremunerative, despite five decades of state 'protection' to this sector. Textile mills are also perennially sick and many have closed down due to their inability to face competition even from the local power loom sector, leave alone cheap foreign textiles that have begun flooding the Indian market. The power loom sector is also facing a grim survival struggle, though it has been able to outperform the organized mill sector mainly due to its ability to bypass most bureaucratic labour, industrial, and taxation laws by staying small, lean, unorganized, and dispersed. But trying to stay out of the account books of the government has stunted its performance as also its ability to give decent wages and working conditions for its employees.

Instead of mediating among the various economic interests and thereby facilitating the growth of productivity for all, our governments have encouraged a constant state of battle among different sectors of the economy to the detriment of each so that the state could project itself as the sole power source to resolve these disputes. In the process it came to acquire dominance over the whole society, which it uses for demanding humiliating forms of deference and vast amounts of bribes from all.

No society can make progress unless there is a deep-rooted sense of 'we' and 'us' pervading all sections of that society, even while there maybe a number of internal differences between them. No country can become economically powerful if the economic and social elites do not feel ashamed of the destitution and degradation of fellow citizens. No society has the right to be called civilized if it fails to provide a life of dignity and opportunities for advancement for all.

Societies make economic progress only when there is a degree of complementarity of interests between agriculture and industry, between wage earners and employers, between small-scale and large-scale industry, between consumers and producers—rather than where each of these sectors are locked in a permanently adversarial relationship with the others. At the same time, we need to have transparent and accountable institutions capable of providing effective and impartial conflict resolution, as and when the rights of one sector or producer are trampled upon or suppressed by the other. Our country lacks such functioning mechanisms so that conflicts keep simmering and frequently erupt in ugly and violent forms.

POLITICAL FREEDOM THRIVES WITH ECONOMIC FREEDOM

While political scientists and theorists in India have engaged extensively with the need for greater political rights and freedom, there has been far less attention paid to issues of economic freedom. Political freedom has thus been understood in a very narrow sense of free and fair elections, right to representation in political institutions and decentralization of decision-making in civic affairs through devolution of powers to state governments, *zila parishads* and *gram panchayats*. The issue of economic rights and freedoms has predominantly been viewed through the prism of class struggle, with the state being projected as the sole 'protector' of the weak and vulnerable sections of society from the greed and exploitation of the rich and powerful. The bureaucracy avidly imbibed this Nehruvian bias because it facilitated the concentration of vast, arbitrary powers in its own hands.

Neither our economists nor our political theorists have tried to come to grips with the often predatory role of the State and how it works hard to wreck people's livelihoods and their self-confidence. Without economic freedom, whatever political freedom we have, becomes an empty ritual. That is a major reason why, despite such an actively involved electorate, our political democracy remains deeply flawed and has become hostage to anti-social elements. Since our intellectuals and media remain obsessed mainly with the political and electoral dimensions of democracy, they have more or less ignored the systematic and routine loot, extortion, violence, and indignities suffered by our people as they go about perfectly legitimate economic pursuits. For example, booth capturing in some constituencies during Assembly or Lok Sabha elections becomes a big issue in media and public discourse but not the fact that our government functionaries loot through violence and criminal means, thousands of crores of rupees every day from our citizens, including the poorest, by way of bribes. Even beggars are forced to cough up a good part of what they get to the police and other *sarkari* agents.

The diagnostic failures of the Left in India and its tendency to see all economic conflicts as a sign of the imminent radicalization of the working masses and as a necessary step towards preparing them to take over political power have led to disastrous tragedies for the very people they claim to represent in different parts of the country. During the freedom movement, Mahatma Gandhi's attempts at defending the carefully circumscribed legitimate interests of Indian industrialists and farmers were dubbed as a sell-out to bourgeois-landlord interests, even though Gandhi, more than any one else, was committed to strengthening the rights of the poor and the weak. After Independence, the orthodox Left parties worked hard to curb Indian entrepreneurial genius through collaborating with the bureaucracy in building draconian and stultifying statist controls over agriculture, industry and every other arena of economic activity, thus preventing the people of our country from generating employment and wealth through honest endeavour. Sadly all this was done in the name of safeguarding the interests of the poor. They opposed the interests of the Indian industrialists when the Indian business classes genuinely needed protection from the onslaughts of colonial policies. But today, when a broad-based consensus is emerging even among industrialists in India that in the name of 'protection' the business classes have been prevented from acquiring a competitive edge due to excessive government controls, many of the Left intellectuals have turned out to be champions of protectionism for inefficient Indian industries and in favour of the bureaucracy retaining tight controls over the economy.

Opponents of Reforms Find a New Alibi

Ever since the economic stagnation, the growing fiscal deficit and debt burden of India forced those in power to initiate a half-hearted agenda of economic reforms in 1991, many of those who have traditionally projected themselves as representing the interests of the rural and urban poor have dubbed the reforms a sell-out to Multinational Corporations (MNCs) and other devious foreign interests who are seen as subverting India's economic and political autonomy. They attribute most of our present day problems and social evils to the increasing spread of consumer culture and attempts at opening of the Indian economy to global competition. The increase in sexual violence, wife murders, escalating dowries, corruption, female foeticide, declining sex ratio, increasing crime rate in our society, the impoverished condition and indebtedness of our farmers, failure of crops due to poor quality pesticides, the growing frustration of millions of unemployed youth in India—all these and more are projected as inevitable outcomes of the process of globalization and the accompanying economic reforms in India. (For a critique of this position see the chapter: 'A Half Step Forward: The Thwarting of Economic Reforms in India'.)

Till about the 1980s organized Left parties and intellectuals were seen as the main representatives of the working classes and rural poor. They exercised tremendous ideological influence in imposing a restrictive environment for economic activities. They were the prime supporters of a closed-door economy and statist controls. However, in the last two decades that space has increasingly come to be shared by a certain category of NGOs that specialize in whipping up frenzied campaigns against liberalization of the Indian economy for which generous political and monetary support is available from certain Western donor agencies that work in close collaboration with their respective governments. According to government sources, the NGO sector received $3 billion in 2003 from various foreign sources. A substantial part of these funds are going to what I call, the Anti-Globalization Brigades (AGBs).

With these fabulous grants, AGBs among the NGOs are forever jet-setting from one exotic destination to another preaching to each other and friendly journalists about the need to protect our people from the evil ways of the West by keeping our country insulated from the global economy and the evil influences of western culture. They seldom bother to explain how any economy can be kept 'closed-door' without a draconian bureaucracy and police establishment to prevent the flow of goods and capital from one country to another. They generate the politics of emotive outbursts and think it can be a substitute for meaningful analysis of social and economic problems and finding ways to set things right. For decades the mantra-chanting Leftists immobilized idealistic young people by telling them that no social problem could be solved without the workers of the world uniting under the 'red flag' to defeat the forces of world capitalism and capture state power. They actively discouraged their followers from finding concrete solutions to concrete problems and made rabble-rousing a substitute for all political activity. That fantasy never materialized because the working class refused to fall in line. Thereafter, some of these disoriented Leftists have reinvented their politics and are now calling upon the NGOs of the world to unite under the aegis of the

World Social Forum (WSF) with generous grants from aid organizations, and the governments of 'capitalist–imperialist' countries to defeat the forces of globalization! Once again they seek to channel the idealism of many dedicated young people towards bloated rhetoric so that they keep away from creative engagement with concrete problems in order to find workable solutions. Fortunately, many sincere and creative NGO activists, including many of those that attended the WSF, know the futility of such empty sloganeering and instead prefer to engage in constructive activities that actually empower marginalized communities so that they can effectively resist being trampled upon. Unfortunately, the many sane voices of such NGOs are drowned in the din and noise made by AGBs.

The entire thrust of AGB politics is to internationalize every local problem that comes to their notice. When there is a riot in Uttar Pradesh or Gujarat, many of them run to European capitals to give fiery speeches on human rights violations instead of being on the scene to protect those under attack or organize relief for them. They want global networks for themselves but insist the rest of us must live like frogs in a well and not be corrupted by the evil ways of the West. They often buy their cheese and chocolates from Switzerland and France but if they see Indian villagers buy a box of *desi* Brittannia cheese or Amul chocolates or a packet of cheap Maggi noodles, they begin to have fits of anxiety over the increasing hold of the decadent consumer culture of the West among Indians.

Since Arundhati Roy has emerged as the most celebrated pamphleteer of India's AGBs, I would like to illustrate the basic features of this worldview by quoting from a speech delivered by her at the WSF meeting in Brazil in 2002.* This represents in a very condensed and accurate form all the key diagnostic clichés offered by this articulate group of our *samajik neem hakims* (quack social scientists) to explain what ails our politics and economy.

India—the world's biggest democracy—is currently at the forefront of the corporate globalization project. Its 'market' of one billion people is being prised open by the WTO. Corporatisation and privatization are being welcomed by the government and the Indian elite. It is not a coincidence that the Prime Minister, the Home Minister, the Disinvestment Minister—the men who signed the deal

*http://www.sustecweb.co.uk.

with Enron in India, the men who are selling the country's infrastructure to corporate multinationals, the men who want to privatize water, electricity, oil, coal, steel, health, education and telecommunication—are all members or admirers of the RSS... a right wing, ultra-nationalist Hindu guild, which has openly admired Hitler and his methods. The dismantling of democracy is proceeding with the speed and efficiency of a Structural Adjustment Programme. While the project of corporate globalization rips through people's lives in India, massive privatization, and labour "reforms" are pushing people off their land and out of their jobs. Hundreds of impoverished farmers are committing suicide by consuming pesticide. Reports of starvation deaths are coming in from all over the country.

The two arms of the Indian government have evolved the perfect pincer action. While one arm is busy selling India off in chunks, the other, to divert attention, is orchestrating a howling, baying chorus of Hindu nationalism and religious fascism. It is conducting nuclear tests, rewriting history books, burning churches, and demolishing mosques. Censorship, surveillance, the suspension of civil liberties and human rights, the definition of who is an Indian citizen and who is not, particularly with regard to religious minorities, is becoming common practice now. Since the Indian "market" is open to global investors—the massacre is not even an embarrassing inconvenience... All this to say that it is a myth that the free market breaks down national barriers. The free market does not threaten national sovereignty, it undermines democracy. As the disparity between the rich and the poor grows, the fight to corner resources is intensifying. To push through their "sweetheart deals," to corporatize the crops we grow, the water we drink, the air we breathe, and the dreams we dream, corporate globalization needs an international confederation of loyal, corrupt, authoritarian governments in poorer countries to push through unpopular reforms and quell the mutinies.... The corporate revolution will collapse if we refuse to buy what they are selling—their ideas, their version of history, their wars, their weapons, their notion of inevitability. Remember this: We be many and they be few. They need us more than we need them.

Ms Roy gave concrete shape to her crusade against MNCs at the WSF meet in January 2004 held in Mumbai by giving a call to the AGBs to target two MNCs involved in Iraq for boycott of their goods in order to drive them out of business. The farcical nature of their boycott is evident from the fact that the previous year the AGBs had issued a similar call against American imperialism by pasting stickers and posters, mainly in and outside their own offices asking people to boycott McDonalds, Pepsi, and Coke. These three companies producing junk food and drinks undoubtedly make for easy and culturally compelling targets but certainly do not represent the full and real might of the imperialist West. If the AGBs are truly anti-globalization, why not include a boycott of foreign consultancies, foreign aid money, foreign TV channels, publishers, Nokia cellphones, IBM computers, Internet services, Suzuki, Honda or Ford cars, fax machines, Sony TVs, and DVDs as well as the aeroplanes they ride while continuously globe trotting? Could it be that they really have not understood that microchips are the real symbols and enablers of globalization—not potato chips!

EXERCISE IN SELF-DECEPTION

The anti-West outbursts of Ms Roy and others that have unfortunately come to dominate the WSF, drowning the voices of many genuine NGOs doing genuine work, remind me of a similar spectacle of self-deception in the form of a Swadeshi Mela organized at Pragati Maidan in 1999 by the Swadeshi Jagran Manch (SJM). The idea was to make a case against integrating India into the world economy by showcasing the supposed superiority of India's indigenous industrial sector.

As one entered the exhibition venue, one was greeted by Bisleri and Pepsi kiosks—both products of multinational soft drink giants. The bulk of the stalls at the Swadeshi Mela were a lacklustre display of several loss-making Public Sector Undertakings (PSUs) who had been coerced into participating and paying exorbitant fees for exhibiting their 'achievements'. Our private sector is often ridiculed for providing shoddy imitations of western goods with outdated western technology. But at least the private sector industrialist makes profits for his company. By contrast, the PSU stalwarts have drained the taxpayer's money and made their companies bankrupt. And yet these relics of the Nehruvian socialist past, which they themselves never tire of deriding, were put on display as symbols of India's economic power and resolve to challenge the might of MNCs.

The only pitiful proofs of India's swadeshi industrial genius were pathetic little stalls selling pickles, poorly packed herbal shampoos, small snacks, and spices made by housewives looking for a side income and, of course, handmade textiles, and other crafts made by our impoverished artisans. One was left wondering: Is this all the weaponry we have to take on the might of the industrial West? A furniture company occupied pride of place in the centre of the big hall where this swadeshi fantasy had been laid out. It had displayed the most garish and vulgar furniture—a cheap imitation of western sofas and dining tables of the kind you would see on the film set of a D grade Bollywood film, depicting the lifestyles of underworld dons. As if that was not farcical enough, the furniture company had a big, prominent board kept in the midst of red and purple velvety sofas which proudly proclaimed: 'Made with 100 per cent Imported Materials!'

There is something similarly comic about representatives of the AGBs warning us about the evils of globalization despite their own politics being altogether dependent on international aid money. They should take their swadeshi fantasies to their logical conclusion by putting up a signboard outside their mega-shows saying: 'Our *Swadeshi* Politics is Manufactured with 100 Percent *Videshi* Aid Money!'

Basic Flaws in AGB's Diagnosis

There are basic flaws in the way the AGB diagnoses India's problems:
  (i) In the AGB's worldview, globalization = privatization = selling off India's assets to some evil marauders. All this is ostensibly carried out by the RSS and other rightwing members of the 'evil' Hindu guild who are Hitlerian fascists out to muzzle the free press and trample underfoot the rights of the poor and marginalized groups. The AGB has hallucinated itself into believing that the opening up of the Indian economy is due to the evil designs of the BJP–RSS combine. The truth is that the position of the RSS outfit, Swadeshi Jagran Manch, on globalization is in fact identical to that of most AGBs. The BJP position is much closer to that of the Congress Party of the late 1980s and early 1990s. Rajiv Gandhi was the first politician to have astutely sensed the need to open up the Indian economy but was successfully thwarted by his own partymen due to inexperience. Therefore, it fell upon Narasimha Rao to give the reform process a major thrust. Erstwhile Prime Minister Atal Behari Vajpayee of the BJP wanted to carry forward the process of economic reforms set into motion by the Congress Party but

was obstructed in his endeavours by influential elements in his own Party, as well as other outfits of the Sangh Parivar who share many of the anti-globalizers' phobic fantasies.

(ii) In their zeal to prove an integral connection between a 'sell-out' to MNCs and communal violence, the AGBs attribute corrupt deals like the one signed with Enron to the BJP regime. In actual fact, the Congress government first signed the deal with Enron. It came to be undone during the BJP regime, not so much by design but by a series of unpredictable events.

(iii) The AGBs have deluded themselves into believing that the forces behind the opening up of the Indian economy are undermining democracy, promoting rabid kinds of censorship leading to a Hitlerian brand of politics. Facts tell a contrary tale. The closed-door economy was synonymous with state controlled servile television and radio, a regime of government controlled paper quotas for newspapers which, along with government's patronage through release of advertisements to sycophants, were used as powerful instruments to coerce newspaper establishments into playing a game of cautious servility. Today we have dozens of private news channels including some foreign TV channels beaming less censored news to our homes than was ever possible in the heydays of state-monopolized TV. Easy access to the internet has made censorship much more difficult. The kind of well-deserved outrage expressed by our newspapers towards the Gujarat government following the riots of 2002 should be compared to the tame newspaper coverage of similar riots of the 1980s or human rights violations in the Northeast during the euphoric days of the closed-door economy when *sarkari* press releases were the stuff news of such incidents was largely based on. The draconian clampdown on the press during the Emergency was not only a sign of political authoritarianism but also a denial of economic freedom to many segments of society, especially the peasantry. Not surprisingly, the toughest challenge to the Emergency came from Punjab farmers led by the Akali Dal who had been fighting against the policy of compulsory procurement of wheat by the government at officially controlled prices. *Shahidi Jathas* of Akalis courted arrest every single day of the Emergency period to protest against lack of economic liberty and muzzling of political freedom, with thousands filling government jails.

(iv) The worst communal outbursts and riots in post-Independence India took place during the 1970s, 1980s, and early 1990s before India began opening up to global markets. During the same period most of the border states witnessed secessionist movements involving virulent popular upsurges. Chief Ministers of almost all states in India were involved in constant battles with the Centre over issues of regional autonomy.

(v) The secessionist upsurge in Punjab and the consequent Hindu–Sikh conflict of the 1980s and 1990s were settled in the post-reforms period. In the Punjab there is even a BJP–Akali Dal alliance signifying the return of pragmatic alliances between Hindus and Sikhs. The BJP led government initiated serious measures to bring peace with dignity in the perennially troubled Northeastern States, including Nagaland that had given rise to the longest and bloodiest secessionist movement in India. The BJP also ensured that Kashmir witnessed a free and basically fair election in October 2002. The popularly elected government started to be successful in restoring the estranged Kashmiri people's faith in India's secularism and its capacity to satisfy their legitimate political aspirations within a democratic framework. The BJP government began a dialogue with the Hurriyat leaders and both agreed that they should talk to each other rather than let the guns do all the talking. They made a major breakthrough in initiating a peace process and trade with Pakistan as well.* It is a fact that the hardcore *Hindutvavadis* and the Islamic *jehadis* did not make peace with this changing face of India. But their influence was substantially reduced while the moderate BJP leaders gained salience and put development issues on the forefront.

(vi) Politicians of all hues have had to learn that they cannot stay in power for long if they are openly associated with fomenting communal hatred and a fascist worldview. This has forced a sea change in the strategies (and perhaps attitudes) of several Hindu nationalist leaders ever since they came to power. They seem to

---

*All these measures have unfortunately suffered a serious setback ever since the Congress led coalition resumed power at the Centre. Kashmiris as well as Pakistanis were in an optimistic mood as long as the Vajpayee–Advani team was leading the peace process. The Congress party has set the process back with its confused and clumsy handling.

have understood that leave alone foreign investors, even the Non-Resident Indians (NRIs) or resident sons and daughters of Mother India will not invest their money in India, if there are deadly outbreaks of violence or recurring inter-community riots in the country. Political leaders such as Chandrababu Naidu of Andhra Pradesh, S.M. Krishna of Karnataka, and Buddhadeb Bhattacharya of the Marxist Communist Party (CPM) are far more vigilant that the country and their state does not get associated with caste, class or communal violence. Bhattacharya has let it be known to his CPM cadres that they cannot create law and order problems through irresponsible and violent trade unionism because he is no less keen in inviting Indian and foreign investment to his state than the BJP leaders.

(vii) As some politicians began to take economic reforms seriously, be they ideologically Left or right, they were compelled to initiate a whole series of political and administrative reforms. It is not a coincidence that Rajiv Gandhi and R.K. Hegde (erstwhile Chief Minister of Karnataka), both of whom sensed the need for economic reforms before most others, were the first ones to implement laws for devolving greater power to panchayats.

(viii) The states that are wooing capital are precisely the ones that are implementing measures for reforms in governance. By contrast, states like Bihar which have not responded to the challenges of globalization remain the poorest and their governance is in the doldrums.

(ix) A helpful outcome of a globalizing economy is that it reduces some of the top heavy powers and oppressive influence of many national governments, making the world relatively more democratic. Many countries where business communities have been freed from the clutches of insular and corrupt bureaucracies, politicians, and army generals, are more democratic today than they were when they had built high walls of protectionism. China, the former Soviet Union, Korea, Malaysia, and Indonesia have all yielded relatively more space in recent years for the voices of dissent than was available before. Even within India we have witnessed important (though not sufficient) democratic reforms in governance during the take-off period of economic reforms and India's feeble attempts to be part of the global economy than in the previous five decades. To cite just a few initiatives that are not yet effectively implemented:

(a) Enactment of the Right to Information Act at the Central level in 2002 with several regional governments passing similar laws in their respective states. The law is not radical enough and lacks teeth but represents an important breakthrough.

(b) Compulsory disclosure of assets for all those entering the electoral arena may start to bring a measure of accountability for politicians.

(c) Law for disclosure of criminal records at the time of filing nomination by candidates.

(d) Open voting for Rajya Sabha to prevent Members of Parliament (MPs) from flouting party discipline and selling their once 'secret' votes to the highest bidder among candidates.

(e) A fairly draconian law against defections to curb 'horse-trading' after elections.

(f) Some of the state governments have taken important first steps towards e-governance, including computerizing land records so that farmers can secure title documents without having to bribe and grovel before the *patwari*. Government rules and regulations are beginning to be simplified and digitalized to reduce the possibility of harassment of citizens by government officials.

(g) For the first time, corporate houses and successful entrepreneurs are taking an interest in law and order issues and beginning to exercise pressure on the government to prevent the outbreak of communal riots. Earlier, such issues were taken up only by small human rights organizations that carried relatively small influence with the government. Now that our entrepreneurs are developing global ambitions, they are anxious to make sure that there is more peace and stability in the country.

The fact that even after a decade and a half of reforms, India commands only a small proportion of world trade and is not getting the kind of foreign investments many other Asian countries are getting shows that the economy of India is still over-politicized and marred by instability, corruption, and red tape. Moreover, the infrastructure is still too poor to inspire enough confidence in investors. Despite all the hype surrounding it, there has only been a small trickle of foreign investments in India totalling no more than $3–4 billion a year as compared to $55 billion a year for China. Between 1980 and 2002, China has welcomed $336 billion in foreign investment; India received only $18 billion.

(x) AGBs happened to have only recently noticed with the excessive zeal of new converts that Indian farmers are committing suicides by consuming pesticides. Unfortunately, the debt-ridden farmers of India have been committing suicide for much longer than the anti-globalization brigade finds it convenient to remember. Till not very long ago, the landowning farmers were labelled as oppressors of the rural poor, especially if they grew cash crops. The chronic economic distress of Indian farmers did not evoke a sympathetic response among the AGBs. It was only when Western governments needed some moral arsenal to oppose globalization which is now moving in favour of Asian countries and hurting First World economies, that they made counting of the dead bodies of Third World farmers into a lucrative career option for all those willing to whip up righteous rage against a freer trade regime envisaged in principle by the World Trade Organization (WTO) and attribute every sign and symptom of economic distress to globalization. That is how the plight of Indian farmers has become a popular subject of NGO discourse. AGB narratives were hitherto confined largely to the 'oppression' inflicted by the landed peasantry on the landless wage earners.

(xi) So mesmerized are the AGBs by their own rhetoric that they fail to notice that the cotton-producing farmers of Andhra Pradesh and Maharashtra choose to commit suicide by consuming the same sub-standard pesticides they are forced to use for their crops to drive home the sad truth that the 'Made in India' poor quality pesticides are efficient in killing human beings but useless for killing pests, even while they are far more expensive than the relatively safer *videshi* pesticides, access to which has been denied to Indian farmers. This is an important reason why farmers kept losing their cotton crops and getting more and more indebted. Indian farmers did not get impoverished after the coming of the WTO or the BJP government. Theirs is a much longer history of oppression and exploitation by almost all governments in post-Independence India—whether of the left, right or centre—which devised no less devious ways than did the British, of depressing the incomes of people in the farm sector. (For a detailed analysis see the chapter 'Cutting our Own Lifeline....').

(xii) One of the big campaign points of the AGBs is that India's natural resources are being sold out to MNCs and corporate interests who are going to monopolize and commodify our forests, water and even our air, making it harder for the poor to survive. Why do they want us to forget that the State's monopoly over our natural resources has already caused deadly environmental havoc for all citizens, but especially poor rural communities? Most of them are well aware that the Indian State prevented farmers from selling their land at market prices through the use of draconian laws like the Land Acquisition Act which gave sweeping powers to force the farmers to surrender land to the government to acquire and corruptly distribute land to 'developers' at absurdly low rates. Even that pitiful compensation did not often reach the hands of uprooted farmers. Nearly 50 million people have been uprooted from their villages and rendered destitute by forcible takeover of their lands by the state in post Independence India. These lands were then handed over at dirt-cheap prices to industrialists, miners, and hoteliers or used for creating housing enclaves for the bureaucrats and other elite sections of society. Similarly the fouling of India's air and other natural resources took place much before India saw the face of MNCs. Poor people in large parts of the country have for long been forced to buy drinking water or walk long distances to fetch pitiful supplies of water so polluted as to be unfit even for animals. All this had happened much before international corporations came into the picture.

(xiii) Those who are today breast-beating about *videshi* MNCs like Coca Cola destroying our water sources by pouring chemical pollutants into ground water or rivers, would do well to remember that all of us *desis* are also allowing the sewage from our toilets and industrial wastes from our *swadeshi* industry, including petty production units situated in our city slums, to poison our river systems and ground water supplies. We would also do well to remember that the *desi* pesticides produced by government-controlled factories have made India's farm produce far more dangerously polluted food with deadly chemicals than any food produced by First World MNCs.

There is no denying that many MNCs indulge in unethical practices and behave like marauders in poorer countries. However, the conduct of MNCs or for that matter even small business establishments and petty shopkeepers depends on the quality of regulatory mechanisms institutionalized in each country and the effectiveness of the legal system in providing sure and speedy redressal when the legitimate rights of citizens are being violated through unethical business practices. Societies that have effective and transparent mechanisms to impose punitive measures for wrong practices in business are able to enforce a sense of responsibility for both big and small market players. The chapter 'Yours Nationally' may appear a light hearted satire but it is meant to be a serious critique of all those who in their zeal to attack MNCs would like us to overlook the fact that several companies get away with gross negligence only because our politicians and bureaucrats do not ensure accountability and ethical business practices. A government, whose various arms are actively violating the rights of its own citizens or helping internal anti-social elements to dominate political and economic life, cannot be an effective instrument for protecting our people from the greed and rapacity of outsiders. A government like ours that cannot prevent state owned industries from poisoning air and water sources is not likely to be able to enforce high standards on private industry—be it *desi* or *videshi*.

ALL IN ONE MESSY BAG

An additional problem with the AGBs politics is that they put everything into one messy bag they call globalization. Opening of borders for world trade is for them the same as being servile to the International Monetary Fund (IMF) and World Bank dictates and hapless surrender of every country's intellectual property rights to rapacious MNCs. The failure of various ruling elites to provide good governance in their respective countries are also projected as part of one grand evil design through which Third World countries will be enslaved by the diabolical corporate giants in full partnership with the World Bank.

There is a world of difference between India becoming an active player in world trade and being hostage to the policies of international institutions. Well-managed economies do not have to listen to the dictates of outsiders. Only poorly functioning, troubled economies require bailouts by international donors and bankers and therefore end up subjected to such conditionalities. Those governments that have played a catalytic role in wealth generation for their people are not beholden to aid agencies and therefore cannot be coerced into following self-harming policies. Countries like China, Japan, Korea, and Taiwan, which have successfully taken on the might of First World industry and have succeeded in dramatic improvements in their national incomes, are not allowing outsiders to dictate policy.

There is not a single example in the world today of a completely closed-door economy which is also wealthy and successful. On the contrary, countries like Burma which are rich in natural resources and had relatively high standards of living a hundred years ago, have been wrecked and impoverished by their authoritarian regimes blocking economic access to the world in the same way that the Soviet rulers led their economy to collapse. It is well-known that countries open to trade and investment grow faster than those that are not. North Korea was once richer than South Korea; after 50 years of hermit economics, it is now 16 times poorer. Per capita Gross Domestic Product (GDP) fell by an average of 1.1 per cent in closed developing countries. In industrialized countries, it rose by 1.9 per cent. Not too long ago, India and China had close to the same per capita income. By 2003, China's per capita income had gone up to about US $900, roughly twice that of India. The fastest growth—at an average of 5 per cent—occurred in developing countries that had liberalized their economies. The simple fact is that the globalizers are catching up with rich countries while the non-globalizers fall further behind. As pointed out by Vikas Singh, from 1780, it took England 58 years to double its wealth. A hundred years later, a vigorously reforming Japan did it in 34 years. Another century later, South Korea achieved it in just 11 years. (*Times of India*, 17 June 2003).

No doubt, there will be some losers and victims of the globalized economy. Unfortunately, the losers will be those very countries that are saddled with tyrannical and authoritarian regimes that deny their citizens economic freedom and have prevented them from acquiring education and other skills. Countries, where bribes and pay-offs are the basis of economic decisions, where there is lack of transparency and where citizens do not have the power to call power-wielders to account, will also lose out to economic marauders in the global economy because their leaders are often too eager to shortchange their own people. This underscores the urgent need for reforms in governance rather than a closed-door economy that will only strengthen the hold of rapacious servants of the state.

The Advantages of the WTO

A great deal of the ire of the anti-reforms lobby has been focused at the economic regime being institutionalized by the World Trade Organization (WTO) which is seen as yet another First World conspiracy to enslave the economies of the poor Third World nations. The phobic propaganda being carried out against the WTO builds cleverly on the memories of colonial subjugation that India experienced when its entire economy was forced to serve the interests of the British economy.

However, the WTO, despite being an imperfect instrument and despite all its current biases in favour of trade distortions through subsidies for some agricultural products, represents a major and historic paradigm shift away from nineteenth and twentieth centuries imperial domination in world trade. This is the first time in history that we have a rule-based multi-lateral regulatory body for trade of goods and services among so many nations of the world.

A unique feature of this body is that it provides developing countries the possibility of using their numerical strengths to bring about more just terms of trade. So far, in all the decision-making bodies of the United Nations, powerful First World countries have had a disproportionate influence because they have the right to veto any decision taken, no matter how big a majority of the members have arrived at that decision. However, under the WTO regime, not even the United States (US) has the privilege of vetoing any decision, including those that go against it. This is not to deny that the US and other First World countries try their best to twist decisions in their favour, or, failing that, try to impose unfair terms of trade on poorer nations. When trade relations are carried out on a bilateral basis between a rich and a poor nation, the wealthy and powerful partner finds it far easier to arm-twist a politically and economically weak nation into accepting unfavourable terms of trade. The big difference that has come with WTO is that trade terms are not any more decided solely by bilateral arrangements but mainly through a multi-lateral forum where the rules of the game are at least in principle to be decided through consensus, where poorer countries can at least stall and obstruct unfair trade practices by effective lobbying, even if they cannot get decisions ruled in their favour expeditiously. The principle of non-discrimination writ into the WTO mandate has enormous potential for benefiting Third and Second World countries, especially if they lobby together for its implementation. When any member tries to use its economic clout to impose unfair rules on others through overt or covert means, WTO provides a forum for grievance redressal. Thus, for the first time in history, world trade is governed by clearly laid out rules, which can be changed and amended through due process, if found to be unfair or discriminatory. Unfair trade deals can be exposed through open scrutiny before the entire comity of nations, most of which have no interest in being satellite economies of a few economic powers. Moreover, internal conflict of interests between various First World economies—countries of the European Union (EU), America, Australia, and New Zealand—allows developing countries to find allies in various permutations and combinations for specific issues. They too are competing with each other and therefore, cannot act as a solid bloc. By effective lobbying, the Third and Second World countries can and have sometimes been able to muster enough clout as a collectivity, on account of their numerical advantage, to take on the might of the superpowers. It is not for nothing that the fiercely self-willed Chinese government, which has hardly ever yielded to arm-twisting by the West, has fought hard to be included as a WTO member.

As we saw at Cancun, the focus of debate has shifted from the trap of 'free trade' to 'fair trade'. Many of the WTO provisions can go in favour of poorer countries. For example, agriculture in First World countries is heavily subsidized. The US and EU together provide more than $440 billion annually by way of domestic and export subsidies to farmers. WTO mandates progressive withdrawal of agricultural subsidies and removal of tariff barriers, both of which distort market forces through political mechanisms. Even post-WTO, the US and the EU are actively resisting withdrawal of cash and other subsidies to their farmers as the farm sectors in those countries could collapse without those subsidies since it is highly capital-intensive. Further, prices of food products in all these countries are extremely low due to over-production. The subsidies are cornered mostly by the industrial-size corporate farms that have also destroyed the small and medium farmers in the US and EU. Fred Bergsten, Director of the Institute for International Economics in Washington, says: 'Our American subsidy system is a crime.' Ian Goldin, the World Bank's Vice-President for External Affairs, says, 'Reducing these subsidies and removing agricultural trade barriers is one of the most important things that rich countries can do for millions of people to escape poverty all over the world…. It's not an exaggeration to say that the rich countries' agricultural policies lead to starvation.' For example, as per the calculations of Oxfam, the US corn growers receive an effective subsidy of $145 million a year, for exporting their produce to Mexico. This amounts to more than the total household income of the 25,0000 corn farmers in Chiapas. America's lavish handout to its 25,000 politically powerful and wealthy cotton farmers comes to nearly $3 billion a year. The produce of this absurd farm economy is then dumped on world markets, harming millions of South American, African, and Asian cotton farmers by driving world prices below the cost of production. Washington is having a hard time defending a programme that costs taxpayers billions to keep in business a few corporate farmers who cannot compete with farmers of Third World countries. West Africa's Cotton Initiative has made a case that America should not only be forced to abolish its subsidies but also be made to compensate poor cotton-producing nations harmed by these subsidies. Since Europeans do not produce cotton, they too supported the Africans. The US delegation was clearly put on the defensive and began proposing 'a grandiose but vague plan' to support the African cotton textile industries, much to the amusement of the African delegation.

As per a recent estimate by the World Bank, scrapping farm protection and output subsidies in rich countries would boost global agricultural production by 17 per cent, adding $60 billion a year, to the rural incomes of low and middle-income states. This could yield gains of $2.8 trillion by 2015, of which $1.5 trillion would go to developing countries. A white paper by the British government on globalization states that a 50 per cent reduction of import duties in industrialized and developing countries would add about $150 billion to the national incomes of poor countries.

As per a *New York Times* report (9 September 2003), in the past decade, industrial-scale farmers in the US have tipped their allegiances decisively towards the Republican Party, which supports the current system of subsidies. No wonder, political contributions from agribusiness jumped from $37 million in 1992 to $53 million in 2002, with the Republicans' share rising from 56 per cent to 72 per cent, according to figures compiled by the Center for Responsive Politics. The subsidies let the big farms get bigger and control markets around the world. Not surprisingly, they are willing to pay such hefty bribes by way of party donations to their political allies for distorting world trade and carry out a price war against the farmers of poorer countries using the political clout of their governments.

Our farmers, on the other hand, have borne the brunt of artificially depressed prices leading to negative subsidies. Negative subsidy is calculated as the difference between the price at which farmers of a country are compelled to sell their produce due to denial of market access and the prevailing international price of that commodity. Indian farmers are likely to be net beneficiaries because their produce would have a price advantage in the international market if First World subsidies are abolished and if they have access to the necessary infrastructure by way of irrigation, safe fertilizers and good roads for efficient transportation of produce and safe storage facilities. It is unfortunate that many of our bureaucrats and politicians have been slow at learning the art of negotiating advantageous deals for India in international trade negotiations. For decades they were not called upon to develop the requisite knowledge and skills and often allowed corrupt considerations to influence their decisions. For example, the WTO regime expected a slow and phased reduction in tariffs and opening up closed-door economies to imports. Our policy-makers went too fast on some imports, especially in agriculture, while they did little to encourage and enable India's exports. To give just one typical example: while exports of Indian fruit grew by 14 per cent in 2002-3, fruit imports grew at 58 per cent during the same period. The US, Australia, China and some other nations disallow Indian fruits such as mango on many a flimsy ground, including the fear that these could be carriers of dangerous pests. But India had no laws to protect its farmers against a flood of foreign fruit eating into the market of local growers as well as the possibility of harmful pests coming in with foreign farm products. When it was found that a mysterious disease destroyed most of the apple crop in Himachal Pradesh in 2003 and an alien pest has struck coconut farms for the last two years, some reactive remedial measures were announced as late as January 2004, to put similar curbs on fruit imports as India has faced with fruit exports. This too was done without proper inspection mechanisms in place.

However, in a few instances where our policy-makers did proper homework and went prepared to battle their case on merit, they have succeeded in getting WTO verdicts in India's favour. The recent moves by the Indian government to forge an alliance with China and the Cairns group of countries at the Cancun meet to lobby that EU and the US play by the WTO rules and cut down their agricultural subsidies and allow market access to developing countries have the potential to bring enormous openings for farmers of Indian and other developing countries. Asian and African delegations were delighted at getting a good hearing at the WTO trade talks where a large coalition of countries successfully prevented the US from getting WTO's stamp of approval for its unfair trade policies.*

WEST DISCOVERS THE EVILS OF GLOBALIZATION SO LATE!

It cannot be a coincidence that a strong movement against globalization and multinationals began to emerge in the West only in the last decade when the following new developments began to get consolidated:

(i) The WTO regime added to the clout of Second and Third World economies by giving them the possibility of influencing decisions and seeking a level playing field. Many decisions on trade-related disputes have gone in favour of the developing world and against the attempts of First World countries' imposing unfair terms on the former.

(ii) Multinational Corporations began shifting their manufacturing base to Asian countries in a big way, leading to flight of capital and job losses in First World countries. The fact that many MNCs owe little or no loyalty to nation-states and move to whichever countries they find profitable to operate from, has earned them the wrath of western professionals and trade union leaders who derogatively refer to them as 'footloose' companies.

(iii) There was no comparable criticism of MNCs as long as they merely sought export markets in Second and Third World countries. Dumping of MNC goods is beneficial for First World economies if the MNCs are based in the First World. However, ever since the MNCs started shifting their manufacturing base resulting in the flooding of western markets with 'Made in Korea', 'Made in China' or 'Made in Mexico' labels, there is legitimate panic in the First World against this reversal in the flow of goods and money.

(iv) While Asian countries are actively wooing MNC investments, the MNCs are facing harsh criticism by people of the very countries that gave them birth. If the MNCs were indeed as evil as they are being projected to be, then the First World anti-

---

*Further gains were made at the 2004 WTO meet at Geneva where EU and the US were forced to agree to phasing out $440 billion annual domestic and export subsidies. In addition, developing countries will get somewhat better market access in western countries.

MNC radicals should be glad to be rid of them. The fact is that they are upset at their mobility and refusal to be bound down by national loyalties.

(v) This is not to deny that many MNCs, especially those involved in defence production or construction activities, stay loyal to the governments of mother countries because they require and use the political clout of their governments to get business deals. But most MNCs do not act at the behest of the White House in Washington especially when their profits are outside of the country and their home government's policy goes contrary to their corporate interests. Witness how the American and West European governments are battling to force a sense of economic loyalty in their MNCs towards some of their respective mother countries. For example, on 23 January 2004 the US Senate passed a law barring American MNCs from sub-contracting to non-Americans the work given to them by the American government, all because of the fear of job losses in America. The very fact that special laws need to be passed shows that a significant proportion of MNCs are not voluntarily complying with the demands of the American government because they realize that if they listen to such governmental dictates, they will not be able to compete with their rivals globally. Therefore, MNCs are battling against their respective governments to allow them to outsource contracts as well as recruit the required human labour power from other countries. Such ongoing battles between First World governments and First World MNCs have provided unique openings and opportunities for countries like India.

(vi) The panic in First World countries is compounded by the fact that several of the Asian economies, including India, which began by inviting MNC investments, have generated enough wealth and expertise to start their own MNCs. These Asian MNCs are starting to give a genuine run for their money to western MNCs in many manufacturing activities barring defence equipment, which is still a western monopoly. China alone now produces 50 per cent of the world's cameras, 30 per cent of the air conditioners and televisions, 25 per cent of the washing machines, 20 per cent of the refrigerators and 80 per cent of the world's toys. Today, China's annual exports are over $ 266 billion compared to $ 62 billion in 1990.

(vii) The EU and US governments are very worried that if they are compelled to withdraw the $440 billion annual subsidy currently being given to their farmers, their respective farm sectors will simply collapse. By contrast, farmers of countries like India which have borne the brunt of negative subsidies and artificially depressed, bureaucratically controlled prices as well as restrictions on export imposed by their own governments, will be finally able to out-compete European and American farmers for certain crops if the subsidy and tariff regime is dismantled as mandated by the WTO.

(viii) Countries like the US are beginning to run huge trade deficits with the newly emerging Asian Tigers. Consequently, these newly emerging economies have brought about a substantial change in global power equations. In the 1990s the pressure to quickly open up was on developing countries. In recent years, the domestic political compulsions in the developed world (fear of loss of jobs and collapse of their agriculture and fear of two-way flow of trade) are driving them towards protectionism. The steel quota and tariff initiative of the US, the US Farm Bill, the recent US ban on outsourcing, the EU Non-Tariff Barriers on food and agro-exports from India are examples of the developed world turning protectionist and moving away from what they preach. The angry scenes at Seattle and Rio, the huge presence of representatives of Western governments at the World Social Forum 2004 in Mumbai and the massive funds being poured into the coffers of Third World AGBs are clear indications of how threatened the First World feels at the change in equations following WTO. They have good reason to feel frightened of its consequences because even a hitherto poor performer like India is beginning to give genuine cause for worry.

It is therefore, no surprise that huge protest demonstrations are being organized by western trade unions, farmer unions, professionals and First World intellectuals, with the full support of many First World governments and western donor agencies who are actively wooing Third World protesters to come and add numbers to give their campaigns the appearance of a vast global movement against globalization! That some First World governments and workers are worried about MNCs shifting their areas of operation leading to unemployment in their own countries is understandable, though if MNCs are as bad as they make them out to be they should be happy to get rid of them from their respective countries. But what is hard to understand is why certain Indian NGOs and intellectuals are upset at the prospect of a dramatic increase in employment opportunities in upwardly mobile jobs for the people of India.

When political parties in India hire buses, trucks, and people for political rallies where the poor are given some freebies, brought in from villages and slums as a show of strength by our *netas,* we tend to frown upon it as an example of political corruption and cynical manipulation of people. Likewise, we look down upon those who sell their votes to this or that party for a couple of hundred rupees or a bottle of liquor. All these are seen as signs of undermining our democracy. However, by contrast, we are failing to register the significance of a new kind of deluded or hired rallyist who has emerged on the international scene. Most of the self-styled radicals, who went and demonstrated against WTO in Seattle and Rio de Janeiro or in Hyderabad, the site of the Asia Social Forum in 2002 or gathered at Mumbai for opposing economic reforms and emoting against globalization, have had their air tickets and per diem expenses paid for by a whole range of western donor agencies and some European governments that are financing the politics of trade barriers and closing borders against the flow of goods and services from Third and Second World countries. It is dishonourable enough that the AGBs in the West want to fire their guns from the shoulders of people of impoverished nations by making out a case that the Third World countries would be devastated by freer trade regimes. But it is even more dishonourable that our self-styled radicals are happy at being thus used for defending the interests of First World farmers, industrial workers and professionals and yet pretend that they are speaking on behalf of the impoverished farmers and the working poor of India.

No to Free Trade, Yes to Tied Aid!

Unfortunately, the very same AGBs who pant and fume at India opening up to foreign investments have very little objection to India being aid-dependent. They are in fact upset at the recent feeble attempts of the Indian government to lessen India's aid dependence. The June 2003 announcement by the Finance Minister that the government is in the process of reviewing its position on external aid flows and that the country will no longer accept any 'tied aid' has apparently caused a great deal of panic among our aid-dependent

NGOs. Harsh Sethi, an old veteran of NGO politics, articulated their concerns in a revealing article entitled 'What Price Hubris' in the *Hindu* dated 20 June 2003.

Admitting that 'whatever the humanitarian impulse behind giving aid, it is difficult to deny that it comes at a price, tied in myriad ways to the interests of the donor country,' Sethi argues in favour of keeping these aid flows going, because the very existence of NGOs is threatened if that money is stopped. For Sethi, the ambition to make India move out of aid dependence is mere 'grandiose' posturing for which he can barely hide his derision. To quote his own words:

> The present regime [in India] more than any other rarely misses an opportunity to flaunt its nationalist credentials. Being classified as an aid-receiving country hardly adds to pride and self-worth. So now that our forex reserves are comfortable, why not return loans (even when not due) and discontinue aid arrangements? ... Possibly, we now want to join the club of aid-givers, not takers, which is more suited to our newly acquired and revised position in global affairs. [Such a] grandiose announcement ... may please our unreconstructed swadeshites; it may bolster our pride that we are no longer a beggar nation. But, there is little doubt that it has alienated many of our external well-wishers and may land us with consequences that our political masters may not have thought of. Alternatively, is it possible that they just don't care. After all, what price for pride?

It is noteworthy that Sethi is not really picking up cudgels on behalf of those aid agencies which support many worthwhile health, education and other development projects run by those NGOs which have made substantial differences to people's lives because those projects are not threatened. He is justifying and defending that aid which is 'tied in myriad ways to the interests of the donor country,' and often involves attempts to undermine the political autonomy of recipient nations. Our aid-dependent political campaigners want to convince us that India's feeble attempts at moving away from being an aid-recipient country will alienate the 'external well-wishers' of the NGO sector and be taken as a sign of 'hubris.' Clearly, they prefer Indians in the role of grovelling supplicants who have willingly crushed all pride. They have no problem in being tied to the apron strings of international donor agencies, to finance their politics but do not trust Indians to benefit from partnership in world trade. Their policy of 'No to Free Trade, Yes to Tied Aid' explains the real worth of their politics.

INDIA CATCHING UP DESPITE ARRIVING LATE

When the reform process started, the doomsday prophets had declared that Indian manufacturing would collapse in the face of external competition. After the initial shock and fright, India's corporate sector has begun to participate as a global player. India's exports doubled in less than a decade of reforms from $26 billion to nearly $52 billion. When we started the reform process in 1991, India was so bankrupt that the government had to mortgage its gold reserves. By 2003, we had more than, $100 billion in currency reserves and the amount is growing. Some of today's star performers are from precisely those industries— steel, capital goods, and automobile parts—that were once synonymous with waste, inefficiency, and shoddy products made with outdated technologies. They are now beginning to capture some export markets after they demonstrated their ability to catch up on quality and efficiency.

Prominent eco-feminists in India had prophesied doom and destruction for India's pharma industry post-globalization. But the speed with which India's pharmaceutical industry has begun acting as a global player has taken the world by surprise. It is already worth $ 6.5 billion and it has been growing at 8 to 10 per cent a year. Its exports have crossed $2 billion, and have increased by 30 per cent in the past five years. India is among the top five manufacturers of bulk generic drugs. In 1971 the share of pharmaceutical-producing MNCs in the Indian market was 75 per cent. Today it is down to 35 per cent! India has grown to be the world's fourth largest pharmaceutical producer with 8 per cent share of global production by volume and 1.5 per cent share by value. Indian pharmaceutical companies have a cost advantage that facilitates the production of drugs at almost one-twentieth the cost incurred by other developed economies. With a number of generic drugs likely to become off-patent in the near future, India is likely to become a large manufacturing base for these drugs. For once, Indian industry has even started investing in research and development (R & D). Exports form a vital component of the growth strategy of most Indian pharmaceutical companies. Their growth over the last five years has been more than 20 per cent. A major share of Indian pharma exports is going to highly regulated markets in the US, Germany, UK, the Netherlands, and others. Now First World pharmaceutical companies are the ones getting jittery.

We have produced at least one Indian company that is globally No. 1 in its field today, namely Essel Propack that manufactures laminated tubes for packaging toothpastes, cosmetics, drugs, and foods. It has already secured 30 per cent of the world market. It has 12 foreign plants in China, USA, Germany, Philippines, Indonesia, Mexico, Columbia, and Venezuela. Its success story as narrated by Swaminathan A. Aiyar goes as follows: Essel's Chairman, Subhash Chandra, was an ordinary rice exporter up to the early 1980s. While searching for plastic packaging for the safe delivery of rice to global customers, he came across plastic laminates at an industrial fair in Germany and immediately grasped their potential for India. Till then toothpaste tubes in India were made of aluminium. But plastic laminated tubes work out cheaper, are more hygienic, better looking and preserve fragrance and taste better. He launched Essel Packaging in the 1980s. By the 1990s he had conquered the Indian market. Having met the needs of top MNCs in India, who demand high standards from their suppliers, he made himself globally competitive. Since Essel invested well in R & D recognizing that even humble products need constant improvements to beat the competition, the company has beaten older and established global players.

This is not likely to remain an exceptional success story. Auto Ancillaries have been following the same path. In the last decade and a half, they gained the know-how and confidence that comes from supplying auto parts to leading MNCs such as Ford, GM, Hyundai, and Suzuki who demand high standards. Fifteen of the world's major automobile manufacturers are now obtaining components from Indian firms. Some of these Indian firms have now begun setting up plants in China. In 2002, exports of auto components were $375 million. By 2003 end they were close to $1.5 billion. Estimates indicate they will reach $15 billion within six to seven years. India's leading bicycle manufacturing company, Hero, after its collaboration with Honda has grown to become the largest manufacturer of motorcycles in the world, with an output of 17 lakh motorcycles a year. One lakh Indica cars made by the Tatas are to be marketed in Europe by Rover, one of United Kingdom's most prestigious automobile manufacturers, under Rover's own brand name. Aston Martin, one of the world's most expensive sports car brands, has contracted prototyping its latest luxury sports car to an India-based designer. This would be the cheapest car to roll out of Aston Martin's stable. Maruti has been the preferred supplier of small cars under the Suzuki brand for Europe. Suzuki has now decided to make India its manufacturing, export, and research hub outside Japan. Hyundai Motors India is about to become the parent Hyundai Motor Corporation's global small car hub. Ford India got its first outsourcing contract in 2000. Within three years outsourcing accounts for 35 per cent of its sales. The parent Ford is sourcing close to $40 million worth of components from India, and plans to increase this in the coming years. France's leading auto and tractor-maker, Renault, has chosen International Tractors as its sole global sourcing hub for 40 to 85 horsepower tractors. On a world scale all these figures remain very small but for India, which lay dormant for five decades, they represent a major breakthrough.

Another significant trend is the emergence of Indian corporates buying companies abroad and becoming MNCs. The Centre for Monitoring the Indian Economy reports that Indian companies acquired over 30 foreign firms from April to October 2003— totalling their acquisition spree to nearly $1 billion. This includes the AV Birla group which has bought companies in Southeast Asia, Australia, China, and Indonesia. Within the last five years pharma major Ranbaxy has acquired an on-ground presence in 30 countries. Among other international players are Tata Motors, Reliance, Wipro, Hindalco, Wockhardt, and Cadilla Health. Again this is peanuts in global terms but significant for Indian industry which used to be an object of disdain till a decade ago.

India may not have attracted much direct investment flows, because of its poor infrastructure and a heavily politicized economy, but there has been a steady and inexorable shift of jobs from the Western economies to India. A Morgan Stanley report predicts that in the coming years this will assume the form of a 'seismic shift' leading to the creation of four million jobs and steer the Indian economy to a trillion-dollar level. According to McKinsey, 203 of the Fortune 1000 companies are already outsourcing jobs to India. Business Process Outsourcing (BPO) is expected to earn $39 billion by 2010. Another report by Deloitte Research says that $35.6 billion worth of the global financial services industry will also move offshore, with much of it likely to come to India. Standard Chartered has been gradually transferring its back office to Chennai. Other institutions may soon follow. Over 100 of the Fortune 500 companies are now present in India as against 33 in China. General Electric (GE) has invested $60 million in India and employs 1600 researchers while it has only 100 in China. Once again, this is a tiny sum for GE. Its significance lies in the fact that a decade ago many of our own scientists felt India was inhospitable for serious research and many of them looked for openings abroad.

Even in the area of food, the powerful mascot of US imperialism, the McDonald's food chain, has certainly not stood up well to the charm and quality of our *desi* Haldiram or Bikaneri chain of snacks and *mithais* or the much healthier fast food provided by Udupis. This when McDonald's spends billions on ad campaigns and our Haldirams and Udupis rely only on customer satisfaction. Haldirams have already started opening chain stores outside India. It won't be long before they offer McDonald's tough competition on it own home turf.

SOME LEGENDARY SUCCESSES

The success of Indian Information Technology (IT) firms has already become legendary. One third of the start-ups in Silicon Valley were by Indians. India exports IT and IT-enabled services to over 133 countries. Our IT professionals provide world-class services at one-tenth of what the same services would cost in the United States. Our 50,000 software engineers contributed to creating $16 billion worth of wealth a year out of which $13 billion came from IT exports. Thus, less than half of one per cent of our population contributed to almost 20 per cent of our exports. To quote the Council of Scientific and Industrial Research (CSIR) Director R.A. Mashelkar, 'If this is what the tip of the iceberg could achieve so fast, imagine what would happen if such openings were made available to all of our people.' This sector is growing at the rate of 20 per cent a year. This is occurring despite the fact that India made a late entry into the world of computers because our trade unions and Leftist intellectuals initially blocked their entry, imagining that computerization would destroy jobs in much the same way that the anti-globalization lobbies want to convince us today that India will be devastated if it engages with the global economy. That doomsday prophecy proved to be far from true. The entry of computers has created far more jobs and self-employment opportunities in India than any other sector in the last five decades. Since IT has become the backbone of the service sector, its effect on job creation is exponential. This sector grew despite poor telephone lines and frequent power breakdowns primarily because they did not have to deal with government controls and regulations.

Similarly, Bollywood has emerged as the only real competitor to Hollywood in the global entertainment market. Its success is even more impressive because it has grown amidst a very hostile atmosphere with the government having kept not only a vigilant eye on it through absurd and rigorous censorship laws but also by keeping it starved of legitimate sources of finance. Since it was denied status as an industry, filmmakers could not get bank or other institutional finance. Consequently, Bollywood filmmakers came to rely on black-money holders to finance their films. Such has been the demand for Indian films that even poor quality prints smuggled out made huge fortunes—a good part of which came to be used to finance more Bollywood *masalas*. The very same trade networks also came to distribute Indian films and music videos in countries across the globe.

The French and German film industries may well be collapsing under the onslaught of Hollywood. Bollywood has not only withstood Hollywood competition on its home ground but also actually offered the latter the most powerful challenge the world over. For example, German films are left with only 10–11 per cent of Germany's entertainment market. The rest has been captured by Hollywood. By contrast, Hollywood's share of the Indian market averages a mere 5 per cent whereas in most other markets it has 60 to 90 per cent of the market. Between 2001–2, Indian film exports grew by over 80 per cent. In 2003, they nearly doubled. Even highly globalized Indians like NRIs prefer Indian films to those made in Hollywood. Mumbai films began their global conquest with the former Soviet Union and Middle Eastern countries. Over the last two decades, our films have come to be sought after even in North America, Australia, New Zealand, Singapore, Hongkong, Indonesia, Malaysia, Japan, and other East Asian countries, as well as the African continent. No Richard Gere or Harrison Ford can today match the committed and large fan followings of Hrithik Roshan, Madhuri Dikshit, Shah Rukh Khan and other icons of Bollywood. TV networks in Indonesia, Singapore, Malaysia, Japan, Thailand, Egypt, Algeria, Morocco, and many other Afro-Asian countries provide a regular diet, often half a dozen films in a day, of Indian cinema. In recent years, whenever I travel to non-European countries—be it Uganda, South Africa, Bangladesh, Indonesia, or Malaysia—everywhere, from the taxi-drivers to kids on the street, I have been greeted with a catchy dialogue or song from a Bollywood film. While Hollywood excites fears of mindless Americanization, and spread of narcissistic individualism among non-western societies, Bollywood films with their emphasis on family loyalties, and assertion of traditional Indic cultural values—even in their caricatured form—are closer to the emotional grammar of Asians and Africans. Therefore, they are popular as family entertainment in most countries where there is a powerful backlash against the 'permissive' western culture that is identified with Hollywood.

Bollywood has in fact helped build vital emotional links with India and influenced the daily lives of people both within diverse regions of India as well as in countries across the globe in many big and small ways. For example, till the 1970s, it was rare to find a woman in *salwar-kameez* in the southern states of India, leave alone in neighbouring countries. Today, the North Indian *salwar-kameez* has become a popular outfit in virtually every country of the subcontinent and every state of India—all through the seductive power of Bollywood. Likewise, the North Indian bridal wear has become a common feature of weddings in Sri Lanka, and Bangladesh as well— though both these countries have had very different cultural and dress traditions.

The colourful, eclectic, and astute mix of western culture with traditional Indian values is aptly summed up in the famous song, '*Mera joota hai japani, yeh patloon Englistani, sir pe laal topi Russi, phir bhi dil hai Hindustani*' (My shoe is Japanese, my pants are made in England, I wear a Russian cap on my head but my heart remains Indian). This has helped Bollywood act as a major vehicle of social transformation by attempting to figure out a workable amalgam of western and Indian values and winning people's interests the world over in the filmy version of Indian lifestyle, social, and family values, fashion, song and dance. So strong is the Indian people's identification with this filmy version that it is actually influencing their lives, values, and behaviour in significant ways.

Bollywood films have also played a significant role in providing the diverse NRI communities an emotional and cultural anchor. For most NRIs, especially those who could not keep a live contact with India through frequent visits, Bollywood films became their main source of information about the changing milieu in India and a fun filled, though often unreliable guide to religious and secular festivals, traditional and modern rituals. The increasing involvement of second- and third-generation NRIs from North America and Europe in the political and economic challenges before India, their efforts to support schools, colleges and technology institutes, their attempts to adopt and upgrade their native villages, and their emergence as effective lobbyists for India with the governments of their adopted countries are oddly enough in part due to the emotional ties with India being nurtured through a regular diet of Bollywood films.

Looking at the success of Bollywood in taking on the economic, political and cultural might of Hollywood better than the film industry of any other country, despite a paucity of legitimate/legal sources of finance, it is reasonable to believe that other sectors of our economy would also flourish and bloom if provided a supportive environment for growth or at least not actively obstructed by the government from growing, as has been the case so far.

Most important of all, the Government of India is starting to make substantial new investments in roads, power, ports, and telecom, thanks to sustained pressure from the Indian and global corporations. Apart from generating lakhs of jobs, these improvements are bound to provide a long-term boost for the economy. The National Highways Development Programme alone is supposed to provide one-and-a-half lakh jobs every day, though all these are short-term project-based jobs. But more than the government, it is the private service sector that is generating more, though still not a sufficient number of jobs than ever before. For example, in 2003 private recruitment companies collectively found jobs for 3.5 lakh individuals and expect their placements to go up by 25 per cent in 2004. These jobs are being created both for the high and lower skilled workers ranging from software engineers to call centres, restaurant helps, security guards, and drivers. Even a cursory look at our cities show a visible and dramatic increase in the numbers of street vendors, auto and cycle rickshaws, taxis, and buses all of which point to greater vibrancy in the economy and more avenues of employment for the poor, post reforms. However, given the informal nature of these sectors, there is no credible and regular method of keeping count of these jobs.

One of the most positive outcomes of the reforms process is the change in aspirations of young people in India. Till recently, except for the big corporate houses, private sector jobs were associated with low wages and a high degree of insecurity. Therefore, most educated young men felt 'unemployed' if they did not have a government job with life long security. This mindset is changing slowly. Many of those who do not relish making extra income through bribes and extortion associated with most government jobs, are beginning to get into entrepreneurial activities and private sector jobs that allow for rapid upward mobility.

Even small firms, at least in big cities, are beginning to pay better. The new role models for today's youth are people like Azim Premji and N.R. Narayanamurthy who made rapid advances through honest hard work and sheer innovation. This change in mindset in a significant section among the educated is likely to have a rapid multiplier effect.

These are just a few examples of how things have finally begun to move in favour of India. All this ought to be seen as cause for celebration, not mournful breast-beating, as is common practice among the AGBs. The speed with which our corporations have restructured and shown the determination and capability to be world-class may come as a surprise to the rest of the world but should not surprise us in India because the entrepreneurial skills of our business communities have been honed over centuries. They suffered serious hurdles and roadblocks in the last 200 years but a society with such a rich legacy of entrepreneurship can come into its own again with speed.

WHO ARE THE SUCCESS STORIES OF INDIA?

The absurd doomsday prophecies with regard to globalization become evident if we take a count of all those who emerged as economically successful Indians even through the heydays of our closed-door economy. The successful were not those who were phobic of the outside world but those who developed live contacts and explored new opportunities in whichever corner of the world they could find a foothold. Even most of those Indians who went as impoverished, semi-literate migrants and took up menial jobs like cleaning toilets, washing laundry, driving taxis or working as dishwashers in Canada, US, England, and other well-off nations have within one or two generations emerged as great success stories of those societies in every field. Far more amazing is the entrepreneurial resilience and innovativeness shown by those who were taken as indentured labourers to inhospitable and hostile places like Fiji, Mauritius, South Africa, Guyana, and Uganda. They too rapidly moved up the economic ladder and came to dominate in business, trade and even professions despite facing political persecution and systematic discrimination. Many have also made a mark even in politics as for example, Bharat Jagdeo, the President of Guyana, Sir Anirudh Jugnauth, President of Mauritius and Mahendra Chaudhry, the former Prime Minister of Fiji.

While globalization has become a very fashionable buzzword with the current government, one of the prerequisites of a globalized economy is not getting due attention. Though efforts are being made to allow free movement of goods, there is no attempt to bring about a global regime in which people are free to move across national boundaries, free to sell their skills and labour wherever they find a good market for them. The many implications of the institutionalized restrictions on the free movement of human beings is analysed in the chapter 'Captive People, Free Trade? Human Rights and National Boundaries,' written in 1991 when the western powers had begun to aggressively peddle a policy of free trade across national boundaries. The First World countries have been extremely restrictive about issuing work permits to Indians and other Asians. While highly qualified people such as IT professionals, engineers, doctors, and nurses still manage to get entry despite tightly controlled quotas, the less educated Indians are mostly blocked in their attempts to get visas even though they could easily find gainful employment. That is why so many end up risking their very lives making hazardous journeys as illegal migrants to First World countries.

Countries like India which have an overpressure on land, and therefore, would gain enormously from a freer flow of people across national boundaries should be vigorous in bringing this issue to the negotiating table in the international economic fora saying, 'We will open up more markets for your goods, if you are liberal in opening up your economy for our people who are looking for markets for their labour and skills.' This could be the bargaining strategy for seeking more work permits for our people in more prosperous economies. Instead of celebrating only the success of the skilled professionals, our policy should be to help our ordinary citizens gain access to global opportunities. They may not have hi-fi degrees from the Indian Institute of Technology (IIT) or Indian Institute of Management (IIM) but they are rich in entrepreneurial spirit and experience and many have become successful within no time even when they began as unskilled labourers in menial jobs. The semi-literate Gulf migrants working in blue-collar jobs sent back to their families in India more foreign remittances than our high flying professionals in the US. These earnings played a significant role in uplifting millions of poor families out of poverty.

IMPACT OF REFORMS REMAINS LIMITED

This is not to deny that the constituency for economic reforms remains small in India, in part due to the consistent propaganda war against it by vested interests. But the main reason for the apprehensions about the reforms among the general public is that the entire discourse on economic reforms has been diverted to an obsessive focus on the entry of transnational corporations, the concerns of the Indian corporate sector, and the fate of government-run public enterprises, as they prepare to deal with a market open to competition. These are valid issues and concerns. But, for all the attention it hogs and the influence it wields through wining, dining, and bribing power-wielders, even the corporate sector has not really benefited from their shortsighted approach because the purchasing power of the majority of Indian consumers, who are their natural market, remains depressed.

Despite the many substantial gains made by the Indian corporate sector in recent years, we cannot afford to overlook the fact that Indian and foreign corporations and the PSUs together provide employment to no more than three per cent of our population. Another three to four per cent is employed in various government agencies. As against about 10 per cent who are self-employed in Europe and America, the vast majority of people in India (more than 90 per cent) are still self-employed; 70 per cent are still wholly or partly dependent on agriculture and allied occupations. The rest are self-employed as artisans or workers in the unorganized sector of industry, or earn their living by providing services in casual or regular jobs. Their economic status, unlike that of the tiny salaried class, depends on the well-being of the whole economy within which they operate as service providers or small family enterprises with few or no employees.

Loosening of bureaucratic controls may have brought some relief to some segments of industry and easy access to a wide variety of consumer goods for people at large. However, running any business enterprise in India is still a nightmare because of excessive red tape, poor infrastructure, and a deeply embedded culture of extortion, harassment, and lethal amounts of paperwork, especially in small towns. People who run small industries in small towns report how, as soon as someone buys a new car or a new machine for the factory, government inspectors will come raiding their premises to claim a bribe. In addition, political mafias start making ransom calls. That is why small town, small-scale industry is collapsing, not flourishing. The rhetoric of reforms is not being implemented with earnestness because politicians and bureaucrats are not willing to end their rapaciousness. Consequently, the entire industrial and corporate sector of India, including the PSUs, have not been able to provide employment to more than 3 per cent of our population. The downsizing of labour in some industries to make them cost effective has not been accompanied by growth in other sectors. In the organized private sector, employment remains stagnant. Industry leaders are only recently forecasting that India Inc. will start hiring again soon (*India Today*, 2 February 2004). The most optimistic forecasters admit that the industrial sector will not be able to absorb more than 15 per cent of our working population, even 20 years from now, that too provided all goes well. In China, Korea, Malaysia, and Indonesia, the loosening of state controls on the economy led to the creation of many new avenues of business and employment. In India, among large sections of the people, reforms are associated mainly with job losses and onslaughts on Indian agriculture and enterprise, rather than wealth creation. Therefore, there is a great deal of genuine anxiety and panic in the organized industrial labour force. This segment of society enjoyed a high level of protection against the vagaries of the market during the days of the command economy. Today, that rigid protection has become the greatest threat to its future. Lack of freedom to hire and fire had prevented entrepreneurs from making changes in staffing and introducing new technologies that bring down costs, and enable them to stand up to growing international competition. Yet, there can be no freedom to hire and fire if India does not have effective social security measures, generous retrenchment benefits and enhanced avenues of employment. Thirteen years after economic liberalization, the government has still to create even a rudimentary social insurance for the vulnerable groups.

We have a large army of underemployed and underpaid people getting more and more desperate about their future because they are denied access to skills that are in demand, while the skills they possess are not marketable. Yet, the budgetary allocation for education remains pitiful—at less than 5 per cent of GDP. Given that more than 90 per cent of the education budget goes into providing salaries of teachers, most of our children whose parents cannot afford elite private schools are not getting any worthwhile education. The vast majority of those coming out of government and low quality private schools are so mal-educated that they are rendered unfit for any worthwhile employment in the modern sectors of our economy. Their aspirations have been raised but not their skills. Therefore, they are unwilling to do manual jobs or pick up traditional skills from their parents while they have not gained any worthwhile new skills through the school system. Millions of such unemployable youth live in despair and provide ready recruiting ground for criminals. There is no sign of our government having woken up to this explosive situation.

Two-thirds of India's export earnings (leaving out the recent leaps made by the newly emerging IT sector) have come from agriculture and handmade products of our traditional artisans. Till very recently, there were hardly any buyers in the international market for the products of our industrial, corporate sector that is only recently learning the value of being competitive. By contrast, the beautiful products of our artisans such as the handwoven textiles of our impoverished weavers, handcrafted jewellery as well as spices, fruits, flowers, *basmati* rice and the long staple cotton produced by our impoverished farmers have for decades been our prime foreign exchange earners. Yet these self-employed groups are not perceived as important players in the economy, leave alone as entrepreneurs requiring economic freedom. The livelihood concerns of the vast majority of our people remain marginalized even in the minds of those pushing for reforms. We think of weavers and artisans only if they commit suicide in dramatic ways, not when their children die prematurely from malnutrition and ill health. Even a cursory glance at newspapers and TV news and discussions will show how little space is given to the concerns of the self-employed poor in our mass media. Even the frequent TV coverage of the WTO negotiations showing the huge effort, resources and energy invested by the US and EU to protect the interests of their farm sector has not brought about sufficient awareness about the potential of India's farm sector. We think of agriculture only when there is a massive drought or a major crop failure that raises prices for urban consumers. Not surprisingly, there has been an alarming drain of capital and skills from rural areas due to the inability of Indian agriculture to provide a dignified living to the vast majority of our people who are still wholly or partly dependent on it.

ECONOMIC WARS ON INDIAN FARMERS

It is noteworthy that all those who go and make common cause with American and European farmers against WTO never showed any inclination to join in solidarity with India's farmers' movements when they waged long drawnout battles against the price warfare carried out by the Indian government against India's own farmers.

The governments of wealthy nations encourage exports instead of discouraging them. Our government has a long history of obstructing the export of farm produce through outright bans or arbitrary quotas. For decades Indian farm produce had ready buyers in the international market because of its quality and price competitiveness. This despite systematic hurdles put in the farmers' way, lack of adequate power and irrigation facilities and denial of access to the best available farm technologies. But the government prevented Indian farmers from raising their incomes by banning or restricting farm exports. Today, our farmers have lost that advantage in some important crops, especially wheat and oilseeds, due to rapid advancement in biotechnology in the West that has led to a phenomenal increase in productivity and fall in prices.

The two chapters 'Cutting our Own Lifeline: A Review of India's Farm Policy' and 'A Half-Step Forward: The Thwarting of Economic Reforms in India' were written in the 1990s when strong mass movements of farmers were protesting against the myriad ways in which our government waged economic wars against them. The essays draw heavily on the information collected and the insights gained through my active involvement with those farmers' movements that have been consistently anti-subsidy and pro-economic freedom. The essays remain relevant because they deal with the processes and policies through which our farm sector has been drained of wealth in independent India causing untold misery for our farmers.

A few of the restrictions on agriculture and agro industries described in these two essays have been dismantled since then but the farm sector has still not become the focus of comprehensive reforms. For example, government godowns are overflowing with food grains for which there are no buyers. And yet, myriad restrictions on inter-state movement of food grains have not yet been dismantled. The government is no longer interested in forced procurement of food grains. But our current laws do not allow direct dealings between traders and farmers. The farmer can sell his/her produce only in a government *mandi* where he is heavily taxed both officially as well as through institutionalized extortion rackets. Likewise, traders purchase their requirements from the government's Food Corporation of India (FCI) at pre-determined prices. On 20 January 2004, more than 13 years after the launch of economic reforms, the government announced that private traders would be allowed to buy directly from the farmers. But the relevant laws which forbid a free market for food grains within India and restrict opening up the export market for the farm sector are yet to be withdrawn or changed. Even the announcement allowing private traders the freedom to purchase from farmers was accompanied by a rider that 'the Central Government will monitor production levels and buffer stocks so that there will be no large diversion to the world market.' This proviso defeats the very purpose of this policy reform. As long as the government can switch off exports at will to bring down domestic prices, the farm sector will remain in the doldrums. Even without formal bans, the government continues to use devious means like refusing to provide railway wagons for carrying food grains to the seaports for exports, thus leading to cancellation of export orders due to delays in ensuring delivery. Most important of all, the draconian Essential Commodities Act—the most patent symbol of Stalinist controls on the farm sector, has still not been repealed.

India is one of the few countries in the world whose government has repeatedly dumped imported farm produce in the domestic market—wheat, sugar and cotton, cooking oil, lentils—in order to depress the prices of the produce of Indian farmers. And yet all those who claim to stand up for *swadeshi* today did not register even a nominal protest against policies designed to wreck the Indian farm sector. For example, in 1992 the domestic procurement price of wheat was fixed at a low of Rs 280 per quintal which led to much resentment among Punjab farmers who wanted to hold back their stocks in the hope of selling their wheat at better prices after the government procurement drive was over. To browbeat them, the government imported three million tonnes of wheat at a landing price of Rs 540 per quintal from Australia and Canada. This, despite the fact that there was no grain scarcity and Punjab had produced a bumper harvest at the time. This naturally had the intended effect on the domestic market—wheat prices were artificially depressed. We did not hear any protest from the anti-globalization, neo-swadeshi lobby at that time.

In 1997 the government procurement price of wheat was announced at Rs 415 per quintal. Faced with protests, FCI conceded a bonus of Rs 60, totaling Rs 475 per quintal. Farmers had demanded Rs 650 as the procurement price. Again, as a deliberate measure of price warfare, wheat was imported at a landing price of Rs 780–800 per quintal. Later that year, at the time of the winter harvest, the government-announced price was Rs 480 against the open market price of Rs 543. Yet again wheat was imported, which cost between Rs 750–800 per quintal. Earlier, in September–October 1996, faced with a temporary *atta* crisis, the government came up with a typical knee-jerk reaction and totally banned export of wheat. At the same time, wheat imports were opened at zero duty. We did not hear any protest from the anti-globalization lobby at this point either.

In 1999, with a big crash in international prices of wheat, the Indian government at that time imported two million tonnes of wheat, even though our FCI godowns were chock-full with 3–4 years of buffer stocks. The domestic producers were paying 11–12 per cent taxes on wheat. But imported wheat was allowed at zero duty. Later a Central Bureau of Investigation (CBI) inquiry had to be ordered to find out who benefited from that deal. This is how our FCI godowns started overflowing. A 50 per cent duty was imposed on wheat imports only after the situation became explosive in the countryside. At this juncture too the silence of the anti-globalization lobby was deafening.

The same flip-flop policies have been at play with other crops too. Take the example of the way onion shortages came to be handled over the last few years, starting with the Big Onion Crisis that brought down the BJP government in Delhi. That year there was a big shortfall in onion production due to the El Nino factor. As expected, onion prices rose dramatically, till they peaked at Rs 60 a kilo. This rise in price created such panic in Delhi thanks to hysterical media coverage of the issue, that the Delhi government went ahead and imported onions at Rs 30 a kilo with the landing price being no lower than the domestic prices at that time. These were sold through government outlets to urban consumers at the subsidized price of Rs 10 a kilo. No *swadeshi* monger then shed tears at the fact that *videshi* onion was dumped to depress prices of *swadeshi pyaz*. The whole issue came to be seen through the eyes of the urban consumer and it was made out as if cooking without onions would cause a serious dietary crisis for the Delhiites. Had we seen it through the eyes of the farmers, we would have appreciated the fact that the temporary high prices of this item would help them recover in part the losses they made due to the big shortfall in the size of the crop that year. Since then onions have been covered under the Essential Commodities Act. This in effect means that their exports can be banned whenever the prices show the slightest tendency to rise. As soon as the price of onions reaches, say, Rs 9 a kilo, and the farmer begins to get a decent return of about Rs 3–4 a kilo, exports are banned and the prices come crashing down. In 2001, when this happened again, a union minister had to face a shower of rotten onions when he went to visit Nashik. He got the message and on his return to Delhi, got the export ban lifted. About a 100,000 tonnes' quota for export was announced. But much before that quota was completed, when 36,000 tonnes were yet to go, onion export was abruptly stopped again. Such devious games continue till date. For example, in February 2003 when the onion crop was harvested and farmers took it to market, onion exports were banned to ensure that farmers do not get good prices and traders could buy them cheap. However, the ban was lifted in April so that traders could export the cheap stocks they had purchased and made good money from selling at higher prices. In January 2004, while the Government made a pretense of offering several pre-election sops to farmers, they again announced a ban on onion export on the eve of the onion harvest. It was lifted within a few days because Shetkari Sangathana led massive protests outside the ruling party's offices in Maharashtra. Since the government was planning to hold early elections, they responded promptly by lifting the ban. Such on and off export policies have meant that our exporters are not trusted as suppliers in the international market and are unable to make a firm place for our farm produce. This also has the inevitable effect of artificially depressed prices in the domestic market. These can sink so low that farmers have to plough back their crop in the soil because the price they fetch does not cover even the transport cost to the market, leave alone the cost of production.

Sugarcane farmers are another demoralized lot. This sector has witnessed real messy interventions even during the reforms period. While *zonebandi*, which forced farmers to bond their crop to the local sugar mills, has been lifted and compulsory levy on sugar is abolished, the sugar mills went into crisis because the government imported huge quantities of sugar from Pakistan and dumped it in the Indian market, thus once again bringing down prices through political machinations rather than allowing for market mechanisms to determine prices. The mills refuse to pay the government fixed minimum support price to farmers because they say they are working at a loss. The ongoing battles between cane farmers and the sugar industry has led to massive unrest and protests among farmers.

'Do-Gooders' Add to the Woes of Farmers

Far from resisting such onslaughts on Indian farmers, most of those who claim to represent the interests of the poor in India seem to have unwittingly played an active role in impoverishing our people through the agendas they pursued. One of the central pieces of their pro-poor demand list has been that the state keep providing subsidized essential foods for the poor through the government-run Public Distribution

System (PDS). Even if we do not pay attention to the mammoth cost of corruption, leakages, and inefficiency inherent in the government-run food distribution system, the very logic of this demand has spelt disaster for our country. Seventy per cent of India's poor live in villages and are either wholly or partly dependent on the farm sector. Whether as farmers or as hired labourers, their income or wages depend on the surplus generated in the farm sector. If the government is compelled due to pressure from ill-informed agitationists to provide wheat and rice at unrealistically low prices, the government has no option but to force the farmers to sell these crops at the lowest possible price, often not covering the cost of production. This has invariably meant use of coercive means and ban on exports. All this makes farming a loss-making proposition with the inevitable effect of depressing labour rates in the farm sector. If the farmers are not getting adequate returns, they cannot pay good wages nor can they diversify into entrepreneurial activities because their capacity to save and invest is impaired.

It makes no sense to first rob the farm sector of all possibilities of generating employment and wealth through unremunerative prices of farm produce, and then try to bring them 'low-cost' food grains through the PDS. This food is first mopped up from villages at artificially low prices, and taken at enormous cost to government godowns. It is then chaotically distributed to various parts of the country at still greater cost—sugar from Maharashtra taken to Andhra, rice from Tamil Nadu taken to Madhya Pradesh, and so on.

According to agricultural economist Ashok Gulati, FCI spends Rs 4 for each Re 1 worth of food grain it provides to a 'Below Poverty Line (BPL)' family. In states like Andhra, the cost is even higher: Rs 6 is spent to get Re 1 worth of food for the poor. The colossal waste of this entire exercise is evident. Following criticism that most of the 'subsidized' food was being supplied to the better-off urban consumers, since 80 per cent of PDS outlets were located in urban areas, the government decided to revamp the system. The Antoyodaya Anna Yojana (AAY) was launched on 25 December 2001 to provide 25 kilos of grain to BPL families. From April 2002, the entitlement was increased to 35 kilos a month. The government calculation is: 26 per cent of India's population is BPL—which comes to roughly 6 crore households. The government's budget provides Rs 10,000 crore for rural anti-poverty schemes. A total of Rs 49,907 crore is spent on subsidies on food, fertilizers, LPG, and PDS kerosene. That is a neat Rs 60,000 crore. As economist Bibek Debroy points out: 'If you include all subsidies, the total bill is a colossal figure of Rs 274, 352 crore. If you transfer this money directly to 30 crore people 'Below Poverty Line', each such individual will get Rs 9,145 a year amounting to nearly Rs 46,000 per household.' If this transfer had actually occurred, there would be hardly any destitution left in India. Instead, we are allowing billions of rupees to be legally and illegally siphoned off in the guise of anti-poverty schemes while, most of those who work in agriculture remain in extreme poverty.

The numerous restrictions imposed by the government on the farm sector and other self-employed poor have led to depressed farm incomes, stagnant agricultural production, distortions in trade and pricing, obstructing the organic growth of agro-industries causing flight of capital and skills from rural areas without any comparable increase of opportunities in the urban economy.

If only rule-based redressal mechanisms of the WTO variety had been institutionalized and made available to Indian farmers to safeguard them against unfair trade practices imposed by the Indian government they would not be as impoverished and debt-ridden as they are today. In the absence of such mechanisms all they can do is wage long-drawn-out struggles and express their resentment through massive protests, which every now and then turn violent, and invite massive repression. Occasionally they have succeeded in pressuring politicians near election time to yield to some of their demands with temporary knee-jerk concessions. Farmers who fight for justice on their own strength receive very little sympathy or hearing from our intellectuals, the media and other sections of the educated elite.

Not surprisingly, many leading organizations of farmers, including the All India Kisan Coordination Committee, led by Sharad Joshi of Shetkari Sangathana, welcomed with enthusiasm the WTO regime because they see vast opportunities opening up for India's farmers if the ruled based, redress providing WTO system is implemented with sincerity. The dramatic, happy change in the fortune of cotton farmers of Maharashtra in 2003–4 after they managed to break down the government monopoly on cotton procurement enforced through draconian laws which led to artificially depressed prices, provides a good example of the potential for the Indian farm sector, if the government gets off their backs and lets them fend for themselves. Restrictions on inter state movement of raw cotton have not been officially removed but farmers en masse are openly defying monopoly procurement in Maharashtra, the State that leads in cotton production. Fortunately the Maharashtra Government has stopped enforcing free trade of cotton through draconian means such as arrests of farmers on charges of smuggling or confiscation of their crops. In November 2003, when the government opened its procurement centres with much fanfare, with big political leaders invited to come and inaugurate the procurement ceremony, the farmers voted with their feet: no one turned up to sell their cotton. The government was offering Rs 2300 per quintal whereas the open market price ranged from Rs 2950 to Rs 3200 per quintal. In sheer embarrassment, the government procurement officials had to make token purchases from the open market for the *mahurat* ceremony. Earlier the government would import raw cotton to bring down domestic prices. However, since the international cotton prices were much higher, this option could not be used. Thus the monopoly procurement programme has collapsed in Maharashtra due to people's non-cooperation and their following market forces rather than government dictates. Our cotton farmers are finally feeling happy and hopeful after long years of losses and mounting debts. They are able to demonstrate their capacity to be competitive both in price and quality even against the heavily subsidized American farmers. This despite the fact that influential campaigners have been against new hybrids and Bt cottonseeds delaying the availability of high yielding, pest resistant seeds to Indian farmers that enable them to bring about dramatic increases in cotton production. However, farmers in Gujarat and a few other places began using these seeds in open defiance of government restrictions. Those who did are registering enormous increase in production and a dramatic reduction in costs: it takes Rs 2300 to produce a quintal of cotton today with ordinary seeds. With new seed varieties the price could come down to a low of Rs 700 per quintal, thus making it possible for Indian cotton to compete internationally.

Another noticeable positive outcome of the breakdown of the monopoly procurement system in Maharashtra is that earlier the Vidarbha region that grows cotton was not allowed to develop much industrial activity for processing raw cotton. All the mills were located in and around Mumbai—the economically dominant region of Maharashtra—all because the government agencies found it convenient to have their headquarters in Mumbai. Now the ginning mills are thriving in the hitherto backward Vidharba region because the government is not able to siphon off the entire supply of raw cotton away from Vidharbha.

We should be proud of the fact that Indian farmers are among the leading voices for economic freedom and have been battling the government to allow them to prove their worth in the international market. And yet, economic reforms in agriculture remain niggardly and half-hearted. This when even the hitherto indifferent business chambers of commerce are also acknowledging that industrial growth cannot be sustained without a big boost in agricultural incomes and production. It was openly acknowledged that the much flaunted 'feel good' factor for 2003 was in large part due to a good monsoon. The advancing of the General Elections by the NDA was an open acknowledgement of the fact that they could not risk the 'feel good' mood give way to 'back to gloom' in case 2004 turned out to be a drought year.*

THE UNORGANIZED SECTOR

The plight of people working as artisans or in the urban unorganized sector is also cause for concern. Most people think that people in the informal sector work outside bureaucratic controls. However, a close examination shows that those who work in the unorganized sectors remain poor precisely because they are among the worst victims of the notorious License-Quota-Raid Raj and a host of needless and harmful bureaucratic controls.

Despite the rhetoric of liberalization, the poor are subjected not merely to simple extortion but to various forms of humiliation, violence, and ill-conceived legislation. They have been forced to seek protection of *goondas* and touts who act as intermediaries between them and the government machinery. The two articles on street hawkers and rickshaw pullers of Delhi—'Blackmail, Bribes, and Beatings' and 'Laws, Liberty, and Livelihood: Economic Warfare against Rickshaw Owners and Pullers'—provide a glimpse into the economic plight and hazards faced by street vendors and rickshaw pullers, who constitute a large proportion of the urban self-employed poor in India. These accounts show how government policies, laws, and regulations often work to wreck these people's livelihoods and facilitate extortion rackets, rather than create an enabling atmosphere for these small-scale entrepreneurs to earn their precarious living by providing security of life, livelihood, and property. They also demonstrate how the government actively discriminates against the poor by enacting laws which make the

---

*The unexpected defeat of the NDA government in the May 2004 elections was in large part due to people's anger at the very limited reach of economic reforms which meant that their benefits too remained confined to small sections of our population, even while expectations and aspirations have risen across the board.

marginalized sections of our society fall easy prey to criminal coercion and routine violation of their human and citizenship rights. The information collected by *Manushi* through close interaction with thousands of street hawkers and rickshaw pullers over the last several years indicates that in Delhi alone people working in these two sectors could well be coughing up nearly 50 crore rupees per month by way of bribes, including regular loss of income due to confiscation of their goods and vehicles as well as enforced idleness for days or weeks due to stoppage of their trade by various authorities.

While the political class gets a great deal of flak from the people because they have to face their wrath at least once in five years at election time (hence their need to placate a section in their constituency through dangling various carrots), the bureaucrats get away with the use of arbitrary laws and regulations which provide them with deadly powers to harass and fleece the citizens without suffering any consequences. Their jobs carry lifetime security and a very high degree of immunity from prosecution for corruption.

The article '*Naukri* as Property' elaborates precisely how most people who manage to secure a foothold in government, be it at the level of a humble municipal sweeper, a peon, or a senior administrator, tend to treat their *sarkari* job as a loot license. Not surprisingly, people are willing to pay huge amounts of money to procure such a safe and lucrative access to siphoning off public funds and fleecing citizens. In recent years in state after state we have witnessed outbreaks of scandals exposing how those presiding over selection and appointments in government jobs have been minting money by virtually auctioning those jobs to the highest bidders. Every state seems to have worked out pre-set rates for various levels of *sarkari* jobs, from the lowly ones such as that of a postman, clerk, and school teachers to administrative cadre. Even those with professional degrees in medicine, engineering, and management have in recent decades been opting for *sarkari* jobs because of the perks, privileges and 'get rich quick' opportunities these jobs bring.

If the quickest, surest and easiest way to become wealthy is to acquire or bribe your way into a government job, is it any surprise that young, educated people are willing to fight do-or-die battles for *sarkari naukris* as became evident during the violent outbursts against Other Backward Classes' (OBCs) reservations mandated by the V.P Singh-led government in August 1990. The chapter 'Beyond For or Against' argues that such desperate hunger for government jobs is an ominous sign of a stagnant economy and proof that the bureaucracy for the most part still has the bulk of our country's economy in its grip despite the rhetoric of liberalization and economic reforms. In a healthy and vibrant economy, aspirations find diverse channels and government jobs—barring the very high powered ones—do not have much attraction for people. In our society, the high value placed on all types of government jobs indicates that there are relatively limited avenues to make a decent living available to our people and hence the bitter battles over pitiful jobs in government. The depth of feeling stirred at the prospect of being denied a few thousand jobs every year in the government shows how despite all the talk of liberalization, the all powerful *sarkar* still rules the main commanding heights of the economy. The chapter on reservation policy also deals with the hollowness of the arguments used by the opponents of OBC reservations who seem to have convinced themselves that they stand for meritocracy, which is threatened by reserving a certain percentage of government jobs for castes considered educationally and socially 'backward'. More importantly, this chapter examines how the survival of democracy in our country is intrinsically connected to the continuing hold and transformation of *jati* identity to modern day caste identity; it discusses how caste has emerged as an instrument of political mobilization and democratic assertion by disadvantaged groups and communities.

It is tragic that during the anti-Mandal agitation there was hardly any awareness among the upper caste urban educated youth opposing reservations and the media that lent support to their hysterical agitation that the castes and communities designated as 'backward' and 'most backward' actually constitute very productive groups in our society. A large proportion of them belong to a whole range of peasant castes engaged in feeding the rest of us and providing vital raw materials for industry. Another important category dubbed as 'backward' belong to a vast array of artisan castes such as weavers, metallurgists making aesthetic art objects, carpenters, including traditional ship builders, architects, goldsmiths and so on. Many of these traditional technologists are still producers of high quality luxury goods and art objects. One third of India's export earnings have come from handicrafts and handmade fabrics (silks, jewellery, bronze images, etc.) made by these traditional artisans. Another third of export earnings are accounted for by the produce of our supposedly backward farmers producing exotic spices, *basmati* rice, long staple cotton, mangoes, coffee, tea and a whole range of agricultural products feeding our industry. However, the skills and knowledge possessed by our traditional technologists and farmers, handed over from generation to generation and honed over centuries, are devalued and denied appropriate recognition. Their labour is so poorly rewarded that an increasing number of them are abandoning their centuries old occupations in favour of menial jobs, including unskilled labour. While they are being compelled by our economic policies to abandon their traditional skills instead of being helped to upgrade them, a majority of them are unable to acquire marketable 'modern' skills due to a denial of quality education to low income groups of our society.

How can a society make economic and cultural progress which devalues its inherited legacy of skills and declares more than 90 per cent of its people as 'backward', 'most backward' and 'scheduled castes' and declares them as lacking intelligence and capability, simply because their knowledge is not acquired through the formal education system and through textbooks written in the English language? The chapter 'Destroying Minds and Skills: The Dominance of *Angreziyat*' in our Education' carries the same theme forward. The most powerful determinant of status and access to opportunities in contemporary India is whether you received education at an elite English medium school. Those who know no English are not even counted. This divide has helped concentrate too much power, knowledge and opportunities for advancement in the hands of the tiny English knowing elite which treats all others as belonging to a lower species. The dominance of *angreziyat* is in large part responsible for the marginalization and devaluation of our traditional knowledge systems. It is also making it impossible for us to improve the quality of education available to the average citizen.

Those in charge of planning and policies tend to exist in a cocoon with very little connection to the world inhabited by ordinary citizens of India. The essay 'Symbols of Mental Slavery' tries to capture some of the bizarre consequences due to this mismatch and the alienation of the English-educated elite from their own environment and their own people's needs. The essay: 'When, Nature's Call is a Crime: Breakdown of Conflict Resolution Mechanisms in India' describes how the elite sections of our society have become callously indifferent towards the most basic human needs of the poor, and how the government creates conditions which inevitably promote civil strife between different strata of society. While the article focuses on some specific incidents in a particular area of Delhi, it has much wider implications because such insensitivity and short-sightedness has become the hallmark of our social, economic, and political life.

WEAK FOUNDATIONS FOR REFORMS

A sure sign of the shaky health of our economy is the high government deficit. It is estimated to be growing annually by more than 10 per cent of GDP. This is among the highest rates of deficit growth in the world. More importantly, most of the money is being spent on unproductive current consumption like paying salaries rather than on building productive assets. This has curtailed government's ability to invest, to enlarge and to boost job creation. Wasteful subsidies are responsible for much of the consolidated fiscal deficit of the Central and state governments, and create even more problems for the economy by distorting investment and consumption priorities. Yet, four-fifths of these subsidies are going to the organized middle-class groups, to inefficient PSUs and industry and even to the very rich, rather than to the poor in whose name they are instituted. At the same time, the social sector and economic infrastructure is starved of adequate investments and support, while the citizens have no power to monitor and ensure that public money is spent with prudence.

These are clear signs that the reforms process has remained very stunted and that the continuing poverty of our people is due to lack of sufficient reforms rather than due to implementing them. The few sectors like telecom and the automobile industry that have actually witnessed significant reforms have given solid benefits to the average citizen, including those in rural areas, by making these 'luxuries' available to citizens at more affordable prices, and eliminating the culture of bribes and shortages. There was a time when even in the capital of India you waited for 10 years to get a phone connection and paid bribes to keep it functioning erratically. Today, thanks to international competition, telecom companies offer you incentives to buy their phones and provide you a connection within hours of applying, even in rural areas. Most important of all, this one sector has created many more better paying jobs even for those with low education than were ever created by the myriad employment generating schemes of the government.

However, such dramatic results are not visible in most other areas. Consequently, the insecurity of various groups temporarily threatened by globalization is being articulated, most often in distorted and mistaken forms, mainly by anti-reform lobbies, most of whom have ended up as defenders of statist controls, tighter regulations and increasing government monopoly in key sectors of our economy. The fears and phobias unleashed by the preliminaries to the process of opening up the Indian economy have made the anti-reformers see the License-Permit-Raid *Raj* as an ally and a necessary instrument for providing jobs and social security for the poor. Their position is bolstered by the fact that the economic reforms agenda has not yet focused on the livelihood concerns of the poor and the economic freedom required by the self-employed in order to move towards prosperity.

TRICKLE DOWN WON'T DO

The reformers would like the vast majority of our people to believe that prosperity will one day just 'trickle down' to them when the reforms attain the right momentum. For five decades, our people were promised an egalitarian and prosperous society, if they patiently helped in building 'socialism'. Now that their patience has run out, they are still being told that wealth will slowly percolate down to them one day, if only they are willing to put up with hardships involved in restructuring the economy. Very few people are willing to buy this dream, simply because the 'trickle down' approach in effect amounts to believing that only the rich need economic freedom. The rest have to depend on state patronage and a few crumbs from the tables of the wealthy. The main concession made for the self-employed poor by the pro-reforms lobby is to demand that the state provide unemployment insurance schemes or similar 'safety nets'. Unemployment insurance can work only if people who once had jobs are temporarily jobless and the currently jobless are relatively a small proportion of the total population. Even in western countries from which we borrow the idea of social security, such systems are providing only partial and limited safety nets to a section of the vulnerable.

But in our country the bulk of our working population is not unemployed. They are not idlers or social dropouts, but among the most hard working people in the world. They are generating social wealth with some even making quality luxury products. Their economic deprivation is an imposition from above and the result of stifling government controls and interventions rather than due to a lack of enterprise and talent. They do not deserve to be abandoned to the mercy of any *mai bap sarkar*. They can create wealth with their own initiative and skills. All they require is the right to pursue their economic activities without being beaten down and parasited upon by those who claim to protect them. That will enable them to move out of the vicious poverty trap sooner than any statist intervention.

A countrywide survey carried out by the Centre for the Study of Developing Societies (CSDS) in 1996 found that more than 80 per cent of our people had not even heard of, let alone experienced, any difference in their economic situation following the initiation of the economic reforms in 1991. Less than 10 per cent of the 19 per cent, who had heard of the new economic policies, approved of the reform process—amounting to less than two per cent of our population. The situation is only somewhat better but not radically different in 2004. A majority of our people has not yet begun to experience the positive benefits of reform in their lives except in some sectors like telecom and having a greater variety of consumer goods available to them at more competitive prices.

The ordinary citizens would consider economic reforms as beneficial:
1. if they did not need to pay bribes to government functionaries for accessing services they are entitled to and for carrying on with their day-to-day activities;
2. if government functionaries lose the power to needlessly harass and obstruct citizens in their economic pursuits;
3. if people feel they have security of life and property and access to a wider range of economic opportunities;
4. if there are efficient dispute resolution mechanisms, when they face situations where their legitimate rights are being violated; and;
5. if there is a distinct improvement in the social infrastructure and civic services.

Clearly very little of this has happened so far proving that economic and governance reforms have not yet taken deep root.

A Decentralized Economy—Our Historical Legacy

Ironically, most of those determined to stall the hesitant doses of economic reforms in India swear by Mahatma Gandhi. They forget that he was one of the most steadfast opponents of state controls over the economic life of our people, as well as over other institutions of civil society. His economic philosophy was not derived from any esoteric western utopian worldview but based on India's historical legacy of self-governance.

One of the special features of Indian civilization has been that, until the coming of the British, the rulers at the top were not usually in a position, nor did they expect to assume the right, to impose their rules and laws over the intimate economic, social, and cultural lives of various local communities. Each village, each town had its own institutions of self-regulation. In ordinary times, the rulers usually had only a right to traditional forms and rates of taxation. If they were on hand, they were expected to adjudicate disputes according to the customs and norms established by the concerned communities. It is with the establishment of the colonial state that this system of self-governance was wrecked and the rulers arrogated to themselves more pervasive powers over the economic, political, and social affairs of our people.

We would do well to remember that India was far wealthier in comparison with other areas of the world as long as its people manufactured what they liked, did business with whom they liked and the world's traders came to buy Indian goods—both industrial and agricultural. We began to get impoverished when the British destroyed our industries as well as agriculture through draconian statist controls on economic resources and activities coupled with ruinous taxation. After Independence, political stalwarts like C. Rajagopalachari, Minoo Masani, Nijalingappa and many others put up a determined fight against the bureaucratic controls imposed in the name of ensuring equity. From the 1970s onwards, strong rural movements, especially in Maharashtra, Punjab, Haryana, Gujarat, and Andhra, saw lakhs of farmers participate in long-drawn struggles to demand dismantling of the regime of restrictions imposed on them by the State and to allow the agriculturists free access to the domestic and international markets. In other words, the urge for economic freedom has primarily come from within and goes hand in hand with the urge for a more decentralized polity.

The numerous bans on the economic activity of the forest dependent communities and the accompanying *sarkari* tyranny has been a major reason for the growth of violent resistance movements, such as those led by Naxalite groups. The industrialists may not have come out as openly as the farmers and tribals against the curbs on their enterprise since they gained some advantages in the domestic market by compliance, but they resisted and sabotaged the system through covert means—bribes, evasion of taxes, and working through the parallel 'black' economy which grew much faster than the 'official' one. If we open up the Indian economy to global competition without thoroughgoing reforms within India that go beyond the narrow concerns of the corporate sector, we will create an absolute disaster for our people. We need a bottom-up agenda of economic reforms if we want people in India to move out of the poverty trap.

Unfortunately, the theoretical debates on issues of citizenship continue to be carried out in the limited framework of civil rights and political equality. It has not yet been fully understood that without universalizing economic freedom, whatever political freedom we have becomes an empty ritual. We can regain a position of pre-eminence in the world only when our people, at all levels, regain economic freedom and the right to be global players rather than remain economic hermits.

Causes and Cures of Ethnic Conflicts

Just as the impoverishment of a vast proportion of Indian citizens is primarily due to the absence of mechanisms to hold the *neta–babu* combine to account, similarly the recurring ethnic conflicts and riots in India that cause severe setbacks to our society and economy are products of increasing encroachments by our national political parties and centralized administrative machinery over the daily lives of communities. Many of our power wielders have played an active role in promoting inter-community conflicts. As a result, India is often in the news as a place where ethnic conflict and riots are common. However, if we look at how ordinary people live their lives without the interference of politicians, India could well be held up as an example of how an incredibly large spectrum of diverse religious, linguistic communities, and *jatis* have worked out fairly sophisticated norms of co-living on the basis of mutually agreed upon arrangements at a people to people level.

Dozens of major language groups, each with hundreds of dialects, coexist in India without these cherished linguistic identities tearing the society apart as has happened in many other parts of the world. Though predominantly Hindu, people from virtually every religion in the world have lived in India for centuries without our society witnessing the kind of religious or denominational wars that Europe experienced—for example, those between Catholics and Protestants.

Pre-British India is not known for large-scale massacres and pogroms, as were directed against the Jews in Europe. This was the case despite the fact that India had the misfortune of being subjected to several invasions, which caused severe dislocations and upheavals in society. The historic clash between the polytheistic Hindu and the monotheistic Islamic worldview was indeed traumatic especially since Central Asian invaders indulged in large-scale loot and destruction of temples whose wealth made them attractive targets for attack. But, as some of the invaders settled down and made India their home rather than a place for loot and plunder, over a period of time even the theological conflicts between Hinduism and Islam were ameliorated through powerful socio-religious movements like Sufism within Islam and the *Bhakti* movement within the Hindu fold which built bridges of communication between the two contrary world views. Many of the *sufis* and *sants* had common followings among people, professing different faiths. Their shrines became common centres of worship for people cutting across religious boundaries. The subcontinent also has any number of communities which described themselves as 'Hindu-Muslim' till very recently and were recorded as such in the census reports.

These mutual adjustments were made possible because traditionally this subcontinent evolved into a society where the rulers at the top were not expected to exercise control over the local aspects of social arrangements, personal beliefs, cultural practices, family organization, inheritance patterns, and intercommunity relations. Our various *dharmashastras* (religious treatises) repeatedly emphasized that the duty of the king was to respect customary practices and beliefs rather than legislate them. Likewise, our society does not have a tradition of any centralized commandments giving religious texts or authority figures that hold socially sanctioned power to issue dictates on modes of worship or religious and social beliefs, or determine the universal and absolute morality or immorality of social practices for all the diverse communities of this land. India has often been described as a society of independent autonomous village republics where local communities were free to evolve their own religious, social, cultural norms of living as well as economic arrangements. As and when conflicts arose, they were expected to be resolved on the relative strength of the local community, its wisdom and practical sense rather than be hostage to any theological or ideological compulsions brought in by outside authority. This allowed the politics of mutual adjustments and enlightened self-interest based on respect for differences as well as acknowledgement of shared interests to play an important role in decision-making.

However, all these cultural strengths could not fully combat the corrosive power of ethnic nationalism as it came to India during the early twentieth century along with the compulsions of building a centralized state following the trauma of Partition—a state which did not purge itself of its colonial heritage, including the legacy of the politics of 'divide-and-rule'.

POLITICALLY ENGINEERED HATE CRIMES

Most people analyse the Hindu–Muslim conflict in India as rooted in religion. Despite the occasional use of religious symbols to mobilize hatred, the communal conflicts between Hindus and Muslims and other religious minorities are not really a battle between secularism and religious fundamentalism, as discussed at length in my chapter 'Majoritarianism vs Minoritarianism'. It is not so much religious leaders who are encroaching into the secular domain. Rather, it is politicians who are using religious leaders as totems and select religious symbols for largely secular purposes such as fighting elections and manipulating vote banks. In sum;

(1) Almost all outbursts of communal, caste violence are engineered because unscrupulous power seekers and anti-social elements have come to exercise great clout in electoral politics. Whatever their mutual prejudices, there is hardly any instance of spontaneous, large-scale outbursts of violence between communities in India. Even when conflicts do break out they remain small and are effectively handled locally, provided politicians do not jump in the fray.

(2) Almost every riotous mob has been led by politicians who invariably get away with such criminal acts without fearing reprisals from the attacked community because they are aided and abetted by the police and the local administrative machinery.

However, Indian voters have more often than not inflicted humiliating defeats on politicians who play such divisive games. It is a tribute to India's unique civilizational heritage that, despite aggressive onslaughts by colonial rule and manipulative and divisive games played by many of our post-Independence politicians and administrators, left to themselves ordinary people soon allow their traditional bonds and mutual adjustments to reassert themselves, no matter how bitter and bloody the divide engineered by those in power.

The future of democracy in India is integrally tied to our ability to work out a satisfactory solution to majority–minority relations that goes beyond temporary palliatives and moral appeals. Instead, we have to devise functional institutional arrangements for power sharing among the different groups that contain mutually agreed upon compacts between different communities on the fundamental rights of individuals and groups in the minority. The answer lies in institutional reforms, which will break the nexus between shady politicians and corrupt administrators rather than simply preach the virtues of secularism. We have to install mechanisms to force the government machinery to provide safety of life and property as well as liberty of livelihood for every citizen along with effective redressal mechanisms if these rights are violated. This is also a sure to succeed recipe for economic resurgence.

I conclude this volume with the chapter 'An Agenda for India' written on the 50th anniversary of India's Independence. The essay delineates the broad contours of political reforms one would like to see implemented in India. I could add many more reforms to those already listed on the agenda in that essay. However, I have chosen not to make any significant additions or amendments to either this or any other essay because if I started that process, it would become a different book.

1

Laws, Liberty, and Livelihood*
Economic Warfare against Rickshaw Owners and Pullers

Imagine the following scenario: One fine morning, the Delhi government suddenly declares that no more than 50,000 cars and scooters will be allowed in the entire territory of our capital city, without ensuring an effective public transport system to make up for private vehicles. It also lays down that the ability to buy a car does not entitle you to own it. People have to have special government permits to own a car or scooter. Also that no family can get a licence for more than one vehicle. Imagine further, that the government enacts a law stipulating that the person who is issued such a permit to own a car, a scooter, a bus, or a truck has to drive that vehicle himself. If he allows someone else to drive it, the vehicle is liable to be forcibly seized by the Municipal Corporation of Delhi (MCD) and sold as junk, after being hammered to pulp. The corporation further legislates that in order to check the number of illegal vehicles, or those without permits on Delhi roads, the corporation employees and police have the right to carry out routine raids, stop any and every car/scooter driver and impound his vehicle, irrespective of whether he/she is able to produce his/her licence or not. It then empowers itself to confiscate and destroy at random, as many cars as and when it pleases under the pretext of facilitating smooth flow of traffic.

And that in order to save this seized vehicle from being destroyed, the owner-licensee has to prove within 15 days of seizure, that he

---

*First published in *Manushi*, Issue No. 125, July–August 2001.

himself was driving the seized vehicle. That even if there is clear evidence that the seizure was *mala fide* and that the municipal or traffic police inspector had confiscated several duly licensed vehicles simply to extract bribes, the owners of seized cars still have to pay a minimum fine of Rs 40,000 each, or 10 to 20 per cent of the cost of their cars to get their respective vehicles released. That in addition, the owner-licensee of the car has to pay Rs 1,000 per day as store charges for the number of days that his vehicle remains confiscated.

Most educated and informed citizens would dismiss the above scenario as an impossibility. They would argue that such economic tyranny does not prevail even under outright dictatorial and fascist regimes, let alone in a democracy like India.

And yet the situation I have just described does not represent any futuristic nightmare. It is the daily life experience of lakhs of citizens in our capital city—a situation legitimized by none other than the Supreme Court of India. The reason no one has taken any note of it is that the victims are one of the poorest and marginalized groups of our society—the pullers and owners of cycle rickshaws in Delhi.

A Vital Public Service

Cycle rickshaws were introduced in Delhi in the 1940s when they were seen as a major technological advancement over the hand-pulled rickshaws. One would have expected them to disappear with the fast growth of modern, motorized transport. But their number has grown phenomenally in the last couple of decades, testifying to a vibrant and increasing demand for this service. Maxwell Perreira, the Commissioner of Traffic Police, says there are about 10 lakh rickshaws in the entire Delhi region. More conservative estimates put the figure at five to six lakhs. In addition, there are at least 20,000 mechanics servicing this sector. Delhi has several thousand contractors owning anything from five or ten to a few hundred rickshaws. Add to it thousands of those in the small-scale sector who are involved in the manufacture of various components used in assembling of rickshaws. On an average, the earning of a rickshaw puller supports five or six others. Thus, at least 50 to 60 lakh people's livelihood is dependent on the labour of Delhi's rickshaw pullers.

Cycle rickshaws provide a much needed and valuable public service, especially for the low-income groups in our cities. Even today, a kilometre-long ride in a cycle rickshaw costs no more than Rs 5. An auto rickshaw charges Rs 15 to 20 for the same distance. In the old city area and in some of the congested colonies meant for the poor, where the lanes and by-lanes are too small for motorized vehicles, cycle rickshaws are the only available means of transport. During my childhood one saw them mostly in old Delhi and in lower middle class colonies in the trans-Yamuna area, as well as in some of the peripheral semi-urban settlements around Delhi. But now, barring a few VIP zones of Lutyens' New Delhi, where their presence is altogether banned, cycle rickshaws have proliferated in every nook and corner of Delhi, including many of the posh South Delhi colonies. This is because they are often the only available means of public transport for short distances, especially within the various colonies which are spread over large geographical areas. In addition, they are convenient, least expensive and available virtually at your doorstep.

PROVIDES INSTANT LIVELIHOOD

Most rickshaw pullers in Delhi are seasonal migrants whose families are still based in their villages. A good proportion of them are from agricultural families with small and shrinking landholdings. The rest are from impoverished landless or artisanal households. With the growing pauperization of India's traditional artisans and technologists like weavers, *lohars, kumhars, sthapatis* (builders), leather-workers and so on, millions are deserting their age-old occupations and gravitating towards occupations like rickshaw pulling, simply because entry into this occupation is easy, requires no capital, and provides immediate instant income without any financial risk. Rural migrants in search of work can hire a rickshaw within hours of reaching the city and start earning money almost instantly. They hire these vehicles from small or big contractors in Delhi on a daily charge ranging from Rs 18 to 22, depending on the state of the vehicle. Even new migrants can hire rickshaws without giving any money deposit, solely on the guarantee of some known rickshaw puller introducing them to the contractor. The rental has to be paid either at the end of the day or on a weekly/monthly basis, depending on the equation between the owner and puller.

A new rickshaw costs Rs 3,500 and a second-hand one can be purchased for as low a rate as Rs 800 to Rs 2,000, depending on the condition of the vehicle. Thus the Rs 600 hire charge that a rickshaw puller pays to the rickshaw contractor from whom he hires the vehicle represents nearly one sixth the cost of a new vehicle or half the price of a second-hand vehicle. The reason for such high rental is not so much due to the 'greed' of exploitative contractors, but more due to the fact that the corporation laws make owning and hiring a rickshaw a very high risk venture and routinely inflict heavy losses on the owners for operating in this sector.

UNREALISTIC QUOTAS

The rickshaw licensing policy was first formalized in 1960 with the introduction of special by-laws for this sector. Phase one lasted till 1975. Under this, the MCD had initially decided on a quota of 600 rickshaws. Later they added another 150 rickshaws for the Shahdara area, bringing the total sanctioned number of rickshaws to 750.

Despite all attempts at controlling the number of rickshaws, they kept registering a steady increase. Thus, the MCD has had to review the sanctioned quota every few years. In 1975, the MCD carried out a survey of this sector that resulted in the implementation of a new policy in 1976, which also resulted in a raised quota of 20,000 rickshaws for all of Delhi. In 1993, the license quota was raised to 50,000—still far short of the actual number of rickshaws plying in the city. In response to a case filed in the Supreme Court by the Rajdhani Cycle Rickshaw Operators Union challenging the arbitrary actions of the MCD, the then Commissioner of Police, Mukund Upadhyay, submitted to the court that as against the 50,000 licences granted by the MCD, there were 4.5 lakh rickshaws in actual operation in Delhi.

In December 1998, the MCD was compelled to raise the quota of sanctioned rickshaws to 99,000 because of the persistent demands of rickshaw operators. However, the deliberate slowness with which the licences began to be issued can be gauged from the fact that for the next three years only 73,000 licences had been issued. For the last year or so, the MCD has stopped issuing new licences altogether, even though the existing insufficient quota is not yet filled. If we take the figure of 10 lakhs provided by Police Commissioner Maxwell Perreira, in effect it means that only one in 14 rickshaws is licensed. The rest are declared illegal. But even the licensed vehicles are tied up in a web of illegality through other devious laws.

The MCD justifies its policy of 'controlling' the number of rickshaws in Delhi by pointing to the growing congestion on Delhi roads due to increasing traffic. The reasoning appears farcical when one considers that there is no comparable limit imposed on the number of cars or other motorized vehicles allowed in the city of Delhi. Two lakh motorized vehicles are being added to Delhi's traffic every year, without any attempt at control. Petrol and diesel driven vehicles have increased at a much faster rate, despite the fact they constitute a serious environmental hazard. By contrast, the cycle rickshaw is a pollution-free, inexpensive vehicle. In a city like Delhi, which is reeling under the impact of air pollution due to an explosion in the number of petrol–diesel based vehicles, this eco-friendly vehicle should have found governmental support and encouragement. Instead, the Delhi government has used archaic and draconian laws to treat people working in this sector as though they are criminals and used the full might of the state to harass, fleece, and hound them through bizarre regulations.

Owner Must be Puller

Apart from attempting to restrict the total number of rickshaws on Delhi roads, government regulations also extend to who can get a licence and the number of rickshaws a person can own. Article 3(1) of the Cycle Rickshaw By-laws of 1960, framed under Section 481 of the Delhi Municipal Corporation Act of 1957, makes the absurd stipulation that 'No person shall keep or ply or hire a cycle-rickshaw in Delhi unless he himself is the owner thereof and holds a licence granted in that behalf by the Commissioner on payment of the fee that may from time to time, be fixed under sub section (2) of Section 430.' Delhi's municipal law further stipulates that 'No person will be granted more than one such licence.' However, some exceptions are allowed. The Commissioner may grant more than one licence to a widow or a handicapped person subject to the limit of five licences. If a person is found driving a car without a licence, he/she is liable to pay a fine of a few hundred rupees. But a person plying a rickshaw without a puller's licence invites confiscation of the vehicle.

The blatant injustice inherent in this provision becomes obvious when juxtaposed against the fact that a person or company may own a whole fleet of cars, trucks, buses, or even aeroplanes but no one is legally permitted to own more than one cycle rickshaw! This, when a new rickshaw costs no more than Rs 3,500 and a second-hand one can be purchased for Rs 800 to 2,000. Thus, someone who owns even 100 rickshaws—new and old—would not have invested more than two to two-and-a-half lakh rupees. In other words, he is still a petty entrepreneur by any standards. This provision was enacted under the pretence of 'protecting' the poor and hapless pullers from the greed of the contractor-businessmen. But in actual fact, this and other draconian restrictions imposed on rickshaw ownership in Delhi have facilitated a vast extortion racket in Delhi.

Despite laws that mandate that licences will only be issued to owners who pull their own rickshaws, very few rickshaw pullers own their own vehicles. The vast majority of rickshaws are owned by petty entrepreneurs who own small or big fleets ranging from five to a couple of hundred rickshaws. These entrepreneurs are disparagingly referred to as *thekedars* or contractors. The owners are allegedly forced to enter into an unofficial agreement with the MCD who issue them licences in bulk in the name of real or imaginary rickshaw pullers, provided they are adequately bribed. The bribe rate allegedly varies from Rs 300 to 600 per licence.

WEB OF ILLEGALITY

However, even after this, no contractor is given licences for his full fleet. A person who owns 100 rickshaws is not likely to have more than 15 to 20 licensed vehicles. The rest remain illegal. A certain agreed amount of 'monthly' payment per rickshaw is allegedly given to the MCD inspectors as well as the local police as 'protection money'. But this does not save their rickshaws from confiscation. By declaring their very existence illegal, the municipal and police authorities hold the rickshaw owners hostage to increasing extortion and blackmail.

A person who lets out his rickshaw on hire is treated as a legal offender. If a person gives his rickshaw on hire or allows his brother, son or any other relative to ply it, the law allows the municipality to seize and confiscate his vehicle. The gross absurdity of this provision glares at us if we consider that a bus, truck, or car owner can hire any number of different drivers to ply his vehicle. But not so a rickshaw owner. This provision has been challenged repeatedly by the rickshaw operators in the court as well as through appeals to policy-makers. They rightly feel that by legislating against their right to own and operate more than one vehicle, the government has violated their very right to livelihood.

The ownership licences issued are valid only for a period of three years but have to be renewed every year. After three years, an owner has to obtain a fresh licence. The going bribe rate for getting a new licence is reported to vary from Rs 200 to Rs 600, though the official fee is only Rs 50. Renewal costs another Rs 25 as official fee and Rs 150 to Rs 200 as grease money.

An owner-puller is supposed to have two kinds of licences—one for owning the rickshaw, the other pulling it. Even getting a driving licence is so difficult that most pullers ply their vehicles without a puller's licence. So they too are dubbed as illegal, thus inviting confiscation of the vehicle.

Even after this, MCD officials are apparently extremely reluctant to give licences to individual pullers. They are far more inclined to give them to contractors who own a fleet of rickshaws. This is an important reason why very few rickshaws in Delhi are owned by the actual pullers. The reluctance to give licences to individual pullers can best be understood by recognizing the logistics of bribe collection. The officials do not allow a rickshaw to be operated in the city without the owners paying a monthly bribe ranging from Rs 50 to Rs 100 per rickshaw, depending on the area. Both these worthies find it much easier to collect bribes from owners who rent a fleet of rickshaws because they have to operate from a fixed location. By contrast, collecting monthly bribes from six lakh individual pullers is a daunting task. Therefore, the few individual pullers who dare approach the MCD for licences are shooed away, unless they come with political *sifarish* of the local corporator or Member of the Legislative Assembly (MLA). The owner displays in bold and prominent letters a code word (often his own name) as a 'password' so that the MCD inspectors know those particular rickshaws are paying regular patronage money. Whether the vehicle is 'legal' or 'illegal', the corporation inspectors expect and extort a certain sum as monthly bribe for each rickshaw he owns. Lower amounts are paid for 'legal' ones and higher for the 'illegal' ones. Thus the officials have acquired a vested interest in keeping the number of illegal vehicles as high as possible.

The licence is granted for a limited zone in the city, earmarked by colour coding of the rickshaw. In all, the MCD has carved out 12 zones of areas under its jurisdiction. Moving out of that fixed and small zone also invites confiscation of the vehicle. Therefore, owners have to 'placate' the inspectors of at least three or four contiguous zones to buy a measure of 'protection'.

FINES, SEIZURES, DESTRUCTION

A far deadlier change in the policy was introduced in 1998 by laying down that all the 'illegal' rickshaws would be confiscated and destroyed. Up until then, the rule was that a certain number of rickshaws were routinely seized under the guise of eliminating 'illegal' rickshaws in the city, but the pre-1998 policy allowed for the release of seized rickshaws after the owner paid the stipulated official fine and a little grease money. Until 1997, the MCD charged a penalty of Rs 100 plus store charges at Rs 3 per day for as long as the rickshaw stayed in the municipality yard. As if that was not steep enough, in 1998, the MCD raised the fine to a minimum of Rs 300 plus Rs 25 per day as store charges for the number of days that the vehicle stayed confiscated in the MCD yard. This policy change introduced in November–December 1998 also lays down that 'unlicensed' rickshaws cannot be officially released. Even where licensed vehicles are concerned, if an owner fails to get the vehicle released within 15 days, by 'proving' that he is indeed the owner-puller, the MCD has the right to destroy the vehicle and auction it as junk.

It is a common allegation that the MCD employees deliberately delay release of seized rickshaws and that the maximum number of rickshaws are seized on a Friday and not released before the next Tuesday, thus inflicting store charges of Rs 125, in addition to Rs 300 as penalty. On an average, it costs Rs 500 to get the seized vehicle back. This does not include the time wasted in meeting all the legal formalities, grovelling, greasing palms, and pleading to get the vehicle released. If we calculate the loss of income to an owner-puller at Rs 100 a day for the average of four days it would take to get the rickshaw released, the total financial drain would come to Rs 900. This when a second-hand rickshaw can easily be purchased for Rs 1,000–1,200. Not surprisingly, many owners do not take the trouble to retrieve a vehicle, especially if it is old.

Since December 2000, the Lieutenant Governor has empowered the traffic police to seize rickshaws without the involvement of the MCD under the pretence of decongesting city roads. Therefore, a good number of these vehicles reach police stations. Getting a rickshaw released from police custody is a far more complicated process and involves similar 'payoffs'.

The penalties for traffic offences are no less draconian. Even within the zone allotted to a rickshaw, there are numerous forbidden zones. 'No Entry' areas are declared arbitrarily. For example, the very popular Central Market in Lajpat Nagar is a forbidden zone for these vehicles, but not for cars, scooters and other motorized vehicles. There is a total ban on rickshaws on the Ring Road. This has created a peculiar problem for a large community of rickshaw pullers living in the slums of Yamuna Pushta, on the banks of the Yamuna river. They cannot move out of their area without crossing the Ring Road. Therefore, the traffic officials make good money by charging them Rs 5 to 10 each time the puller has to cross the Ring Road.

Rickshaws are altogether banned from entering the New Delhi Municipal Corporation (NDMC) area, the Delhi of the *sarkari* VIPs. Any rickshaw caught there is to be seized, crushed and sold as junk. The law does not allow for its release even after paying a fine.

If a car goes into a 'No Entry' area, it is subjected to a mild fine of Rs 100. But for rickshaw owners, the punishment is nothing short of seizure of the vehicle. The rickshaw can be legally released after paying a minimum fine of Rs 325, that is if it is a permit-holding rickshaw driven by a licensed puller. This in effect means a fine amounting to 10 per cent of the cost of a new rickshaw or 30–40 per cent of the cost of a second-hand vehicle. In the case of non-licensed rickshaws, the MCD staff enter into an informal agreement with the owner and take anything from Rs 200–400 (depending on the value of the vehicle) for release of the vehicle.

ONLY RICKSHAWS CONGEST ROADS?

Even duly licensed rickshaws driven by actual owners are routinely seized under one pretext or the other. People in the trade allege that owner-driven rickshaws and licensed rickshaws are targeted for confiscation more vigorously because the MCD officials want to discourage individual ownership.

The most common pretext for seizing rickshaws is 'decongesting' the road. The municipal authorities along with the traffic police enact this drama routinely. They arbitrarily swoop down on busy areas and start seizing both licensed and unlicensed rickshaws on the excuse that these vehicles are cluttering the road. Some of these seized vehicles are released before they reach the municipal yards if the owners comply with the demand of Rs 200–300 per vehicle. But those that are entered in the municipal records involve the usual fine of Rs 325 plus store charges plus the cost of affidavits and other paper work required to get the vehicle released. Even if it turns out that the seizure was illegal or *male fide*, as per the MCD rules and provisions, and that the vehicle was being driven by a duly licensed owner, the *sarkari* inspectors are not held accountable for it and the owner has to pay a minimum of Rs 350 for release of the vehicle.

Even though the rickshaws are forcibly snatched from pullers, in police and municipal records they are invariably entered as *'lawaris'*, found without owner or claimant.

LICENCES NOT GIVEN

Among the many tactics used for discouraging individual ownership is that the MCD does not accept applications for licences all year round while on the other hand, licences for cars, buses, or trucks can be applied for and procured year round. But for cycle rickshaws, the municipal licensing authority invites applications only for two months in a year. Notifications to this effect are issued in newspapers but since most pullers are illiterate or barely literate, they rarely find out about it. Many complain that even if they do know, the MCD officials make it very hard for them to get application forms which are sold in the black market and given to the favoured few. By the time people become aware, officials have already made their deals with select *thekedars* and let them apply for licences in bulk. The rest are kept dangling and insecure year after year.

How this small strategem adds to the risk of owning a rickshaw becomes obvious from the following account: On 22 April 2001 Deepak Suri (age 45), a very poor rickshaw puller from West Delhi, purchased a second-hand rickshaw for Rs 1,200. On 21 August 2001, it was seized by the MCD during one of its routine raids to decongest the city roads. Even though he was the owner-puller, they would not release his rickshaw without a payment of Rs 400 on the ground that he did not possess an owner's licence. His argument that they made it impossible for him to get a licence considering that applications for getting an official permit are accepted only in October–November, not year round, fell on deaf ears. Since he did not have Rs 400 to give them, he grew so desperate that he borrowed Rs 20 to buy petrol and threatened to burn himself to death if they refused to release the only bit of property he owned in the world. Needless to say, his pleas fell on deaf years and he would have probably carried out his threat but for *Manushi's* intervention. We forcibly took away his rickshaw by raiding the municipal yard in a large group. For this act, the MCD inspector threatened to lodge a case of dacoity against us, but did not go ahead because the whole episode was recorded on film by *Manushi*.

All this fleecing plus the soul-destroying harassment means that very often the owner does not claim the rickshaw, especially if it is an old vehicle. If the MCD can show that no one came to claim the rickshaw within 15 days, they have the right to junk it all and sell it as scrap. The whole exercise of cutting up rickshaws after 15 days of seizure provides additional opportunities for corruption. A large proportion of confiscated rickshaws are sold in the market after MCD employees inflict token damage to the vehicles to show in their records that they have dutifully seized 'illegal' vehicles.

The Cycle Rickshaw Operators' Union secured a Supreme Court order which spells out clearly that any time a rickshaw is confiscated, the owner should be given a proper *challan* (receipt). But many operators allege that often MCD employees refuse to give official receipts. Thousands of rickshaws are seized every year without any entry in official records.

The MCD admits to destroying more than 60,000 rickshaws in the last three years. In the year 2000–1,23,000 vehicles are shown as being destroyed in municipal records. In addition, 33,000 rickshaws are recorded as seized and released after paying fines. However, people in this trade allege that at least 50,000–60,000 rickshaws per year are not returned to the owners. While 20,000-odd are entered in records, the rest are surreptitiously sold by MCD staff. The Supreme Court has repeatedly instructed the MCD not to seize licensed vehicles. But these orders are being violated every single municipal working day in Delhi. This serves a dual purpose: they can show on record that they are actively engaged in performing their duty of removing 'illegal' vehicles from the road; at the same time the *babus* are able to issue a powerful threat to rickshaw owners that they can stay in business only if they placate the all powerful agents of *mai baap sarkar* through regular offerings. Virtually every one of the contractors I interviewed asserted that the licensed rickshaws are specially targeted so that the owners are not lulled into complacency and begin assuming that no bribes need be paid for legal rickshaws. Many allege that there is, in fact, less chance of 'illegal' rickshaws being seized as long as the owner pays a fixed monthly bribe to the corporation, because then there is an assured income from it for them. By contrast, people with genuine licences offer relatively greater resistance to paying bribes. Thus the MCD employees have acquired a deep vested interest in encouraging the proliferation of 'illegal' rickshaws.

Manushi's survey of rickshaw pullers and rickshaw owners indicates that police and MCD employees are siphoning off nearly Rs 10 crore per month by way of bribes and fines from the sector. This is not counting the losses incurred due to junked and destroyed rickshaws.

In Conclusion

Over 90 per cent of India's workforce is in the informal sector. Rickshaw operators are among the most visible groups of self-employed people of our country. They provide a vital service for the city. Their entrepreneurial activity should have received all possible encouragement from the government, especially considering that neither the government, nor the organized sector generate enough jobs to absorb the existing workforce in our country. The existing policy of trying to either 'control' the number of people who enter this trade, or abolish this sector altogether—as many policy-makers want to do—will only add to the large army of unemployed people in our country, which in turn will lead to an increase in the crime rate.

Those who are worried about increasing congestion in Delhi, would do well to remember that if these migrants are not able to earn and send their savings to their village-based families, their survival in the village will become unviable and lead to further depression in agricultural production, since these small cash incomes provide the needed investments for the small and marginal farm holdings. In such a situation, whole families will begin migrating to cities, causing much greater congestion than at present.

Demands of this Sector

(i) Abolish the licence-quota system and replace it with on-the-spot registration.

(ii) Stop seizure of rickshaws and punitive fines.

(iii) Abolish restrictions on the number of rickshaws a person can own. Renting rickshaws as a commercial activity should be legalized.

(iv) Create separate tracks for cycles, rickshaws, and other slow-moving vehicles so that they do not have to compete for road space with fast-moving traffic.

(v) Declare all congested market areas 'No Entry' zones for motorized vehicles and allow only cycle rickshaws to operate in such areas. This will reduce pollution and congestion far more effectively than the present policy of banning entry of rickshaws.

Postscript: A Public Hearing of people working in the cycle rickshaw sector was organized by *Manushi* in August 2001 at the India International Centre. The then Prime Minister, Atal Behari Vajpayee intervened personally after reading press reports of *Manushi's* campaign on behalf of street vendors and cycle rickshaw pullers and announced a new policy framework for both these sectors. This document is perhaps the first serious attempt in India to extend the reach of economic reforms to the self-employed poor in India and free their livelihoods from needless and harmful bureaucratic controls. The new policy drafted by the Prime Minister's Office (PMO) responds to many of the concerns raised by *Manushi*. Therefore, we demand its sincere implementation.

The story of *Manushi's* longdrawn out struggle to get this policy implemented will be narrated in a follow-up volume.

2

Blackmail, Bribes, and Beatings*
Licence-Quota-Raid *Raj* for Street Vendors

Over 90 per cent of India's work force earns its livelihood in the informal sector, which accounts for 63 per cent of the country's GDP. Street vendors and hawkers are among the most visible and active parts of this large informal sector. Most of them come from impoverished rural families. Given the poverty in agriculture, they are unable to feed, clothe, and provide other basic necessities for their families by working on the small landholdings they own, or as wage labourers in rural areas. Street vending absorbs millions of those who come to cities as economic refugees from villages, because they can enter this occupation with very small amounts of capital. They not only create employment for themselves through their own entrepreneurial skills, but also help generate employment in agriculture as well as small-scale industry. They are the main distribution channel for a large variety of products of daily consumption—fruit, vegetables, readymade garments, shoes, household gadgets, toys, stationery, newspapers, magazines and so on. If they were to be eliminated from the urban markets, it would lead to a severe crisis for fruit and vegetable farmers, as well as small-scale industries which cannot afford to retail their products through expensive distribution networks in the formal sector. Hawkers provide a low-cost, decentralized and highly efficient system of distribution covering an incredible variety of products, at prices far lower than those prevailing

---

*First appeared in *Manushi*, Issue No. 124, May–June 2001.

in the established markets. They reach the consumer at convenient locations, even at their doorsteps. Middle-class people buy a large proportion of their daily requirements from street vendors, whereas for the poor, hawkers are often the only affordable source for items of daily consumption. Thus, they are a vital link between consumers and producers and make a valuable contribution to the economy. But for their enterprise, urban consumers would have to travel long distances by buses, cars, and scooters to procure their daily necessities, and this, in turn, would lead to more vehicular pollution and congestion.

A detailed study[1] of street vendors selling food on the streets of eight cities in Asia and Africa documents the important service rendered by vendors, who provide the poorer sections of society with nutritious food at affordable prices. It was found that street food is not only far cheaper than restaurant food, but actually costs less than even home prepared food, especially if we take into account the time spent on shopping and cooking. In large and congested cities working people have to spend more and more time on travel. They tend to eat out more often because cooking proper meals at home takes a lot of time and energy. The study also showed that in terms of nutritional value, street food offers far better bargains than restaurant food. Most surprising of all was the finding from Pune that the cheapest street meals, cooked under the most abysmal conditions by the poorest of vendors, were often less contaminated with bacteria than samples taken from restaurants. Even a cursory comparison of the hygiene levels in the kitchens of most Indian restaurants bears out the relative neatness of street food suppliers. Despite lacking basic amenities like regular water supply and place to wash, the arrangements they devise are far better than available in most restaurants where filth is cleverly hidden from sight.

Moreover, as road safety expert Dinesh Mohan pointed out at the Lok Sunwayi organized by the Manushi Nagrik Adhikar Manch for vendors and hawkers—by their very presence, street vendors bring safety and security to the neighbourhoods they work in. Deserted streets and neighbourhoods facilitate the job of criminals. But wherever there are clusters of open shops on pavements, the crime rate is also low.

A group in IIT, Delhi has studied the space requirement for Delhi's vendors and found that all the existing vendors can easily be

---

[1] Tinker, Irene, *Street Foods: Urban Food and Employment in Developing Countries,* New York: Oxford University Press, 1997.

accommodated in the available space, provided the city authorities are willing to plan space allocation in an efficient and rational manner.[2]

The importance of this sector cannot be undermined, especially considering that the government does not have the capacity to provide jobs to the millions of unemployed and underemployed people in India. Even the corporate sector is able to absorb only a tiny proportion of our expanding workforce. Overall employment in the formal sector is actually declining. This means most people in India have to fend for themselves. People in the informal sector ought to be encouraged to grow and prosper if the government wants to reduce unemployment and poverty in our country.

ECONOMIC WAR ON HAWKERS

Instead of creating an enabling environment, government policies are wrecking the livelihoods of these people, depressing their incomes and thwarting their entrepreneurial potential. Street vendors, for example, are treated as legal offenders, as a 'public nuisance' routinely beaten and driven out of public spaces. All this is done 'legally' in the name of cleaning up the city by clearing it of 'illegal encroachments'. Our colonial municipal laws make it unlawful for anyone to vend on the streets without a valid *tehbazari*, which is a legal permit for stationary vending. But, getting a *tehbazari* from the municipality without strong political patronage and massive bribes is near to impossible.

The municipal and police laws are heavily loaded against people working in the informal sector. On the face of it these laws appear to bestow powers on the police and municipal authorities to promote civic order. But in actual fact, arbitrary powers vested in the hands of municipal officials, police, and other related departments have enabled them to establish a vast extortion racket. The figures speak for themselves. Municipal officials claim there are over five lakh vendors in the city of Delhi, out of which only a handful have been issued *tehbazaris*. (Other estimates put the figure at 2.5 lakhs.) In the NDMC area, only 778 persons have been granted this legal status while in the MCD zones, till date this precious document has not been bestowed even on all of the 4,128 persons who, according to an absurd yet stringent criteria used by the government, were supposed to have

---

[2] Tiwari, Geetam, 'Encroachers or Service Providers?', *Seminar*, 491, July 2000.

qualified for getting a *tehbazari*. Thus, lakhs of vendors are doomed to remain illegal encroachers.

The authorities know that declaring the vendors illegal will not make them disappear, in part because there is a massive demand for their services. Moreover, as the hawkers have no other means of livelihood, they too have no option but to carry on with their trade, even if it means facing police beatings and harassment by municipal staff, who have a vested interest in keeping the vendors insecure and grovelling. They use the illegal status of the vendors to fleece them of a good part of their earnings. If any one of them resists paying, that person is beaten out of the market. In order to keep them frightened as a collectivity, municipal authorities and the police carry out frequent raids in the informal 'natural' markets created by these hawkers and vendors. In the guise of removing illegal encroachments, they seize their goods and *rehdis* (push carts) and lock up all the confiscated property in municipal yards.

Even those who have licensed stalls are not spared. Their stalls and wares are likewise destroyed or confiscated. They are then expected to pay hefty fines to get their push carts and goods released. The going rate of penalty in 2001 was Rs 1,450 plus Rs 300 as 'removal charges' and Rs 100 per day as store charges for the number of days their *rehdis* stayed in municipal yards. Thus a vendor spends a minimum of Rs 1,900 to get his *rehdi* released from the municipality, that is, if it is released the very next day. Often the vendors cannot pay the exorbitant fines and bribes demanded of them for releasing their goods. So they have to start from scratch again.

There are times when entire markets are demolished. It takes them at least a few weeks or even months to resume work by arriving at a new settlement with the police, municipal employees, and local corporators, who are often complicit partners in this extortion racket. Most of these raids are meant to terrorize them into paying the ever escalating bribes demanded of them.

'SARKARI' EXTORTION RACKET

During my survey at various markets in Delhi, I found that the current monthly extortion rates for pavement sellers range from Rs 500 to Rs 3,000 a month for ordinary markets. In locations like Connaught Place, many are even paying Rs 10,000 and more per month. A majority of the small vendors pay between Rs 500 and Rs 800 per month to the MCD, police and local *goondas* as 'protection money'. Those with regular *tehbazaris* pay less if they have not encroached on extra space. Nor are they spared the humiliation of having to placate the tyrannical deities of the licence-permit-*raj* through regular cash offerings. In addition, the police often take away their goods without payment, whenever they so desire. This results in a major loss of income for them. Thus, if we calculate at a modest average of Rs 500 per person per month by way of cash bribes and Rs 300 per month for loss of income due to open robbery of their goods by government servants, the five lakh vendors of Delhi are being fleeced of Rs 40 crore a month, by the government functionaries.

Many of them, especially the fruit–vegetable vendors and chicken–fish sellers, lose a lot more by way of forced offerings in kind allegedly demanded by the police and MCD staff. Add to it the loss of income when they are uprooted and prevented from carrying on their trade for days or weeks on end. If an average of 20 working days is lost every year at Rs 100 a day, the vendors of Delhi alone are likely to be losing another Rs 100 crore per year due to frequent disruptions in their work. They also suffer additional losses when their goods and *rehdis* are seized. Calculated at a modest Rs 2,000 per person per year loss on this account, even if we assume that only two lakh vendors bear this loss, it totals to another Rs 40 crore per year.

All this information is based on hundreds of interviews I have personally conducted since 1995, when I made my first film on street vendors of Delhi. In that film I estimated the bribe amount to be roughly Rs 6 crore a month. Since then the number of vendors and the bribe rates have both gone up substantially, as also my information level about this sector. Therefore, my estimate that Delhi's vendors are currently paying collective bribes of nearly Rs 40 crore a month is not likely to be off the mark. I do not claim infallibility for these figures and would happily correct myself, if the government or some other agency can come up with more reliable information. However, for the time being, I have to trust the figures I collected, because numerous street vendors have given this information on film and many have even provided written affidavits to *Manushi* about the money each one of them is forced to pay. Given the tremendous risks involved in their speaking out so openly, it is unlikely that the information they have provided is exaggerated. My experience tells me that the vendors tend to understate the bribery amounts because of fear. Moreover, they have come to accept a certain amount of financial squeeze as inevitable and, therefore, do not keep count of it. In this context it is noteworthy that though *Manushi* has released these figures to the press, no one from the government has contradicted or denied their validity.

BEATINGS AND ABUSE

On top of it all, many of them, especially the new entrants into this occupation, are routinely beaten, humiliated, and abused by the police. These constant economic and physical assaults not only depress their incomes, but also destroy their self-esteem and confidence. This routine violation of their fundamental and human rights takes place at the hands of the very same people who ought to be ensuring the safety of their lives and property.

This growing violence and insecurity is an important reason why very few women take to vending and hawking in cities like Delhi. The few who dare to venture into this occupation are either widows or older married women whose husbands cannot earn enough. Most families do not allow young girls and women to join this trade because they are far more vulnerable to abuse and violence than men. Thus, women lose out on the few available sources of livelihood and are prevented from developing entrepreneurial skills.

If things are allowed to continue like this, many frustrated young men are likely to gravitate towards theft and take to crime as a way of earning a living. This is already beginning to happen, as is evident from the increasing crime rate in Delhi which is jeopardizing the safety and well-being of all the citizens—rich and poor alike. It is making Delhi more and more unsafe even for business investment.

RIGHT TO LIVELIHOOD

Hawkers and vendors of various cities have fought long-drawn battles, both in the streets as well as through the courts to assert their right to a dignified livelihood. The Supreme Court itself has upheld this right numerous times, but the administration continues to flout it with impunity. In 1985, the Supreme Court, in the *Bombay Hawkers Union* vs *Bombay Municipal Corporation* case, directed that each city should formulate clear-cut schemes which earmark special Hawking Zones after which they could declare certain areas as No-Hawking Zones.

This was followed by a landmark judgment in 1989: the *Sodhan Singh* vs *NDMC* case. It held that 'Street trading is an age-old vocation adopted by human beings to earn a living...[and] comes within the protection guaranteed under the Article 19(1)(g) of the Indian Constitution which guarantees the right to earn a living as a fundamental right.' Therefore, city administrations were directed to facilitate hawkers in acquiring a legal status. Unfortunately, the Supreme Court orders have been flouted with contempt, not just by municipal authorities in Delhi, but in other states as well.

In the Lok Sunwayi held on 25 June 2001, N. Vittal, the then Central Vigilance Commissioner, who presided over the Public Hearing, was visibly moved on hearing first-hand accounts from female and male vendors of the indignities and brutalities they routinely suffer while carrying on their humble trade. He immediately took up the matter with the municipal authorities, the Chief Minister of Delhi and the central government's Ministry of Urban Development. He supported *Manushi's* demand that this trade be de-licensed, since the track record of our municipal and police authorities makes it abundantly clear that they use the licensing system only as an instrument of terror and extortion. Leading columnist Tavleen Singh noted, 'One feels ashamed as an Indian to see how our fellow citizens are tyrannized and robbed of their earnings by the government machinery.' She pledged full support for *Manushi's* campaign to end blackmail, bribes, and beatings suffered by street vendors. Leading neurosurgeon Dr Vijay Sheel Kumar was shocked that fellow citizens of Delhi were getting such a raw deal. He also emphasized the need for rational monitoring mechanisms to ensure that our public spaces are run in an orderly manner. Dr Dinesh Mohan's brief speech was a real booster for the demoralized vendors, when he spoke about the important role played by vendors in making our cities safe, how they save valuable time and money for urban consumers and reduce vehicular pollution in cities.

MAKING COMMON CAUSE

Our holding this Lok Sunwayi in the air-conditioned FICCI auditorium puzzled some of *Manushi's* friends, who felt that this was politically incorrect and bound to give the wrong impression to potential sympathizers. However, ours was a well thought-out decision. The street vendors had been invited to share their *dukh* (grievances and grief) with us fellow citizens, who are better placed than them. It is our duty to share our *sukh-aaram* (comforts) with them. Why do we assume that clean and comfortable environments are meant only for the middle and upper classes? These vendors work under extremely harsh circumstances, braving the hot sun in summer, icy winds in winter, and many a watery deluge in the monsoon every day of their lives. The least we could do was to provide them cool comfort for one day when they came to pour out their grievances before us. They are rarely treated as fellow citizens by middle and upper class people, leave alone the *babus* and *netas* before whom they have to constantly kowtow and grovel.

Ours was a small gesture to communicate the message that we consider them fellow citizens. We are not condescending to 'help them' but wish to make common cause with them.

Give Them Their Due

Through this Public Hearing, *Manushi* appealed to the citizens of Delhi, especially those who carry influence with policy-makers and administrators, to help make Delhi a bribe-free, terror-free city. It is in the interests of all to make common cause in removing corruption and the inevitable violence and crime that accompanies it.

The following demands were made on behalf of vendors:

(i) At a time when big industries are being de-licensed, and factories worth crores can be set up without complex licensing requirements, street vending should also be de-licensed.

(ii) Instead of treating them as a 'public nuisance', services of vendors should be given due recognition. The Supreme Court order requiring every city to clearly demarcate 'Hawking' and 'No-Hawking' zones should be expeditiously implemented, taking the actual requirements of every city's population into account, rather than based on arbitrary, bureaucratic whims. A 'Pay and Hawk' scheme would also increase the revenue collected by municipalities, provided that payments are allowed to reach government treasuries.

(iii) As long as the Delhi government fails to evolve and implement a viable policy for street vendors by allocating proper Hawking Zones, raids by the municipality and clearance operations should be altogether suspended.

(iv) Keeping in view the importance of the 'natural markets' developed by street vendors, the city administration should be pressured to provide them with water and sanitation facilities so that they can maintain cleanliness and hygiene in their markets.

(v) Since the police *danda* is used mostly on honest citizens while the anti-social elements actually get protection from the police, the policemen should be disarmed of their *dandas*. In no functioning democracy is the police allowed to wield *lathis* (batons) on innocent citizens, the way it is done in India. Today citizens of India, especially the poor, need to be protected from the police. One small step in that direction would be *danda*-free policing.

(vi) In addition, the police should be given better training and better pay packets, along with establishing effective accountability in their functioning, if they are to act as an instrument of law and order, rather than promote crime. They, too, need help in restoring their self-respect, so that they do not behave like thugs and looters.

(vii) We urge residents' associations to join the vendors to form *Nagrik Sahyog Samitis* (Citizens' Cooperation Committees) to curb the abuse of power by police and bring municipal officials to account. *Manushi* will attempt to facilitate residents and vendors working together to ensure cleaner and orderly markets.

The meeting ended with an appeal to the concerned citizens of Delhi to help resettle thousands of uprooted vendors who have not been allowed to resume their trade for weeks or months because they have resisted the continuing escalation in bribe rates. Many such families are facing destitution and are sinking under debt.

It is only when well-off citizens join in solidarity with vulnerable groups that we can effectively curb the extortion rackets we are trapped in. That is bound to lower the market prices of the products sold by vendors and bring down the crime levels in our cities.

Note: Following the announcement of the Prime Minister's New Policy for Street Vendors of Delhi in response to *Manushi*'s campaign, a National Task Force set up by the Ministry of Urban Development and Poverty Alleviation has drafted a national policy for street vendors. In the meantime, *Manushi* undertook two pilot projects in collaboration with the MCD to show by concrete example how street vendors can be accommodated with dignity in the city with due care for aesthetics by proper planning and rational allocation of space for various categories of road users. *Manushi* has also undertaken the responsibility of collecting taxes on behalf of MCD as well as ensuring cleanliness and discipline in these Model Vendor Markets. The story of this long-drawn battle is being continually reported through *Manushi* (October 2004).

3

Cutting our Own Lifeline*
A Review of India's Farm Policy

*We may not be deceived by the wealth to be seen in the cities of India....
It comes from the blood of the poorest.... I know village economics. I tell
you that the pressure from the top crushes those at the bottom. All that is
necessary is to get off their backs.*

—*Mahatma Gandhi*

The decision of the government of India to import nearly 3 million
tonnes of wheat from Canada, the US, and Australia in 1992 at the
cost of Rs 1,500 crores to be paid in foreign exchange, calls for a debate
on the agrarian question. Import of foodgrains on this scale after years
of boasting about self-sufficiency in food, merits attention in itself.
Farmers' leaders who opposed this decision were particularly incensed
by the fact that this wheat was purchased in the international market at
a price higher than the domestic procurement price of Rs 280 per
quintal fixed by the government for domestic wheat producers. The
landing price of this wheat, which included a freight charge of about
$30 per tonne, was about Rs 530 per quintal, almost twice as much as
the domestic procurement price.

According to the Prime Minister's own admission, that was not a
crisis year for Indian agriculture. There had been no major drought or
crop failure. How then did our policy-makers rationalize import of

*First published in *Manushi*, Issue No. 73, November–December 1992.

wheat amounting to half of that year's wheat procurement? The food secretary, Tejinder Khanna, justified this decision, saying: 'If the same quantity was purchased from the domestic market, the prices would have shot up' (*Times of India,* 14 November 1992). This was a clear admission that the import was part of a strategy of price warfare against the peasantry, an attempt to browbeat the Indian farmers into selling their produce at artificially depressed prices.

This measure comes as a retaliation against the reluctance of the wheat-producing peasantry of north India, especially Punjab, to sell their produce at the government-fixed below-market price of Rs 280 per quintal. Even before the above mentioned import, the Punjab government had forbidden the *artias* (private grain traders) from operating in the *mandis* of Punjab while the government was carrying out its procurement operations, in the expectation that the farmers would be compelled to sell more of their stocks to the government. The district administrators were asked by the Chief Minister of Punjab to let the grain dealers know that no trucks carrying grain would be allowed to move out of the state and if they flouted this 'order' their licences would be impounded. The farmers of Punjab tried resisting this illegal coercion to some extent. Many held back their stocks until they could sell in the open market. As a result, the year's grain procurement, which had been declining in the last few years, touched a record low. Two years before it was 10 million tonnes while in the previous year it came down to 7.7 million tonnes. In 1992 the government could procure no more than 6.35 million tonnes. Government stocks had indeed touched the very bottom with less than 2 million tonnes of wheat left in state godowns. Yet, it is noteworthy that the open market price went no higher than Rs 330 per quintal—substantially lower than what the imported wheat cost us. Subsequent to the arrival of imported wheat, the prices fell further even in the open market.

Poorly Thought-Out Bluff

It was argued that this was the best option for meeting the requirement of the public distribution system. The Prime Minister defended the decision to import wheat as one based on 'timely anticipation' (*Times of India,* 14 November 1992). He said the government was advised to import wheat in July–August the previous year, when shortage of rainfall created fears about the likelihood of a drought. But then he admits that the conditions changed dramatically in September. That this was a poorly thought-out bluff becomes obvious when one considers the following:

(i) The contract for the wheat import was finalized in October—that is, after the predictions about a likely drought were proven wrong with a good rainfall in August–September.

(ii) The *kharif* rains of July–August have little to do with the *rabi* crop of wheat. In fact late *kharif* rains in August–September brighten the prospects of a good *rabi* crop. Therefore, the decision to import in October seems absurd. Our policy-makers were probably not aware of the nuances of the agricultural calendar.

(iii) The delivery for the American wheat was scheduled for March–April 1993, the harvest time of the *kharif* wheat crop in Punjab. Thus, it seems that the decision to import was not really linked to an anticipated shortage in domestic production.

Is it likely that it was motivated by factors similar to the ones that prevailed in the Bofors deal?

Tejinder Khanna, when specifically asked this question, gave a reply that should win him an award in naivete. 'The wheat has been bought directly ... through the government agencies and there is no question of involvement of any middlemen or agents at any stage' (*Indian Express,* 9 November 1992). Does that mean the commissions were coming directly to those in the government who make these deals?

In fact, now it is being admitted that due to a good monsoon the country was set for a record production of more than 176 million tonnes of foodgrains in 1992–3, though this is still below the official target of 183 million tonnes. However, our policy-makers insisted that the country might still have to import more wheat because farmers may be reluctant to sell their produce at the government fixed price (*Economic Times,* 16 December 1992).

Even for government spokesmen it would have been difficult to pretend that the import of wheat was in tune with their much flaunted liberalization policy, since our government is using the might of the state to subdue our farmers through unfair competition. Nor does the government decision seem rational if it still wanted to attain the objective of achieving self-sufficiency in foodgrains.

It is strange that despite having become enthusiastic new converts to the internationally fashionable *mantra* of free trade as a key to economic prosperity, our policy-makers were not too embarrassed to resort to such harsh interventionist measures against farmers. The import of foreign wheat might have been justified had it cost less than the domestic wheat. This decision to import seems particularly inexplicable when one considers that it was paid for in foreign currency. To fritter away our borrowed foreign exchange in a dumping operation of wheat, of all things, cannot be considered proof of good economic sense.

BETTER ALTERNATIVES

The situation created by inadequate procurement response could have been met more effectively and with far more grace by any one of the following three measures, or a combination thereof:

(i) Pruning the list of the beneficiaries of the PDS to exclude the well-to-do. For example, by linking the PDS to the Food for Work programmes we can ensure that food and other essentials reach the poor, especially those living in villages.

(ii) Quiet purchases of wheat in the open market.

(iii) Procurement and issue of coarse grains like *bajra* and *jowar* to make up for the deficit in wheat procurement wherever possible.

No doubt grain prices would have risen had the government agreed to purchase at the open market price, but that would have had some good consequences as well. Higher prices would have given a boost in the coming years to wheat production, which had stagnated at 54 to 55 million tonnes, even while the demand is continuously going up. For a number of years foodgrain production has been stagnating in our country hovering between 170–174 million tonnes. Unremunerative price of foodgrains being one of the major reasons for this stagnation.

DISINCENTIVES TO FARMERS

Our past experience has shown that imports, unless they bring in new technology, have invariably discouraged production, as for instance happened with PL 480 food imports from the US. Only when we cut down on food imports did we get going with our green revolution in the late 1960s.

In his address to the first Agricultural Science Congress organized by the Indian Agricultural Research Institute, the then Prime Minister Vajpayee had cautioned the nation about the fall in foodgrain production due to diversion of land to relatively more lucrative crops. He said the country needed to double or even triple its food output in the next five to 10 years, given the rate of population growth and called upon agricultural scientists to find ways and means of performing this task.

Scientists do not produce grain. Farmers do. No matter how good the scientific input in devising high yield variety seeds and how successful their laboratory experiments, if farmers are not enthusiastic about growing foodgrain and are shifting to relatively more lucrative crops, foodgrain production cannot go up. In the short run, the government may squeeze the farmers into selling at below market prices; ultimately it cannot force them to produce crops they consider uneconomic.

It is a myth created by the urban elite that only rich farmers grow cash crops, whereas the poor grow only foodgrains for their own subsistence. That amounts to considering the poor too foolish to know their own self-interest. They would be even poorer if they stuck to this scheme. It is common for poor farmers, even in dryland agriculture, to grow whatever cash crops they can manage—potatoes, peanuts, bananas, tobacco. Thus, it is not just the much abused rich farmers who will shift away from foodgrains if they do not get adequate returns, even the poor farmers will do so.

These days our policy-makers are never tired of saying we need to bring about economic efficiency and close down loss-making industrial units. Why then are farmers expected to stick to those crops which they find unprofitable? Our policy-makers ought to remember that they do not possess the kind of instruments that Stalin wielded to make the peasantry accept state diktats. It was only by exterminating large sections of the peasantry that even Stalin could force his will on the peasantry. In the process, he destroyed the economic viability of the Soviet Union.

EFFECTS OF GOOD AND BAD PRICES

Prices play a crucial role in the production decisions of farm families. Even at the national level we have had clear proof of this. During the 1950s when India was heavily dependent on food imports, agricultural prices stayed depressed and production stagnated or declined. The Indian government abandoned its policy of food dependency only when India experienced arm twisting tactics by the US during the Indo–Pak war. In the spring of 1966, the government imported from Mexico 18,000 tonnes of a high yielding variety of wheat, to be used as seed. The international market price of wheat at the time was Rs 54 a kilo. The Indian government announced a procurement price of Rs 76, thus giving the farmers of Punjab the required incentive to bring about a revolution in grain production. After six years, however, the price incentive was withdrawn on the plea that the farmers should now share the gains of the Green Revolution with the consumer. The result of protecting the interest of the urban consumer at the cost of the peasantry is that over the past few years foodgrain production has begun to stagnate.

The experience of milk production is equally telling. During the period 1971–85, Gujarat, which was the hub of Operation Flood and the biggest beneficiary of the huge quantities of milk and butter-oil imported from the European Community (EC) countries, lagged far behind in milk production with a mere 4 per cent per annum rate of increase as against an average of 6.5 per cent for the rest of the country. This, despite the much touted achievements of the government-sponsored cooperatives of milk producers in Gujarat. It was dry and arid Maharashtra which produced the best results in milk production with a 10 per cent per annum increase during the same period. This was because Maharashtra's milk producers had obtained better prices, particularly for cow milk. The academic debate on Operation Flood in India has avoided answering this question: why is it that the European Economic Community (EEC) continues to offer milk producers attractive prices rather than slash milk prices, even if it means dumping the surplus 'mountains of butter' and 'lakes of milk' as gifts to takers like India? As a direct contrast to the EEC, India's response is to gratefully accept these gifts to bring down milk prices even at the cost of discouraging domestic production.

RICH COUNTRIES HEAVILY SUBSIDIZE AGRICULTURE

The policies followed in the developed countries present a stark contrast to those followed in India. In a well documented article reviewing world agriculture (*Economic and Political Weekly*, 26 September 1992), Ashok Gulati and A.N. Sharma establish a long-standing contention of the farmers' movement, that many of those countries which are supposed to have performed economic miracles have one thing in common. They all heavily subsidize their agriculture. In marked contrast to the policies in economically advanced countries, government policies of poor countries such as India, Bangladesh, and Pakistan result in negative subsidies, that is, the peasantry is actually being economically drained through price controls, rather than subsidized. This is a major reason for the continuing rural poverty in South Asia. Most professional economists have hitherto denied or ridiculed the basic fact that Indian farmers are getting an unfavourable deal through government interventions in agricultural prices.

Among the advanced countries, Japan tops the list in extending farm subsidies, amounting to 72.5 per cent of the price of its agricultural produce. The comparable figures for some of the leading exporters of agricultural produce are:

USA	26.17	per cent	Canada	33.50 per cent
EEC	37.00	per cent		

Even the newly emerging industrial powers of Asia give huge subsidies to their agriculture. The figures for the two leading giants are:

Korea	60.67	per cent	Taiwan	22.33 per cent

However, India's peasantry bears a heavy negative subsidy of minus 2.33 per cent. Negative subsidy is calculated on the difference between the price at which the farmer has to sell the produce within the country and the price he would have got, if there was free international trade. Pakistan does even worse than India and taxes its farm sector to the tune of minus 21.80 per cent.

The crop-specific figures are no less revealing. The United States, Canada, and the EC countries are among the largest exporters of wheat, primarily due to protection. Their subsidy figures are:

USA	40.67	per cent	Canada	36.17 per cent
EEC	32.27	per cent		

Once again, the poorer economies are the ones to impose high taxation or negative subsidy on their wheat producers.

The figures for negative subsidies based on the average of 1982–7 prices are:

Pakistan	32.20	per cent	Bangladesh	28.50	per cent
USSR	30.00	per cent	China	5.50	per cent
India	3.83	per cent[*]			

[*][In its submission to the GATT secretariat in 1994, the Ministry of Commerce admitted that in respect of just 20 commodities, Indian farmers have a negative subsidy of Rs 24,000 crores per year—a loss of nearly 69 per cent of the total value of production of these commodities. Thus the negative subsidy of 3.83 per cent calculated by Ashok Gulati would be a gross underestimation.]

Since 1987, the tax or negative subsidy for the wheat growers of India went up due to the devaluation of the rupee. It is the same story for rice, cotton and other crops. It is noteworthy that those governments which impose negative subsidies through price controls are mostly the ones which have to import food.

The main instruments of the US government have been direct payments to farmers, market price support programmes, and input subsidies. The EC intervenes mainly through its Common Agricultural Policy (CAP) and uses border measures, market support prices and export subsidy mechanisms for helping farmers. The price support element of the CAP now accounts for about two-thirds of the entire EC budget. Japan's agricultural policy concentrates on food security, narrowing the gap between farm and non-farm incomes and on improving productivity. It uses price support programmes and restrictions on imports for carrying out these policies. As the leading industrial power it would be far cheaper if Japan were to import food. Yet, the Japanese emphasize the social and political role of agriculture rather than its strictly economic role and treat rice almost as a 'defence item'. There is a total ban on rice imports in Japan despite the fact that its price is five to six times that of the international market.

Thus, in most developed countries, the governments give all manner of economic incentives to farmers to help them find foreign markets, at the same time protecting them from agricultural products from other countries. In almost all developed countries, the farmers have enough clout to be able to resist imports, including those of cheaper and better quality commodities. For example, in the summer of 1992 the French farmers blocked highways to protest against the import of beef from England at rates cheaper than prevalent in France and were successful in stopping those imports. Then the French government was locked in a major battle with the US government because of its refusal to cut down on oil subsidies to French farmers, thus making it difficult for American soyabean growers to sell their product at competitive prices. The American government's threat to impose a 100 per cent import duty on French wine entering the US triggered off a massive protest by the French peasants. Whatever the outcome of this battle, some things are certain.

(i) Despite the peasantry being a small proportion of the overall population in developed countries (in the US it is no more than 2 per cent of the total population), it exercises tremendous clout with the government of its own country.

(ii) No developed country subjects its own peasantry to unfair competition. Mostly, they are not even expected to prove their worth in the international market, but rather given enormous subsidies for their protection.

(iii) Agricultural development is very central to the thinking of economic planners in advanced countries, rather than regarded as an unfortunate nuisance as in India.

The *Research Observer,* the half-yearly publication of the World Bank, has documented how advanced countries are increasingly invoking anti-dumping laws to restrict exports from developing countries. It speaks volumes for the sorry plight of the Indian peasantry that, despite constituting 70 per cent of our population, it lacks the clout to successfully prevent our government from dumping foreign food products in India—after purchasing them at higher than domestic prices.

PRICE CONTROL THROUGH CRIPPLING RESTRICTIONS

In India, in contrast to Japan and other developed countries, crushing state interventions impose a variety of restrictions on the peasantry in order to prevent them from selling their goods at market prices, both within the country and outside of it. This method has become the key instrument of taxing the peasantry, leading to a situation of negative subsidy. For instance, in the case of wheat, the government retains the right of pre-emption in states like Punjab and Haryana, and informally even bars private traders from buying. There have been phases when severe zonal restrictions were imposed, that is, inter-state movement of wheat within the country was forbidden. Even now, there are informal controls imposed on the movement of grain out of the states of Punjab and Haryana.

Rice is procured through a levy on traders and millers at a price fixed by the government. While there are no restrictions on the movement of non-levy rice, some states impose informal restrictions on the inter-state movement of paddy/rice to facilitate procurement in the state. For example, in Thanjavur district in Tamil Nadu, the government has a monopoly over procurement and paddy is not allowed to move out of the district.

Thus, for the farmers, as a result of government intervention, India is not a unified single territory. Economic borders are created for them arbitrarily. In Maharashtra, cotton is procured under the monopoly procurement scheme and farmers are forbidden from selling in other states and have to pay hefty bribes to the police if they want to 'smuggle' their produce to neighbouring states when prices are higher there. The same is true for farmers from Andhra Pradesh or Madhya Pradesh wanting to sell their produce in Maharashtra.

No less crippling are the restrictions on processing of farm produce. Rice growers are forbidden from husking their own paddy without getting a licence from the government. Ginning of cotton is a simple process and was traditionally done at the village level. But today only licensed gin mills are allowed to gin cotton. Cotton growers cannot gin the cotton they produce even though this simple activity would enhance their profit margins considerably as well as give them useful by-products. Likewise, if the apple producers in Himachal Pradesh were allowed to make cider and milk producers of a milk surplus state like Maharashtra were permitted to process the milk, they would not face a seasonal marketing crisis as they do now. The list of restrictions on the agricultural sector are endless.

HIJACKING OF SUPPORT PRICES

The Agricultural Prices Commission (APC), appointed by Lal Bahadur Shastri in 1965 with the view to providing the requisite price incentives to farmers, functioned according to Shastri's vision only in the first few years. With the end of the political and economic crisis after the Indo–Pak war, the usual bureaucratic inefficiency, complacency, and anti-farmer bias crept into the functioning of the APC. Defective and inadequate collection of data, erroneous methodology and deliberate undercalculations in the prices of agricultural inputs became the hallmarks of its price fixation policy. The cost data of APC contains such absurdities as the following: In 1977, the cost of spraying insecticide was put at 1 paisa per 1 hectare of wheat while determining that year's support price for wheat!

Its estimates of irrigation costs to farmers have often been so low that they would not even cover the cost of electricity charges (even at subsidized rates) for running their lift irrigation pumps. In the last decade, a great deal of the wrath of the farmers' movement has been directed at the functioning of the APC and its successor, the Commission for Agricultural Costs and Prices (CACP), because it was often found to recommend prices that prevailed in the market two to three years back, rather than perform the task it was meant to—namely fix prices realistically so that farmers get adequate returns for their crops. Today, the support/procurement prices announced by the CACP have the effect not so much of providing the basic minimum that a farmer must get for a particular crop, but rather of ensuring that even in the 'open market', traders need never pay more than the prices determined by the government.

AGRICULTURAL EXPORTS DISCOURAGED

Worse still are the restrictions on agricultural export. The export of cotton is tightly controlled with yearly quotas released in small instalments over the cotton year. In addition, such exports are subject to a minimum export price fixed by the Textile Commissioner. Thus Indian cotton producers are not allowed to compete freely in the international market. This despite the fact that there is a big demand for the new varieties of long staple cotton now being produced in India and our cotton fetches higher prices than that of most other types of cotton available in the international market.

If these two controls were to be removed, India could be exporting a minimum of 15 lakh bales of cotton. Why is this not allowed? Simply to ensure a cheap, assured supply of cotton to our forever sick textile industry, which has remained sick despite government provided protection—by forbidding import of foreign textiles while allowing it to freely import synthetic fibre to cut down prices of raw cotton produced in India.

In fact, in 1992 the price of cotton slumped by Rs 300 to Rs 400 per tonne as compared to the same time previous year because of low domestic demand. The weak textile industry is neither in a position to buy fresh cotton nor pay the overdues of the previous years without massive subsidies.

The experts in Punjab and Haryana as also the Northern Indian Cotton Growers Union apprehended that if the government delayed allowing the export of surplus cotton, farmers may stop growing cotton even in the districts covered under the World Bank-aided intensive cotton development programme (*Economic Times,* 16 December 1992).

Even where permitted, external trade is subject to stringent government regulations. Export of wheat is subject to a ceiling fixed by the government and administered through the Agriculture Processed Food Products Exports Development Authority (APEDA). *Basmati* rice can be sent out under open general licence but is subject to a minimum export price. Non-*basmati* rice cannot be exported beyond the ceiling fixed by the government. Export of onions and cotton have to be channelized through the bureaucratic and corrupt National Agricultural Cooperative Marketing Federation of India (NAFED). Even the export of nigerseed, for which there is no domestic demand, has to be channelized through NAFED and TRIFED despite complaints from foreign buyers of poor quality supplies and unprofessional approach to exports, leading to stagnation of export volume.

Excuses for Discouraging Agricultural Exports

The policy of export restrictions on agriculture is based on two tenets which have had extremely adverse consequences not only for agriculture but the entire economy. The agricultural produce is supposed to be exported only when the production is perceived as being more than adequate to meet all the local demands. Pressures by secondary and tertiary sectors of the domestic economy to keep the prices of their raw materials low have generally resulted in bans on the export of even surplus production. Mill owners have systematically manipulated production and consumption statistics to create a bogey of scarcity to justify imports and bans on the export of cotton. This now-on-now-off-with-a-small-trickle quotas export policy has been disastrous for the credibility of Indian exporters of agricultural produce. The vicissitudes of this policy have cost India precious markets.

The second tenet holds that export of value-added articles is to be preferred in all cases to that of primary produce. The hypothesis is not necessarily true, particularly if the cost added exceeds the value added—as happens in most cases where the plant, machinery, and technology are imported, making our supposedly value-added goods uncompetitive on account of both their high price and their being a shoddy imitation of western industrial goods. In reality, there is no conflict between the export of value-added goods and raw agricultural produce. The USA leads in both these categories. So do France and Italy. This policy of encouraging the crippled industrial sector and discouraging the competent agricultural sector has resulted in India today being counted as one of the world's basket cases.

All this, when the governments of most developed countries aggressively pursue the interests of their farming communities by helping them find export markets through various devices. In our country, the government has been actively blocking the way of farmers, preventing them from competing in the international market. Instead it has been providing all kinds of incentives to the industrial sector, such as protected markets within India through high tariff walls and supplies of cheap raw materials, encouraging it to become parasitic and incompetent. Even after the recent reduction, India's tariff rate for industrial goods, at 85 per cent, is the highest in the world. For years industrialists were even given cash incentives if they managed to export. But there is hardly any demand for Indian industrial goods as they are extremely shoddy and uncompetitively priced. It is our *basmati* rice, wheat, cotton, mangoes, new varieties of seedless grapes, and a host of other agricultural products which are capable of competing successfully in foreign markets and earning the foreign exchange necessary to bail the country out of its economic crisis.

ECONOMIC DRAIN OF PEASANTRY

The British colonial *raj* was based on the direct economic drain of the peasantry through brutally high taxation which led to large-scale pauperization and landlessness. The brown *sahibs* who took over from the British were smart enough to remove land revenue as a form of taxation. Instead, they opted for indirect forms of taxation through forcing unfair terms of trade on agricultural producers.

According to an estimate by Dilip Swamy and Ashok Gulati, in the decade of the 1970s the peasantry was drained of Rs 45,000 crores (at March 1986 prices) through unfavourable terms of trade manipulated by government controls. This is a form of indirect taxation. They estimate that at present this form of economic drainage is likely to be close to Rs 7,000 to 8,000 crores a year. Sharad Joshi, the leading spokesman of Indian farmers and founder of Shetkari Sangathana had calculated the quantum of economic drain at around Rs 12,000 crores per year because the former estimate is based on the highly inadequate APC data.

Yet the bureaucracy and the urban intelligentsia never tire of complaining against the pampering of the peasantry and justifying controls on the farmers on the grounds that the farm sector does not pay income tax. Some of the leading voices within the peasant movement like that of Joshi have for long been demanding the 'honour and privilege' of paying income tax. The government has avoided imposing an income tax on the peasantry because it will bring out the sad truth that only a minuscule section of farmers have incomes large enough to qualify even for the bottom rungs of the tax paying bracket.

Today it is only the black money-possessing urban elite (doctors, lawyers, politicians, bureaucrats, and businessmen) who are benefiting from income tax exemption of the farm sector. They invest their ill-gotten wealth into buying huge estates and build luxurious palaces of the kind that have mushroomed in Delhi's Sainik Farm area. They escape paying taxes on this by having phoney poultry or dairy farms with five-and-a-half chickens or one-and-a-half cows or a small patch of land set aside for supplying to five-star hotels exotic vegetables such as avocados and asparagus, grown by hiring low-paid *maalis*. If income tax is introduced in the farm sector, it is these worthies who are going to be adversely affected—not the real farmers, because those who are really living by working on the land are too poor to be tax worthy.

PRODUCERS STARVE: CONSUMERS THRIVE

Our policy-makers are never tired of repeating that they follow these policies with a view to protecting the interests of the poor, helpless consumer, for if they lifted restrictions on agriculture, prices of food would shoot up. Grain procurement, in particular, is justified in the name of providing cheap food through the PDS. That this is far from the truth becomes evident when we consider that 80 per cent of those living below the poverty line live in villages, whereas the vast majority (80 per cent) of PDS outlets are in urban areas. The cheap ration hardly ever reaches the poor landless labourers in whose name government justifies its anti-farmer policies. Instead it is cornered by the urban upper and middle class and their servants, lower middle classes and a small segment of the urban poor. It is common for well-off families in cities to enter into an arrangement with their servants whereby they take the servant family's ration sugar in return for allowing the latter to take their quota of cheap foodgrains.

If the government were serious about reaching the really poor it should withdraw the benefits of PDS from the better-off urban groups and focus mainly on the rural poor because the incomes of the urban poor are far higher than those of the rural poor. By linking the PDS to Food for Work programmes, the government can ensure that the subsidized food actually reaches the needy. If it has to provide cheap foodgrains to the urban poor, it can do so by supplying low priced but highly nutritious coarse grains such as *jowar* and *bajra* which currently sell at far lower prices in the international market than wheat and rice.

The truth is that food prices are being kept low in order to confer on urban industrial interests the advantages of low wages and cheap raw materials. Those who complain against rising foodgrain prices need to remember that the prices of industrial goods have risen much more in this period. In 1990–1, the purchasing power of wheat was only 67.6 per cent of its 1970–1 value. In comparison, wages in the organized urban sector have risen far more substantially to counter this rise.

Who Benefits from Fertilizer Subsidies

For years the government has propagated the myth that the farm sector is heavily subsidized by being supplied cheap electricity, water, and fertilizers. The fertilizer subsidy in particular has been cited as an example of the unhealthy clout of the peasantry. Actually, far from helping the peasantry, this subsidy is designed to help the already bloated fertilizer industry as well as the urban consumer get foodgrains at artificially fixed prices.

Chemical and petroleum-based fertilizers were pushed down farmers' throats through a massive propaganda campaign by government agencies in order to ensure a certain level of self-sufficiency in food production. Fertilizer prices were kept controlled in order to coax the farmers into using them to bring about dramatic increases in food output. That is why there was no increase in fertilizer prices from 1981 to 1991. On the other hand, the fertilizer industry was assured large subsidies to meet the deficit between the fixed sale price and the supposed cost of production. This is called the Retention Price Scheme (RPS). In order to extract more and more by way of subsidies, the fertilizer industries began to devise ever newer tricks, such as quoting inflated figures for the initial investment as well as various running costs of operation. They had no incentive to be economically efficient. From a Rs 500 crore subsidy in 1981, the figure shot up to Rs 5,000 crore in 1991. During this period fertilizer consumption doubled.

Despite this heavy subsidy (which is now being withdrawn), the fertilizer prices in India are higher than those prevailing in most parts of the world. If we base our calculation on the number of kilos of wheat or rice required to purchase one kilo of fertilizer, we find that our fertilizer prices are higher than even in neighbouring Bangladesh and

Pakistan, let alone in those developed economies which give heavy subsidies to agriculture.

The following table shows the amount of paddy required to pay for 1 kg of nitrogen-based fertilizer by farmers in various countries during 1988:

Pakistan	1.97 kg
South Korea	0.76 kg
Japan	0.34 kg
Philippines	2.25 kg
France	1.82 kg

Indian farmers paid the highest at 3.19 kg for 1 kg of nitrogen-based fertilizer.

The policy of RPS has resulted in insulating the fertilizer industry from internal competition by assuring it of a guaranteed return on capital investment. This has resulted in an unviable expansion of the production capacity of the fertilizer industry and encouraged a very inefficient utilization of resources. Industrialists can afford to inflate plant costs as long as they meet government set quotas. This policy rewards bad investment instead of penalizing it and discourages the industry from upgrading technology to be cost-efficient. By permitting it to produce fertilizers at a cost much higher than its import parity price, the government is providing it implicit subsidies.

In addition, this industry receives an explicit subsidy by receiving its feedstocks (such as naptha and fuel oil) at prices much lower than the ones being paid by non-fertilizer users. Thus, the withdrawal of the subsidy on fertilizers will not harm the farmers. It will have the beneficial effect of forcing a closure of all those units which function inefficiently and whose output costs the Indian farmer more than a comparable product in international markets. So far the farmers have had to bear the burden of keeping them artificially alive.

IRRIGATION SUBSIDIES

As for irrigation and electricity subsidies, they are indeed heavy and need to be withdrawn but the withdrawal will not serve any useful purpose unless the entire system of management is made cost-efficient and viable. Our irrigation potential, which was increasing at a much faster rate in the 1960s and 1970s has begun to decline dramatically. During the 1980s both the government's investment as well as the farmer's investment in agriculture were on the decline. That is really a danger signal for agriculture. The farmers are unable to invest because the return on investment is very low for most crops and the risks too high.

Government investment is coming down because it has frittered away huge amounts in the inefficiently run water and electricity boards. Today even the operational and maintenance expenses of these two inputs are not being recovered, let alone the capital cost. It takes about Rs 60,000 to 70,000 to irrigate a hectare. To run the system as per economic principles, the government ought to recover at least 10 per cent of the amount annually, whereas the actual recovery is no more than Rs 250–300 per hectare. In Punjab, farmers pay about seven paise per kilowatt as electricity charges. It costs the state government about Rs 1.08 per kilowatt to distribute electricity. Yet, the farmers are not the real beneficiaries of these subsidies because they are not able to recover fully the costs of these inputs even at subsidized rates from the prices at which they are compelled to sell their produce. In fact, they feel cheated, because the bureaucratic management of irrigation and the power sector is indeed faulty and wasteful. Corruption and very poor maintenance ensure very low productivity of the system. Erratic supplies keep farmers forever on tenterhooks about when and how much water or power supply they will get. These prices could be easily increased if the farmers could rely on it and recover the costs.

Who Subsidizes Whom?

Even if one were to concede, for argument's sake, that Indian farmers are actually subsidized, our bureaucrats and politicians have no moral right to oppose subsidies to agriculture. If subsidies are defined as the difference between what you contribute to and what you take out of the social cake, then the salary earners in the government services are the recipients of the heaviest subsidies. Their overall economic contribution to society is, if anything, negative because of the enormous nuisance value they have acquired and the mess they have made of our economy. They are recipients not just of huge subsidies but also free luxuries, which include palatial bungalows, telephones with bills running into thousands of rupees every month, cars, prime land provided to their housing cooperatives at far below market prices, cheap house loans and car loans if they want to buy one of their own in addition to the free official vehicles and homes provided. All this comes along with fat salaries and a million opportunities for loot and plunder.

Likewise, teachers, bank and public sector employees get a variety of perks, including free holiday allowances for their entire families. Their children get highly subsidized university education (the fee charged by the colleges and universities for children of the urban elite does not cover even 5 per cent of the costs involved) and even subsidized transport (bus passes for students of metropolitan cities are so low priced—it amounts to virtually free travel) and yet nothing gets these sections more agitated than the supposed subsidy to the farm sector. This is a good example of our tendency to despise those whom we exploit most. The relationship and attitude of the urban elite towards the peasantry is typically that of colonizers. It is immoral for us to use the sad plight of the landless and urban poor as an excuse for continued exploitation of the peasantry for our own direct benefits.

If Only Farmers were Rich!

It is not just the landless who work as wage labour. A large proportion of those who seek wage labour are poor peasants. This is due to the fact that the prices they get from the sale of their produce do not ensure year-round subsistence. They would benefit more by a rise in the price of crops they produce rather than food prices being kept low. The government's own records show that dryland farmers holding up to 25 acres have come to seek work at Employment Guarantee Scheme sites during drought years. Why? Because during 'normal' years they are not able to save enough to last out even one bad harvest. Compare this to the European farmers, who cannot do any farming for almost half the year because of heavy snow and yet are assured of a year-round decent standard of living.

What is the maximum income an honest, hardworking, efficient farmer can attain? For example, let us take the case of a cash crop growing farmer in Maharashtra, for whom the land ceiling is fixed at 18 acres for irrigated land. Out of this, theoretically only one-third can be used for sugarcane plantation because irrigation water for more than that amount is not possible. But even if we calculate on the basis of the entire landholding being under sugarcane, a proficient farm family can get no more than Rs 3,000 per acre as their profit margin, amounting to no more than an annual income of Rs 54,000 or Rs 4,500 per month. This is on the higher side. Thus, this cash crop growing 'rich farmer' earns no more than a bank clerk. The income involves the labour of the entire peasant family, including children, not just that of one earning member, as in urban families. For a dryland farmer, the land ceiling is fixed at 54 acres. For such a farm family a net income of Rs 300 per acre per year, amounting to Rs 16,200 for all of 54 acres, would be considered exceptional. In Delhi a cycle-rickshaw puller probably earns that much by his own labour alone.

In the case of wheat, the best estimates of profit per hectare (two-and-a-half acres) does not exceed Rs 2,000 per crop per acre. Thus, the half yearly income for the maximum permissible land holding of 18 acres in Punjab would amount to little more than Rs 14,000. The maximum permissible landholding of 18 acres even in a fertile and prosperous state like Punjab would represent a value of Rs 18 lakh at the most. This is equal to the value of an ordinary middle class flat of the kind owned by section officers in the government of India.

Why do our policy-makers not impose similar 'ceilings' on urban incomes, including their own salaries and perks, for that will at least ensure the removal of obscene economic disparities in our country?

ONLY FARMERS MUST STAY POOR

But that is obviously not the goal of our 'socialist' pattern of development which puts the interests of urban consumers above the interests of rural producers.

The food secretary defended the recent wheat import thus: 'If at all this import has adversely affected anybody, it is the handful of big farmers who held back wheat in anticipation of rise in prices in the post-*rabi* marketing season' (*Times of India,* 12 November 1992). He could get away with such trivialization of the problem because of a deep-seated prejudice against the peasantry among the urban intelligentsia, who have for long justified destructive anti-agriculture policies in the name of curbing the power of the rich *kulak* farmer. In fact, the term 'rich farmer' is almost always used by urban intellectuals as a pejorative. They would never think of opposing the efforts of the urban working class to become well off.

We do not mind rich teachers, rich lawyers, and rich doctors, rich journalists, rich bureaucrats, or well-off bank employees. But it is politically fashionable to dread the prospect of farmers becoming rich. Do we want the peasantry to stay poor forever? Farmers getting rich by farming alone is not even a distant prospect. All over the world, people in the industrial and service sector have relatively far higher incomes and opportunities for accumulating wealth than those confined to agriculture. Yet any sign of prosperity among the farming community upsets our policy-makers as well as the urban elite and brings forth harangues against the deadly power of the 'rural elite'. The sight of Amul Cheese or Maggi ketchup in a village shop is for them a sign of spread of a degenerate consumer culture, even while they import their own cheese, sauces, and dressings from France and Italy. They justify their anger at the farmers, saying they do not pay adequate wages to their farm labourer. This is phoney concern because they are not willing to pay them statutory minimum wages when the impoverished peasants and landless poor come to cities and work as domestic servants and *chowkidars* in the homes of the same urban elite who claim concern for the poor while they are in faraway villages. They will haggle for every 50 paise with a rickshaw driver but do not feel pinched paying Rs 25 for a pot of coffee in a five-star hotel. It is very convenient to rave and rant about low agricultural wages because they have to come out of the peasantry's pockets, not our own. If we want to contribute to the desired increase in the wage rates of agricultural labour, we have to be willing to pay higher prices, at least in the short run, for farm produce. In the long run, food prices are likely to fall if production rises significantly.

Undoubtedly, there is a small number of big landlords who hold vast estates. But these are not farmers. They are mostly rentiers who have managed to defy ceiling laws because of their political clout. Such people ought to be dealt with as law-breakers, not farmers.

Natural way to Economic Growth

Rather than mopping up the agricultural surplus for industrial development in urban centres by following the Soviet model, if our policy-makers had minimized the obstacles in the way of our farming population, our country's economy would not be in the shambles that it is in today. The innovativeness and the enterprise of the Punjab farmer during the late 1960s when he was provided with price incentives effectively smashed the stereotype of indolent Indian farmers lacking entrepreneurial spirit and skills. It has been commonly observed that when allowed to retain surpluses, farmers use the incremental incomes in a fairly rational manner.

Their order of priorities tends to be as follows:

(i) Pay off private debts and discharge obligations like marriages, especially of daughters;

(ii) Increase acreage under the paying crops;

(iii) Invest in improvement of land, water, energy supply as well as in improvement of the quality of other inputs.

These investments in agriculture have an extremely positive consequence insofar as they lead to a significant rise in rural wages, accompanied by increased availability of work. In addition, the resultant increase in agricultural production brings in greater stability in prices by lowering of off-season prices. Retention of surpluses in rural areas allows farmers to diversify into non-agricultural activities as happened in Japan and also nearer home in Punjab. The latter represents a model of people-based small-scale industrialization leading to dramatic increase in wages and incomes to the extent that people from diverse states migrate to Punjab for work. In contrast, wage rates and employment potential in both rural and urban Bihar remain dismally poor despite this state being the heartland of heavy industry and a possessor of rich mineral and forest resources. It is noteworthy that Bihar has the maximum state investment in the industrial sector and Punjab the least.

Societies which pursue pro-farmer policies have been able to industrialize much faster and better than those that do not. For example, in Japan the support prices of paddy were fixed in 1921 at three times the international prices. The results are there for all to see. Within no time the Japanese farmers began diversifying into cottage and small industries, laying a solid foundation for the large-scale industrialization of Japan. South Korea, another example of the same phenomenon, is equally instructive. Between 1951–71, South Korea received massive aid from the US and yet remained poor. In 1971, the government of the country launched a deliberate pro-farmer policy with heavy subsidies and fixation of remunerative prices for paddy. That is when the South Korean economy began its take-off to become a formidable force in the world economy. This is a more organic and natural route to economic growth, as opposed to the Stalinist or Nehruvian policies of forcibly extracting rural surplus for enforced, top-heavy industrialization which has resulted in large-scale pauperization of the rural population.

Consequences of Anti-Farmer Policies

Apart from causing rural poverty, anti-farmer policies have endangered the economic and political health of our entire society. It is the prime reason for runaway inflation which is aggravated as our dependence on foreign loans and aid increases. The more we become a dependent economy and the more we borrow, the more we experience the foreign exchange crunch. In addition, the top-heavy artificial industrialization necessitates centralization and bureaucratization. Exploitation and neglect of the agricultural sector has resulted in large-scale unemployment and underemployment, leading to a sick variety of urbanization and painful transfer of population from the over-burdened rural sector to urban areas.

No country in the world has made economic progress by following policies which inevitably promote pauperization of its agriculture-based population. The millions who flock to cities to live in slums and work as rickshaw pullers, domestic servants, rag pickers, or stone-breakers and take on sundry low-paid occupations, are economic refugees from our villages, mostly from poor peasant families. Even the sons of so-called middle and high income peasants come to the cities and work as bus conductors, drivers, peons and so on, since they earn more in these low-paid occupations with relatively less arduous work, than on their own farms. In short, anyone who can escape agriculture does so. As a result, only those with no options and opportunities are stuck to the tarbaby of agriculture and are left behind to take care of that vital sector of our economy which supports about 70 per cent of our population. It is common for men to migrate to cities and leave behind women and children to take whatever care they can of their family land. The resultant small flow of cash incomes earned in cities is crucial for the survival of farm families.

Take the case of Jharna, who along with her mother works as a domestic servant in Delhi. She comes from a peasant family of West Bengal. Most members of her family are working in low paying, menial jobs. The only reason one or two adult members (out of seven) of her family have to stay back in the village on a rotation basis is that if they rent their land and all of them together stay away from the village for an indefinite period of time, their small holding might be taken away on account of their being declared 'absentee landowners.' Apart from the economic consideration that the income from their land is not enough to provide year-round subsistence to her family, Jharna herself does not want to live permanently in the village. Her reason: she finds cooking, cleaning, sweeping and mopping floors, washing clothes, and performing endless domestic chores for urban middle class families much more 'easy' than agricultural work.

A traditional saying, common to many of the Indian languages, grades different occupations thus: *kheti utkrisht,vyapar madhyam, naukri kanisht*, meaning earning one's livelihood by agriculture (*kheti*) was considered the most superior of all vocations. Business (*vyapar*) was of middling value. Service (*naukri*) was considered the worst of all. The economic policies of our erstwhile colonial rulers and our present-day masters have succeeded in making the traditional value system turn on its head. Today, being a *khetihar* (farmer) is considered a curse, while having a *naukri*, especially if it is *sarkari*, is considered the biggest boon. People are waging do-or-die battles for even low level government jobs, as was demonstrated by the violence accompanying the anti-reservation agitation. Hundreds of students tried burning themselves to death to protest against caste-based reservations in government employment.

POWERLESSNESS OF INDIAN PEASANTS

Today our rural population is not only deeply disgruntled but also extremely demoralized because despite decades of powerful peasant movements, both old and new, they have not yet acquired enough clout to oppose the anti-farmer policies of our government and the accompanying misleading propaganda against the peasantry. This despite the fact that more than half of the Members of Parliament hail from rural backgrounds. Evidently, farmers' sons cease to be interested in agriculture as soon as their economic interests are divorced from it.

Farmers have had to organize massive agitations mobilizing lakhs of people for protest demonstrations to get their voices heard by policy-makers sitting in the various *bhavans* of Delhi. They have had to organize themselves into large vote banks to wrest even nominal concessions for agriculture. However, our industrialists manage to manipulate government policies in their own favour and extract large concessions through simply bribing, wining and dining bureaucrats and politicians—and that too not out of their own pockets. These expenses are included in the 'cost of production' of the goods produced and incorporated as 'entertainment allowance' given to their business executives and passed on to the consumer.

BRIDGING THE RURAL–URBAN DIVIDE

Given the terms of trade between urban and rural India and given the artificially depressed prices of agricultural produce in relation to industrial goods, even a farm family with a maximum holding permissible under the ceiling laws and producing the supposed lucrative cash crops cannot become 'rich' unless it has other sources of income.

Over the years I have visited scores of villages in India but have never come across a single instance where a rural family was able to amass wealth *solely* through agriculture. The 'rich' families in any village are those in which at least some members have employment, professional or business interest, or political power, that comes with outside connections. A study done in a Gujarat village by Priya Deshingkar published in *Manushi* highlights that the wealth of the Patel community is linked to its political clout and its involvement with diamond polishing, paper mills, real estate and other business and industrial ventures, as well as overseas connections, which bring foreign remittances. An average peasant family in Punjab or Haryana would prefer to have a son employed in a low level government job as a peon or a driver rather than working on the farm. Even a supposedly 'big' farmer cannot earn as much as a government school teacher, if he is dependent only on agriculture.

Unless our farmers have the possibility and opportunity to improve their life, on a par with urban citizens, India will not be able to make any substantial progress. Let us not practise our radicalism at the cost of the peasantry. Given the hard work that goes into farming, the peasantry deserve to be well-off more than anybody else. It is they who are being denied this opportunity more than anybody else. For if there were indeed enough rich farmers, our villages would not be in the sorry state that they are in, lacking in even basic amenities like an assured year-round supply of drinking water and facilities for primary health care.

In 1951, the ratio between agrarian and non-agrarian incomes was 1:1.4. In the decades after Independence, this gap between rural and urban incomes has increased substantially. In 1988, it was reported to be 1:2.8 at constant prices and 1:6.2 at current prices. The gap is likely to have increased further. Between 1951 and 1989, the GDP in agriculture as a proportion of total GDP came down from 66 per cent to 27 per cent. As against this, during this period the agrarian population remained steady at around 70 per cent. Over the 1980s, the gross capital formation in agriculture as a proportion of total capital formation in the economy has tended to decline markedly from 18 per cent in 1980–1 to less than 10 per cent now.

The rural sector, which caters to almost 70 per cent of India's population, gets 25 per cent of the total electricity produced in the country, one-third of the education budget and less than one-fourth of health facilities. The child mortality rate in villages is almost double that of cities. The rural literacy rate is less than half that in urban areas.

Several studies have shown that the average length of each work day for most peasant women across the country, including those in the supposedly wealthy Punjab, is 15–16 hours. This includes about six hours on domestic work, including tending the animals, and 8–10 hours of work in the fields doing extremely arduous work. This backbreaking drudgery cannot be reduced unless agriculture becomes more of a paying proposition. Likewise, children, especially girls from agricultural households, cannot make use of educational opportunities, even when they exist, if the majority of peasant families remain so poor that they cannot afford to dispense with the labour of their children.

ADDITIONAL MEASURES

Our rural economy has been so severely exploited, especially since British colonization, that it has resulted in the denudation of capital stock in agriculture over a prolonged period. We need to make amends for this by rehauling our overall economic policies in favour of the agricultural sector, even if it means a *short-term* setback to the interests of the well-off urban consumers. After a brief upsurge during the years of the Green Revolution, investment in agriculture has been falling and moving towards the urban sector because the rate of returns in trade and industry are disproportionately high as compared to that in agriculture.

A change of investment pattern is urgently required. This cannot happen unless we allow agriculture to generate more profits. Hence this examination of the agrarian question focuses overwhelmingly on the price question. This is not to argue that lifting of price controls will take care of all the problems of the agrarian sector. In fact, the wild fluctuations in international prices of farm produce have ruined many small farmers in many countries. Therefore, some amount of state intervention is necessary. But these interventions ought to function more as a protective buffer for our farmers rather than act as crippling restrictions on them.

Apart from removing market restrictions, we need urgent action on two additional fronts: infrastructural development and technological innovation. Among other things, this will include much greater emphasis and investment in agricultural research, not through bureaucratic-run institutions but through direct involvement of the farming community in both conceptualizing and carrying out the research. The farmers have the ability to help upgrade agricultural technology more than the best of mere lab-smart scientists. Unless the farmers, especially the women among them, are allowed full opportunity for further upgradation of those skills which they have honed over generations, we cannot effect meaningful improvements in agriculture. Research specialists ought not to be 'government servants' but rather work as field-oriented consultants advising farmers on a 'share in incremental production' basis.

Simultaneously, we will need to rehaul our transport system in a way that villages have easy access to markets and services. In addition, better storage facilities at the village level will help the farmers to diversify into processing of farm produce thus taking some of the pressure off agriculture to fully support our rapidly growing population, and shifting into small-scale industries.

Our irrigation system also needs substantial expansion and freedom from the bureaucratic stranglehold. Farmers ought to be made co-sharers of the local irrigation networks through the issue of water bonds so that they are involved in planning, maintenance, supervision, and expansion of the system. This will help farmers undertake effective environment conservation programmes which also need to be freed from bureaucratic mismanagement.

Given the heavy risks involved in agriculture, there ought to be widespread introduction of commercial insurance on a field-to-field basis for all crops as well as more scientific input into accurate weather predictions.

This is by no means an exhaustive list but only a rough indication of areas that ought to receive priority attention in our planning processes.

In Conclusion

No country in the world has made economic progress without ensuring the economic sustainability of agriculture. We can no longer afford to ignore the danger signals. Our top-heavy model of industrialization through the 'commanding heights' theory of the economy has proven a dismal failure.

(i) If we want to escape our constantly recurring economic crises, we have to change the unfavourable terms of trade imposed on agriculture. This will help bring about a change of investment pattern and help resources flow towards the relatively more efficient agrarian sector. Neither our industry nor IMF and World Bank loans can bail us out of the resource crunch. The agrarian sector shows the capacity to do so by being able to produce a range of products at internationally competitive prices, despite all the hurdles placed in its way.

(ii) The peasantry needs to be freed from the clutches of the bureaucracy far more than do our industrialists, who have thrived on the licence-permit *raj* by perfecting the art of corruption and bribery to manipulate economic decisions in their favour. The bias against agriculture and rural India is a major reason for our present economic crisis. Unless we combat this bias actively, India will continue to be counted as one of the major economic failures in the world.

(iii) The present regime of restrictions on agriculture in India have only benefited the much better-off urban population at the cost of the agriculture-based population—both the peasantry and the landless. They will not need 'development aid' nor do they need 'subsidies' if the urban elite stops putting obstacles in their attempts to struggle out of poverty. Subsidies have not done anything but harm the farmers because through price controls and unfavourable terms of trade we have extracted far more than what is given through subsidies. All those who wish to see our villages rich and prosperous and not on the brink of subsistence, as the self-serving urban elite would have them remain, need to help the peasantry get the government off its back.

(iv) Those of us who are concerned with the plight of the landless poor ought to realize that their wages can rise only if farming becomes a remunerative activity. If agriculture is in shambles, there is no way we can implement statutory minimum wages in rural areas. If agriculture is prosperous, the landless poor can get year-round employment in the villages themselves and not have to migrate to the cities in search of work. If the flow of immiserized people from our villages does not halt, our cities will become even more unviable than at present.

(v) The excessive pressure on land can be reduced only if agriculture begins to yield enough surplus so that farmers begin to diversify into other forms of productive activity such as food processing and other small-scale industry. Easing the excessive pressure on land is also a precondition for effective environment conservation programmes.

(vi) We need to link the PDS of subsidized food with Food for Work Programmes, and link the latter to building permanent social assets in rural areas, such as roads that last (not the kind that get washed away with every rain) and locally controlled environment conservation programmes.

(vii) Food prices cannot come down if we stay dependent on imports. They can come down only if domestic production goes up substantially, which can happen only if the farmers are allowed their legitimate share in the economic advancement of the country.

The opposition of urban intelligentsia to freeing agriculture from crippling state controls seems motivated by short-term self-interest parading as 'national interest'. The long-term self-interest of even the urban elite lies in supporting the interest of those who constitute the majority of India's population. For if the living conditions of 70 per cent of our population do not keep pace with that of the urban elite, the latter will have to deal with pauperized, disgruntled millions invading those urban centres in which there are islands of opulence. Since all of these millions cannot be absorbed in cities even as domestic servants and rickshaw pullers, many will inevitably take to crime as a way of survival.

Our film industry has been giving us warning signals of the consequences of allowing people's disgruntlement to go beyond safe limits by churning out a whole flood of films depicting the poor resorting to crime as a way of dealing with social injustice because their attempts at seeking justice through peaceful and legal means are consistently thwarted. The takeover of the peaceful Akali movement of the 1970s and early 1980s by criminal brigades of terrorists inspired by Bhindranwale is the political real life counterpart of the shabbily depicted warning coming through our film industry. A key demand of the Longowal-led Akali movement was that Punjab farmers be freed of numerous price controls imposed by the central government, especially with regard to wheat. Our policy-makers refused to heed the Akali demand for economic decentralization, which would allow the farmers more say in marketing their produce within the country and outside. The failure of this massive, peaceful mobilization of the Punjab peasantry to get its demands accepted resulted in the movement being hijacked by the lunatic militants. Despite the disaster of Punjab, we do not seem to have learnt to heed the warning signals. Our government continues to resort to cheap gimmickry and token concessions rather than respond to the legitimate grievances articulated through farmers' movements in different regions of the country. If we fail to reform our agricultural policy in favour of producers, we are likely to unleash many more forces similar to the ones running amok in Punjab.

I owe much of my own education on farm policy issues to my long and valuable association with Shetkari Sangathana. I am indebted to Sangathana cadres and leader Sharad Joshi for giving me the opportunity of learning through participation in their numerous struggles.

4

Captive People, Free Trade?*
Human Rights and National Boundaries

Ever since the collapse of communist party regimes in the Soviet Union and Eastern Europe, the proponents of 'liberalization' have become ever more aggressive in advocating a market economy as the panacea for all problems related to economic prosperity and political and social justice. We are told that this magic *mantra* will pull the erstwhile Second World as well as the Third World out of the economic and political morass in which they find themselves. The assumption is that removing the restrictions imposed upon private enterprise within a country and free flow of capital from one country to another are the most effective ways to remove poverty. The IMF, World Bank, and other powerful international funding agencies backed by western governments are banging at the ruling elites of the Third World, making them cringe and crawl to obtain good character certificates regarding their liberalization measures.

Apart from the pressure to 'liberalize' their economies, countries like India are also being pressurized to adopt more stringent and effective measures to control the rate of growth of their population. The internationally fashionable ideology of the day is that most Third World countries are poor because, in addition to their economies being choked by state controls, the resource base of these countries is overburdened by the size of their populations. Curbing population growth is thus being presented as an essential pre-condition for the removal of poverty.

---

*First published in *Manushi*, Issue No. 67, November–December 1991.

First World countries are not averse to massive statist interventions in Third World population policy because they see the Third World poor as responsible for jeopardizing the environmental safety of the globe due to their 'uncontrolled breeding habits'. Unfortunately, the ruling elite in most Third World countries, including India, have accepted this diagnosis as accurate and are desperate to adjust their population policies to this world view, even if they have not been able to figure out how to do so effectively.

The basic problem with this world view is that it sees the problem of poverty not from the point of view of the poor but from the perspective of the wealthy.

THWARTED FROM FENDING FOR THEMSELVES

How is it that so many people are poor? In the vast majority of cases, poverty is not due to any fault or disability on the part of the concerned group or individuals. Mostly people get to be poor because they are actively thwarted by others more powerful than them in their attempts to fend for themselves. Therefore, the most effective and dignified way of attempting to combat poverty is to accurately identify and remove the hurdles placed in the way of currently vulnerable groups when they strive to fend for themselves. Throughout human history, people have been thwarted in different ways from taking care of their economic well-being; for example, rapacious rulers and military chiefs taxed and plundered in order to drain peoples' wealth from them. Those who have been remembered as 'good' rulers are usually those who kept warfare at a distance from the people, snatched the least from their subjects through taxes or other means, and put the least number of hurdles in the way of people organizing themselves to take care of their own economic well-being.

Till very recently in history, one simple way people had of dealing with poverty conditions and overpressure on land was to move from areas of scarcity and greater oppression to areas of relative flexibility and relative abundance. This is how continual migrations took place from one part of the world to another. Whenever there was, for instance, prolonged famine or drought, people would eventually start a move to a place where the land was more hospitable, more fruitful, where there was less pressure on it. Undoubtedly, great risks were involved in this process. Transportation itself was often a hazardous affair. In addition, problems of security and the enormous amount of coordinated labour required to bring new land under cultivation made it necessary for them to move in large numbers willing to work together as a closely knit community and evolve security arrangements.

Lack of an efficient and systematically enforceable set of political restrictions on migration served another very important purpose. It allowed people an escape route from tyrannical rulers. If, for instance, rulers turned oppressive, then a significant number of people, to the extent it was viable, voted with their feet and moved to territories outside the jurisdiction of oppressive rulers. Since there was a more favourable land–person ratio in earlier times because of the smaller population due to the low child survival rate, there were enough under-used territories to settle on if they were willing to put in enough hard work to turn it into habitable land. This created some restrictions on rulers, often causing them to behave with some restraint towards their subjects, because otherwise they might not have any subjects left to oppress. Often rulers were known to encourage migration from other territories and organize settlements on their own territories, offering all kinds of incentives for doing so. This provided another important exit route from more tyrannical rulers.

SEALING OF BORDERS

The twentieth century saw the culmination of a long process initiated by modern European states from at least the seventeenth century onward of building a world system of restrictions on human migration outside the boundaries of growing colonial empires and later on, the nation-states. This became a role model for all other societies as well, as they sought to transform themselves into nation-states on the European model.

In the post-World War I period we have the systematic completion of the system of introduction of passports, sealed borders, and need to get visas prior to setting off for another nation in a world rapidly becoming completely divided up into a world system of nation-states.

It is important to remember that European nation-states began to impose these restrictions only after Europeans in the colonial period had taken over by force, fraud, and other means large parts of the richest lands in the world. Europe's conquests in the Americas, Australia, New Zealand, Africa, and Asia, were some of the biggest and bloodiest land grab operations in history. The migrations led by imperial powers were different from other migrations insofar as the Europeans (in those places they chose to settle) were not content with just making a space for themselves alongside the local populations. The indigenous people in many places, such as most of the Americans, were brutally subjugated, marginalized, made to live on reserves, or altogether eliminated through violence, diseases, and brutal coercion. The conquests often had genocidal characteristics. In many cases whole civilizations together with their peoples were made extinct. While the extinctions and subjugations were underway, Europeans declared themselves exclusive owners of some of the most bountifully endowed lands in the world. Thereafter they not only forced the tiny surviving indigenous populations to live on small reserves but also began to restrict the entry of other non-European peoples, both into these colonized countries as well as into Europe. This regulation of people's movements across the new boundaries is an important weapon used by the so-called First World countries to become exclusive citadels of power, privilege, and plenty.

Simultaneously, the European colonizers were also instrumental in affecting large-scale population transfers between different colonies. This was carried out under their own severe restrictions and controls designed to provide them with a cheap and reliable labour force in areas where there was a shortage of native people willing to work under harsh conditions imposed by the colonizers. For example, the British took Indian indentured labour to Africa and Fiji, among many other places. Despite brutal working conditions it was possible to recruit Indians for this labour because the impoverishment of the rural population in India under British colonial rule left people with no choice. These population movements were permitted only to the extent that they met the economic and political requirements of the European colonizers. It did not take long for the colonizing powers to choke even this rigorously monitored flow by imposing more and more restrictions on new entrants. For example, in the early phases of setting up plantations in America, Africans were captured and forcibly carried in shiploads as slaves to America. In the nineteenth century, many Indians were forcibly carried by the British as indentured labour to Africa. However, by the early twentieth century, they were already putting restrictions on even wives joining their husbands, as happened with indentured Indians in South Africa. This trend continues more ferociously today. For example, in the 1960s and early 1970s highly skilled Indian professionals, especially doctors and engineers, were encouraged to migrate to the US because it was experiencing a shortage of skilled professional manpower. But as soon as the US requirements were met, stringent restrictions were imposed. Today, getting a visa for an Indian wife to join her immigrant husband in the US may take years or never materialize.

It is ironical that all these oppressive restrictions on migration have come to be fairly effectively implemented at the same time when, during the same period in world history, due to tremendous advancements in technology, travel has become easy, relatively inexpensive and swift, when local travel risks are fewer and when resettlement is not as hazardous and arduous an enterprise as it had hitherto been.

For example, getting an immigration visa to Australia is an extremely difficult, almost impossible affair for an ordinary Asian today. Even getting a tourist visa to America or Germany comes as a boon bestowed upon a select few. Getting a work permit is a blessing that comes only to the very lucky and to the most privileged among the excluded millions. This is the first time in human history, in all likelihood, that fending for oneself outside certain political boundaries is made to appear a crime. For example, if one is seeking a tourist or study visa to the US or Australia, one has to sign all kinds of pledges promising not to work in these countries to earn a livelihood before one will be given an entry permit. If one were to be 'caught' working for a living, one is likely to be put behind bars or deported or punished in some other way.

In recent years some of the First World countries, for example the US, have introduced a more blatantly biased immigration criterion for a select few. They offer to admit people who undertake to bring very large investments along with them. Thus an already wealthy society manages to keep its doors shut to most of the ordinary working people from poor countries who are most in need of economic opportunities, while picking out a few very wealthy applicants for special treatment.

CHOKED AND CONFINED

This tightly controlled immigration policy has resulted in a very imbalanced situation. The people of what are now called Third World under-developed countries are compelled to live under conditions of poverty because severe obstacles are placed in the way of their attempts to make a decent living for themselves, whether internally or externally. They appear to live in over-populated areas because people in these societies are denied the right to move outside the political borders of their nation-states. It is important to remember that most of the so-called under-developed, over-populated Third World has evolved out of societies which were colonized by the Europeans during the seventeenth, eighteenth, and nineteenth centuries. The Europeans had not come in search of poverty. They came originally to trade with them because many, like India, had highly evolved economies which were able to go beyond meeting survival requirements of their populations, and to produce a large variety of high quality luxury goods. These economies could support the largest populations of any societies in those days. But western imperial domination of these highly organized societies led to a systematic draining away of economic wealth, leaving them extremely impoverished. Having destroyed the economic, political, social, and ecological balances in these societies today, the western powers are deliberately thwarting the movement of Third World people to other areas controlled by the Europeans that are better off. Thus an important aspect of the very process through which Europeans had themselves emerged as a strong economic power is denied to Third World people.

The ideologists of the western powers make it appear as though the restrictions on people's movement across borders is based on some God-given principle of natural rights—as though those who now live in Australia, New Zealand, or various parts of America have acquired some divine right over that territory. By claiming exclusive rights and excluding others from crossing their borders, they make us believe they are performing some high patriotic duty. But in actual fact this has resulted in the ghettoization of poverty. Bangladeshis, for instance, would not remain poor, nor would the country be 'over-populated' if Bangladeshis could easily migrate to Australia or Canada—countries which are clearly 'under-populated'—as did Europeans to these same lands in the eighteenth and nineteenth centuries. Even while governments in Canada and Australia want white people living there to produce more children in order to be less 'under-populated', they do not want to solve the problem more equitably and rapidly by allowing entry to people from over-populated countries. It is precisely by choking and holding populations as virtual prisoners within the colonial world's creation, the borders of nation-states, that overwhelming population pressures are created in some areas which then become so hopelessly poor.

In order not to appear to violate their commitment to human rights and democracy, the US and many European countries are trying to develop a new definition of what gives a person a right to enter another country. Most of them have slowly come to a consensus that individuals suffering from particular acts of political persecution in their respective countries must be allowed entry in order to escape being killed or jailed or persecuted by repressive regimes. At the same time, however, they are trying to clamp down heavily on what they call 'economic refugees', that is, those persons who are trying to escape poverty conditions in their countries and want to make a living for themselves and their families in other countries. For example, the Haitian boat people seeking entrance to the US were trying to escape the economic devastation resulting from Haiti's almost endless succession of brutal and corrupt dictatorships. As more of these people tried to come in, the US government put them into detention camps and forcibly sent back as many of them as possible. They rejected what they call 'economic refugees' and only accepted those individuals who could prove to the US government's satisfaction that they were being actively persecuted for their political activities in Haiti.

The tragic story of the Vietnamese boat people is well known. Many of them perished at sea by drowning, starvation, murder, and rape because they were shunted from one shore to another for months without being allowed into any of the countries to which they tried to gain admittance. The treatment meted out to Albanian refugees is another poignant example of this process. As long as Albania was ruled by a ferocious dictatorship which forbade Albanians from leaving their country, in the early stages of the ensuing flow of refugees, Italy allowed in with much fanfare the very few who managed to escape—for that served a political purpose. But as the dictatorship disintegrated and young Albanian men began leaving in ever larger numbers by ships across the narrow strip of water that separates their country from Italy, they were handled quite brutally. The refugees were put in camps, were denied adequate food and kept as malnourished, ill-treated prisoners until they were forced out of Italy.

All these and many other similar examples demonstrate how the dividing line that the more prosperous nations seek to draw between economic and political refugees can be very deadly when applied to groups who are escaping harsh economic conditions.

THIRD WORLD POLICIES EVEN WORSE

However, this madness has spread beyond the western world. These very stringent immigration policies which were initiated by the First World countries against the people of the erstwhile Second and Third World for fear of loss of wealth, jobs, income, power, and privilege are being unfortunately emulated by Third World regimes with no less vigour.

For example, we ignore the news of Bangladeshis being shot dead almost every day by our security forces on the border as they try to sneak into India. India's ruling elite presents this immigration as a kind of 'Islamic invasion' of India. What is actually occurring is essentially a movement of people from areas where the economy has been so devastated by its own ruling elites that people cannot earn enough to meet even their survival needs, no matter how hard they work. They try to move out to wherever they can make a relatively better living. Since they do not have the access or resources to reach more opulent societies, they try to move somehow to India or Pakistan. They mostly come and work at such low paying jobs as domestic servants, rickshaw pullers, ragpickers—that is, work at the bottom rungs of our survival economy. In the same way, many Indian migrants to the West find they can earn a better wage and look forward to a higher standard of living in the US or Germany than in India. They do work few citizens in the country would undertake such as washing dishes, cleaning public toilets or vending newspapers.

Both these groups are willing to do extremely arduous and menial jobs in foreign societies because they nurture hopes of improving their economic prospects, gaining some upward mobility from however low an initial level through this physical movement to a relatively better off society. But in most cases they can enter only as 'illegal immigrants' who can be arrested and punished for daring to work for their living without permission. In India we are forever demanding the deportation of Bangladeshis as the Europeans and Americans do to most Asians. Indians yearn to have the right to travel and settle freely in First World countries but cannot conceive of conceding the same rights to poor Bangladeshis.

The First World countries use discriminatory policies mostly against non-First World people. Travel for Europeans within Europe requires no visas. Likewise Americans require no visas for travel to Europe and vice versa. The Third World regimes do not even treat their own similarly disadvantaged neighbours any better. It is more difficult for an Indian to get a Pakistani visa and vice versa than it is for a traveller to get a visa to England. At least a few privileged Indians are able to secure immigrant and citizenship rights to the First World countries every year but India's own policy does not allow this right to virtually any foreigner. Not only that, we are fairly stringent even towards our own people. Even Indians settled abroad have to apply for visas, which they are not automatically granted, when they want to visit their families.

While there may still be some kind of justification for putting restrictions on entry of people into India from outside its borders, it is hard to understand why our government has made issuing of passports to Indians to go elsewhere such a complicated business. It is made out to be such a boon that many people have to use touts, pay bribes, go through humiliating police enquiries and what not simply to acquire a document that is an absolute pre-condition for even applying for a visa for other countries. This is one important reason that makes forging passports such a lucrative business.

CAPITAL MOVES FREELY, PEOPLE CANNOT

There is undoubtedly some merit in the argument that if at this point of time one accepts the right of people to settle for short or long periods anywhere they desire to go, and be free to make a living there by their own work, then it would set into motion conditions of great turbulence, especially in the First World countries. Hundreds of millions of people would be ready to go across national borders if they were not restrained by guns and barbed wire. It seems at first justifiable that the First World countries should have the right to use their own criteria to restrict migration.

However, the devastation caused to the millions who are being forcibly confined in areas of great poverty is no less important a cause of great turbulence and misery the world over, threatening to destroy the very ecological balance of our planet. The First World cannot escape its responsibility for this mess not just because of what it did during the era of colonization but also for its current policies. Given the present power balance, their dominating power in military, political, and economic terms makes it easy for the First World countries to impose discriminatory trade policies in the Third World leading to further economic drain from these societies. Thus the big powers have no moral justification for choking the flow of people into territories controlled by them while bullying the whole world into agreeing to their version of free trade.

The aggressive moves by the First World countries to get the Third World and erstwhile socialist countries to allow free movement of goods and capital investments and the acceptance of this *mantra* by most Second and Third World regimes will acquire a much greater potential for removing economic stagnation and poverty only if this formula is consistently applied to include free movement of people across borders.

It is absurd that while pressing for various national economies to become integral parts of the larger world economy, the First World countries are simultaneously tightening their immigration policies, making it harder and harder for immigrants to get into their countries. The humiliating treatment meted out to Indians when they queue outside the American, German, Australian, or even the Philippines Embassies to apply for visas, the rate of denials versus admissions makes nonsense of the attempts to 'liberalize' economies—just as it would be hypocritical for Indians to demand more open entry for business deals in the Middle East or wherever but continue shooting down Bangladeshis as they try to 'intrude' into India.

The free flow of capital will mostly benefit the big business houses and multinational companies if it does not come along with allowing a freer flow of people across borders. Allowing multinationals to set up industrial plants or enter into joint ventures to explore mineral or oil deposits without too many hindrances must be accompanied by the lifting of restrictions on ordinary Asians setting up a small newspaper kiosk, a food stall, or a laundry shop in New York or Sydney—or for that matter washing dishes in Paris or Frankfurt. Most people of Third World countries are not likely to have investment capital for setting up even small businesses. 'Liberalization' of the economies must include being free to seek work wherever one can find it—without too many hindrances.

All these checks and restraints against the flow of human beings work not just across international borders but in subtle ways even within each country. For instance, when the rural poor come into cities in search of work they have no capital to buy the exorbitantly priced land or homes in the city. They have no option but to squat on whatever piece of empty land they can find and build shelters for themselves or put up roadside vending stalls. They are then treated as illegal encroachers whose poor dwelling places are forever being demolished by municipal and police squads. Their wares are taken away by the corporation to prevent them from selling where they are not officially 'permitted'—all this when official permits are impossible to get without paying big bribes and grovelling before dozens of officials. They are compelled to live at the mercy of police, corporation employees, and other officials who extract regular cuts from their tiny incomes while holding the threat of eviction and demolitions constantly over their heads. We never care to ask: 'Does a government have the right to forcibly prevent people from fending for themselves through hard work, especially if it has no other alternative to offer them?'

RISKS AND PROBLEMS OF FREE MIGRATION

This is not to argue that the freer migration of people from the countryside to cities or from one country to another will magically end poverty or that this migration will be a problem-free phenomenon, now that technological advances have made travel and resettlement relatively easy. Nor is it true that migration or freer flow of people is a policy devised only to protect the interests of ruling elites. We know from our own experience that migration from outside can cause severe dislocations and stress for vulnerable groups of any area. For example, the migration of the relatively more 'advanced' Bangladeshi peasantry into Assam meant the local populations were being pushed off their land. The large-scale migration of people from north Bihar and other areas into tribal pockets of south Bihar, after this area was opened up for industrialization by the British, meant the alienation of local tribals from their land and other means of survival. At the same time they did not gain adequate access to the new jobs that were created because more 'skilled and educated' outsiders moved in to take up those jobs. Likewise the relatively low paid workers in the First World countries are likely to be the first ones to feel threatened, and rightly so, if a large number of Asian labourers were allowed into those countries. It is rare that a situation like the one in Punjab comes to prevail, whereby the poor Biharis migrate to take on the job of agricultural labourers in Punjab while the sons of the Jat peasantry and even some Mazhabi Sikhs who used to do those agricultural jobs migrate to other parts of India or even to places like Canada as labourers and petty entrepreneurs.

In most cases there are tensions and conflicts produced between the new incoming and local groups. This raises a very fundamental question: Do those who claim to be indigenous groups have the right to determine who comes in and who does not? Do we accept the principle that only indigenous people have the right to decide how the resources in the area they inhabit are to be used?

If we are consistent in applying this premise then we have to be willing to accept that Punjabis have no right to go in search of business opportunities to Manipur, Kerala, or even Uttar Pradesh. But that would be considered absolute heresy because most people have been led to assume that there is something noble and moral about the unrestricted movement and right to free settlement of people within national frontiers, for it brings about 'national integration'. Any move to the contrary is seen as thwarting this process and leading society towards narrow parochialism, no matter how much economic, cultural, and social stress such a movement causes to the local, indigenous populations of different regions within a country. The question is, if we are not willing to accept restrictions on the right of a Tamilian to settle in Mumbai, why are we not willing to be consistent and accept the free movement of people across frontiers as a no less sacred human right?

No 'Free' Trade without Free People

Likewise those who advocate the removal of obstructions in the way of trade, money flow, technology, and activities of corporations are being dangerously inconsistent in not allowing for a free flow of people across national frontiers. Their argument that this will cause economic stress within the host economies is undoubtedly true. There is no escaping the fact that such a free flow will adversely affect the poorer sections of the working class populations in those countries. Wages may fall as a result of such migrations. They may even have to face unemployment in the immediate future, among other things. However, the free flow of capital and technology is also known to cause similar economic stresses in the vulnerable economies. The entry of multinational corporations very often pushes the small businesses out and has other adverse effects on the host economies. Yet the liberalization enthusiasts see those as acceptable risks in the supposed interest of economic laissez faire as the most efficient route to worldwide prosperity.

Laissez faire is no laissez faire if people cannot move freely and only big money can. The evil effects of putting severe state controls on trade and business are recognized. Somehow we are not yet willing to face the fact that severe state controls on the free movement of people results in much greater evil and substantially reduces people's ability to throw off the shackles of exploitation and poverty. No doubt there are risks and problems in opening the gates to people—but these are far less or no more than those that come with removing restrictive controls on trade, technology, and business. In short, truly free trade can only be carried out by truly free people.

5

Naukri as Property*

Causes and Cures for Corruption in Government

When I moved to my flat in Lajpat Nagar in the late 1980s, I was distressed to find that the central square in our block, originally designated as a park, was being used as a garbage dump. Many people from a neighbouring slum would even come and defecate in it. The tap supposedly meant for watering the non-existent garden in the supposed park had a broken faucet. The water gushed out intermittently all day, leaving huge pools of stagnant water. Stray cows came to quench their thirst and rest in the puddles. In the morning several poor labourers from the vicinity used this bountiful flow of water as an open air bathing place. The whole place stank and in certain seasons became a breeding ground for mosquitoes.

Several residents complained to local municipal authorities against this abuse of our public space, but to no avail. Finally, some of us decided to take the matter into our own hands and develop the area into a proper park using our own collective resources and initiative. Within no time, thousands of rupees were collected as an initial fund. Each family subsequently paid Rs 30–50 per month. A few residents did not cooperate and refused to pay. But on the whole, the enthusiasm level was high. We hired a private *maali* (gardener), bought a pump for our own regular supply of water, and a lot of plants. We simply took charge of the upkeep of the park.

*First published in *Manushi*, Issue No. 100, May–June 1997.

Suddenly, a whole army of corporation officials descended on us, including the official *maali*, supposedly responsible for the upkeep of this particular park. We had never seen him before. We were told that by creating a park we were 'encroaching' on government land, that we had no right to hire gardeners for our park. It was not our property. It was government property and its maintenance was the job of the government! Naive residents like me were outraged. However, wiser heads prevailed. They had understood the message correctly—these employees and their superiors wanted to be paid off for allowing us the privilege of doing the job they were hired to do.

They were well aware that nobody in the government ever loses a job for not doing any work, especially if in the files a reasonable amount of paper work has been duly entered, salaries are regularly withdrawn and money spent on various officially sanctioned works. However, if these *naukri wallahs* (job holders) had to officially acknowledge that the civic jobs they are responsible for are being done by others, were actually arranged for by citizens without any help or support from the Municipal Corporation and its workers, they would have no rationale for holding on to their jobs. Therefore, they interpreted our work at developing the park as a coup of sorts—an anti-government activity—and so seemed determined to obstruct our functioning in every possible way.

The wise ones in our Residents' Association, however, understood what was really at stake and worked out a deal with the *maalis* and their supervisor. The Association would pay them a certain monthly amount plus a bottle of liquor every month just for keeping off our backs, and for letting us develop and take care of the public park with our own money. Our Residents' Association in-charge also assured them that we would never raise the issue of their dereliction of duty or complain against them.

As soon as the space started to respond to our efforts and began to look like a pleasant pocket park, the Corporation officials unilaterally declared it an 'ornamental' park. This special status was bestowed on it for a purpose. According to Corporation rules, in ordinary local parks, residents are allowed to hold marriages and other similar functions by paying a fee (and a bribe) to the Corporation. However, in an ornamental park local residents are not supposed to be allowed to hold any private functions. Our non-ornamental park space for years had been intermittently cleared of its rubbish for holding marriages and other functions, especially since the government-owned local community hall meant for such purposes had been taken over several years ago by encroachers with full help from the government, under the garb of setting up a refugee camp for Kashmiri migrants (There is barely one Kashmiri family there now. But those who are in possession of the hall cannot be asked to vacate for obvious political reasons). Therefore, the declaration that our local park could no more be used as a venue for residents' family functions, even if they paid for cleaning up and restoration work after each function, upset many residents. They began petitioning and pressuring for relaxation of this rule. Thanks to the perseverance of an active and influential political worker in our neighbourhood, permission began to be given on a case to case basis.

But we well know that every government 'don't' implies a larger price tag for creating an exception. In effect, as a result of reclassifying the space into an 'ornamental park', the bribe rate for getting permission for holding marriages or other functions went up substantially. But that is not all. We were told, to our shock and amazement, that Corporation officials had been withdrawing approximately Rs 70,000 every quarter from the Corporation funds to 'maintain' this ornamental park! They did provide us four benches and some lights as a token of their involvement. But in the government records they claimed to have developed the park all by their own efforts and initiative. We were also informed that the Corporation employees had similarly pocketed a huge sum for a bore well, which the residents themselves actually bought and installed with their own money, as well as for ostensibly providing all kinds of facilities in the park, for working overtime on it, and for similar imaginary activities.

This story would be laughed off as a fantasy, an unbelievable farce in many parts of the world. But in our country, we have come to accept such situations as routine. They cause neither surprise nor indignation. Our local Corporation *babus* and *maalis* are merely emulating what is being systematically practised at every level of the supposedly 'organized' sector of our economy.

LICENCE TO LOOT

The moral of the story: a government job in our country does not involve any responsibility to work because such a job is treated as property. It gives you an official licence to extort money, to grab public property, to embezzle public funds. In addition, you get a lifelong salary and even a pension after you retire for having done nothing except move files at a snail's pace, or block their movement, harass the public, hide information from the people, and devise ways to siphon off public funds.

Actually, if the government employees did nothing, that would be a blessing. It would work out better for the rest of us if they collected their salaries and just stayed at home and let people fend for themselves. However, as things operate now, the ownership of their jobs entitles them to legally obstruct people who try to get our public facilities to function. They have an unchallenged right to make a nuisance of themselves, and to harass citizens. That is where their real income comes from. Their salaries are a mere licence fee which the government pays its employees to confer on them the right to make the life of citizens as difficult as possible so that they do not forget the power and might of our *mai baap sarkar*.

Here is an example far more sinister than the one quoted above. We are all familiar with the sight of men, women, and children from poor families picking through garbage outside private houses and on the streets as well as from municipal garbage dumps. According to reliable estimates, two-thirds of the city's garbage is collected, sorted and sold to scrap dealers by hardworking poor people who actually at their own cost and by their own labour do the work that Corporation employees and officials receive regular salaries for doing. However, very few of us know that the Corporation employees are not content at letting these people be, even though they do much of their work for them for free. They actually collect a fee from these garbage pickers in return for letting them take away the city's refuse at their own cost. The logic is simple: garbage pickers are eking out a living from collecting and recycling garbage; Corporation officials treat whatever is in the garbage as their own property as soon as it yields a return, though they shirk garbage handling as it is a burdensome and sickening task. Therefore, they demand a regular commission from the garbage pickers, much in the same way that a person leasing out property expects rent.

For instance, I found out that in a nearby market, shopkeepers have made a private arrangement with certain cycle-cart pullers to get the day's garbage collected and taken to municipal dumps because the Corporation does not perform this task nor has it made any other arrangements for garbage removal. The municipal employees who are supposed to do this job charge a fixed fee for every cartload from these rickshaw *wallahs* for permission to dispose of the garbage. A large number of sanitation employees in Delhi appear on the work scene *only* to make these daily or weekly collections, a good part of which goes to their bosses. They beat up and harass garbage pickers every now and then just to keep them frightened and insecure. The police, for their own mercenary reasons, join in to tyrannize and beat them and, at times, even put them in the lock-up on trumped-up charges and extort additional payoffs. Go to any garbage pickers' slum and you will hear tale after tale of how they are beaten, arrested on trumped-up charges, put into the police lock-up and freed only when they agree to pay up whatever sum the police demands of them.

Even at the level of 'humble' municipal sweepers, many are known to have leased out their jobs to other people who are willing to do their work for a pittance. A sweeper who draws approximately Rs 2,300 per month often hires someone for as little as Rs 500 per month for that work so that the *naukri* owner can spend his time elsewhere in more remunerative occupations. The supervisors, whose job it is to check, get a percentage cut so that they too shut their eyes to such frauds. If by chance, some sincere enthusiastic official were to try and fire an employee who regularly evades work, the sweepers would be sure to inundate the city with garbage by going on an indefinite strike till the employee is reinstated.

Employees of the electricity, water, and telephone departments are likewise known to openly use their duty hours for doing private jobs while they neglect their official duty. Yet, if one were to be fired, the unions would bring the entire department to a complete halt to protect such an employee from 'victimization'.

Similarly, Doordarshan and All India Radio have many employees who collect their salary while doing work at the same time for private channels, or who have set up their own businesses while being on the government payroll. Many show up only once a month to sign the attendance register and to pass on a certain percentage from their salaries to their bosses for letting them retain their *naukri* for life while doing real jobs elsewhere. Not one person has ever been fired for this racket. Many of those who actually work for Doordarshan have also converted those jobs into a business: they get a percentage as their cut for any programme they sanction, and for every bill they pass. Very few private producers who work for Doordarshan escape this extortion.

That this mentality of *naukri* as property has come to pervade the entire government was eloquently brought home by the recent Air Traffic Controllers' (ATC) strike. As per newspaper reports, a senior level ATC was suspended from his job after it was discovered that carelessness or a lapse on his part nearly led to a major air disaster. Hundreds of people could have been killed if the pilots of the planes had not saved the situation by handling this emergency in a few split seconds. Yet, the mere act of ordering a temporary suspension pending an investigation provoked a total lightning strike by the ATC union all over the country, demanding unconditional reinstatement of the employee under suspension. The entire air traffic in India ground to a halt for three–four days, inconveniencing lakhs of passengers. No other government worth its name would have succumbed to such crude blackmail but ours did because the entire bureaucracy and the political class have come to believe that a government job is indeed the most inviolate form of private property.

NAUKRIS ON SALE

No wonder that many of these *naukris* and postings are actually purchased exactly in the same way as one would buy a piece of property. The going rate for a postman's or peon's job is Rs 40,000–50,000; a school teacher's job in many states can be bought for Rs 1 lakh or more; a policeman's job at the lowest level costs a couple of lakhs. All *sarkari naukris*, at the lower levels, have fixed rates. They keep escalating just as prices of property do in India. So also with transfers: a Regional Transport Officer's posting at a lucrative highway could cost anything from Rs 5–20 lakhs. To get posted as a Station House Officer (SHO) to a rich business district like Karol Bagh or to a red light area like G.B. Road, police officers are known to pay several lakhs as bribes to their own bosses. Appointments, postings, and transfers are in fact a big industry—with politicians and bureaucrats routinely making crores of rupees from it. If one were to audit a senior bureaucrat's or a chief minister's working day, one is likely to find that 90 per cent of their workload pertains to handling these job auctions and transfer deals.

When Indira Gandhi amended the Constitution during the Emergency to eliminate the right to private property from among the list of fundamental rights of citizens, our progressive intelligentsia hailed it as yet another step towards an egalitarian social order. Similarly, when land ceiling laws were enacted during the heyday of Nehruvian socialism, giving the state unregulated power to take over anyone's supposedly surplus land at will, the only complaint these intellectuals made was that the laws were not being applied stringently enough.

The Land Acquisition Act—a hangover from our colonial days—has given the government the right to snatch away vast tracts of land at throwaway prices (not always paid in reality) and uproot hundreds of millions of farmers from their villages by a mere administrative order with very little redress available to those who are thus being robbed of both their homes and means of livelihood. However, the entire might of the Indian state cannot risk taking away the job of one sweeper, one ATC, one *sarkari babu* or one government doctor, teacher or pilot—no matter how gross their dereliction of duty! The understanding is that once you have secured a foothold in a *sarkari* job by hook or crook, no one can take away this sacred gift from you, even if in the process the government ends up bankrupt and the entire economy is ruined.

In the early 1990s the government, under threat of bankruptcy, announced that it would reduce the size of our over bloated bureaucracy by cutting down on government jobs and closing down loss-making PSUs. However, several years later, jobs have still not been cut—instead, thousands of employees have been added. PSUs, including those that are performing disastrously, have not been freed from government control.

CAUSING BANKRUPTCY

In 1994–5 alone, the central government subsidized 246 PSUs (not counting the numerous state government-run PSUs) to the extent of Rs 4,667 crore. Their losses are mounting every year. Paying the salaries and perks of lakhs of job holders in bankrupt enterprises has thus become a financial millstone choking the entire economy. The PSUs really exist not to provide any product or service but simply to provide salaries and loot for *naukri* holders and their *sarkari* patrons.

No matter how poorly run the services provided by a government organization, the employee salaries and perks keep increasing to keep up with the *naukri* owners' expectation of constant improvements in their standard of living along with their increased seniority in their job. For example, our government-run airlines may be bankrupted due to the inefficiency, incompetence, fraud, and corruption of those who run and work in them, but the salaries of their pilots, engineers, and managers must keep increasing. It indeed requires some cheek for our airline managers and pilots to go on strikes to demand that their remuneration be at par with that provided by international airlines, when their performance standards are so far below those of other airlines that the only sensible thing to do with these airlines would be to close them down.

Due to malfeasance and incompetence, a recently built bridge may collapse, causing the deaths of hundreds of people, a dam built to last 40 years may silt up in five years or collapse in two, causing havoc, death, and ruination for lakhs of people; yet, such is the power of our *babu*dom that barring a few days of suspension, no action will ever be taken against the guilty.

GOVERNMENT MONOPOLIES

The nuisance value of these *naukri wallahs* arises from the fact that they have a monopoly. Even where the government allows private operations and enterprise, it is well controlled through the licence-permit-quota system with enormous arbitrary powers to grant or deny permits and licences in the hands of officialdom. Such a system can only result in vast corruption, especially as it also officially allows those in power to put a veil of secrecy over all their misdoings.

For example, when our bureaucrats and ministers in charge of telecom claim the right to charge crores of rupees for 'granting' telecom licences in select circles to those companies willing to oblige them with suitcases full of currency notes (or better still hefty amounts deposited in foreign accounts) and denying them to all others who do not meet their terms and conditions, what does it all actually amount to? They are auctioning in small doses the right to do the job which our *sarkari* telecom department failed to do in all these decades while retaining their power to squeeze out the largest possible cuts and bribes despite the facade of liberalization. Instead of citizens demanding that the telecom ministry be shut down for being such a disaster, there are many in this country who endorse its right to obstruct citizens from getting an efficient, functioning telephone from whoever is willing to provide the service at a competitive and affordable price. Why should this right to select and reject companies vest in our *babus* and *netas* anyway? Why should it not be left to an independent regulatory system that would benefit the people rather than the *babus*? Why should the Department of Telecommunications be allowed to 'earn' and loot thousands of crores as licence fee and bribes from private telecom companies, thereby making telecom services far more expensive than they need be if the government were good enough to just move out of the way? Whose interests are they protecting by acting as licensees except that of the *naukri wallahs*, the army of *babus* who provide us with the worst telecom system in the world, and the *netas* who preside over this inefficient system as deities of corruption? To defend the existing system in the name of *swadeshi* is to make a mockery of the concept.

ARTIFICIAL SCARCITIES AND PARASITIC *NAUKARSHAHI*

This system of *naukri raj* thrives on creating artificial scarcities. Anything our *sarkar* brings under its control and 'management' automatically becomes scarce—water, trees, electricity, fuel, gas, telephones, housing, land, and whatever else they can hold as a monopoly. When new competitive private companies offer to provide fully functioning telephones to every person on demand within a year or two of their setting up operation, they are perceived as a big threat by our telecom ministers and *naukri* holders, because under such conditions our incompetent *sarkari* telephone departments without a monopoly would go broke and their employees inevitably lose their jobs and, in turn, their means of collecting vast bribes.

The *naukri* owners would not even be content if they were assured of employment at comparable or even higher pay in the private sector in exchange for closing down these *sarkari* outfits, because their extortion power would have been snatched with the end of monopoly, poor service, and artificially created scarcity. So desperate are the babus to keep the culture of scarcity alive that our petroleum ministry prefers to burn hundreds of thousands of tonnes of gas every month at Bombay High rather than let it be used and distributed by private companies as fuel in India. This, when our country is facing a grim fuel crisis.

The votaries of *naukarshahi* do not mind technology imports because apart from earning commissions and cuts on every import deal, they know the management genius of our *swadeshi naukarshahi* can make the best and the worst technology perform at par—make it dysfunctional and become part of the rot. But they resist the entry of competitive companies because they know that they will be redundant as soon as things start functioning.

The ideology of *naukri raj* is leading to economic breakdown, civic chaos and all pervasive criminalization of our society because it subverts the very purposes for which public institutions were created. Government hospitals function as if they were set up to provide jobs to doctors rather than to treat and cure sick people: our primary schools seem to exist solely for the purpose of providing ever increasing salaries to ever more teachers who seldom, if ever, teach rather than cater to the educational needs of students. Special departments and ministries are created so that officials can obstruct the efficient functioning of industries and collect money by harassment. Public sector units are not allowed to be closed down even if they are incurring thousands of crores in losses every single year just so that a few ministers and lakhs of *babus* and *naukri wallahs* can go on acting as parasites on the system.

The neo-*swadeshi* mongers claim that allowing private, especially foreign, companies into India will compromise our national security and create unemployment. In fact they are defending a system whereby a few lakh *sarkari naukri wallahs* are allowed to hold the entire society to ransom, a system whereby government has come to resemble a vast, organized extortion racket—and nothing else. They oppose the dismantling of government monopolies using the specious plea that competitive privatization will mean surrendering to the greed and exploitation inherent in the capitalist market system.

They obviously prefer a system whereby every citizen has to feed the greed and power mania of *babus* and *netas* who control the *sarkari* machine. They humiliate the rest of the people in this country, parasitic as they are, reducing us all to the status of colonial subjects. Think of the way even the supposedly mighty Tatas and Birlas cringe and crawl to placate every petty official in every ministry they have to deal with. Our 'big bourgeoisie' has to organize 'public relations departments' and armies of *liaison* officers in order to offer *salaamis* to and grease the palms of every *sarkari* representative from the peon to the ministers and their secretaries.

In actual fact, a *sarkari* mode of privatized loot and plunder has already been in operation for many years—indeed, Leftist rhetoric has helped provide a large fig leaf for this process. For instance, if you want a water or electricity connection, you don't just walk into a government office, fill out a form, deposit a fee, and get the connection. You look for a tout who will charge you a fee to identify the right palms to grease inside those government offices for the sanction to come through. This is the most venal form of privatization because government employees are using a state monopoly for private gain, and you have no other option. Our electricity departments are in the red because the employees are privately selling electricity by providing more illegal connections than legal ones. Their inspectors will happily tamper with meters and lower your bills in return for a fee. A consumer who has been charged a fraudulently exorbitant bill dare not refuse to pay up because they will have his/her telephone or electricity connection cut off altogether. It will take months or even years to get it restored and that too only after these *sarkari* thugs have been propitiated with all kinds of offerings.

In our *naukri raj*, if there is a power breakdown, it does not mean those in charge of running that electricity station will be called to account. Far from it. What actually happens is that enterprises or farmers in that area whose production is affected by the power breakdown will come, plead, grovel, and beg before the *bijli babus* and pay them whatever they demand in order to get them to restore the power supply as soon as possible.

SARKARI SOCIALISM

Our *sarkari* version of socialism thus amounts to providing state protection and government space for allowing its employees to carry out self-serving personal deals with resources paid for by the people, and making government offices commission collection centres for politicians, employees, and managers who have been provided with every possible incentive to keep things dysfunctional, to promote inefficiency and breakdown. This is the kind of extortion racket our Leftists wish to defend by keeping intact the state monopoly in key sectors of our economy.

Every time some enthusiastic bureaucrat talks of making the laws more strict and calls for a rigorous implementation of the law to prevent misuse and theft, the attempt usually brings in a bigger bonanza for the *naukarshahi*. For instance, when Mr Tejinder Khanna took over as Lt Governor of Delhi he took up the challenge of removing unauthorized constructions and encroachments over public land. A special task force was set up for the purpose of carrying out demolitions. A few high-profile buildings were indeed demolished to show our *babus* meant business and a few of those among the government engineers who had connived in the illegal construction were temporarily transferred to other posts. For a few days the demolition squads went around making a pretence of breaking down illegal constructions: a few theatrical hammers pounding at fancy buildings were duly photographed for the media coverage and for government records. All this provided an opportunity to collect another round of bribes from the building owners. Net result: the overall bribe rate for illegal construction has gone up considerably in Delhi.

ENCOURAGING CRIME

The assumption behind creating the special task force was that the law-breaking public ought to be punished. However, anyone who has had anything whatsoever to do with any kind of building—from a *jhuggi* to a palace—knows that the *sarkari babus* will not let you proceed an inch unless they have been propitiated first. Anyone who wants to build lawfully—that is, follow the building laws faithfully, would be harassed beyond all limit. You simply cannot get such a plan sanctioned. The *babus* want you to, in fact they encourage you to, flout the laws because that will bring them more money. The amount the engineers and sanctioning clerks can extract out of a person depends on what extent the rules are being flouted. Therefore, they themselves encourage people to undertake illegal construction, and to occupy public land.

In recent years, the Municipal Corporation engineers have started moving around with hired *goondas* in order to facilitate the task of extortion from city builders. The *Indian Express* of 11 June 1997 reported that 'with salaries not more than Rs 7,000 a month, junior engineers in Delhi pay between 15,000 to Rs 20,000 a month plus one per cent share for their protection'. Deepak Datwal, the MCD junior engineer who was arrested for the murder of his boss, R.P. Singh confessed to the police that he was paying his bodyguard Rs 80,000 a month. The bodyguard in turn had three more *goondas* on his payroll solely to protect Datwal. The lucrative protection business has attracted a large number of unemployed youth from Delhi's villages. Armed with long knives and countrymade revolvers, they threaten the builders when they do not pay up. At times sophisticated weapons are arranged for by the Uttar Pradesh mafia dons. There are times when the junior engineers are paid but they fail to get the builder's work done. As no legal records are kept of the payments, builders send their goons to teach the junior engineers a lesson. In such situations, hired bodyguards come in handy. Datwal claims to have got his boss murdered because the latter was beginning to make excessive monetary demands—that is, demands for a higher cut from the booty Datwal collected. The money collected per building ranges from a lakh to several crores. A number of murders have taken place in recent years because of conflicts over sharing of bribes.

CORRUPT AND INCOMPETENT

What we are facing today is not merely organized corruption in government but something far more deadly—plain and thoughtless criminal appropriation of public funds without restraint. Our *netas* and *babus* in fact feel persecuted if this right is challenged as the behaviour of the Sukh Rams and Laloo Yadavs testify. There are numerous examples of societies with a fairly high level of corruption. Yet they have not become as dysfunctional. Their governments manage to perform many of the essential public tasks with a measure of responsibility. Take the case of Malaysia. There too people have come to take it for granted that politicians and bureaucrats will pocket a certain percentage by way of cuts and bribes in any government-sponsored project. Yet it is one of the booming economies of Asia today. It has a relatively developed and functioning infrastructure, far better civic amenities, and provides substantially better health care and education to most of its citizens than does India. The difference is that the political and bureaucratic leadership in Malaysia has a long-term vision beyond loot and plunder and a worked out programme of actions that can lead their whole society to a better life. They have aspirations to lead their entire society to prosperity—not just to amass personal wealth. Therefore, if a road is to be built, those in charge will make a good deal of money out of it, but they will also have built a relatively decent road as well. However, in India, the money is likely to be pocketed without any trace of a road or at best a road of such poor quality that it will not last two months. We are in a hopeless mess because most of our bureaucrats are not just corrupt—they are also hopelessly incompetent. Over these years they have developed hardly any skills or training for doing anything but stealing public money.

On a recent visit to Batala in Punjab, I saw large parts of the town dug up to resemble a vast disorganized chaos. My friends in that town narrated how they had gone in a deputation to the Deputy Commissioner (DC), requesting him to first finish constructing the already dug up roads before the Corporation dug up more. Without a hint of shame the DC explained his operation thus: 'The government has just released several crores of rupees for road works in this area. Who knows how long my posting will last? I may be transferred in two-three months. I want to make sure that I have spent the entire amount before that.' Mindless digging was indeed the quickest and the easiest way of spending and siphoning off a large percentage of the money whereas building a road would take planning across a wide variety of *naukri wallahs,* and lots of time and effort, as well as reduce the amount *naukri wallahs* could pocket.

Thus the *naukri raj* is criminalizing our society, sapping the vitality of our economy, and destroying whatever base we might begin to construct for developing a sense of responsible citizenship, a public morality. The concentration of crooks, pimps, and thugs is highest in and around government offices. From *naukri* as property we have now come to a stage where those who hold government jobs have come to believe that public money put under their charge is actually there only so that they can find ways of channelling the money into their personal accounts. Rajiv Gandhi as Prime Minister had openly admitted in the mid-1980s that no more than 15 per cent of the government money ever reaches where it is meant to go. Today, the figure would be close to 5 to 8 per cent. That too is spent inefficiently. When one reads reports of so many crores of rupees lying unspent under this or that head in a government department, what this in effect means is that the *naukarshahi* has not yet found ways of siphoning off those funds. Only such projects are undertaken, only such dams or roads begun, which provide for large-scale loot and plunder.

The nuisance value of our *naukarshahi* has grown by leaps and bounds also because it has bloated magnificently in post-Independence India. The British were here to make money so they were careful about how much they spent on administration. Our *naukarshahi,* by making *naukri*-holding a lucrative business, has gone on expanding recklessly. For instance, the number of central government employees has increased from 14.4 lakhs in 1948 to 38.7 lakhs in 1997 while the number of secretaries in various ministries has increased from 8 to 92 in the same period. Our jumbo ministries attract criticism, but the gargantuan bureaucracy goes unnoticed because the *babus* remain faceless. Agriculture is a state subject and yet the Agriculture Ministry in Delhi which has no rationale to exist has 11,738 employees. The Information and Broadcasting Ministry whose only function is to block information flows and hamper the functioning of Doordarshan and All India Radio has a strength of 59,155.

The less they do, the more they obstruct, the more money they extort. The bureaucracy has just given itself a massive salary hike which is estimated to add Rs 40,000 crore to the central and state government's expenditure. The Pay Commission which recommended the salary increase has also recommended cutting down the size of the bureaucracy by a third. Needless to say the pay hike has been implemented but the downsizing of the bureaucracy rejected.

PRIVATE SECTOR MESS

This culture of *naukri* as property also permeates the private organized sector. Our tax, company and labour laws and their implementation are so perverse that they make it virtually impossible for an industrial employer in the organized sector to operate a business according to their strictures without losing vast sums of money every year. In order for most organized sector firms to survive, they demand and receive hefty hidden and explicit subsidies from the government. They refuse to undertake production unless the government protects them from real competition; they see to it that there is a guaranteed market for whatever they produce, however shoddy and obsolete the goods they produce, however inefficiently they operate. In a practical sense, there is little competition among the major firms in the organized sector. Much of our industrial plants that turn out our capital and consumer goods are more than a generation behind ordinary (not cutting edge) work organization practices and product technology easily available in most of the world, and falling farther and farther behind every day. On top of all these deficiencies, the political impossibility of working out a viable exit policy for those firms that, even with all these protections, are actually bankrupt, makes all parts of the economy totally dependent on the *sarkar*.

Many in the small-scale sector avoid increasing their workforce, avoid making the transition to the scale of the organized sector, though they have the capital and technology available to them to scale up, just to escape figuring in the government records and coming under the evil gaze of the tax and labour officials. They do not want to grow big and be noticed by the *sarkar* because they will no longer be competitive if they are required to follow the same rules as the organized sector firms. Thus, even though our workers in the informal sectors are paid so little and produce an enormous but little recognized proportion of the national product, our infrastructural industries that are monopolized by the organized sector hog our national resources but nevertheless remain backward in terms of technology, product quality, and organizational skills.

Privatizing *Desi* Style

In recent years, an active lobby has emerged which advocates liberalization and privatization as the panacea for all the ills of our non-functioning, non-competitive economy. However, whatever little we have seen of attempts to encourage large-scale private enterprise in the Indian context has not proved much of a boon even to the consumer so far. Businessmen function responsibly only in those societies where the government also functions somewhat competently and rationally. It must have some larger sense of strategy beyond blind loot and plunder. It must ensure that as liberalization begins and grows, well-functioning, independent, and rational regulatory controls are put into place to supplement the disciplines of the market and to mediate conflicting claims—as well as to call to account those whose short-term greed attempts to undermine the market.

While no reforms will remove the entire burden of crookedness and corruption from any society, many countries in the world that were once as poor as India have shown that it is possible to reduce the scale of loot and plunder of the *naukri wallahs* by leaving them with less discretion and decision-making authority, by making easily available the information the public needs to evaluate the performance of its government.

In our society, neither the police nor the law courts provide much protection to those whose rights are violated. Private businesses of any size tend to function only in terms of what they can get away with in the short run, however much it may harm their firm on a longer term basis; the rule of the *naukri wallahs* over generations has resulted in businessmen not believing there will be a tomorrow when they will be able to make long-term decisions about profits and investment in a stable and fair competitive environment without being fleeced and trampled upon by the *naukri wallahs*.

One example will suffice. In Delhi, the state monopoly over the city buses was brought to an end a few years ago by opening up this sector to private operators. However, the licence-permit *raj* stayed intact. People were granted these private bus licences and issued remunerative routes largely on the basis of payoffs to ministers and bureaucrats. The largest fleet of buses in Delhi however is owned by a politician who has also been the Transport Minister of Delhi.

Overnight, scores of companies and hundreds of individuals turned transporters and tried to make a quick killing by fiercely competing with each other to pick up as many passengers as they could by disregarding route designations and safety regulations.

A new system of bribes and payoffs to the police and politicians who were supposed to control their operations let bus services resort to the type of competitiveness that is supposed to characterize the jungle. Their ill-maintained buses observe no speed or traffic rules. They hire inexperienced drivers and conductors on a commission basis to drive and operate their vehicles for long hours without proper shift breaks. They drive like maniacs. They have killed and maimed thousands of people without paying penalties that would discourage them from continuing to maximize their loot in a competitive environment without any effective regulatory mechanisms. These buses are packed far beyond their capacity, making travel in them a nightmarish experience. Within a short period, these vehicles came to be known as killer buses. Despite this corruption-ridden competition, they charge arbitrary fares; they have pushed up the prices of tickets far beyond what they would be in a properly functioning competitive system.

They are getting away with such irresponsible and even murderous behaviour because those in charge of overseeing their operations are so busy milking them for bribes that they need fear no sanctions. Buses are not impounded, nor permits cancelled despite repeated accidents because the police and political bosses are routinely paid off. The traffic policemen posted at different strategic points all over the city never bother to enforce speed limits provided they get their *haftas* regularly. The licensing authority is willing to sell licences without as much as the formality of a driving test so that many who take up driver's jobs have no such qualification or training. Many of these drivers are colour blind or have impaired eyesight. But the licensing authority could not care less.

Likewise, the inspector of the anti-pollution department stands on the road only to collect his dues and turns a blind eye to the poisonous fumes these ill-maintained buses belch out in lethal quantities. They are one of the gravest threats to the safety and well-being of Delhi citizens. The government-owned transport corporations that are the only other available alternative, provide even poorer service and the government agencies encourage mismanagement by keeping various levers of control in their hands and refuse to get out of the way to allow an independent regulatory body that would encourage rational competition to come into being.

Similarly, in the health sector, private practitioners get away with fleecing patients while providing abysmally low quality services bordering on criminal neglect and wilful malpractice because the government sets very low standards in state-run hospitals. Moreover, it does not encourage and support independent regulatory bodies that would help protect the rights of medical consumers.

SETTING THINGS RIGHT

How do we set things right?

(i) To begin with, government monopoly over essential services has to be replaced by a system of service provision that encourages competitive alternatives so that there are profit incentives for companies to provide quality services at a competitive price. There must be a system of sanctions to make service providers behave responsibly.

(ii) Our government servants need to be transformed into genuine public servants by giving citizens real power to understand and monitor their functioning and retain or dismiss them if they do not perform. This means replacement of the culture of life-time *naukris* with a system of jobs offered contingent on actual performance.

This restructuring process has to start at the village level because our rural population is the worst victim of *naukarshahi's* tyranny. The power to hire and fire employees—from school teachers, to local police, and electricity department employees—ought to rest with local *panchayats*.

(iii) The work of the government should be restricted to those tasks that cannot be better done on a competitive basis in the non-government sectors. Whatever jobs remain within the government should be linked to work actually done under public supervision. A *naukri* within the government should not be treated as a licence to obstruct and fleece people. Instead, to the extent feasible, incentives should be in built to enhance job performance. For instance, if the salaries of our telephone employees were given or cut according to the number of telephone lines under their group's charge that they could keep in functioning order, they would have a strong personal incentive to keep the system functioning smoothly.

(iv) We need to frame laws in such a way that they reduce the enormous discretionary powers of our unaccountable government employees.

Today, our system bestows sweeping ill-designed and ill-defined powers on law-enforcers to punish citizens with thousands of unenforceable laws which make law-breaking the only effective way of surviving and making money. We should reverse this altogether.

Our laws should primarily target law-enforcers for punishment if, under their jurisdiction, the few necessary clear and rational laws are not being correctly implemented. For example, building laws should be restructured so that they are widely known to all interested citizens, are enforceable without allowing the police or municipal officials wide discretion, and there are as few of them as are required for basic social health, safety, and commerce. Failure to honestly implement those few clearly stated laws ought to be treated as proof of connivance with law-breakers and should merit dismissal of officials in charge of ensuring compliance.

(v) The different classes of services—class I, class II, class III and IV—ought to be replaced by a system that assigns job classifications according to job functions. The current system is just another mindless continuation of the former colonial government that provided an army of peons, clerks, and section heads for each class I officer. In fact we have mindlessly increased the numbers of unnecessary government employees at all levels, leading the country towards bankruptcy.

Such overstaffing and lack of clear job duties encourages irresponsibility, demoralization of workers, and obstructionism. There is no reason why public officials should not deal directly with the public, type their own letters and handle their own files so that work does not have to move from table to table, room to room, and clerk to clerk, at snail's pace.

There should be a realistic time frame prescribed for every task to be performed. Failure to stick to deadlines should lead to automatic sanctions against the poor performance of the officials concerned.

(vi) The Official Secrets Act ought to be replaced by a Duty to Provide Accurate Information Act which would make it mandatory for government officials to provide correct information to the general public (without a citizen having to make any special requests or follow any difficult procedures) to learn what happens to money allotted and expenditures incurred for each activity of the government.

For instance, the officials of every municipal corporation and *zila parishad* should be obliged by law to put on easily available public notice boards every month the money under their charge, where it comes from and what exactly they spent it on. Failure to do so should result in automatic suspension and even dismissal of the officials concerned. Citizen Committees should have the right to check and examine the veracity of these accounts. In cases of possible fraud or misinformation, the official concerned should be automatically suspended and if a hearing demonstrates in a time limited period that he is responsible, he should be dismissed.

(vii) At the same time, the salaries of government employees should be increased substantially. By giving them unrealistically low salaries, the government is facilitating corruption. However, this can be feasible only if the size of the *naukarshahi* is reduced drastically. This will automatically increase its efficiency and make this an affordable proposition.

(viii) Finally, and most importantly, while cutting down the bloated size of the government, dismantling the monopolistic *naukarshahi* and making space for a more competitive system, we need to overhaul our legal system from the bottom up so that it is actually able to provide timely and enforceable judgements to protect citizens from unscrupulous wrong-doers—whether in government or in the private sector.

6

A Half Step Forward*

The Thwarting of Economic Reforms in India

The whole agenda of economic reforms, as put forth by a section of the Congress leadership led by Narasimha Rao in 1991, came more as a response to a crisis situation of bankruptcy and total depletion of foreign exchange than as a well worked-out plan of economic resurgence. Rao and his team were unable to provide a coherent action plan on economic reforms because they became hostage to their primary agenda—how to cling to their power at any cost. In fact, most Congress politicians did their best to sabotage attempts to restructure our economy because that would curtail their vast discretionary powers and hence their ability to loot and plunder the people and resources of this country.

Instead of opposing the one step forward, two steps backward approach of our government on economic reforms, and criticizing Rao's very limited vision and agenda, the opposition parties on the whole opposed liberalization because criticizing the liberalization programme gave them yet another stick with which to beat the fragile government headed by Rao. By focusing their attacks obsessively on the central government's tentative relaxations on the entry of foreign capital, they depicted the Rao government as having sold out to the MNCs and evoked paranoid fears of the *phoren* hand colluding with the Congress to re-enslave India. Unfortunately, neither the proponents nor the

*First published in *Manushi*, Issue Nos. 92–3, January–April 1996.

opponents of liberalization have shown real conviction by initiating a thorough public debate on this key issue of public policy. None of the main opposition political parties are offering the country a coherent alternative set of economic policies.

A whole range of NGOs who claim to be working for the disadvantaged sections of our society are trying to fill this ideological vacuum. Though initially NGOs began by working at the micro level on particular projects, in recent years some of them have been responding to macro level issues. Some even claim to speak on behalf of the entire society as though they represent its moral voice even though they have never sought or received any such mandate from the people.

Range of NGOs

NGOs can be divided into four broad categories:

(i) Those providing valuable services to specific vulnerable groups and communities or sections of our society. Outstanding examples include Self-Employed Women's Association (SEWA), headed by Ela Bhatt, Anna Hazare's work in Maharashtra and so on. Even though some of these service-oriented NGOs depend on grants from international aid organizations and some receive assistance from the government, their work is well-rooted among the people. They have made appreciable differences in the lives of those they serve. Such NGOs have well-functioning structures to ensure accountability of their workers and have demonstrated their capacity for disciplined work in their areas of specialization. They tend to stick to their own well-defined agendas and do not move from issue to issue in a hit and run fashion, nor are they swayed by changing political fashions or rhetoric.

(ii) NGOs floated by plain opportunists who have set up these outfits simply to make money. Such organizations exist mostly on paper and have proliferated in recent years because of the desperate problem faced by international aid organizations and the government of India in disbursing money credibly for 'development work'. One of the pet peeves of aid organizations (e.g., the World Bank) is that they allocate billions of US dollars to India that the government has asked for but never gets around to using. Hence, the government is increasingly using NGOs as a fig leaf in order to keep getting a foreign dole. However, so many of these NGOs are so blatantly corrupt that Council for Advancement of People's Action and Rural Technology (CAPART [created by the central government to help facilitate the growth of

NGOs]) has ended up blacklisting hundreds of its recipient NGOs on charges of misappropriation of funds.

(iii) NGOs floated by activists affiliated to political parties for whom the NGO cover is useful because it provides them with a do-gooding facade while it facilitates access to money and influence in the corridors of power. Most such NGO leaders have roots in political parties who proclaim themselves as anti-western, anti-capitalist, and anti-imperialist. However, most of them seem to have no problem in accepting whatever money they can gather from western funding agencies.

(iv) NGOs whose main tasks seem to be to hold and participate in conferences and workshops, undertake 'networking' and propaganda campaigns in the media, and lobby at the national and international level. They are flush with both foreign and government funds. Their leaders are far better known in international and diplomatic circles than in the cities or neighbourhoods in which they say they are working; they wax eloquent decrying India's poverty in international conferences but you will seldom, if ever, meet their leaders in the villages or slums of India unless they are on paid assignments with handsome per diem allowances. They are accountable to no one except their foreign funders. The volume of their aggressive harangues against the dangers of western consumer culture rises in direct proportion to their own level of consumption. Their western lifestyle is wrapped in Kanjeevaram sarees and other ethnic chic. They are usually represented on all the important social welfare committees of the government and also often serve as consultants to the UN and international aid agencies.

However, they are not content with running this or that project. Often their own organization is in shambles but they arrogate to themselves the right to determine for all of India not just its economic and political agenda, but also its foreign policy. They voice naive critiques of how different nations ought to run their affairs. You can recognize these NGOs by their stereotyped pseudo-Leftist Third World rhetoric about the evil conspiracies of the capitalist/imperialist West even while their own livelihood, globetrotting and lobbying activities are more often than not dependent on western aid agencies.

If one studies the position papers produced by our NGOs on economic reforms, it becomes obvious that the last two NGO categories have emerged as the most influential voices within our NGO community because of the resources at their command and the fact that they have very little real work to their credit. Had it not been the case, they would have offered more responsible, better informed and specific proposals to reform our economy rather than the patently absurd stances they have taken.[1]

Unlike political parties, who can be called to account and even defeated in elections if they propagate foolish and impractical ideas, there is very little political accountability for NGOs. They are in no way responsible to the people on whose behalf they claim to speak, since the sources of their support lie outside our society. Therefore our NGOs can indulge in ideological fantasies and even recommend disastrous policies with impunity. Their response to economic reforms reminds me of a popular saying, *Neem hakim khatra-e-jaan* (Quacks are dangerous for your life).

DOOMSDAY SCENARIO

Many of these NGOs predict that doom and destruction will follow if liberalization gets seriously under way. They are worried that if our government allows joint ventures between Indian and foreign capital this will destroy our non-viable *swadeshi* industry; that MNCs will enslave India economically and politically; and that liberalization will be worse for Indians than was living under the regime of the East India Company. They fear that removal of restrictions on the export of agricultural products will lead to commercialization of agriculture and a shift from food to cash crops that will compromise India's security and sovereignty, leading to widespread hunger, illness, and death.

---

[1] The most comprehensive set of NGO documents opposing economic reforms currently available has been prepared by NGOs led by women, mainly because of the funding made available by international aid organizations for those selected by them to participate at the UN Conference on Women held in Beijing in September 1995. Several preparatory conferences were held here before September in order to work out a common agenda for the Indian NGO delegation. Two major documents came out of this process. The first document is entitled *A Perspective from the Indian Women's Movement*, prepared by seven convening organizations that included the CPM women's wing, All India Democratic Women's Association; CPM-oriented Centre for Women's Development Studies; a church-funded Christian organization, the Joint Women's Programme; Socialist Party's Women's Wing, the Mahila Dakshata Samiti; the Congress Party's Women's Front, All-India Women's Conference; and the Young Women's Christian Association of India. The other document, entitled *The Economic Agenda*, was prepared by the Coordination Unit (CU) for various NGOs set up in India by international donors to prepare for the Beijing Conference.

In their view, privatization of the public sector via deregulation and delicensing will lead to large-scale job retrenchment, unemployment, insecure lives for workers, and an increase in the power of criminal gangs. They maintain that working conditions will deteriorate and many welfare benefits will be withdrawn, that there will be a fall in real wages, leading to longer working hours, and that many more workers will nevertheless slip below the poverty level. The ending of state monopolies in telecommunications and the power sector will, in their view, jeopardize India's security. Some enthusiasts among them even approached the Supreme Court with a public interest litigation (PIL) petition asking that the government be prevented from inviting the private sector to enter the telecom sector.

Major cuts in government spending and government employment schemes will, they allege, mean worsening health services and denial of access to the poor, increases in child mortality, deterioration of civic services, worsening of access to education, and more unhygienic living. They claim that following liberalization the poor will no longer have any safety net or social security.

This doomsday scenario of the supposed consequences of economic reforms is, unfortunately, not a futuristic nightmare. The unhypnotized reader will recognize that what these groups are predicting will be the future plight of our people is actually the existing reality for today's Indians, thanks to over four decades of *sarkari* socialism that our bureaucracy so assiduously fostered. Vast unemployment, under-employment, low wages, millions working under conditions of servitude, high infant mortality rates, widespread preventable epidemics, more than half the population living below the official poverty line, millions being ejected out of the agricultural sector as destitutes and coming to urban areas to eke out a miserable living as beggars, garbage pickers, scavengers, and *coolies*, the inability of Indian industry to absorb the population pressures on the land, and the notoriously shoddy goods forced on Indian consumers at exorbitant prices—all this has already happened—not *because* of economic reforms but in the *absence* of them.

THEIR CREED: STATISM

Their vigorous opposition to economic reforms shows that for all their pro-poor rhetoric they are essentially statists. By statism, I mean a world view which subordinates civil society to the dictates of the state and its bureaucracy. Statists are those who believe in the government playing an overarching, omnipresent role in controlling social and economic affairs because they do not trust ordinary people to behave sensibly nor to have the innate capacity to resolve social conflicts among themselves without petitioning the *sarkar* for its wise interventions of the kind we witnessed over the Ayodhya *mandir–masjid* conflict. They believe that the state is the primary vehicle for societal engineering and that those in positions of state power ought to determine organizational principles for the entire society. They seem convinced that if they can prevail upon the state to pass what they consider proper laws, people can be made to behave in ways approved by these self-appointed reformers and social engineers.

Thus they borrow lock, stock and barrel from the agenda of the Nehruvian Congress and its pet child—our 'socialist' bureaucracy. State socialism may be discredited the world over and violently disowned by those who lived under socialist dictators and suffered the tyranny of those systems. Strangely enough, its ideological hold is still strong in India.

Our present Constitution makes it mandatory for every political party seeking to be registered with the Election Commission to swear an oath of fidelity not just to democracy and secularism, but also to socialism—an ideology whose principles are vague enough to provide good cover to our bureaucrats, politicians, and 'licensees' in looting the country for personal gain.

It is understandable that our bureaucracy is feeling threatened by the prospect of losing its power as our economy sinks further and further under the dead weight of the corrupt and bloated government machinery and people begin to demand that those governmental controls which have wrecked our economy be removed. Being aware of how discredited and mistrusted these *sarkari babus* are on account of the mess they have made of our country, they dare not fight their battle openly on their own behalf. With no one else willing to defend them, our bureaucrats have found a valuable ally in certain NGOs who have valiantly risen to their rescue by declaring a *jehad* against economic reforms. Their alliance with the bureaucracy should hardly come as a surprise since for all their 'anti-government' rhetoric, the statist NGOs depend on the sarkar for their very survival. They get their funds either directly from the government, or from various international donor agencies that require prior clearance and sanction by the government with due bribes and cuts paid to *babus* who clear the files.

Physician Heal Thyself

Most NGOs that campaign against liberalization have focused obsessively on the need to prevent the entry of foreign capital and collaborations between Indian and foreign companies. Here an ethical issue is involved. If they think bringing in western money and intellectual know-how is so harmful, they ought to start their campaign by refusing to apply for or accept grants for their political work from various western donor agencies. Or is it that our statist NGOs want us to continue presenting ourselves before the world as beggars requiring endless doses of foreign aid rather than aspiring to become active participants in the world economy? Is it because a good part of foreign aid money gets routed through them that they prefer foreign aid to foreign trade? The money that would enter our country as business investment would bypass the NGOs altogether. How can we hand over the entire Indian economy to those whose own small organizations are not economically independent, whose livelihood comes from encashing on India's poverty abroad, peddling the misery of the Indian people and gathering crumbs on their behalf? Any self-respecting Indian would prefer that we do business with foreigners as equal partners than appear before them as grovelling supplicants as do many of our NGOs.

When discussing economic reforms, liberalizing the entry of foreign capital ought not to be the key issue. The far more important, though neglected, aspect of liberalization is ending the continuing soul-destroying harassment inflicted by government agencies on ordinary citizens of this country when they undertake any independent economic activity—all so that a whole range of unaccountable *sarkari* thugs can parasite on the people and extort huge bribes from them.

From the Bottom Up

The worst victims of this licence-permit-quota *raj*, which grew out of the colonial machinery of governance in alliance with some of the destructive aspects of Soviet style socialism added on during the Nehru dynasty era, are the poor and the vulnerable groups in our society. Instead of opposing economic reforms, we need to ensure that the purposes and objectives of reforms do not stay vague and abstract, do not remain confined to the top layers of our economy. We need to expand their scope to include the numerous governmental restrictions which thwart the economic initiative of the vulnerable groups in our country, thus keeping them trapped in poverty.

Our statist NGOs oppose privatization on the plea that the market marginalizes the poor. If they were less caught in clichés and were to look carefully, they would discover that the poor are already enmeshed in the market, except that various state interventions make the market in which they try to survive much more skewed against them. Even small, primarily subsistence farmers try to grow whatever cash crops they can manage such as groundnuts, vegetables, bananas, cotton, grapes, and fruits. How else would they meet their cash requirements for buying clothes, soap, footwear, utensils and other necessities? Those who oppose the commercialization of agriculture forget that even the poor have needs other than staving off hunger with plain *dal* and *roti*. Those who are compelled into subsistence farming cannot grow enough food for year-round survival and have to seasonally migrate in search of wage work. For instance, an unpublished 1995 SEWA survey of six villages in Sabarkantha district found that though 93 per cent of these families live below the poverty line (with 97 per cent of the families possessing less than five *bighas* of land), all of them grow vegetables like tomatoes, brinjals, onions, potatoes, and even some fruit like watermelons as cash crops.

In remote tribal areas, women bring chickens they rear, homemade rice beer, and forest produce that they gather to local markets. But here, too, state interventions make things worse for the poor. For example, forest dwellers who survive by making products from bamboo, cane, and other fibres have to get licences to buy this raw material and to transport the finished product from their homes to the market. The government sells these products to these poor crafts families at a price which is often 200 to 300 per cent higher than what the paper mills pay for the same forest produce. Thus government monopolies actually rob the poor to subsidize the rich. Poor villagers earning their livelihood from collection of *tendu* leaves need licences to hold stocks of even one bag of these leaves. They cannot freely sell the leaves in the open market or even use them to make *beedis* in their homes. A 1995 SEWA survey provides another concrete instance of how the licence regime works against the interests of the poor by keeping them out of the market economy. The women living in desert areas (*Santalpura taluka*) of Banaskantha district survive mainly by gathering gum from the *babul* trees owned by the Forest Department which insists on licences for gum collection. As long as the women had no licences, they were collecting this gum 'illegally' and selling to private traders. After joining SEWA they formed Development of Women and Children in Rural

Areas (DWCRA) groups and demanded licences so that they could operate 'legally'. However, this meant they can now only sell the gum to the Forest Corporation at rates arbitrarily fixed by the latter at much lower than market rates.

As the rates of gum were reduced by the Forest Corporation from Rs 20 per kg in 1990 to Rs 8 per kg in 1995, the average earnings of women dropped from Rs 25 per day to Rs 12 per day in the last five years, though their working hours have increased. The rates of gum range from Rs 25 to 30 per kg in the open market but the Forest Corporation will not allow them to enter the open market. They have to sell their gum to the Corporation for one-fourth the market price.

SEWA conducted a study of 80 women from nine villages and found that, as a result of the lowering of rates, these women were near starvation. For 93 per cent of them, gum picking is their main occupation with 68 per cent of families earning less than Rs 500 per month; 25 per cent earn between Rs 500 to Rs 1000 per month. As a fallout of 'licensing', poverty levels have gone up. Seventy-seven per cent of families have children also engaged in picking gum. Many have consequently left school. Seventy-six per cent men have become bonded servants to farmers in other villages; 64 per cent of women have had to pawn their jewellery; 70 per cent have mortgaged their land while 63 per cent of families have had to sell their land.

Even when these rural destitutes come to urban areas as migrants, various state controls continue to hound them and obstruct their economic initiative, despite the kind of work they attempt to do. To survive, they must act illegally at every turn. Poor migrants to the city cannot afford to rent a 'legal' accommodation, thanks to the land monopoly that the government enjoys. They pay exorbitant rents for miserable *jhuggis* built by slumlords with political patronage by encroaching on government land. Even the government-sponsored organizations created to promote better housing for the people's sector such as Housing and Urban Development Corporation (HUDCO) and National Housing Board are restricted from giving loans or materials to 'illegal' or 'unauthorized' dwellings—with the result that the poor, whose housing conditions need urgent improving, are altogether ignored. The electricity connection they use is illegal because they are denied a regular connection, on the plea that they are living in unauthorized colonies. They are compelled to pay regular *haftas* to the electricity department employees in return for the privilege of 'stealing' electricity. The list of extortions is endless. When an eviction is threatened they cough up more money and get to be used as captive vote banks of local goons.

While the government is lifting some restrictions on large-scale business and trade, the small traders (for example, the hawkers and the vendors) are still subjected to restrictions which make it illegal for them to carry on their trades. Although there are no reliable figures of the total number of persons engaged in vending in the country, it is estimated that in the city of Mumbai alone there are 250,000 vendors. This gives us a glimpse of the vastness of this sector. Yet almost all the vendors in our country are 'illegal' and therefore subject to archaic licensing laws. They live in mortal dread of the staff of local municipalities, licensing authorities, and local police who systematically parasite on them. Even after making regular payoffs to all these *sarkari* tyrants, they are subjected to frequent round-ups, *challans*, confiscation of their goods, fines and then pay even more bribes—all this for the ostensible purpose of clearing the city of unauthorized encroachments. However, the real purpose of this harassment is to get still more money out of them and keep them in a state of fear so they will not resist paying even larger protection amounts in the future. SEWA of Gujarat had to fight a long drawn-out legal battle which went up to the Supreme Court to defend the right of women vegetable vendors to ply their trade where they had been selling vegetables for generations. Yet even after a mutually agreed upon settlement and payment of mutually agreed upon fees, their status is still not 'legally' regularized.

Take the allocation of credit as another example. Our financial institutions and public sector banks were nationalized ostensibly as a 'socialist' measure that would provide credit at reasonable rates to the poor. In actuality they provide loans to the rich at relatively moderate rates of interest—moderate, that is, when compared to what others are forced to pay (if they are lucky enough to get any loans at all). Indian industrialists, in fact, have perfected the art of getting financial institutions to invest public money in their enterprises while management and ownership remains with private businessmen. As for the poor, even opening a savings account in our nationalized bank is made so difficult and humiliating, that they even fear to enter bank premises.

Our government even provides low interest car loans as well as concessional house building loans to bureaucrats and *babus*. But the poor who need credit the most are denied access to credit through the government-controlled banking system on the ground that they have no collateral. Even those who do have property to mortgage to banks end up paying hefty commissions to bank staff for getting even pitiful amounts sanctioned. Farmers who get small amounts as crop loans from the government-controlled rural banks have to face the prospect of imprisonment without trial for 40 days for any default in payment. Bank staff are authorized to arrest them without as much as lodging a First Information Report (FIR). They have the power to confiscate and auction property the indebted farmer owns, including household goods and utensils that are seized by bank officials if they default or delay in paying back loans. In fact, the money spent on their food while in jail, the Travel and Dearness Allowances of bank staff who go to arrest them is added to their loan amount. This happens even when the default is due to drought or crop failure. But our industrialists get away with defaulting and embezzling crores of rupees as unpaid loans.

The poor generally are left at the mercy of market sharks in the informal sector. Even in Delhi, poor slum dwellers borrow from local money-lenders at rates ranging from 60 to 200 per cent per annum. The government has a virtual monopoly on banking in the rural sector through nationalized or government-controlled cooperative banks. Private money lending at usurious rates is officially illegal. Yet the majority of the poor borrows money from these illegal sources at ruinous rates of interest. SEWA, an organization known for its pioneering work in providing cheap and easy credit for self-employed women in Ahmedabad, applied for permission to the Reserve Bank of India in 1984 to extend its services to rural areas as well. They had conducted a survey that found poor rural families were paying interest rates ranging from 45 to 180 per cent per year for minor loans. It took SEWA 12 years and much effort to secure permission to provide credit despite the enormous influence and respect they have at the national and international levels. The reason offered for the endless delay was that rural banking is the government's monopoly even though the nationalized banks have failed to reach the poor, especially those in rural areas. Thus the licence-permit *raj* actively obstructs the growth of competing or potentially competing institutions which can genuinely serve the economic interests of the poor.

SEWA Gujarat is one of the few NGOs to demand widening of the scope of economic reforms instead of mindlessly opposing them. They want debureaucratization extended to many of the state-owned Corporations supposedly created for the benefit of the poor—such as the Forest Corporation, Handloom and Handicrafts Corporation,

Fisheries Corporation, Khadi and Village Industries Corporation. Because of the financial backing of the government, these corporations have become notorious for wasting money, inefficient functioning, and outright corruption. Despite all the money that is being pumped into them by various ministries, they are still unable to compete with small private traders. Almost all of them run at huge losses and are known to harass and exploit the artisans worse than any private trader. They need to be freed from government control and ministries and handed over to the artisans whose interests they are supposed to serve and made to compete in the market.

AGRICULTURAL SECTOR

The prescriptions of our statist NGOs for the agricultural sector, which provides a livelihood to more than 70 per cent of our population and meets the food and raw material needs of the entire society, are truly disastrous. In their entire analysis there is not a word about the growing rural–urban divide in incomes and other facilities. In 1951, the ratio between agricultural and non-agricultural incomes was 1:1.4. However, by 1988, this gap had reportedly increased to 1:6.2, at current prices. By now, the gap has widened even further.

Our statists seem both unaware and unconcerned about the myriad ways in which the farm sector has been subject to crippling restrictions in order to force farmers to sell their produce cheap in the interest of the industrial sector and urban middle class consumers. They seem mainly concerned with the wage levels of agricultural labourers with no concern for farm incomes. They pay little attention to the problems of farmers except to demand that the government use its *danda* to make the farmers even more subservient to its dictates than they already are. Their key demand is that land reforms be carried out to alleviate rural poverty. They have not updated their data or else they would know that barring a few pockets in places like Andhra and Bihar, there is very little land available for appropriation by the government in order to distribute among the landless. Those who own land above ceiling levels are not farmers but politicians and bureaucrats who have invested their ill-gotten wealth acquiring palatial farm houses such as the ones in the Sainik Farms in Delhi.

In most parts of the country, the problem is the increasing fragmentation of agricultural land, making most holdings uneconomical. The land ceiling levels are such that within one generation a farmer family with two to three children ends up as marginal farmers. Many of our landowning small farmers, including those in states like Haryana, are poorer than those who are working as wage labourers, if the former rely solely on farming the land they possess. If anything, our landholdings need consolidation in order for investments in agriculture, like using tractors, to become more viable.

GOVERNMENT'S LAND MONOPOLY

Our statist radicals also oppose what they call 'emergence of land monopolies' following liberalization, when the heart of the problem is actually the government's monopoly on land. This occurred following British colonial rule which left behind a vicious land policy whose underlying assumption is that the government owns all land and people have a right to use it only if the government bestows a form of leaseholding on them, which it reserves the right to snatch back at will.

The Land Acquisition Act provides the government draconian powers. It can take away anyone's right to land without adequate compensation, and can uproot hundreds of villages by an administrative fiat ostensibly for 'development' purposes. This is often actually an excuse to simply rob the poor of land only to award to themselves and their favourites that same land. That is how posh bureaucratic colonies like Vasant Vihar and Shanti Niketan in New Delhi got built. The villagers were simply told to remove themselves in return for pitiful amounts as compensation. The land was developed and carved into housing plots for bureaucrats at throwaway prices. They built palatial mansions whose market price now runs into many crores.

The government can get away with all this—as it can with snatching the land of the poor and giving it to industrialists or even building golf courses on it—because it has a virtual land monopoly. Our statist radicals have not a word to say against this. Nor do they demand that the Land Acquisition Act be scrapped as a first step towards land reforms so that if the government needs any land it at least has to pay the market rate and negotiate a deal, rather than just declare the takeover of their lands unilaterally.

FARMERS MUST STAY POOR?

Furthermore, our statist NGOs fear that liberalization might lead to agricultural exports—something that most well-off societies work hard to enhance but our statist radicals wish to obstruct by whatever means necessary. They allege that exporting agricultural products will lead to a shift towards cash crops, a rise in food prices and a fall in the nutritional status of our people. So they clamour for the government to immediately stop farmers from producing cash crops for export and exhort them to restrict themselves to producing subsistence food crops, especially coarse grains for the poor. All of this is demanded in the supposed interest of 'food security'. Cash crops are believed to benefit only 'rich peasants'. In their world view, Indian farmers becoming well-off is a reprehensible crime that ought to be put down with a heavy hand.

The entire statist analysis is based on the mistaken assumption that any farmer who grows cash crops automatically becomes a rich peasant. In reality, the way agricultural prices are controlled by the government, even those who grow cotton or sugarcane often stay poor. Many farmers with substantial landholdings end up at Employment Guarantee Schemes performing unskilled labour at minimum wages during certain seasons.

Food production is stagnating in most of India. It is an unprofitable and often losing proposition for most, especially dryland farmers. These farmers have been left to bear the main burden of the PDS by providing it with subsidized food. The policy of forcing the farmers into selling foodgrains to the government at arbitrarily fixed low prices and supplying it cheap to PDS outlets has been the key factor in the continued impoverishment of the peasantry and the consequent shrinking of food grain production.

Farmers in different parts of the country are switching over from foodgrains to other crops precisely because in their particular circumstances, growing these subsistence crops yields such poor incomes that they can neither meet their own basic requirements nor pay competitive wages to the agricultural labour they may employ.

Income levels from agriculture. rather than government laws, end up determining which crops a farmer will opt to grow and what wage rates he can pay. In Kerala, a large proportion of farmers have abandoned paddy cultivation in favour of coconut plantations precisely because of the relatively high wage rates for agricultural labour due to militant trade unionism in the state combined with artificially depressed prices of paddy. Many logically prefer to simply leave their land fallow rather than grow a crop involving losses.

It is erroneous to think that export of agricultural produce leads to food scarcity, except if it happens under conditions such as those under

British rule, when farmers made distress sales in order to pay ravenous land revenues which were mopped up by traders for international export. Wealthy nations are those whose governments encourage exports instead of discouraging them. The European, American, and Canadian farmers receive huge subsidies from their respective governments in order to help them compete in the international market. Our government, on the other hand, puts enormous hurdles in the way of our farmers and subjects them to negative subsidies in order to prevent them from exporting. In its submission to the GATT secretariat, the Ministry of Commerce admitted that in respect of just 20 commodities, farmers had a negative subsidy of Rs 24,000 crores. Negative subsidy is calculated as the difference between the government-controlled price and the international market price—leading to an indirect tax on farmers. This loss to Indian farmers on 20 commodities comes to 68.88 per cent of the total value of production of these commodities. As farmer leader Sharad Joshi argues, this, in effect, means that all these years farmers have been required to pay 69 per cent of gross proceeds as tax to the government. 'While the highest rate of income tax for the non-agricultural sector is 60 per cent of the *net taxable income*, even the humblest *kisan* is subjected to a tax of 69 per cent on the *total turn-over*' (Sharad Joshi, 'National Ulti-Patti for Kisans', *Business India*, the *Times of India*, 23 May 1994).

In less distorted economies where farmers have had the freedom to make rational choices, exports have led to higher incomes and hence higher investments in agriculture. This has led to a rise in productivity and consequently an overall lowering of prices, as has happened in areas such as Europe, America, Australia, Taiwan, and Korea. If cash crops are more profitable, it might even be better to import cheap food. You do not have to grow your own food and starve. India has the highest number of hungry and malnourished people in the world, despite restricting exports of foodgrains for a half-century.

It makes more sense to produce cash crops where our farmers have a comparative advantage in the export market (e.g., cotton) so that rural incomes rise. We could then import produce which is grown cheaply elsewhere, such as oil seeds. The USA's largest export throughout the nineteenth century was cotton and other agricultural products; the profits from agriculture helped finance their industrial revolution. The export of Indian cotton in the nineteenth century failed to achieve a similar result primarily because the colonial rulers thwarted the developing market economy in India, draining away India's wealth through statist interventions so that England's industry became the primary beneficiary of India's cotton exports. Even today the US and other industrial countries are leading exporters of farm produce. If today our own farmers can compete successfully in the international market, we should rejoice in their ability for they will bring much needed foreign exchange into the country. If we become net exporters rather than remain the net importers we are now, the rupee will be strengthened and the overall economy will improve.

Despite all the handicaps imposed upon Indian farmers, they, more than any other sector, are capable of earning the much needed foreign exchange that can save the country from bankruptcy, raise rural incomes and make the government's welfare pretensions redundant. Despite all the protection our industrialists get, most of their goods are despised and shunned in the international market. By contrast, our farm produce is in great demand—*basmati* rice, wheat, long staple cotton, turmeric and other spices, a whole range of fruits, especially mangoes, apples and grapes, and now even flowers are competing successfully in the international market, despite the numerous hurdles put up by the government against the farm sector. Our farmers have the ability not only to feed the people of our own country but also to make a place for themselves in the international market if only the government would get off their backs. Rural poverty cannot be removed without dismantling the licence-permit *raj*.

Yet statists defend this system and feel that moving away from our anti-farmer policies will compromise or threaten 'the sovereignty of the nation'. They want farmers to do farming in the spirit of selfless sacrifice for the nation—their business being only to provide cheap food to others even if they ruin themselves in the process.

STALINIST CONTROLS

Those who argue that farmers should not have the freedom to grow remunerative crops nor be allowed to export their produce are, in effect, asking for Stalinist controls over the peasantry. Those who preach crippling state controls for others might begin by imposing at least some of them on themselves. For instance, what if we proposed that those who preach this kind of statism for others:

   (i) cannot take consultancies with foreign aid organizations;
   (ii) cannot write books for foreign publishers;
   (iii) cannot earn money by taking teaching or research assignments

in foreign universities (because a country as poor as India cannot afford to let its educated elite add to the knowledge pool of rich developed nations); and

(iv) must only work for government educational institutions and write textbooks only for village school children rather than for exploitative western intellectual markets.

But we know better. If the government were to ban their foreign trips or consultancies or the general flow of foreign funds to them, these statists would go screaming all over the world that their fundamental rights and civil liberties were being violated. Yet they want the peasantry to accept restrictions that would further pauperize them—all in the name of food security and providing cheap subsidized food to all as was attempted in the erstwhile Soviet Union. Even Stalin could not succeed in enforcing this policy except by exterminating large sections of the peasantry, which led to a permanent and severe breakdown of agriculture in the Soviet Union. Our statists have obviously not learned the most elementary lessons from the collapse of the Soviet economy and polity.

Illogical Authoritarianism

Apart from objections to their authoritarian proposals, what is amazing is the utter lack of common sense and logic in what they demand. On the one hand, they want farmers to be confined to coarse grain production, without growing cash crops—that is, to stay in the realm of subsistence farming. On the other hand, they want everyone (except for farmers, I presume) to be supplied with cheap foodgrains since they cite erstwhile Andhra Pradesh Chief Minister N.T. Rama Rao's Rs 2 a kilo rice scheme approvingly. Those who practise the kind of agriculture they propose, such as subsistence farmers in tribal areas, cannot produce enough even for their own year-round subsistence and have to send off one or two family members to migrate in search of work at pitiful wages in order to meet their own cash and food requirements. Those who oppose commercialization of agriculture need to realize that it is not just crops like cotton which come under the category of cash crops. Any crop which is grown for the market is a cash crop. For the Punjab or Haryana farmers who feed the entire country, wheat and rice are as much cash crops as are cotton, sunflower seeds, or sugarcane.

Commercialization of agriculture has nowhere led to shrinking of agricultural employment, as the statists fantasize. They believe the shift to commercial crops is leading to 'less work and lower wages', especially for women. On the contrary, it has led to much greater demand for labour and consequently much higher wages as compared to areas practising subsistence agriculture. For instance, the daily wage in Punjab ranges from Rs 60 to Rs 100 a day (far above the minimum wage of Rs 28) whereas in non-cash crop growing areas work is harder to get and fetches no more than Rs 15 to Rs 20 a day. Punjab and Haryana are providing employment to millions who migrate from Bihar, Madhya Pradesh, and other poorer regions.

INCAPACITATING OUR FARMERS

The real issue facing the agricultural sector is that ever since British rule it has been subjected to far more draconian restrictions than has the industrial sector. Without freeing agriculture from deadly restrictions, it is meaningless to talk of democracy, decentralization of power and *panchayati raj*. If our statists want to decide what farmers should grow and at what price they should sell their produce, it means they want the bulk of India's population to live in permanent servitude. The consequences of this mode of Stalinist thinking are frightening and dangerous.

For decades, farmers have been fighting hard to free themselves of government controls and have organized massive protests about being forced to sell their produce at unremunerative prices to keep the urban middle class and industrialists happy. This anti-farmer policy has been implemented through a whole range of government mechanisms. For instance:

(i) The farm sector is subject to procurement of foodgrains at government fixed prices which do not give the farmers a remunerative return, making agriculture a poverty-ridden sector.

All over the country, paddy is subject to a compulsory levy at a price fixed by the government (i.e., rice mills have to sell the government 40 per cent of their produce at below market prices). In certain districts of India, only the government can buy paddy from farmers. Private trading is simply not allowed. This monopoly procurement at rates fixed by the government translates into artificially depressed prices for farmers.

(ii) Economic borders are created arbitrarily for farmers. For instance, Maharashtra farmers cannot sell their cotton crop outside the state. The state government enjoys a monopoly of purchasing cotton. If farmers take their crop to neighbouring states, they can be arrested for smuggling. The government imposes both formal and informal restrictions on the inter-state movement of paddy and wheat to facilitate procurement in the grain producing state. This system goes to such absurd lengths that rural migrants who come to work in the city are not allowed to bring their own farm produce from their villages, even for their family's own personal consumption. The police search trains and buses to check if they are carrying bags of rice or *dal* with them. The police has the right to arrest them for inter-state smuggling if they are caught carrying even one tiny bag of rice. Punjab and Haryana farmers were for decades forced to sell their produce to the government. Private traders were prohibited from purchasing wheat till the government was through with its procurement drives. Nor could Punjab farmers take their wheat outside the state borders.

An important reason for the disgruntlement of the Sikh peasantry which made them gravitate towards separatist politics in the 1980s was that they were forced to sell their wheat to the government at such artificially low prices that they got into a vicious debt trap. No one paid any heed to the demands of the Punjab peasantry even while they launched massive protest movements and the government unleashed widespread repression in Punjab in order to carry out its wheat procurement drives. Our statists reacted with alarm only when the issue was hijacked by religious fundamentalists demanding a separate state of Khalistan.

(iii) Our government frequently resorts to the import of farm produce which includes foodgrains, dairy products, cooking oil, cotton, and sugar at prices far above domestic levels and dumps them in the market at below market prices in order to force down the price of Indian farm produce. Right now Australian farmers have been given a big contract to supply pulses to India. Those statists who are crying *swadeshi* are not known to protest when our government launches price warfare against our *desi* farmers while benefiting European or American farmers.

In addition, Indian farmers face crippling restrictions in exporting farm produce. The export of cotton continues to be tightly controlled by government interventions to hold down the domestic price. The government not only arbitrarily fixes the quota for cotton exports, but reserves the right to cancel or lower it arbitrarily at the behest of Indian industrialists. In addition, it is the government which decides the minimum price at which farmers can export—usually fixing it deliberately at a price that renders Indian cotton uncompetitive in the international market. Timing of exports is related to the harvest season and international market situation. However, in our country, farm exports are hostage to politics.

Early this year, suicides by cotton-growing farmers were reported from Andhra Pradesh following a drastic reduction in cotton prices due to a curtailment of the export quota by the government leading to severe economic distress for cotton growers. The export cut has come despite there being a near glut situation in the country. Various state governments, including those of Gujarat and Maharashtra, had requested the central government to allow export of cotton to enable an increase in prices in the domestic market so cotton-growers who were getting low returns this year could benefit. However, the textile industry blocked this move and was even able to influence the Election Commission into ordering the central government not to allow the export of cotton till elections were over, making it seem that this would influence voters in favour of ruling parties in cotton-growing states. It was absurd for the central government to even refer this matter to the Election Commission. Obviously, their intention was to block exports to help textile industrialists who can in turn reward the Congress with election funds. When cotton prices were slightly high, the same lobby was successful in influencing the government to allow it to import raw cotton to bring down domestic prices. But they would not allow imports of cotton cloth so that their own shoddy products enjoy a protected market.

Similarly, exports of wheat and rice are subject to a ceiling fixed by the government. Most important of all, exports of farm products (except fruit and flowers) were routed through bureaucratic institutions created by the government (such as APEDA, NAFED, and TRIFED) whose only purpose is to cause delays, confusion, corruption, and red tape, leading to the stagnation of export volume. Even after easing some restrictions only government-licensed traders can export commodities like rice and wheat. Even export of non-essential items like castor seed is subject to arbitrary on–off quotas to be routed through MMTC and select licensed traders. In 1994–5 castor seed exports earned Rs 330 crores. Certain interested industrialists are trying hard to get it restricted so that they get an assured low priced supply.

Restrictions on the processing of farm produce prevents the emergence of small agro-industries in rural areas, thereby stagnating farm incomes and restricting the growth of employment. To mention just a few examples: cotton-growers cannot gin their own cotton—only licensed ginning mills can—even though this simple activity would enhance farmers' profit margins considerably, as well as give them useful by-products. Grape-growers have to obtain licences if they want to sun-dry their produce to make raisins. The list of restrictions is endless. Needless to say, none of these licences come easily without paying large bribes.

In many areas sugarcane growers are prohibited from making jaggery and their crop has to be bonded to the local sugar mill. Paddy-growers cannot husk their own paddy which would provide them with useful by-products and enhance their income. Only licensed mills are allowed to undertake this operation. Setting up a milk-processing unit (above 70,000 litres capacity) requires getting clearance from both central and state governments. This involves such complicated licensing procedures that only those with exceptional political clout succeed in getting them. In many states, units set up by the state government have been allowed a virtual monopoly of the purchase and processing of milk, thus keeping the prices of milk depressed for producers, resulting in low milk production and continuing scarcity. This culture of scarcity allows the few government patronized licensed companies to keep high profit margins at the cost of consumers.

In 1990, milk was briefly decontrolled for a few months. During this period several milk-processing plants came up in different regions giving some boost to milk production. Milk producers got higher prices and the competition led to an increase in quantity. In Punjab alone, four milk producing plants came up in those few months of delicensing, making serious dents in the state-owned Markfed monopoly in milk. For instance, even though producers are getting nearly double the price they got when Markfed had a monopoly, *ghee* prices stayed stable at Rs 100 per kilo and even declined later. This is because competition has forced the factories to cut down their profit margins, benefiting both producers and consumers. However, in 1991, a Milk and Milk Procurement Order restored all the earlier restrictions that come with requiring licensing. As a result, no new processing units have come up since 1991.

India is the world's second largest grower of fruits and vegetables. Yet only 1 per cent of our production is commercially processed while one-third of all its produce is wasted due to poor distribution and storage facilities, as well as absence of food processing units. This criminal waste at a time when millions go without adequate food is primarily due to the fact that government policy has systematically thwarted the emergence of agro-processing units in rural areas. This has kept incomes low and kept too many people dependent on the land while forcing farmers to sell their perishable produce at dirt cheap prices for lack of processing facilities.

FOOD SECURITY

The NGOs opposed to destatization argue passionately that the Structural Adjustment Programme (SAP) will lead to withdrawal of the state from providing food security and cutbacks in the PDS, leaving the poor to the presumably ruthless forces of the market. But exactly what kind of food security has the government provided in its non-liberalized *avatar*? According to an expert committee of the Planning Commission set up to estimate the number of poor people in India, there are 312 million people below the officially designated poverty line. Most other estimates put the figure at 50 per cent of the population. This means they are both malnourished and underfed. This is despite more than four decades of socialist bureaucratic measures which created institutions like the FCI. The role of the PDS in the total consumption of foodgrains in India is relatively marginal at about 15 per cent.[2] The majority of the Indian people, especially the poorest, remain outside its purview. The distribution of foodgrains has not been allocated to states in proportion to their levels of poverty. Bihar, Madhya Pradesh, Rajasthan, Orissa, and Uttar Pradesh combined obtain less than 16 per cent of the rice and wheat distributed through the PDS, though over half of the poor live in these states. Eighty per cent of PDS outlets are in urban areas whereas 80 per cent of the poor live in rural areas. A study done on the PDS by D. Ahluwalia showed that the richest 40 per cent of the population get 30–5 per cent of the food distributed through PDS.[3] In many of the really poor districts of India, villagers have never even seen a PDS outlet.

The PDS, in fact, needs total dismantling. It is a hub of corruption and inefficiency. Leakages alone amount to about one-third of the total distribution. The stocks are usually either too low or too high without any thought given to storage capacity or the requirements of food security. According to government experts, foodgrain stocks should be

---

[2]For a review of the PDS I draw from an article by Gulati, Ashok, 'Changing Gears', *Seminar*, 433, September 1995.

[3]Geetha, S., quoted in Gulati, 'Changing Gears'.

around 15.4 million tonnes. During the last few years the government has accumulated more than 37 million tonnes; much of it is rotting in FCI godowns. A large amount has become unfit for human consumption. An expert on PDS, S. Geetha, has calculated that carrying the buffer stock costs nearly Rs 1,400 per ton annually.[4] In 1995 alone, the FCI spent nearly Rs 200 crore for letting thousands of tonnes rot and become unfit for humans.

When private traders buy and sell food, they make profits. FCI, like all other government undertakings, is constantly losing money. The government subsidy to FCI increased from Rs 661.54 crore in the fiscal year 1980–1 to Rs 3,674.46 crore in 1992–3. The budgeted subsidy in 1995–6 was to the turn of Rs 6,500 crore.

Whether foodgrains reach their destination in time or in the right quantity is of no concern to the FCI. Since all its losses are automatically covered by the government, it has no interest in controlling costs. Its callousness in promoting waste surpasses even its propensity for corruption. Sugar levied in Gujarat is taken to Uttar Pradesh for distribution while sugar procured in Uttar Pradesh may be distributed in faraway Andhra Pradesh or Maharashtra—all so that those handling it can get more opportunities to pilfer stocks and make money at each stage of the numerous transactions involved. Losses that are a result of improper storage, pilferage, and damage due to careless handling are conveniently categorized as transit losses so the FCI officials are not held responsible for poor management or even theft.

If our statist NGOs were really serious about providing food to the needy, they would not have demanded Soviet-style food subsidies for almost all of our over 900 million people—a totally impractical and economically bizarre proposition. A better way of reaching food to the poor is to have year-round guaranteed food-for-work programmes in rural areas. But leaving this important task to a government so corrupt and inefficient is a risky proposition. Hunger and malnutrition can be alleviated only when we stop helplessly petitioning the government. Instead, as a society, we have to take responsibility for ensuring that no one stays hungry in our country. For instance, one sees few signs of hunger in Punjab largely because of the vast network of rural and urban gurudwaras which provide free *langar* (cooked food) every day to anyone who wants it. It is a common practice in Punjab for farmers to offer a portion of their produce to the *gurudwara* before they take it to

---

[4]Quoted in Sainath, P., 'Food for Thought', *Seminar*, 433, 1995, p. 22.

the market for sale. Urban Sikh families also make regular contributions to their gurudwara for this same purpose. Thus, the entire Sikh community in Punjab tries to ensure that no one in the state (Hindu, Sikh, or anyone else) needs to go hungry. This tradition was also once followed by Hindu temples but was destroyed systematically during British rule. The idea is not to push back the problem of hunger from the secular to the religious domain but to make the entire society take responsibility so that not one person needs to go without two decent meals a day which come to them unconditionally and respectfully in the *Guru ka langar* spirit rather than as demeaning state 'welfare'.

RACKETS PROMOTED BY THE ESSENTIAL COMMODITIES ACT

Nothing shows the absurdity of our farm policy more than the case of the sugar industry. For reasons best known to itself, the government treats sugar as an 'essential commodity' and hence subjects it to ridiculous controls and restrictions. It is well known that white sugar is like white poison and its consumption has more harmful than nutritional value. Instead of encouraging and assisting farmers to improve the quality and shelf life of the more nutritious *gur*, which has traditionally been an important farm related cottage industry in India, the government discourages *gur* making in some areas and even bans it at the behest of sugar producers. The Sugarcane Control Act allows the government to arrest and lock up any farmer undertaking *gur* making in areas where it is prohibited. For example, no one is allowed to make *gur* (except through the wasteful open pan method) within a 20 km radius of a sugar factory to ensure that the sugar mill has an assured supply of sugarcane. Besides licensing, every other aspect of this industry, ranging from price fixation, use and movement of byproducts, supplies to the PDS, monthly releases in the market down to exports is controlled by the central government. These controls have stunted the functioning of the sugar industry, which is in addition saddled with obsolete technology leading to perpetual sickness and avoidably high production costs (*Business India,* 26 February 1996, pp. 54–5). No sugar mill can be set up anywhere in the country without clearance from the centre and state government. In Maharashtra, sugarcane farmers are subjected to zone bandi, that is, they are not allowed to sell their sugarcane to anyone except to the sugar factory under whose jurisdiction they are placed. They have no choice except to become members of that particular cooperative mill, often run by political barons. Being a member means that the crop is bonded to the mill and they have to accept whatever price the factory arbitrarily decides to give them. Even if a neighbouring factory is offering higher prices, they cannot go and sell there. All over the country mill payments to farmers are delayed for months on end. Moreover, farmers wait helplessly for mills to accept their bonded crops after harvest and suffer enormous losses due to these delays.

Sugar factories are subject to yet more controls. All over the country they are subject to a compulsory levy of 40 per cent of their total production, which means that the government buys this amount from them at far below their cost of production for the PDS outlets. They are permitted to sell the rest in the open market. However, the free sale amount is subject to monthly quota releases by the government. The easiest way to bring down general sugar prices (as opposed to enforced levy method) would be to allow more sugar mills to come up. Applications for new licenses from the sugar licensing committee do not get approval for years, despite the incidence of sickness in the sugar industry. If sugar was treated as a byproduct and not the main product of the industry, prices would also decrease. Bagasse and molasses are valuable products but the industry is not allowed to use them as well as they might. Bagasse is used for making paper, cardboard etc. as well as as an industrial fuel. Molasses feeds the liquor industry and is also used for making industrial alcohol, citric acid, ethyl alcohol, and cattle feed. The Molasses Act empowers the government to claim the entire molasses production of every mill at arbitrarily fixed prices. One of the managers of the Batala Sugar Mill in Punjab told me that till recently the government would take molasses from them at around Rs 12 to Rs 14 a quintal and then give it to liquor manufacturers at Rs 200 a quintal. Getting a licence for making industrial alcohol is as difficult as getting a sugar factory licence. Batala Sugar Mill applied for the conversion licence in 1988 but has not yet managed to secure it. Thus factories are prevented from diversifying and functioning economically. If they could profitably use their by-products then sugar prices would come down considerably.

Batala Sugar Mill produces 1 lakh quintal of molasses, out of which the government has allocated 30,000 quintals to be supplied to a liquor factory. The rest of the production has to be stored by the sugar factory at its own cost till the government allocates more quota for disposal. Excise inspectors come to check these stocks and inspect daily production reports. This offers ample room for harassment and abuse of power.

Even the levy sugar has to be stored at the mill's cost for as long as the government chooses not to lift the levy. If there is surplus production, the government often refuses to lift the stock it claims. If there is a shortage the government could demand that the mills give it a larger proportion as levy and threaten to use the frightening Essential Commodities Act to ensure compliance. All these needless storage costs result in huge losses.

This factory has a total share capital of Rs 2.17 crore. Out of this the government had invested a mere Rs 25 lakh. The rest of the shares belong to the farmers. Farmers of the region have to become shareholders whether they like it or not. Their initial 'shares' came through automatic deductions from the price of cane they brought to this factory when it was first set up in 1963. Yet the farmers are treated as virtually bonded producers for the mill. The state government, not the factory management, determines the prices at which sugarcane is to be purchased. This wreaks havoc on cane production. For instance, in 1994, sugarcane production was 40 per cent less than the 1993 peak production because in 1993 the government increased sugarcane prices by a mere Rs 1—from Rs 49 to Rs 50 per tonne despite rising costs of production. Farmers got demoralized and cut down production. The next year they increased prices by Rs 12 per tonne but as usual announced it too late—not at the time of sowing but at the time of crushing—so that by then the down turn in production could not be arrested.

The Sugar Act requires that once a year a meeting of the shareholders must be held to approve the factory's balance sheet. This has never been done. In 1982 BKU, a farmer's organization, approached the High Court to demand that the mandatory annual meeting be held and proper balance sheets produced. The High Court, in fact, presided over that first meeting held under its order. Till date the decisions taken in that meeting have not been honoured, nor any follow up meeting held. The Sugar Act also provides for the withdrawal of the government provided its share capital is returned. The farmers offered to return the government's share capital of 25 lakhs but the government refuses to give up its control. Thanks to all this mismanagement, the factory whose net worth at today's prices is about Rs 7 crore, has an outstanding loan of about Rs 10 crore! It is the same story for most other sugar mills in the country.

To top it all, the government works hard to create artificial sugar scarcities and does not allow for sugar exports even if there are surplus stocks lying with factories. However, that does not prevent it from every now and then going in for sugar imports—usually at higher than Indian prices, ostensibly to bring down domestic prices but actually to provide opportunities for kickbacks and embezzlement of the now infamous sugar scam of 1994 variety in which 20 lakh tonnes of sugar was imported even though there was no short fall in cane production. Even in 1995, despite signs of a bumper crop, the government imported another two lakh tonnes and authorized forward contracts for import of another four lakh tonnes all with a view to carrying out a price warfare against domestic producers (*Business India*, 20 November 1995, p.32). Strange that our *swadeshi* enthusiasts never object to such imports nor have ever demanded de-licensing of the sugar industry which would automatically lead to a spur in production and lowering of prices as well as technology upgradation.

THE ORGANIZED SECTOR

In the anti-liberalization campaign literature there are warnings galore about the likely decline in wage levels of workers, especially of women, and hence the importance of keeping foreign business interests out in order to prevent the exploitation of Indian labour. However, we hear nothing about how our *desi* industrialists have become corrupt, wasteful, and inefficient due to lack of competition and over-dependence on government. Indian industry is notorious the world over for its obsolete, high cost-low quality shoddy products. Our home-bred industrialists have acted even more irresponsibly and callously where the rights of the Indian people are concerned than any MNC would ever dare.

Poor management and rapacious short-term thinking of Indian industrialists along with extremely irresponsible and dull-witted trade unionism have contributed to the mess that is the Indian economy. Indian industrialists have used the concept of *swadeshi* to demand ridiculously high protective tariffs which gave them a virtual monopoly over the vast Indian market where they proceed to sell the cheap junk they produce at exorbitant prices. Even today our import duties are among the highest in the world.

Public and private sector industries pour poisonous waste materials in our rivers or wherever they please without any safeguards, and pollute the air. They have successfully resisted attempts by citizens asking them to clean up their poisonous filth. No MNC dare do what the government-owned Agra refinery is doing to the city and to the Taj Mahal. No Enron management, for all its greed, is likely to foul up the air as much as our public sector managers at the Indraprastha power station have in the heart of Delhi.

Control over economic activities in the name of building socialism and protecting our national sovereignty provides grand opportunities for bureaucrats and politicians to amass huge fortunes at a faster pace than any businessman could ever achieve. Despite all the talk of opening up the economy, the restrictions are, by and large, still intact—as the Enron affair and the Jain *hawala* scandal demonstrated. Jain was acting as a broker for many of the foreign firms, bribing virtually every minister and bureaucrat who held power to give clearance to projects.

'The new industrial policy of July 1991 did not bring about any drastic changes with regard to private foreign investment. All it did was to change the foreign equity limit from 40 to 51 per cent without changing very much the list of "core" industries which had been opened earlier to the Foreign Exchange and Regulation Act (FERA) companies. This was for the so-called "automatic" route.... At the same time the government also opened some discreet bylanes through the so-called "non-automatic" route for "non-core" industries involving discretionary case-by-case disposal' (Suresh D. Tendulkar, *Times of India*, 15 April 1996).

This is still the norm, allowing large scope for corruption. Our *babus* and *netas* still control all the entry and exit points to business and commerce.

That is why thugs are flocking to politics and the bureaucracy. Even our richest businessmen have to grovel before the pettiest government *babu* or politician, to satisfy his every whim in addition to providing regular offerings. On a recent trip to the industrial city of Surat, one of the big mill owners told me that the excise inspectors collect Rs 25,000 per month from each of the 450 textile mills in Surat. This amounts to Rs 1.25 crore every month in bribes to one government department from just one segment of the business community. K.J. Alphons, an IAS officer known for exposing corruption in the government, has written in his autobiography that bureaucrats get away with making far more money than even the most notorious of our politicians: 'An officer who pays a lakh of rupees to his political bosses for a posting would make at least a 100 lakh during his tenure in that post. The equation is simple: for every lakh which goes to the politician, 99 lakh goes to the bureaucrats.' He cites instances of officials who are worth more than

Rs 3000 crore even though their income from their salary is no more than a few thousand rupees a month.[5]

Our industrialists and traders succumb to extortion by government officials because the corrupt and incompetent among them have benefited enormously from this licence-quota regime of favouring those who grease the right palms. In addition, they have become dependent on the protection from competition through underhand government price fixing, rather than competing in the market. Some of our major businessmen even use criminal mafias as a routine way to make money. The underworld links of many industrialists, real estate developers and builders have been exposed in recent years. However, many other underhand means they use to influence government policy are accepted as normal lobbying. In such a scenario, healthy competition is bound to be feared and despised and the cry of *swadeshi* used as a protective shield.

The problem is not the entry of foreign companies but the lack of transparency in government decision-making. Shady deals continue to be made with kickbacks being the chief criteria for selection. This usually means either that relatively responsible foreign firms will shy away from doing business in India, while only those willing to indulge in corrupt practices come here. When firms do come to India, they are likely to expect their Indian business partners to handle all bribes and underhand deals so that they do not get into trouble with the laws of their home countries. In many countries, businessmen or officials convicted of corrupt practices can actually be punished. It is not just we Indians who are worried about this inability of our government to enforce the rule of law. Foreign business firms are even more frightened of doing business with us because our regulatory and legal machinery either does not function effectively or does not function at all.

The anti-economic reforms lobby seems content to let a system of doing business continue which allows an Arif Mohammad Khan to get a kickback of Rs 7 crore in just four months of being a minister, and an additional Rs 46 lakh when he was a mere Member of Parliament (MP) from just one French company desirous of his *sifarish* that was seeking just one contract in the power sector. No businessman can make so much money without investing a single rupee of his own. These amounts are merely the tip of the iceberg.

---

[5]Alphons, K.J., *Making a Difference*, New Delhi: Viking Penguin India, 1996.

Most of our business houses are neither socially responsible nor competent as enterprises. That is why only a small proportion seem willing to fight against the evils of the bankrupt licence-permit *raj*. The economic reforms agenda in our country has remained limited and half-hearted because each sector demands that restrictive measures on other sectors continue while simultaneously demanding a loosening of controls for themselves. At the same time very few groups are willing to give up the lure of special 'concessions' and subsidies that the government routinely throws them as crumbs to keep them servile.

Even those of our businessmen who demand a measure of liberalization for themselves want many restrictions on agriculture to continue. While sugar mill owners want the government to do away with the system of compulsory levy on sugar and control over the production and sale of sugar by-products like molasses, they still want the government to continue controlling sugarcane prices in their favour.

It is time our industrial sector stands on its own feet and learns to function in the market. If, in the process, the inefficient producers of shoddy, overpriced goods lose out, we need not shed tears for them. If *swadeshi* for them simply means producing poor imitations of western goods at the same or at a higher price—Double Seven or Campa Cola—as our *desi* versions of Pepsi or Coca-Cola, then the western companies are bound to emerge triumphant. These are known to be harmful drinks. Therefore, competing with Coca-Cola to produce a *desi* version of the same junk is pointless and only shows mental slavery. It is only our *jaljeera, mattha, kanji, neembu-pani, thandai, lassi* and various other genuinely desi drinks that are both far more delicious as well as nutritious which can help us withstand the onslaught of Pepsi and Coca-Cola. Similarly, Indian made synthetic fabrics are bound to lose out to more efficiently produced and quality conscious foreign products. However, the fabrics and designs produced by our poor handloom weavers even today remain unsurpassed in beauty and quality. It is from them that our Ambanis and Mafatlals will have to seek inspiration, guidance, and expertise if they are to survive as industrialists in an open economy rather than grovel for *sarkari* favours in a protected market.

RETRENCHMENT AND JOB LOSS

Here the approach of the anti-reform lobby is no different from the stereotypical trade union response. They claim that 'opportunities for employment in the organized sector in general and more specifically for women have actually decreased as a result of structural adjustments', that 'women workers are being pushed even further into the informal or unorganized sector', and that 'the notorious exit policy allows employers to fire workers easily and lead to mass retrenchment.' (*A Perspective from the Indian Women's Movement*, p. 14.)

All this is as ridiculous as the kind of 'facts' and 'figures' they quote to build a case against reforming our industrial sector. For instance, the mentioned document tries to prove that exploitation comes with export-oriented industries by telling us that in the garment export industry in Mumbai, they found women workers earning between Rs 2.50 to 12.50 per day. This is followed by similar examples from the leather and shoe industries. These figures are so dubious as to be laughable. Not even in remote tribal pockets will you find it easy to hire someone for a daily wage of Rs 2.50, leave alone in Mumbai in the garment exports industry, a city with one of the highest wage rates in the country. Even if, after much toil, they found one or two rare cases of such low wage rates in Mumbai, the authors of this document ought to mention the entire range of wages available to women. In cities like Mumbai and Delhi, women who perform piece rate work commonly earn Rs 60 to Rs 120 a day. The real question is: are the wages of men and women working in export-oriented industries higher than for work in other sectors available to those women?

Even with the pitiful trickle of economic reforms, there has been a visible spurt in the availability of jobs for both women and men in the organized non-government sector. Wage rates (discounting for inflation) have risen both in rural and urban areas. Women in cities have taken up new jobs that have been created in the service sector and in various industries including garments, leather, pharmaceuticals, electronics, and small-scale trading. Wage levels in most export-oriented industries remain unsatisfactory. However, they are still far better than what women earned before these export industries made their appearance in India.

The statists also build a case that liberalization will lead to the closure of vast numbers of small-scale enterprises. In the All India Democratic Women's Association (AIDWA)-CWDS sponsored document they allege that four lakh small businesses have closed down in the last few years since liberalization began. It would be far more useful if they also gave us figures for how many more new small-scale industries or production units were started during the same period. Even before liberalization, a closure rate of four lakh small enterprises would not be considered significant since they are likely to have been replaced by many more. From 1991–2 to 1994–5 employment grew from 129.30 lakh to 146.56 lakh in the small-scale sector, or about 4.5 per cent a year. The number of small-scale sector units has increased from 20.82 lakh to 25.71 lakh, an average annual increase of nearly 8 per cent.

Even small steps towards delicensing have led to large-scale mushrooming of small-scale manufacturing units as well as a vast development of ancillary units for bigger industries. The country is actually already in the midst of a shortage of skilled workers in many areas.

The key question that our statists needed to answer is: why is it that after more than five decades of a fairly closed-door economy, keeping multinationals at bay, our government-organized *swadeshi* industry has provided so little employment to women that more than 90 per cent of the female labour force remained in the unorganized sector? According to their own figures, only 14 per cent of the workforce in the organized sector are women and their main employer is the government. In the organized sector for more than the last half-century, women were being constantly eased out which led to a steady decline in employment of women in virtually all large-scale industries (1975, Status of Women Committee Report). That trend was operating in the heyday of Nehruvian socialism under the vigilant leadership of Indira Gandhi.

The fears of Maria Mies (a German feminist who is very influential among Indian feminists) with regard to economic reforms in countries like India gives us a glimpse of why certain international forces are lending extraordinary support to our statists. In an interview with the *Times of India* on 12 February 1996, Mies is reported to have said that the flexibility of capital following reforms will lead to MNCs preferring countries like India for investment: western business houses are 'increasingly opening production centres in third world countries where wages are low and female labour even cheaper'. She admitted that the majority of employees in low wage units and export processing zones were women. Mies disparagingly calls them 'footloose industries' because they are committed to maximizing their profits, not to any nation-state, and hence employ whoever serves their interests best.

That some First World feminists are worried about MNCs shifting their areas of operation leading to unemployment in their own countries is understandable—though if MNCs are as bad as Mies makes them out to be she should be happy to push them out of Europe. But what is hard to understand is why certain Indian feminists are upset at the prospect of a dramatic increase in the employment opportunities of women in India. If MNCs offer much lower wages to Indian women workers than to their western counterparts it is precisely because the existing wage levels and opportunities for work in India are so poor. As more economic choices become available for workers with the destatization of the Indian economy, including for women, wage rates will go up and work conditions improve. No multinational would dare pay the kind of wages our bonded labourers currently get in the indigenous brick kilns, stone quarries, glass, and match industries.

Our statist NGOs are upset that nearly 65,000 workers have taken the offer of voluntary retirement with the benefits that go with it. Only in a few sick and dying industries, such as textiles, are jobs likely to undergo a serious decline. In a functioning economy such mills could never be allowed to continue to lose hundreds of crores of rupees annually, simply because they provide employment to a few thousand workers. Yet in India, our government and trade unions raise all manner of obstructions to prevent even the sickest mills from closing. If nothing else, they could at least be handed over to the workers with the proviso that they are to run them without state subsidy or patronage. Apart from the needless subsidies to this loss-making sector which raise consumer prices, cotton growers are forced into selling their produce at artificially depressed prices due to the political manipulations by the powerful owners of this forever sick industry. Its products are too high priced for the poor quality cloth they provide. Yet our statists want such parasitic industries to continue while they oppose the emergence of other companies willing to be competitive and viable under a less stifling state, not to mention providing employment to millions hungering for it.

Unfortunately, the only type of employment that meets the standards of our statist NGOs, no matter how parasitic or exploitative the enterprise, is that provided by the government. This is due to a voracious clinging to the Soviet ideology that private business and industry are exploitative by definition, no matter what the wages and working conditions they provide. In their view, state and public sector units provide the only desirable jobs because they alone can keep the greed of capitalists under check. Therefore the only employment they want to see expand is in the government sector.

Worst of all, they oppose disinvestment and dismantling of wasteful public sector units as well as retrenchment of our incredibly bloated bureaucracy. The AIDWA-CWDS document, for instance, bemoans the fact that 'there is a virtual ban on recruitment in the public sector, thus drastically curtailing job opportunities.' They are rising to the defence of the utterly indefensible. Even our bureaucrats and politicians are embarrassed to publicly defend the public sector or the vast *babu*dom they have created. We need to ensure that the government stops running so many losing businesses—hotels, banks, airlines, mines, electricity power plants, fertilizer, cement, and other industries—and starts learning how to perform its most primary task: law enforcement. It defies logic how our statists can oppose government getting out of these businesses when the public sector is accumulating losses worth tens of thousands of crores of rupees every year. For instance, to give some notion of the vast extent of the losses, each employee of our nationalized banks made an average loss of Rs 81.7 lakh during 1993–4 alone. The government-run Delhi Transport Corporation employed 21 persons for each bus. No wonder it ran crores of losses every year while private operators made a neat profit of at least Rs 30,000 to 40,000 per month per bus, despite thousands of rupees they have to pay as bribes to the police and other officials. In our country virtually no one can be fired from a government, public sector job—even if they indulge in outright robbery and do no work.

Our statists oppose privatization without telling us how the country is to continue to bear the mounting losses from government and the public sector. The entire public sector has become a heavy millstone for the rest of society and will make the whole economy sink if allowed to continue in this fashion. The telecom controversy in the 1990s proves the corruption of the public sector very aptly. Now that the government is taking a few reluctant steps towards surrendering its total monopoly in the telecom sector, we find that the government can earn billions of rupees and actually get us a functioning telecom system merely by simply letting our bureaucrats and *babus* sit back, stay out of the way, and not even pretend to work. Mahanagar Telephone Nigam Limited (MTNL) always runs huge losses. In the 1990s, for example, Himachal Futuristics offered to provide a functioning phone system to consumers in Delhi and a revenue of Rs 85,000 crore to the government for simply being allowed to do the work which MTNL claimed to do but made such a corrupt mess of.

Today we have a disastrously large public sector whose sole business seems to be a parasite on the economy. Even the finance ministry in its Economic Survey for 1994–5 admits that government expenses have run wild. The 1994–5 budget showed a fiscal deficit of Rs 57,600 crore, which was one-third of the total budget. The interest on public debt is estimated at Rs 52,000 crores in the year's central budget. This is more than half of the entire revenue receipts of the government for the year. These figures point towards a breakdown of the official economy.

The sad truth about disinvestment and retrenchment is that it has not even begun. The 1996 budget had hoped to net Rs 7,000 crore from disinvestment in PSUs. So far the government has been able to collect only around Rs 168 crore. Far from encouraging retrenchment, the government has no exit policy worth the name. In fact, in recent years, despite all the phoney talk of cutting down government expenses, bureaucrats and politicians are not willing to let go; the bureaucracy continues to grow. The central government alone has actually increased employee strength by taking on 1.7 lakh more people in the last year. The story is no different at the level of various state governments.

We desperately need a policy that will end non-viable government enterprises and government-subsidized companies in both the public and the private sector. The bureaucracy needs to be cut down to less than a tenth of its present size if we are to make India a functioning society. More than 25 per cent of our official budget is spent on government salaries alone. The figure would be at least double if we included the salaries of defence and defence-related personnel. In fact, these government salaries and perks gobble up most of the money meant for development projects. Actually it would be a mammoth savings for our country if the bulk of our bureaucracy were given not just a golden, but a platinum parachute, provided that they permanently sign away their right to claim control over further government *naukris*.

THE POOR BEAR THE BRUNT

Where does the money for all this waste and corruption come from? Clearly not from the pockets of the rich but by fleecing the poor—who are paying proportionately much higher excise, sales and other indirect taxes than our rich businessmen. The indirect systems of taxation in our country efficiently yet invisibly burden the poor with a disproportionate level of inescapable tax. Income tax, which the middle and upper classes are supposedly subject to, contributes far less than a tenth of total government (state and central) revenue. The bulk of our national and state revenues comes from sales tax, customs, and excise duties. In

1994–5, 57 per cent of all state and central revenue came from customs, excise, and sales taxes, while only 6 per cent came from income tax. Since virtually every consumer item that the urban and rural poor buy—from a matchbox to hair oil to a cycle—is subject to sales tax and a substantial excise duty, they are paying every day of the year while most of our businessmen specialize in evading almost all of their income taxes. The farmers pay an additional indirect tax by being forced to sell their produce at below market prices.

In order to stop this continued haemorrhaging of our economy, the closing down of non-viable PSUs, and the subsidy requiring are both necessary and desirable.

DEFENDING THE NON-EXISTENT SOCIAL SECTOR

The statists, upset at the proposed half-hearted liberalization measures, remind me of the response of some of the deeply disturbed battered women I have known. How would one respond to a woman who keeps complaining for years that her husband earns nothing, snatches away a good part of what she earns, gets drunk routinely, is a drug addict, and frequently beats her up along with her children and yet expects unconditional obedience and *sewa*? He has taken away her self-respect, all her jewellery, and blown all her money on buying liquor. He has pawned her kitchen utensils and mortgaged her house, incurring debts which she has to pay off.

Then one day she comes to us desperately crying that he has threatened to leave her because he has started an affair with another woman. Anyone with a grain of sense would advise her to thank her stars for being able to get rid of him, that she would be better off without such a man. Instead, the woman goes back to him wailing and falls at the feet of her husband, saying, 'How can you abandon me? You are my *pati-parmeshwar*! You are the *daata* and earner of this family. Our children and I will starve without you. The evil world outside will descend on us. You are our protector, our benefactor. Please remember, it is your duty to provide me with a comfortable house, all kinds of luxuries, good clothes and jewellery, love and care, money for the children's education, holidays, and all the other good things in life. How can you abdicate this responsibility?'

I would undoubtedly sympathize with such a woman, understanding that she perhaps has legitimate fear of the world outside which she believes is unsafe, that even the pretence of marriage gives her a minimal measure of physical and emotional security from some forms of external violence.

It is also understandable that many of our statist NGOs might fear freedom from dependence for undoubtedly many of them will collapse if government patronage and support are withdrawn from them. But they need to realize that most ordinary Indians do not share their fears and are yearning to break free of government tyranny.

When our statist NGOs argue against the SAP on the ground that it will lead to a deterioration of health and civic services, make education inaccessible for the poor, and leave people to fend for themselves which will allegedly lower their chances of survival, one wonders why they are pretending these services exist and are provided by our government. When they argue that 'there was a noticeable drop in poverty levels during the 1980s as public expenditure on anti-poverty programmes and employment guarantee schemes insulated poor households from the worst effects of a restructuring market', one wonders whose poverty alleviation they are referring to. The illegal incomes of bureaucrats and *netas* undoubtedly rose during this period with new opportunities to siphon off public funds.

As for the ordinary poor citizens of this country—their conditions also improved, but this was due mainly to their willingness to avail themselves of the slight increase in economic opportunities that opened up due to the expansion of economic activity that occurs with even the slightest relaxation of control.

The ill effects of privatization on social welfare were indeed felt in countries like England, France, and the US which had functioning welfare programmes, relatively decent schools and hospitals provided by the government, and a functioning public transport system for some regions at affordable prices.

In India, our government has never demonstrated its ability to perform any of these essential tasks and responsibilities. If we had a bureaucracy that was capable of providing health services and education to those who cannot afford private arrangements, India would not have the largest number of illiterates, nor have among the worst health care delivery systems in the world. Our government has not even provided clean water in our major cities, leave alone in remote villages. Public health centres in rural areas seem to exist only for the purpose of providing salaries to incompetent and indifferent doctors, nurses, and Auxiliary Nurse Midwives (ANMs)—they do not even see to it that medical staff show up to work. Our shamelessly high infant and maternal mortality rates and the widespread prevalence of preventable diseases like jaundice, malaria, polio, and gastroenteritis speaks volumes of our dysfunctional health care system which the statists want to protect. Two million children out of 25 million born every year in India die within a year.

The government claims a shameful female literacy rate of around 36 per cent, yet its definition of literacy does not even include the capacity to read a children's textbook or write a letter. Most of India's poor are denied access to schools because firstly there are not enough schools, and secondly, most government schools that exist provide so little education that even the poor (who are otherwise desperate for education) reject them as useless. Given the quality of these schools, it is not surprising that we have such a high drop-out rate even at the primary school level. Most schools in our country function to provide salaries to teachers and *babus* of the education ministry in much the same way that the Bihar Husbandry Department's chickens and buffaloes existed to provide salaries and opportunities to government employees to steal public funds. The British at least geared their education system to train and produce clerks from among Indians to man their colonial machinery of governance. Our post-Independence *sarkari* schools are capable of producing only *chaprasis* (peons) incapable of any useful function. Consequently, our problem today is not so much that of unemployment, but that the millions who are coming out of our *sarkari* schools are literally unemployable. The urban elite, however, indeed have a heavy stake in the government's continuing involvement in education because our universities, medical, and engineering colleges provide virtually free education for the children of the middle and upper classes.

India is placed 134 down the list of nations on the Human Development Index (*Human Development Report*, 1995) only marginally ahead of a few civil war-ravaged sub-Saharan African nations and a few other war-ravaged Asian countries like Afghanistan.

When Rajiv Gandhi was Prime Minister, he himself admitted that no more than 5 to 10 per cent of the money meant for development and social welfare actually reached the people. The rest found its way into the pockets of *babus* and *netas*. The little that trickled down was not even spent imaginatively or sensibly. In many instances, the projects remain on paper while the money is siphoned off according to a 60:40 formula. The bureaucrats and politicians who sanction these projects take 60 per cent and the contractors meant to execute projects simply pocket 40 per cent. Yet the statists advocate further expansion of the welfare functions of the government.

The list of interventions the government is urged to undertake is awe-inspiring. People do not even have such unrealistic expectations from their gods! If our NGOs had their way, the government would take care of all our needs including bringing up our children, inculcate the 'correct' gender-sensitive, anti-consumerist values in them, feed, educate, clothe them, and then provide them jobs. However, they conveniently forget that as yet our bureaucrats and politicians have not even learnt the ABC of sensible governance, nor can they even moderate their own rapaciousness. Nevertheless, they are expected to act like benevolent gods answering every prayer that we address to them. Moreover, our state-enamoured NGOs do not indicate where the resources and skilled well-structured administration for all this are to come from. Sometimes an enhancement of taxation is suggested as one source. But if we were to follow their economic advice, nobody except bureaucrats, politicians, and criminals will have incomes enough for taxation.

At the core of this controversy is the question of how we view poverty. The 'development' philosophy that has come to us from western donor agencies and was imbibed by our statist NGOs is based on the assumption that people are poor because they are underdeveloped. Hence outside intervention by donor agencies and government leads people to 'develop' themselves and move out of poverty conditions. Thus poverty is seen as some kind of a natural habit of those who are currently poor—hence the need for governments and NGOs to play a paternal (or maternal) role and make the aspiring poor appear as helpless children.

Remove the Obstructions

Poverty is not a natural condition. People all over the world have a natural tendency to better their material conditions, and struggle against scarcity and deprivation. Whenever you see a group of people unable to fend for themselves, it's wise to look around and see who or what is obstructing them. When you see water go up a slope it is obvious that there is some external force like a booster pump which is making that happen. Similarly, when you see people in a state of destitution or grinding poverty, it is safe to assume some person or group has worked hard to reduce them to that condition by obstructing them from taking care of their own needs. The only effective way to alleviate poverty, therefore, is to remove the hurdles in the way of people fending for themselves in a dignified fashion.

Poor, middle class, or even rich, there is literally no activity you can carry out in any area which involves contact with the government without greasing palms or being humiliated and made to appear like a grovelling supplicant before an imperial authority. You have to pay off for everything—getting a house plan sanctioned, getting an electricity or a water connection, getting a driving licence, a phone connection or even getting a death certificate! For instance, the going rate for buying a licence in black for a *coolie*'s job at a small town railway station is about Rs 15,000. At Delhi railway station the rate is over one lakh rupees.

Just ask the poor how they fear going near a government office or near a police station. It is well known that even beggars pay regular *haftas* to get police clearance to beg or else they will be arrested under the Vagrancy Act or under some other law. Beggars are frequently rounded up and jailed because the government assumes the right to prevent people from seeking alms, even if they are destitute.

Our police are known to extract large regular *haftas* from brothels. According to a survey conducted by the Indian Health Organization, a Mumbai-based outfit, the monthly police earnings from brothels in Mumbai run into many crores of rupees. The 300-odd brothels in Parwalla Lane, for instance, pay Rs 1,000 each per month as *hafta*. On Falkland Road about 3,000 brothels pay Rs 300 each per month. This money apparently reaches even departments like the CID. These payoffs continue despite the fact that prostitution is legal in Mumbai. In Delhi, to get a posting as the SHO for G.B. Road, where many brothels are situated, policemen are reported to be paying Rs 10–15 lakh as a bribe to their seniors in charge of transfers.

In fact, crime in our society is directly proportionate to people's proximity to government offices, courts, and police stations. The closer you come to these institutions, the more crime and corruption you witness. The further you go from them, the more you witness the innate honesty of most people in this country. Even today, remote villages which are inaccessible from district headquarters witness far less crime.

Today, the biggest obstacle to our economic and moral well-being as a society is the licence-permit *raj* which makes all of us, but especially enterprising working people and the poor, into helpless supplicants before all of those who man the government machinery. Our bureaucracy has been allowed to trample on our self-respect for too long and has cultivated habits of dependency and passivity in our people. This grovelling dependency has destroyed the inner health of our society as well as its power of resistance against evil in much the same way as the AIDS virus destroys a body's immune system. This is perhaps why even those who claim to speak on behalf of the poor cannot go beyond encouraging people to hope that somehow the *sarkar* will take care of all their needs.

Towards Solutions

When I oppose our licence-permit regime, I do not imply that moving towards a market-driven economy will usher in *Ramrajya,* nor am I a votary of the 'free' market economy. Such a thing does not exist in today's world, as all nation-states have built selective barriers, including those that officially believe in the superiority of market-driven economies over state-controlled economies. Competitive markets, no doubt, bring in their wake great insecurities, fierce brutal competition and unscrupulous profit seeking. Therefore, virtually every market-driven economy depends on instruments of regulation and conflict resolution that provide some measure of protection to those whose interests are being violated by others, ensuring that business is conducted by somewhat predictable and open rules and norms. It is a cause for worry that our political and administrative machinery does not have the capacity to perform this role effectively, as our government is primarily an instrument of extortion, harassment, and tyranny. We have little redress available when those who rule violate our rights as citizens with impunity or when a powerful person or group violates the rights of vulnerable individuals or groups. The Union Carbide case is a good example. Our government first let them run the plant without requiring adequate safety measures because the inspectors were interested in bribes rather than inspection. When thousands died from the gas leak, the government prevented people from suing the company by usurping the victims' rights to reparations by insisting that the government alone had the right to sue Union Carbide on behalf of its citizens. It then sent the case to a US court on the plea that our courts were not able to handle such a case. The government thereby admitted that our legal machinery does not function, even in critical situations. When the US courts refused to entertain the government's petition on the ground that the offence had been committed on Indian soil, our rulers went on to make a miserable settlement and pocketed most of the small settlement that Union Carbide coughed up for the poor victims.

We are in even greater danger from the corruption and lack of accountability of our government machinery than from the forces of the market or the MNCs. If a company like Union Carbide finds it harder to get away with murder in the US than in India, it is because our government officials and politicians are willing to overlook even the most flagrant acts of commission and omission of business firms if they are suitably bribed.

Our agenda, therefore, ought to be ensuring that the government fulfil its most primary task—that of maintaining law and order and providing democratically monitored well-functioning institutions for regulating and arbitrating in case of conflicts. It is not the business of government to run businesses.

The leading and responsible proponents of economic reforms in India have consistently argued that as far as basic social and welfare services are concerned, the answer is obviously not privatization, for these are precisely the services that the entire society must pay for itself through public sharing of the burdens of providing the most basic public goods. Even in the market-driven economies of Europe and North America, most governments traditionally took some responsibility for providing somewhat competent basic education, health and other necessary services that offer a minimal safety net for the poor. They continue to develop and become wealthy in large part because they invest heavily in improving the life and job skills as well as the quality of life of their people, including many of the poor, for example by providing them with subsidized or free health care and education.

However, our bureaucratized, over-centralized government cannot be trusted with these important tasks anymore. Instead, democratically worked-out, locally accountable institutions must take direct charge of defining, funding, and managing these services. If we want good education to reach the poor, schools must not be run by *babus* in the education ministry sitting in Delhi *durbar*, state capitals, or even in district headquarters. They should be run directly by village *panchayats* (as opposed to *sarkari panchayats*) who ought to have the power to both hire and fire teachers as well as have a genuine say in the curriculum. Similarly, our own primary health care centres should not be under the charge of health ministry officials, but rather controlled and managed by the *panchayat* in each village. The same principle should apply to sanitation, water supply, electricity, and other services, especially the police.

This arrangement is bound to have many difficulties because our society has lost the habit of self-governance. However, it will have many advantages. People will have the power to make and correct their own mistakes and over time evolve functioning institutions which meet with their common requirements. Most important of all, it will help restore our *swabhiman* (self-respect) as a people so that we can actually work towards Mahatma Gandhi's vision of *swaraj*—with each village functioning as an autonomous and self-governing unit.

7

When Nature's Call is a Crime*

Breakdown of Conflict Resolution Mechanisms in India

When the United Nations declared 1995 as the Year of Tolerance, many a seminar and conference was held on the subject with our political leaders, bureaucrats, and various celebrities extolling the virtues of tolerance. A similar resurgence of conferences on the theme took place following the Babri Masjid demolition. Leftist secularists suddenly discovered the *sufi-bhakti* tradition in their attempt to combat the culture of intolerance and inter-community violence in our society. As a result, audiences were subjected to grand music festivals of medieval *bhajans, dohas* and *sufi* songs in several cities of India in attempts to wean them away from the hate-mongering communal propaganda of the Sangh Parivar.

Conflict among human beings and among groups is inevitable. There is no evidence that people become tolerant if you subject them to pious speeches, or even offer them deeply moving *sufi-bhakti* songs. Men like Kabir, Tukaram, and Nanak had such a powerful effect on their contemporaries not primarily because they composed good verses or gave stirring sermons, but because their life was their message. People were moved by their love, compassion, and deeds—all of which challenged the prevalent prejudices and sought to bridge the divide between the rich and the poor, the high caste and the low, Hindu and

*This article was originally published in an issue on 'Tolerance' in *Seminar*, 4(135), November 1995, © Madhu Kishwar.

Muslim. It was their actions and deeds which sanctified their poetry and their verbal message.

Today, when their *dohas* or *shabads* are recited by power-hungry politicians whose own lives run totally contrary to the original message, people are naturally left untouched. Similarly, when an avowedly Stalinist party like the Communist Party (Marxist) (CPM) resolves to 'use' the *bhakti* and *sufi* traditions to combat the growing influence of the BJP in the Indian polity and gets involved in organizing festivals of *sufi-bhakti* music, its impact cannot go far beyond providing high quality entertainment for a day or two to a select audience. Attempts to use Kabir's message without attempting to live one's life in tune with it would inevitably ring hollow. The CPM's politics would have to embody not strife but love and compassion if people are to take its words seriously. However, even powerful voices like that of Kabir could not inspire people to become mutually tolerant merely on the strength of their own inspiring lives. People have to see the advantages of tolerance over intolerance.

Tolerance flourishes in societies and polities that are able to provide effective, workable means for conflict resolution in a way that every individual and group can count on as a measure of protection for their specific interests. For this to happen, it is crucial to have effective mechanisms for mediation, as well as skills at evolving a measure of consensus on conflicting claims and rights of different groups. In times when such institutions no longer function well and begin to collapse, people become increasingly intolerant of the claims of others and begin to resort to aggression and violence in order to deal with conflicts.

Unlike Europe, India has no comparable history of inter-religious or denominational conflicts spread over centuries such as those between Jews and Christians, with the latter intermittently attempting to virtually wipe out the former, or denominational wars which went on for centuries and only subsided recently (but consider the Balkans) such as those between and among various sects of Catholics and Protestants. In fact, ethnic cleansing has been a frequent response of western societies whenever they are confronted with ethnic groups different from mainstream society. Modern western nations were built in some parts of Europe only after those countries did their best to get rid of groups professing different religious dogmas or belonging to different ethnic stocks. Western Europe cleansed itself of almost all Jews through centuries-long violence and persecution. When European settlers went to the New World, they did a fairly thorough cleansing job for that era, considering the technologies available at that time for wiping out the native inhabitants. In India we have no comparable history of any groups being targeted for ethnic cleansing or of centuries-long hostility among ethnic groups being acted out in day-to-day living.

For instance, there is no history of Hindu–Muslim riots or pogroms in pre-British India. The various communities living here were able to evolve fairly sophisticated norms for co-living in the same society while at the same time preserving their distinct cultures. This was in part due to the fact that we in India generally lacked a centralized authority structure both in the religious and in the political realm. For example, in India there is no counterpart to the Roman Catholic Church with its ambitious attempts to determine inter-personal and inter-community behaviour at the local level. Nor did political rulers in India sitting in distant capitals try to govern the lives of people at this ground level. Each region's villages were self-governing on most issues, abiding by their internally evolved social norms for working out conflicts among its various *jats* and *biradaris*. Thus no matter who ruled at the top— Hindu, Muslim, or Sikh—the conflicts among various rulers did not necessarily disturb people at the village level. Consequently, various groups and communities had the space to work out norms of living together without much interference from outside and from above. That is why you have the unique feature of Hindus, Muslims, and Sikhs joining together in each other's religious festivals at the local level and even, at times, having common places of worship. As long as the responsibility for ensuring law and order, dispute settlement, organizing security, and taking care of common needs such as sanitation, water, and education rested at the local level, *jati* and village *panchayats* functioned effectively, even though they did not and were not meant to ensure egalitarianism.

With the imposition of the British Empire's version of a modern state machinery, the traditional systems of conflict resolution and taking care of common civic needs began to crumble. This form of the modern state claimed that all powers ultimately came from the top, from itself, and took away whatever local decision-making powers it desired leaving the rest of the structure of community living to rot. While it destroyed the old, it failed to evolve a functioning system of conflict resolution to distribute social wealth and rights over natural resources, and to manage religious and civic affairs. This colonial history is one of the major reasons why we see a dramatic rise in social conflicts in our country in our time and consequently, a growing intolerance.

I illustrate this growing intolerance in our time by narrating the story of an ongoing conflict in Delhi between a group of slum dwellers and a neighbouring upper middle class colony. The manner in which this particular conflict has been allowed to fester because the two sides are trying to use the machinery of the government to press their respective claims, has only escalated it further and strengthened hostility between the two groups. The degeneration of this small conflict into a mini civil war situation has many common features with some of the larger conflicts in our society, such as that between Kashmir and the Central Government over power sharing, between Punjab and Haryana over Chandigarh, Karnataka and Tamil Nadu over water sharing, between Hindus and Muslims over Babri Masjid, between the government of Gujarat which wants the Narmada dam completed and those who oppose it. In fact, many of these conflicts have been actively instigated by various politicians as a tool in their electoral political struggles.

Shaheed Sukhdev Nagar is a *jhuggi-jhopri* (JJ)cluster in Delhi adjoining D Block of Ashok Vihar in north-west Delhi. This area of Ashok Vihar has wealthy middle class people living in bungalows, some of which are owned by Wazirpur industrialists. The 5000-odd families of Sukhdev Nagar live in shanties constructed illegally on railway land by the side of the railway line that separates Ashok Vihar from the industrial area of Wazirpur, which faces it.

The government has shifted its policy in recent years from forcible resettlement of JJ clusters to improving and upgrading existing squatter settlements by providing some minimal amenities to them with the consent of the agency on whose land they have encroached. However, since the Railway Ministry, which owns the Sukhdev Nagar *basti* land, is averse to any permanent construction on its land, the *basti* has even fewer amenities than many of the regular JJ colonies. The children of the *basti* attend government schools either in Wazirpur industrial area or in neighbouring Ashok Vihar. There is no medical facility in the *basti*. The nearest dispensaries are in Ashok Vihar or further up in Azadpur while the fair-price ration shop used by the Sukhdev Nagar residents is also in Ashok Vihar. Therefore, for many of their basic needs the residents have to go to Ashok Vihar.

The slum wing of the Delhi administration has a provision for installing one water tap for every 100 *jhuggis* and one toilet seat for every 25 *jhuggis*. This is evidently inadequate, for it means one toilet seat for nearly 125 people, calculating an average of five persons per *jhuggi*. However, in Shaheed Sukhdev Nagar the city administration has provided for no toilets whatsoever. Given the overcrowding in the *basti* and the minuscule size of these *jhuggis,* there is no way the dwellers can build toilets alongside their own *jhuggis*. The nearest latrine complex, with 60 toilet seats, is nearly a mile away in Wazirpur. This is run by an NGO—Sulabh International—which also runs two other latrine complexes for the entire Wazirpur industrial belt. The users have to pay 50p per visit to the toilet. Its distance as well as the cost makes this latrine complex unviable for the *jhuggi* dwellers. A family of six, for instance, would have to spend Rs 90 a month for one visit per day per person to the pay-toilet. This is clearly prohibitive, considering the family incomes in this area. According to a survey undertaken by the slum wing of Delhi administration in 1987, only 4.4 per cent of households had a family income of Rs 1,000 per month. Another 26.2 per cent earned between Rs 700–1,000; 63.4 per cent earned Rs 500–700 per month and another 6 per cent had an income of Rs 200–500. Even if we assume incomes doubled between 1987 and 1994–5, Rs 90 per month for toilet use for one use a day would be considered prohibitive by most of these families. Given the frequency of diseases like diarrhoea in such settlements, one use a day would clearly be impractical. The distance adds to its impractically, especially for little children.

Given the total absence of toilet facilities inside their *basti,* the residents began to use the slope on the other side of the railway line for defecation, as well as the nearby park facing D block of Ashok Vihar; these areas became vast open latrines as a result. In addition, the park began to be used as thoroughfare for easy access into Ashok Vihar for *basti* residents needing to go to the ration shop or dispensary, for their children to go to school, or for women to go to work as domestic maids in the nearby middle class houses of Ashok Vihar.

This 'misuse' and 'abuse' of the park became a major source of conflict between the Ashok Vihar residents and Sukhdev *basti* dwellers. Apart from the terrible stink that enveloped their neighbourhood, the Ashok Vihar residents were also concerned about the likelihood of various diseases spreading from the filth and faecal matter the *jhuggi* dwellers left there as litter every day. They prevailed upon the Delhi Development Authority (DDA) to build a wall to block the access of the *jhuggi* dwellers, but the *jhuggi* dwellers would break the wall in no time and continue as before. In 1990, the Residents Welfare Association of Ashok Vihar filed a writ petition in the Delhi High Court asking the

Court for protection against their park becoming an open toilet and offered to construct a boundary wall around the park at their own cost. DDA, as one of the respondents, claimed that it was unable to perform the task of protecting that park from daily encroachments because the *basti* residents thwarted all its attempts to maintain the space as a park. The High Court not only upheld the plea of the Ashok Vihar residents, but went so far as to direct the SHO of the local police station to render all possible assistance to the DDA and its contractors.

The police were assigned the responsibility of ensuring that the DDA did not face any obstruction in raising a six-foot wall, with obstacles on top such as embedded pieces of broken glass, to prevent unauthorized entry into the park. In addition, the police were ordered to ensure that 'unauthorized persons' did not use 'the said part of the park as a public lavatory'. The Court also ordered that some lavatories be constructed for the use of the JJ dwellers. This part of the order was not put into action because the administration had the excuse that the railway authorities would not allow their land to be put to such use. However, the other directives of the Court regarding the misuse of the park were indeed implemented. The local *thana* began to provide round-the-clock police vigilance at the newly constructed boundary wall.

The *basti* dwellers apparently did not think they were expected to honour Court orders forever. Sections of the wall were pulled down continually. Each time the wall was broken, the DDA repaired the breaches. Towards the end of 1993, constant police presence ensured that the *basti* dwellers were effectively barred from the park, which began to be well maintained by the combined efforts of the DDA and the Ashok Vihar residents. However, the residents still resented the fact that, though the *basti* people no longer used their park as an open latrine, they still used it as a thoroughfare.

On 30 January 1995 this conflict erupted tragically. Eighteen-year-old Dilip had come from Allahabad to see the Republic Day Parade in Delhi and stayed over with his relatives in a Sukhdev Nagar *jhuggi*. The residents claim he ventured into the park because he did not know it was 'illegal' to go there for defecation. He was apparently beaten up by the policeman on duty and later died of his injuries. This caused a great stir in the *basti*. Thousands of people gathered and prevented the police from taking away Dilip's body. They insisted that a political leader or a senior official come to the spot before they would allow the body to be removed for a post-mortem. The police retreated for a while but returned around 9.30 a.m. with heavy reinforcements to forcibly remove Dilip's body. The *jhuggi* dwellers began to pelt stones at the police, some of which hit the houses of Ashok Vihar residents, since the police had positioned themselves on that side of the divide, after which the police 'charged' at the *jhuggi* cluster. One can argue that the police could have resorted to milder measures to disperse people including the use of tear gas rather than opening fire, in order to quell the angry crowd. Among those injured was a woman who was hit by a bullet inside her house—she had given birth merely a month ago.

Fifteen days after the event, when I visited the area, I saw little boys and even children with broken bones wrapped in plaster due to indiscriminate police beatings. In addition, the police arrested 123 *basti* dwellers, who were later released on bail. The *jhuggi* dwellers were both angry and frightened. Ashok Vihar had become like enemy territory, literally guarded by police guns. I was rather pained to hear the reaction of the residents of Ashok Vihar. They were completely on the police's side and aggressively justified all the actions of the police. In their view, the police were their saviours. Many said they were convinced that if the police had not opened fire that morning their homes would have been attacked and looted by the *jhuggi* dwellers.

Even though women and children from this *jhuggi* cluster provide cheap domestic labour to virtually every house in the area, and many of the men work in the nearby factories owned by Ashok Vihar residents, the residents wanted these *jhuggis* removed, or at least that the *jhuggi* occupants should be denied access to the colony. Even the death of young Dilip and the serious injuries suffered by many *jhuggi* dwellers had not moved their hearts. Almost all the women residents in Ashok Vihar that I talked to denied that the police were responsible for the killing. They claimed they had heard that the boy had died of a 'heart attack', that he had originally come to Delhi for treatment for this condition. The residents welcomed the policemen on duty with supplies of food and tea and wanted even more police protection for their area, especially for the wall.

For days after the firing, the domestic servants from the *basti* had not come to these bungalows to do their customary washing and cleaning. The Ashok Vihar housewives attributed this temporary absence to a vindictive boycott by the *jhuggi* dwellers, whereas the *jhuggi* dwellers explained their temporary withdrawal as caused by fear. They were too afraid to go into Ashok Vihar with nearly 100 armed policemen camping in the park to guard the border area. After the dramatic clash, several politicians visited the area and made appropriately populist speeches, depending on which of the two groups they addressed, leaving both the Ashok Vihar residents and the *jhuggi* dwellers seething with rage and mutual distrust. It would appear as if the police guns were the only means of mediating between the two groups.

Could such a situation happen in a traditional village? By 'traditional' I do not mean a modern-day village with convenient access to the police and bureaucracy. I mean a village which is sufficiently remote either in time or geographical location so as not to have experienced the paraphernalia of modern-day governance. This is not to claim that traditional villages do not have their own share of inequities, social tyranny, and conflicts over the use of natural resources, including the possession of land. But in a traditional setting, the two sides would have decided the matter through consultation and negotiation. In all likelihood, they would have first held their respective *biradari panchayats*—then perhaps a joint meeting of the two *biradari panchayats*—and eventually would have evolved some kind of a mutually acceptable solution. The solution may not have been fully equitable but the emphasis would have been on workability.

This is not because people in traditional societies are necessarily more tolerant or generous but that they have to act with a measure of accommodation towards each other because they know the consequences for all the villagers if a tyrannical force from outside was called upon to adjudicate their disputes. No villager in medieval India, for instance, could get or would want the *badshah* sitting in the Delhi *durbar* to send his army to prevent a fellow villager from grazing his cattle on the village common, or from drawing water from a particular well.

If force had to be used to prevent someone from exercising a particular right or to obstruct a group from doing something that others did not like, it had to be organized locally by the individual or group concerned. And by resorting to violence against another person or group, there was always the risk of their retaliating. Most violence in pre-modern societies had to be carried out face-to-face without much help from weapons that destroyed others from far away, that operate in a way that you yourself are not in danger if you have a monopoly on these weapons. Only those who commanded huge personal armies, at great personal expense, had a special clout in the larger society. Caste and *biradari* cohesiveness provided another buffer. You could not attack a member of another *biradari* without running the risk of all his kinsmen coming back to retaliate against you. Therefore, there were some checks on local tyranny.

Group rights were better accommodated, even if the group was not considered an equal in social or economic standing.

However, with the interference of modern state machinery under the aegis of colonial, and later, our home-bred rulers, most of these restraining influences have collapsed. At present, local landlords or upper class or caste groups can be far more unrestrained in their tyranny because they can call upon the might of the state to intervene on their behalf without any risk to themselves. The Ashok Vihar residents do not need to take into consideration the very basic needs of the neighbouring *jhuggi* dwellers when seeking to prevent them from defecating in the public park, they do not need to bother about thinking out alternative arrangements. Neither do they fear retaliation, because of their relatively easy success in getting government machinery to act in their favour.

Similarly, on the other side, the *jhuggi* dwellers thought nothing of creating a nuisance for their wealthy neighbours by defecating right in front of their homes, as long as they enjoyed political patronage. Either of the two groups could act against the other's interests with impunity, depending on who had greater confidence in gaining the support of the government machinery. Near election times, the *jhuggi* dwellers would probably have a temporary upper hand. At all other times the upper class residents—because of their education, wealth, social status, and political contacts—could make the government machinery protect their interests while trampling on the rights of their poor and relatively disorganized neighbours.

The level of intolerance is going up in our society because today we have very few means of effective conflict resolution. Consequently, most protests tend to become lawless (e.g., the AIIMS doctors' strike, the anti-Mandal agitation). In fact, a majority of our present-day conflicts are being actively instigated by our rulers from the top to make us more vulnerable, and therefore more dependent on them. Most of our ethnic and inter-group conflicts today are more a product of this failure of our government machinery to work out consensual solutions rather than of any deep-seated, innate hostility between various communities. Those who are authorized to make decisions are at most times too remote from the scene of conflict either to have a sensitive, thorough knowledge of the situation or any stake in ensuring that problems between different groups are amicably resolved. It would seem that the High Court took no notice of the practicality and implementability of their order. It merely banned people from defecating in the park without saying where else they could perform this essential function.

The incident I have narrated goes to show how most middle and upper class people believe that the poor are an unwanted nuisance in the city rather than fellow citizens whose basic human requirements ought to be a matter of concern for all, especially for those who benefit from the cheap labour they provide in that area. In this respect modern-day urban elites in India are more callous and intolerant of the claims of the poor than were traditional elites in a village setting. The latter recognized their interdependence with others in their community, and knew they could not wish away the poor as the modern elites tend to do.

The hallmark of the state machinery we have inherited from our colonial rulers (and thereafter failed to overhaul) is its lack of accountability to the people at large. Consequently, those in positions of power can manipulate it to their advantage at will. Earlier, the upper castes enjoyed a monopoly over its use and abuse. The logic of universal adult suffrage and caste-based reservations has now made it possible for even lower castes and poorer groups to manipulate the state machinery in limited ways to suit their ends. Let me illustrate this by giving another example at the other end of the spectrum.

A family well-known to me (let us call them Kapurs) lives in a wealthy west Delhi colony neighbouring an urban village called Madipur. Children from Madipur attend a government school which is situated right opposite the Kapur family house. These children often jump over the gates of the houses near their school to steal whatever they can lay their hands on and vandalize their plants and gardens, causing a great deal of annoyance to the residents. One day the Kapur family caught one of the Madipur boys stealing from their courtyard. They grabbed hold of him and without hitting or abusing the child, told his accompanying friends to call his parents so that they could report his thieving to them. This boy happened to belong to the sweeper caste. Within minutes more than a dozen outraged men and women of his family and *biradari* descended on the Kapur family. Even before the Kapurs could explain what had happened, the boy's relatives began to beat up male members of the Kapur family, accusing them of holding their child in captivity. The neighbours then phoned the police but the policeman who arrived turned out to be a *biradari bhai* of the sweeper community. Instead of intervening to stop the fight, the policeman joined the aggressors and threatened to arrest the two sons of the Kapur family who had already been beaten. He forcibly took them to the police station as though they were criminals, all along threatening to book them under all kinds of absurd charges. Even though the Kapurs are reasonably well-off and respected in the neighbourhood, they had to put up with insults from the constables at the police station because they refused to pay the bribes being demanded. Even after they called a lawyer, the Kapur family was bullied into not only withdrawing their charge of assault against those who had beaten them up but were also forced to apologize to them for 'keeping their child in captivity'.

Thus, far from resolving the conflict by fair-minded action, the police action ended by creating mistrust and hostility. The supposedly lower caste sweeper community could get away with unprovoked aggression because they could count on the support of local police, thanks to *biradari* ties as well as connections with local politicians who cultivate them as a vote bank.

The above two incidents show that in today's India neither the rich nor poor are safe because the 'law and order' machinery functions in the most lawless manner. Therefore, today it is in everybody's interests to need to work out local, community-based arrangements to prevent local conflicts from going out of control.

When people begin to feel insecure about their physical survival and property, they tend to become more aggressive and intolerant. Our politicians and government machinery thrive on making people insecure. If we want a tolerant society, we must promote the culture of solving local conflicts through mediation and arbitration locally and directly by the communities concerned. We have to develop the skills needed for working out mutually acceptable arrangements, involving give and take on both sides, without resorting to the intervention of those elements of the state machinery whose interest lies in exacerbating conflicts. Even if these locally worked out arrangements do not end up providing exactly egalitarian outcomes, if the emphasis is on consensus, the parties to a dispute would have to give due recognition to the legitimate interests of others for it to become workable.

8

Symbols of Mental Slavery*
Of Toilets, Tubs, and Drains

We had the rare good fortune of being led in the anti-colonial struggle by Mahatma Gandhi. For him, ending the direct political subjugation of India by the British was a small part of a larger struggle to win back for the people of India a sense of confidence in themselves, to shake off mental slavery and to rediscover themselves as a people. He was acutely aware that mental slavery was not less but even more deadly than economic and political subjugation.

It has been more than four decades since India got rid of British colonial rule. Yet, despite Gandhi's creative use of *swadeshi,* we are more enslaved to the West now than when we were under the direct rule of the British. At the rhetorical level, the Indian elite is ridiculously paranoid about western domination. They are forever hysterically screaming against sell-outs to multinationals and other power centres of the western world which are perceived as bulldozing us into following policies which are threats to our political, social, cultural, and economic autonomy. This mindset is all-pervasive. Leftists, rightists, centrists, all join the chorus of self-styled defenders against western conspiracies to enslave and bully India into following the evil ways of the West. Yet even when left alone, the best that this elite does in any field is to imitate the West mindlessly and produce cheap and shoddy imitation of western lifestyle, norms, and products.

---

*First published in *Manushi*, Issue No. 72, September–October 1992.

One unmistakeable symbol of our mental slavery is the continuing spread in India of preference for the western mode of defecation and waste disposal. Its salient features are:

(i) A chair-like commode for defecation which probably is related to the cold climate in the western hemisphere which made it necessary to perform all activities away from the floor, especially when there was no central heating. In India, the same task is performed squatting on one's haunches. That is why a toilet with a chair-style toilet seat is popularly called 'western commode' in India and the one which has a bowl for the squatting posture is considered 'Indian'.

(ii) The flush toilet (water closet) as a system of faecal and other waste disposal which is linked to large drains which are then emptied out into rivers. This is perhaps one of the most ecologically destructive of all the 'advances' made by the western world; it amounts to the wilful pollution and poisoning of the earth's water resources.

When the British left India, they left behind WCs (meaning 'western commode' not just 'closet') in a few select places such as in colonial mansions of the *gora sahibs, dak* bungalows and circuit houses, fancy hotels and restaurants and in a few private bungalows in the Civil Lines area of every city meant for *gora* and brown *sahibs*. Today the western commode has spread like the plague—and with equally disastrous results. You now see WCs in train toilets (even those attached to second class compartments), cinema halls, student hostels, government housing complexes, cheap and fancy hotels—and of course in the private homes of the lower middle and higher urban strata. Likewise, the system of pouring raw sewage into rivers in the name of building a modern drainage system is no longer confined to big metropolitan cities. It has spread all over the country, to small towns and even to urbanized villages.

Its spread is proof that the western educated elites who run the affairs of the country are so mindless in their efforts at aping the West that they are not even aware that they are covering themselves with and ingesting shit in the process. These power wielders are thoroughly alienated from their own culture and environment, in short, even from their own being. Yet they enjoy such tremendous influence over the colonized minds that they can mesmerize vast sections of the population into doing with eagerness things that would have revolted them before being mentally colonized.

For instance, there is no evidence that the World Bank or any powerful multinational has conspired to facilitate the spread of the 'western commode' and the drainage system—both extremely inappropriate and ugly, unhealthy transplants from the West—and major health hazards to boot. It's our own elites which have done so. Contrast this with self-respecting Japan. Japanese homes mostly have eastern style toilets for their own use. But foreigners are culturally distanced and respected by being provided WCs for their exclusive use.

IMPERIAL THRONE OF BROWN *SAHIBS*

Why do I call the western style commode unhealthy and inappropriate? For several good reasons:

• Most Indians, especially those from rural areas, are used to the squatting posture for defecation. The Indian commode[1] serves that purpose very well. In addition, the Indian commode provides good exercise for one's hip, knee, and ankle joints—important for fending off arthritic joints. The squatting posture facilitates bowel movement because of the pressure on the stomach. It also provides pelvic-floor exercise and minimizes the risk of perineal tearing in childbirth. Many Indians, unused to defecating on the WC's throne in a sitting posture, tend to squat on the commode, thus creating a big mess all over it. In addition, one gets up feeling unclean because of the dirty water that comes splashing up from the receiving end of the western commode.

• Given the perennial water shortage in India, the WC becomes a liability wherever it is installed. The Indian commode can be kept clean with a relatively small amount of water to get the shit down the drain. For the western style commode you need more than a cistern full, amounting to almost 30 litres of water to flush off the waste after every use, including urination. If the water supply is irregular and the water tank does not get filled up, which is a frequent occurrence even in cities like Delhi, you have to pour bucket after bucket to get the mess down the drain.

• The use of the WC presupposes the use of toilet paper—something most of us in India are not comfortable with. In any case, in this age of ecological crisis, it is stupid to waste so much paper, involving the cutting down of thousands of trees, just to keep one's bottom clean—especially when the best of toilet papers doesn't do the job as efficiently as does water. When using the western WC which does not allow for an easy

---

[1] What we call the Indian toilet goes under the name of 'Turkish' in France and 'Moslem' or 'Arab' in Britain these days. In Japan it is called the 'Eastern' toilet.

wash, Indians tend to use far more toilet paper than do westerners because of the need to 'feel clean'. In addition, the use of toilet paper causes irritation and is likely to cause haemorrhoids.

• When the WC is used for urinating by men, it ends up with a spray all over the seat. It is very unpleasant and unhealthy to sit on a sprayed seat cover. In the West, they are beginning to recognize this problem and in select public toilets, disposable seat covers are being provided so that the users' bottoms do not have to touch the pee sprayed toilet seat. However, this means more paper wastage and cutting down of even more trees.

• Given the prejudice most Indians have about cleaning toilets themselves (unfortunately there is less prejudice against using unclean toilets), the task is left to poorly equipped sweepers. As a result, even in middle class homes the WC is filthy. You can actually see them coated with dark brown sediments of excreta settled at the bottom under the water. In contrast, the Indian commode can be easily cleaned with even a simple broom and the dirt carried totally out of sight. Even if not cleaned properly, it is not as much a health hazard as is a WC because there is no need for body contact with the commode.

• In public places, the WCs are an even greater health hazard than in private homes. It is a common sight to find excreta floating in urine-sprayed commodes in cinema halls, in student hostels, railway stations, airports, restaurants, office buildings, and practically everywhere where there are WC toilets. Except in five-star hotels, I have rarely found a really clean WC especially in public places in India.

As a result it is becoming increasingly difficult in the cities to relieve oneself outside the house. The problem is most acute for women, who unlike men do not ordinarily urinate standing and are very hesitant to relieve themselves in open public places, an art well mastered by the men of this subcontinent.

Even though the WC is a positive inconvenience from every point of view, it seems to have become a status symbol for any 'modern' home or building.

How did millions of Indians get conned into using the WC? Making a 'modern' home or building requires hiring 'modern' specialists—architects and engineers—whose planning for any 'modern' construction must include a WC. Why? Because the text books and syllabi used in our colleges of engineering and architecture are a copy of what used to be taught in British or American universities several decades ago.

It is the same with the manufacturers of bathroom and toilet fittings. Their energies are focused on copying models of bath tubs and toilet seats designed in the West. Our designers/manufacturers have never thought of making the slightest improvement in the design of what we consider as the 'Indian' commode, though it could do with some modification such as an easily removable cover on top of the commode. Since the reigning style in the West is to use a chair like commode, they keep introducing newer copied models of the WC which are then vigorously pushed into the market through advertising companies which in turn lift ideas and ads from western magazines.

Rarely do I recall having seen an Indian commode in any advertisement of bathroom fittings. The advertisements present pictures of luxurious bathrooms in pink and blue with 'modern' fittings presided over by the WC. It is projected as a veritable *Takhte-e Taus*. These bathrooms obviously have nothing to do with real living conditions in Indian homes, including upper class homes. Their come-hither appearance in advertisements seduces gullible Indians into installing this nuisance in their homes. So strong is the association of a modern bathroom with a western commode that today it is unthinkable for an urban family building a house to do without the WC. The architects, the contractors, the ceramic manufacturers are all part of the conspiracy to project the WC as the final hallmark of having arrived at modern living. We sit on a WC, therefore, we are.

Americans who invented the idea of the bathroom as a 'temple' at least figured out effective ways of keeping their 'temple' clean. In India, because we have forgotten our own culture's notions of hygiene and have begun copying western designs and lifestyles without regard to the wherewithal that goes with it, including getting over our hangups against touching anything connected to excreta, our bathrooms have become dens of filth and stench.

The disease spreads, and unlike any ordinary disease, which is avoided, if at all possible, by those who are in an area where there's a high risk of contracting it, these disease carrier commodes are avidly sought after. People pay fancy prices for having them installed. I am told the price of a good quality WC is 10 times that of an Indian commode.

To have or not to have a WC in the house is to define one's social status in the social hierarchy. It is another matter how you use it! This is considered the most authoritative certificate and proof of being modern (often used as a synonym for being westernized) as well as being above the riff raff. For instance, bungalows of our brown *sahibs* must have WCs but their servants must use Indian commodes. Likewise, Lower Income Group flats built for peons and clerks shall have Indian commodes but those meant for officers and class I employees shall be installed with WCs as status symbols. In the college where I used to teach, the Principal's bathroom and the toilet room for the teaching staff have WCs, but the toilet for Class II, III and Class IV staff have an Indian commode. No five-star hotel will ever allow an Indian commode on its premises but *dharamshalas* meant for ordinary *janata* are not 'honoured' with WCs. An elite university like the Jawaharlal Nehru University (JNU) has to have a certain number of WCs even if it means that half of the toilets are unusably filthy all the time, but a school in a harijan *basti* will be sanctioned Indian commodes.

This madness will go on and on, spreading filth and disease even in middle and upper middle class homes because the primary consideration for installing it is 'status', not convenience. It makes hundreds and thousands of our public toilets unusable, a source of filth, disease and discomfort. They will only stop being used when the Indian style commodes, which are more hygienic and easy to maintain, are discovered by a Jane Fonda in America who will make a videotape on healthy toilet habits, displaying how she uses her own commode. Or maybe if the Green Movement in Europe adopts it, then the health movement activists in India and the appropriate technology *wallah* will start holding international and national workshops in Bangkok, Berne and Bonn to devise strategies for weaning the Indians away from the unhealthy western toilet and getting them to adopt the previously despised Indian commode.

Or perhaps when the Ford Foundation, the World Health Organization (WHO), the United Nations Development Programme (UNDP) and the World Bank will begin to give liberal grants for holding workshops on the art of 'ethnic squatting', some of our innovative dancers and musicians will happily devise specially choreographed pieces on the theme. It is then that our papers will bring out special colour supplements to convince us of the virtues of Indian commodes.

Hand in hand with the spread of the WC goes another architectural monstrosity—the joint bath-cum-toilet room, something altogether alien to our cultural norms. No matter how hard one tries to kill the smell with deodorants, it's not really pleasant to bathe in a room from which someone has just emerged after using the toilet. As homes and bathrooms become smaller with the shortage of space, one ends up having to literally rub shoulders with the WC while bathing.

Add to it the proliferation of bathtubs requiring almost 200 litres of water per bath. They are a cruel joke given our perennial water scarcity.

In any case, most Indians do not feel properly bathed by merely soaking themselves in soap water. Most of us end up taking a shower after a session in the tub. Mostly people just sit in the tub and have a bucket bath! Worse still is the plight of housewives and maids who have to wash and scrub clothes inside the tub because there is little space left for such necessary functions after 'modern sanitaryware' has been installed in cramped bathrooms.

The 'Modern' Sewerage System

While the WC messes up people's homes and their personal hygiene, the modern sewerage system is a threat to the entire ecological system.

I remember years ago when an eight-year-old son of a friend from a Punjab village came to Delhi on his first visit to a big city. One of the first things he quizzed me about was Delhi's big *ganda nallas* (sewerage drains). When he learnt that these big *nallas* carried faecal and other waste to the Yamuna, he was aghast and said: 'But in the villages they use all kinds of faecal waste (human and animal) as manure. Why are they making a *ganda nalla* out of it here? How do you drink Yamuna water if all this filth is poured into it?' This eight-year-old child had more wisdom than our engineers and town planners because he had gained his knowledge from lived experience and not from imported books and syllabi. The millions of drains that go to form the big *ganda nalla* are constructed at phenomenal cost. Laying down underground sewerage pipes is very expensive. The raw sewage in these drains and *nallas* is poured into rivers, thus making their water polluted not only for human beings but even for fish. Many of the world's rivers are totally dead because even fish and other water creatures cannot survive in them, leave alone reproduce. Thus, raw sewerage systematically turns the life-supporting bounties of nature into sources of disease and death even while we have to still depend on the very same river waters for drinking and other needs. Countries where sewerage water is beginning to be first treated before being allowed back into the river have to spend huge amounts of money for the purpose. So we have the absurd system of first dirtying them mindlessly, spending billions in the process and then having to spend many more billions to 'purify' the filth-choked water to make it potable—in the process adding all kinds of chemicals to it. In a country like India which is forever facing water shortages, where millions of people do not have access to clean drinking water, it is a crying shame that billions of tonnes of 'purified' water are used in our flush toilets and poured into rivers which become filthy.

Millions die every year due to water-borne diseases. The infant mortality rate in India is amongst the highest in the world. Almost 80 per cent of these child deaths are caused due to water-borne infections which are primarily due to pollution of our country's water resources. In fact water-borne diseases account for a very large proportion of all diseases in India.

The western sewerage system has been adopted despite the fact that we can ill afford the expensive processing plants required to make the system work. Consequently, we are pouring untreated sewerage water into our rivers. This callousness is all the more appalling given that in our culture, rivers are treated not just as sources of water but as objects of worship. The myths and legends which bestow a halo of sacredness to the rivers of India are not a thing of the past. Even today millions throng for a *snan* at Haridwar, Varanasi, Nashik and various other pilgrimage centres that grew around our sacred rivers, testifying to the continuing veneration for rivers at the popular level. But our own policy-makers act with the same irreverence towards them that our British rulers did. They do not know that urban centres in ancient India (even pre-historic ones like Mohenjodaro) had well-developed drainage and waste disposal systems.

Of course we do not need to recreate in the twentieth or the twenty-first century what was done at Mohenjodaro thousands of years ago. But surely we need to evolve these systems keeping in mind our natural resources, our social values, and our cultural habits. Gandhiji did precisely that when he developed simple but efficient and sophisticated dry latrines which required very little water and effort to keep them clean. They do not require a full cistern of water to flush away the faecal matter. In addition these latrines have the advantage of recycling all of human waste matter into energy. The faecal matter goes into septic tanks and gets converted into manure and gas—thus contributing to the solution of another perennial problem, that of fuel and fertilizer shortage. Gandhiji demonstrated this to be a viable system. Despite the availability of such an appropriate waste disposal and reusage system for several decades now, it has not been taken seriously. It exists only at the peripheries, propagated by voluntary organizations such as Sulabh International—but only for the poor and marginalized groups of our society, who are not seen as deserving the 'modern' sewerage system. That is precisely why it has failed to spread. No five-star hotel, cinema hall, university or elite residential area would ever think of installing it, for it is seen as being appropriate only for JJ colonies or poor villages. It will get to be taken seriously only when London or Paris suburbs decide to adopt it.

Recently, on a trip to Kanpur, I had occasion to visit friends in a new, though not yet fully 'developed' suburb called Vikas Nagar. The friend whose house I was visiting explained somewhat apologetically that their colony did not yet have all modern amenities such as underground sewerage pipes. Since this friend lived in a fairly modern house, I asked how they managed to have their flush toilets function. He showed me the septic tank they had built wherein all the water and faecal matter flowed. This septic tank cost no more than a few thousand rupees as initial investment. The cleaning and maintenance cost of the septic task is offset by the rich manure and biogas it yields. This septic tank made the sewerage system redundant—no need for underground sewer pipes and all the rest of the paraphernalia. It would be functional for five to seven years after which a new pit would be dug right next to the old one which would be emptied out beneficially because by then all the faecal waste would have been converted into high quality manure while the water would have seeped out of the pit to replenish the pool of ground water underneath. This system is clearly not only much more hygienic but also incredibly cheap in comparison to the underground sewerage system. In addition, it has the advantage of usefully recycling waste matter without much cost. Yet, within no time this will be overtaken by the 'modern sewerage' system as soon as the Kanpur municipality can direct its 'development' activity towards this new suburb. Those of you who are familiar with Kanpur would know that the main city is like a sprawling slum with open sewers which carry the city's filth to the holiest of our holy rivers—the Ganga. Modern development of Vikas Nagar will inevitably entail its joining the network of filth-carrying drains, polluting the city environment as well as water supply sources.

MINDLESS INCONVENIENCES

The spread of these mindless inconveniences symbolizes our mental slavery; we fear thinking through things for ourselves, we do not take our social and cultural environment seriously when planning not just the country's economy, but even our own day-to-day living. Even our dreams and aspirations of the good life and our ideas of cleanliness are not our own; they are mere imitations of western commercial advertisements.

For those who find this statement rather fanatical and hyperbolic, it would be interesting to recall that our lawyers and judges still insist on wearing black cloaks which make them look like bats, apart from causing physical discomfort, especially during the summer months. They dare not think of a more appropriate dress code. Our elite clubs still have rules left behind by the British about not allowing entry to anyone wearing Indian clothing. The brown *sahibs* dare not change the rules or then they would not know who to model themselves after.

Fashionable Indians have taken to eating with knives and forks even though our *roti-sabzi* or *dal-chawal* do not lend themselves to these appliances. Our modern office buildings are designed to resemble those in Toronto and New York with sealed windows and no provision for ventilation or natural light, making it necessary to have lighting and central air-conditioning function all through the day with no regard for our weather conditions and our perennial power scarcity. In our eagerness to ape western architecture we forget that we are a sun-rich tropical country.

When Hindustan Machine Tools (HMT) recently introduced special children's watches in India it did not occur to their 'designers' to use one of the playful characters from the *Panchatantra*. Their inevitable choice was Mickey Mouse. Our industrialists aspire to nothing better than giving us potato wafers and other western junk food for snacks and aerated drinks resembling Coca-Cola in the name of providing 'modern' foods. It is worth remembering that even the radical *samajwadi* George Fernandes, when he was the Minister for Industries could go no further than replacing Coca-Cola with Double Seven—a poor imitation of 'the real thing.' Even he dare not think of encouraging *mattha, kanji* (carrot), *thandai* or *sattu* as drinks, unless some American multinational discovers their virtues and *mattha* can come back as 'buttermilk' and *sattu* as Horlicks, through foreign collaboration. We begin to discover the virtues of *yog* only when it returns to us from the West as *yoga* performed by Hollywood actresses to the tune of Beethoven.

This colonized mindset is no longer the bane of the urban educated elite. They have vigorously ensured its spread through their control of the government machinery with its myriad rules, procedures and the hegemonic influence of the *babus* who run it. This is borne out by the following story told by a friend who was doing a study on *panchayat* institutions years ago. In a Tamil Nadu village, the people complained to him they had not been able to hold *panchayat* meetings because the government had not constructed or provided a *Panchayat Bhavan* in the village. My friend asked: 'Why can't you hold the meetings elsewhere, for instance in the school building during periods when it is not being used?' The reply was devastatingly simple: 'The school is in use every day except Sundays. How can we hold a meeting on a Sunday? Government rules do not permit conducting any official business on a Sunday.' Why not on Sunday? Because it is the Lord's Day! And which Lord? The western Lord bequeathed by our colonial masters. In recent years, the British have relaxed the rule about not conducting official business on the Sabbath day. However, the rule has stuck on in India merely because the Indian ruling elite is too frightened to make its own rules and laws.

Today, our biggest handicap is that we as a people, especially our ruling elite, suffer from a poverty of native imagination. We have lost the habit and confidence of being able to think things through for ourselves. Unless we rediscover that strength and confidence, all the noises against western imperialism that our political and social elite are so fond of making will continue to sound hypocritical and appear as the childish tantrums of a slavish and infantile people.

9

Destroying Minds and Skills*
The Dominance of *Angreziyat* in our Education

Societies which have put vast amounts of energy and thinking into providing good quality education and opportunities for acquiring diverse skills for their people are today not only prosperous but also well ordered. We seem to have done the very opposite. On the one hand, our policymakers have helped destroy—through wilful neglect and contempt—the vast reservoir of indigenous skills and knowledge systems acquired and nurtured over centuries by our own people. On the other hand, they have failed to create a viable system for the acquisition of modern skills and education for all those who abandon their traditional occupations. Consequently, it is not just corruption but also sheer incompetence which is leading to a breakdown in our society.

THE NEW COLONIZERS

So far, the world knows India primarily as a country which has earned the dubious distinction of producing the largest number of illiterate people in the world. In the next 50 years we will also be able to claim that we are among the distinguished few nations of the world which has the largest number of people illiterate in their own mother tongue! By retaining English as the medium of elite education, professions, and government functioning even after being formally freed from colonial rule, we have ensured that the schism that was deliberately created by

---

*First published in *Manushi*, Issue No. 102, September–October 1997

our colonial rulers between the English-educated elite and the rest of society has grown even further and acquired deadly dimensions. A hundred years ago our intelligentsia, even when it learnt English, still remained rooted in its respective regional languages and mother tongues. Tagore knew English but chose to write in Bengali, thereby nurturing his language as well as the overall intellectual climate of Bengal. Likewise, Mahatma Gandhi could express complex ideas in English more simply, elegantly, and effectively than most British. Yet he wrote with even better grace in Gujarati and even Hindustani. However, the great-grandchildren of our Tagores, Ranades, Premchands, and Gandhis are today all writing mostly in English. Worse still, even our scriptures and ancient literary texts are read by our educated elite mainly in English. Consequently, the mental, emotional, and intellectual colonization has proceeded with greater rigour and pace in post-Independence India than during colonial rule. The brown *sahibs* of the British era spoke English only in office. The brown *sahibs* of today have let English become their language for love-making, talking to their infant children, and even scolding their pet dogs!

However, this does not mean that they have acquired enough proficiency in the language for it to act as an effective instrument of knowledge acquisition and communication. Far from it. The quality of teaching is so poor, even in our English medium schools that, barring a few exceptional institutions, too many of our students are ill-equipped to make sense of even newspaper reports, leave alone read serious books in English. The few who have a good command over the English language consequently behave and get treated like an imperial race and others who cannot are viewed as a sub-human species. The former are largely cut off from the lives, feelings, problems, and aspirations of the non-English knowing population. Their aspirations are directed either towards migrating abroad or attempting to create small pockets of affluence for themselves so that while being situated, for example, in New Delhi, they can pretend they are living in New York.

In well-functioning societies, the educated elite tend to provide intellectual leadership to the rest of society. In our case, our colonized intelligentsia is so alienated from its own people that it has made our society resemble a body whose head has been severed from its torso. However, the head is arrogant enough to pretend it can manage on its own. In reality, both are rotting, the headless body and the bodiless head.

This communication gap exists not just between different strata of society but also within families. The elderly, especially grandparents, have traditionally played an important role in the socialization of children, giving them *sanskars* and an initiation into their community's culture, values, and knowledge systems. Today's English-educated children tend to treat their non-English speaking relatives as ignorant and illiterate. Tarzan comics and cartoon films are taken more seriously than grandmother's stories. Thus the future generations of the educated minority may be more information rich about computers and business opportunities but will grow up lacking wisdom which can best be imbibed from a close intergenerational interaction.

This dual system of education has taken away so many opportunities from the vast mass of our people that the new generation which is being denied good quality education in English is going to grow up feeling even more demoralized, incompetent, and inferior than the present cohort. In the next few decades, as India integrates more with the global economy, the lifestyles of the Indian elite will become even more alienated from the rest of the people. Since the moneyed elite of today flaunt their opulence more and more before the deprived through television, cinema, and even the print media, the anger and rage of those excluded are going to get far more explosive than at present. They will avenge themselves in the Laloo Yadav way through politics. A person who knows no English at all is virtually unemployable except as a peon or labourer. However, he/she can, like Phoolan Devi, become an MP or like Laloo Yadav hope to become a chief minister and get power and money through politics because he/she cannot hope to get it through education and talent.

DESKILLING OF INDIA

The tragedy we have created for our society through this educational policy is of epic proportions. India was not too long ago known the world over for its industrial skills and crafts. Indian steel was world famous and so much in demand that ancient Roman historians are known to have expressed concern that their coffers were getting emptied buying steel swords (and silks) from India. Our architectural tradition created many more wonders than the famous Taj Mahal, the temples of Khajuraho and Konark, perhaps more than the rest of the world put together. Our weavers produced fabrics which have been the envy of the world for centuries. Our craftsmen produced jewellery, icons, and art objects which are unparalleled in beauty of design and exquisite workmanship. Yet none of our engineering colleges would condescend to admit sons of *lohars* even as students, leave alone teachers, in their metallurgy departments. This, when their practical knowledge, honed through centuries of practising that craft would be far superior to that of our formal degree holders. Why? Because they do not have the English medium education necessary for 'studying' today's science and technology books. Likewise, our traditional *sthapathis* who inherited the skills required to design and make architectural wonders like the Jantar Mantar, the beautiful ancient temples, *havelis,* and palaces found in every corner of India—that too made with environment-friendly materials—have no place in modern colleges of architecture. They have been degraded to the level of masons, *mistris,* and labourers at the lowest rung of our building industry only because they do not have access to English medium public schools. Similarly, our traditional weavers capable of designing and making fabrics of a spectacular variety, do not find jobs as textile designers and engineers in modern factories because they could never hope to get the degrees required for those jobs. Our agricultural universities can be blissfully ignorant about the vast knowledge reservoir of our farmers whose produce—long staple cotton, varieties of spices and fruits, wheat, and rice—have eager buyers in the world market. Their knowledge of food storage, soil conservation, use of safe pesticides, biodiversity, and medicinal values of plants has hardly any takers in the scientific establishment because they cannot write research papers in English. We learn to value *neem* and turmeric only when the international scientific community endorses their many wondrous qualities.

Thus, by making English education the hallmark of qualification for careers, we have marginalized and impoverished all those who carried the rich legacies of our traditional skills and technologies. We have destroyed the self-respect of the majority of our people, making them feel worthless and despised. All we are giving by way of 'social justice' to a few among these deprived millions is reservation of a few thousand government jobs of peons and clerks.

The children of these skilled technologists are deserting their inherited occupation at a rapid speed because they earn pitiful wages for their work. The makers of Kanjeevaram sarees would rather have their children get a peon's job in a government office. Children of our traditional metallurgists have taken to menial unskilled jobs like rickshaw pulling and street vending. Those who merely buy and sell gold make crores of rupees but a skilled goldsmith, after 20 years of being on the job, even in a city like Delhi, does not earn more than Rs 3,500 a month. A bank clerk earns at least four times as much. His only advantage—he has acquired a smattering of the English language.

When sons of skilled weavers turn rickshaw pullers, children of *sthapathis* become busdrivers, and skilled shipbuilders take to vegetable vending, it amounts to a genocide of skills. Stalin destroyed the economic base of his country by physically exterminating the peasantry in the name of collectivization. We may not have physically killed our farmers and other skilled groups, but we have, by undermining their skills and knowledge, destroyed their self-respect, marginalized them economically, and destroyed their capacity to compete by making English the magic key which opens the doors to opportunity. If we take away the disadvantages that ignorance of English brings with it, our traditional technologists—ironsmiths, weavers, carpenters, *sthapathis*, and other metallurgists—would fare much better in gaining entrance to scientific and engineering institutions as well as in the world of manufacturing.

THE COSTS OF NEGLECT

The entire society is paying for this crime. Our modern architects functioning with borrowed knowledge make unliveable and ugly buildings and homes. Our modern offices need to use artificial lights even in broad daylight in a country where sunshine is abundant. There is no provision for ventilation, with windows sealed for air-conditioning in a country where power breakdown is a daily occurrence. All these stupid buildings result from simply copying designs from western books and magazines. Our Ambanis and Singhanias produce fabrics whose designs are either straight copies of western designs or so garish that their own wives would not be seen dead in those sarees. In fact, they are seen proudly wearing the 'ethnic chic' produced by our traditional weavers. It is not a coincidence that only the products of our illiterate or semi-educated, poor artisans have eager buyers in the international market. India's foreign exchange earnings come primarily from exporting cottage crafts, handloom textiles, traditional jewellery, leather goods, handmade fabrics, spices, raw cotton, mangoes, *basmati* rice, and other farm produce.

It is our traditional artisans' products which act as reminders that we were once a great civilization. The famous iron pillar of Qutab Minar in Delhi made centuries ago by our traditional *lohars* still stands proudly without rusting or corroding. The steel being produced by our modern degree holders is of such poor standard that even the not too quality conscious railway ministry has alleged that tracks made of Steel Authority of India Limited (SAIL) steel crack up and corrode within months of installation, causing numerous rail accidents. Temples and houses made by our traditional *sthapathis* have withstood the ravages of centuries. Even as ruins they look aesthetic and grand. The housing colonies designed and constructed by our modern degree holding architects are eyesores from the day they are built and start falling apart before they are occupied.

The modern sector of our economy is not an earner but a guzzler of foreign exchange. Our industries have become a dead weight on our economy and dare not face international competition. They are either grovelling for government protection or foreign collaborations—often both, and yet not able to put their act together. This is the reward our western-educated elite get for treating their own people like colonial subjects. There was a time when only the West treated us with derision and contempt. Today, even our Asian neighbours laugh at the pretensions of our educated elite. The Japanese, Chinese, and Korean elites may not speak as good English as the products of our Doon School and St Stephen's College, but they communicate much better with the world and are more respected in international fora than our self-styled representatives. After all, what do they represent? Grovelling poverty, mass illiteracy, a sickly malnourished population, a rich land turned into one of the worst environmental disasters, an inefficient and corrupt government! And its callous elite which does not even believe in sharing a language with its own people, leave alone wealth and education. Today, we are merely ridiculed and spurned in international fora, treated as pompous failures and self-righteous beggars. If we continue in the same manner we will be treated as virtual untouchables by the rest of the world. Our leaders will be put through quarantine before being allowed to attend international meetings for fear that they may be carrying the many deadly disease germs India is so famous for. Today, our educated elite laugh at and express disdain for the likes of Laloo Yadav, his rustic manners, his *dehati* accent, his strong-arm tactics, his semi-literate wife brought in as a dummy chief minister. If we do not start fixing our education system immediately we will be saddled only with such tragi-comic figures for our leaders. Our Chidambarams and Jaswant Singhs might as well forget about coming to political power through the electoral route. After all, a man like I.K. Gujral could not win a seat in the Parliament on his own strength. He had to be beholden to Laloo Yadav for his seat and to the Akali Dal for winning his previous election.

FROM CLERKS TO PEONS

Actually, the problem is not just that the educated elite are divorced and alienated from their country's people. Our education system is poor even from the point of view of the elite themselves. The British are accused of having introduced a system of education designed primarily to promote an army of clerks Indian in colour but English in habits, tastes, and values. They at least functioned to a purpose and produced efficient clerks. However, our post-Independence schools and colleges are not even producing clerks but people whose skills do not qualify them for anything more than a peon's job. The following extract from a letter we received from the secretary of an NGO gives an idea of the communication skills of our college educated:

> Yours consolidary and collaboration may kindly be solution to the [XYZ] Yuvak Sangha... Which works in the filed of education, Adult Education, pre School Health and Family Planing. Forest and Environment to check the Environment pollution, Sport and cultural activities. Social developments, Women development, Youth activities and tribal development etc.
>
> For the wide spread functioning of the above said activities. The organisation seeks your concolidation and collboration in the above said activities. If your organisation is going land with hand. Intimation maybe requested to
>
> Yours sincerely, XYZ

Many of our court judgements sound similarly like total gibberish. The following sample is an extract from a judgement by a session's judge in a case of child sexual abuse:

> Besides all these, how it seems to be unnatural that the thing for concealing to which the accused was hiding himself here and there and was frightened in coming home, on call only he came to the house, on coming not before anybody else, except before those persons who were bent upon to punish him immediately and further were furious on him and tried to assault him, and who could have sent him in jail for the statement givenby him against himself, has confessed before them his offence willingly. In the back ground of this, the accused who is not only literate but is doctor and is living in the present atmosphere, and confession of such offence by him in this manner seems to be unnatural in itself.... More unnatural to

these all is the confession of the offence before his father which he made before his father... in presence of five persons stated above. The family of the accused is also the family of the learned persons. On account of the last night's incident they would have not become purturbed rather they had so much time they would have come under the influence of the shock as of the family of Madan Gopal Kakkar and would have thought of the saving themselves, and out of them atleast one would have been who would have not admitted the offence again. In this way the story of confession of the offence by the prosecution by the family of Kakkar and Bhasin family is wholly unnatural, fabricated, and product of legal advice. This could not at all be trusted.

One can well imagine what brilliant grasp of law such a linguistic genius would have acquired. This particular judgement, in fact reads as if the honourable judge neither knows nor respects the ABC of law. It is not surprising that he went out of his way to exonerate a medical doctor accused of child rape.

Very few of our policemen know how to register a FIR in legible hand leave alone one that is factually accurate and grammatically correct. Their ignorance of the law is frightening though expected. Their low educational skills make it virtually impossible for them to read and understand even bare Acts, leave alone legal treatises in antiquated Victorian English. But they take no time to pick up those provisions of law which help them fleece money. A linguistic analysis of the petitions filed by our lawyers even at higher levels, leave alone district courts, would show that they read like products of a deranged brain. Here is an extract from an FIR drafted by a Chennai lawyer in a murder case:

> ...two members going to received the money...at the Time of medicine of mind effect and drinking methyl Alcohol for compulsory husband over drinking.. This person Elumalai over drinking and tired staying my house. Again Drinking of Methyl Slcohol for my husband. After my husband wanted meals please take it by Anunchalam. But overtake of again and again attacked the Neg. Suddenly my husband Rolled to Land and earth. Retenched husband again and again attacked. Over attack for snag for my husband place.... Husband sounded stoned some place. Ramaraja... warming Drinking of person attack for Arunchalam unattack of call to go and Sang removed... Five members joined attacked for my

husband Head, mouth nose, attacked things of goods for stones. Some place suddenly number of husband....

My husband's sister Lands of aggiculture lands buying try to Arunachalam. But my husband overtake same Land buying my husband another sister's husband for 9 months. The problem dated warning for my husbands dated 27th April 1993 murder to my husband. The 5 members of speeches of my husband murder to doing ease for you. Also warning for me. My husband murders above 5 members promised. Related persons but deployed for me. Department of police something rupees alloted for received anybody. No action and Responses.

Respected Sir, this problem solved for me. The murder of my husband and brother Annamalai warning. Enquired for the problems solved please, Sir, Thanking you...[XYZ]

LINGUISTIC CRIPPLES

I hear similar gibberish even in elite business chambers and ministerial pronouncements. Most of us Indians sound mentally retarded when we propound our ideas in English. We are today becoming a nation of linguistic cripples which is an important reason why the work calibre of our professionals is so shoddy. A person who cannot handle any language competently is unlikely to be able to handle concepts or ideas required to think things through. Most of even our MBBS doctors are so poorly equipped in English that they cannot possibly follow the latest medical information already available in international journals, even if they are inclined to access it. Therefore, too many of them practise quackery after procuring medical degrees of doubtful worth.

While we are churning out millions of unemployable matriculates, BAs and MAs, the country is facing a real shortage of skilled electricians, plumbers, and a host of such technicians because we are simply not investing any money or energy into this area. Under our traditional occupation-based caste system, every child picked some valuable skill from his or her parents, a skill which had been developed and perfected through generations. Today everybody wants to be a white collar pen-pusher because that alone brings status and money. Only those who cannot make it, take to blue collar occupations but without the required skills for them. The electrical wirings in our public buildings are a virtual death trap; our water treatment plants are a scandal; our power stations are forever breaking down; our municipal sewage pipes frequently leak into water pipes. Most of those actually operating these services could not spell the word 'hygiene' leave alone know how to provide a clean water supply. The fault is not theirs. The children of our impoverished farmers and artisans learn what they can by simply watching other ill-trained people. Their own educational skills are not such that they can acquire this knowledge through self-study.

Our colonial rulers could at least run their exclusive enclaves efficiently and provide functional civic amenities for Civil Lines areas. Our post-Independence elite cannot even ensure clean water supply or regular electricity in the opulent and exclusive New Delhi areas. Frequent tragedies like mid-air collisions of planes, collapse of newly built bridges, breakouts of fire in public buildings, along with power breakdowns, dysfunctional telephones and general civic chaos are as much the products of sheer incompetence and inefficiency as they are the offshoots of corruption.

Destroying Minds

Thus while our policy-makers have destroyed the traditional skills of our people, they have denied them good quality modern education and opportunities for acquiring new skills necessary for running today's economies. The *sarkari* school system meant for the poor is a mockery in the name of education. These schools function mainly to provide *naukris* for the teachers and a host of *babus* of various grades who man our education departments and ministries. Consequently, there is very little teaching going on in them today. The little that happens is of such poor quality that anyone who has gone through a dozen or so years of that exercise has for all practical purposes become a dysfunctional human being, and is unlikely to be able to think coherently on any subject except those areas of life not touched by school education. To top it all, they acquire contempt for any manual work. A son of a farmer or *lohar* who has studied up to matriculation or BA is likely to despise his father's occupation even while he himself is skilled for no other and therefore, likely to end up adding to the large army of unemployable youth.

Among the many very saddening exposures to how our schools are destroying brains, I would like to cite one. While I was on a visit to Vitner village of Maharashtra some years ago, the people there proudly introduced me to a teenage boy as the brightest and most diligent student of that village. I asked him to write an essay on himself and the boy sat down dutifully to do the exercise. After about 45 minutes he brought a two-page neatly written essay on Mahatma Gandhi. I was puzzled and asked him why he didn't write about himself. Somewhat embarrassed he told me that they had not 'taught' him to write on 'that topic' in school. If this is what our school system is doing to our brightest and most hardworking, we can well imagine the fate of our not so bright and less than average students.

I have been experiencing the products of the devastation year after year in the Delhi University college where I teach. As with that village student, my first assignment to even my BA students is an essay on themselves. Most of them (except the few from really well-functioning schools) look as bewildered as that village boy and many simply cannot write more than 6–7 lines that do not go beyond giving the student's name, father's occupation, the area he/she lives in and a couple of other identification points. Their excuse is the same: this topic was never a part of their curriculum. Over the years only a handful have given me something resembling an essay. This was the case even though many of them came from non-*sarkari* schools.

Even our private sector in education functions abysmally because of the very low standards set by government schools. Most private schools, especially those that have mushroomed in small towns and villages, are worse than teaching shops because, for all the money they charge, they give students very little in return.

Brain Drain

Nehruvian socialism has wrecked our economy with its policy of nurturing the supposed commanding heights of our economy by exploiting and depressing the farm sector and other segments of the vast unorganized sector. Its counterpart in education was the belief that a handful of institutions like Mayo College and St Stephen's will provide us the talent to run our entire society and economy for one billion people. The result is there for all to see. The few talented people this country produces are desperate to find a foothold in foreign countries largely because they feel threatened and choked by the inefficiency and corruption all around.

If we do not begin to put our act together in the field of education, think beyond a few elite schools and colleges, and aspire to *high quality* secondary level education for every child in this country and opportunities for acquiring real skills, in a few years we will need to start thinking of importing skilled manpower and well-trained professionals to run even our basic services and civil amenities—as well as our universities and colleges, perhaps even our primary schools.

Our leaders have given us a sickly legacy of substituting ideology for ideas, using radical rhetoric as a substitute for sensible politics. We the educated elite not only swallowed phoney rhetoric avidly and were deeply mesmerized by it as long as it was being mouthed in correct Oxonian English. Today, when Laloo Yadav or Rabri Devi use similar rhetoric of 'social justice' we feel outraged because they are speaking in *dehati* tones we so despise. No democracy can be made to function meaningfully by a tiny informed elite who shut out all information and knowledge from others by speaking, reading, and writing in a language no one outside their charmed circle understands.

Those who feel convinced that the country cannot manage without English should at least have the good sense to ensure that it becomes the language of mass literacy and education and that there are enough schools and teachers available to provide quality English education to our people. Today's ruling elite may not know how to manage our economy and society but at least can appear as respectable 'suited-booted' beggars before IMF and the World Bank and do a bit of crisis management. Tomorrow's ministers and bureaucrats will not even know how to write a coherent letter to various aid agencies asking to be bailed out. Fifty years from now we might have to hire foreigners to beg on our behalf just as today we hire western professionals to lobby with foreign governments because our diplomats know little diplomacy.

10

Yours Nationally*

I am a true nationalist. I want to serve my nation not only in my lifetime but even in my death. I am told that one way of doing this is to join the army and die fighting and killing for the nation so that I will be honoured as a national martyr. Much as I would love to be a national martyr, I hate weapons and have an aversion to killing. Surely, there must be a way that sissies like me who abhor violence can become national martyrs.

Also, I have a feeling that not all soldiers are selfless sacrificers for the nation. So many join the army as people join other professions. They do it for money, not for the love of killing or dying. I want to be a more selfless servant of the nation. I do not want to cost the government several years of salary, food, uniform, free booze and various other expensive benefits which army men get. The government would also have to spend money on buying me weapons if I joined the army. I want to serve the nation without causing any expenditure to the government, which, after all, is the owner of the nation. I want to leave the nation and the government richer by my death. That is how profound and selfless my nationalism is.

And from where do I draw my inspiration? Not from ministers and bureaucrats, nor from government servants, all of whom want others to serve the nation while they themselves rule and loot the nation. I draw my inspiration from the simple and poor people of Bhopal who, even in their death and devastation, served the nation most admirably.

*First published in *Manushi*, Issue No. 105, March–April 1998

First, they made sure that overwhelmingly they were the ones who lived in the vicinity of the plant and therefore inhaled most of the poisonous gas from the Union Carbide plant; they saw to it that the rich did not have to suffer much from the effects of the poisonous leak. For, after all, it is the rich who are the real nation builders. The poor are but a drag on the nation. Thus, those who died voluntarily lightened the burden of the nation.

Those who died from the Union Carbide gas also did so in the most profitable way for the nation and the nation's keepers. Imagine how much inconvenience and unnecessary embarrassment they would have caused the nation if they had been foolish enough to die on such a large scale from the various acts of commission or omission of our venerable government—such as the leaks from *sarkari* nuclear plants, fertilizer factories or in one of the routine epidemics of cholera, hepatitis and a host of other diseases that come bountifully with an unbountiful supply of municipal tap water. Neither would I have liked to inconvenience the nation by being murdered in sponsored massacres, such as the one in Meerut in 1987 or of November 1984 in Delhi. Our *mai baap sarkar* would have been needlessly stigmatized for acting against the people. Such irresponsible criticism would unnecessarily weaken and impoverish the nation. The government would willy nilly have had to announce an ex-gratia payment of at least Rs 50,000 for the dead and Rs 10,000 for those with serious injuries. True, the people would not receive more than half the amount; the other half would be more suitably pocketed by politicians and government functionaries, those who serve the nation by serving themselves.

But, since the Bhopal martyrs were sensible enough to die of an American company's poison, the nation's owners got an opportunity to claim millions of dollars in compensation for the loss of 'national' lives. Indian lives are cheap if Indian poison or police destroys them, but Indian corpses become valuable if a claim can be made abroad.

Thus, not only did the nation's owners make a lot of money for themselves directly by coming to various unpublicised deals with Union Carbide. They also siphoned off the bulk of the money received officially for relief and rehabilitation of the survivors. Our venerable *netas* and *babus* are only too aware how easy money corrupts people easily, especially the poor. That is why the government passed a law disallowing individual victims from claiming damages, and has made sure that all the money came through the nation's owners. At first, many survivors staked their claims for compensation through lawyers who would fight for them for a fee. But the government, through an ordinance, taught them the sheer presumptuousness of their actions. The survivors had to accept the all enlightened nation's servants as their proxy in their suit, for they are truly government fearing and nation-loving citizens.

Had they dared to do otherwise, I am sure the government would have been wise enough to pass an ordinance declaring them anti-national.

In addition, think of all the sympathy the Indian nation and government gather internationally by the fact of these deaths. Our prime minister can actually hold his head high in self-righteous indignation whenever he talks to the foreign press about the Bhopal tragedy. But those who were foolish enough to be massacred at Arwal, Bhiwandi, Ahmedabad, or in Delhi, prove as much of an embarrassment and liability in their death as they were a burden on the nation in their life. So, it is from these poor, government fearing and nation-loving citizens that I draw my inspiration, and pray morning, noon and night for the following opportunities to serve the nation:

- May I be blessed with the opportunity of being poisoned to death at the hand of a foreign company and not an Indian one.
- If I have to die in an accident, may it not be an Indian train or bus. They seem to have a special fondness for plunging into rivers and valleys every time they see a half crumbling bridge or mountain road. I would rather die in an air crash on a foreign airline so that my death can bring much needed foreign exchange to the nation.

Shame be on all those who have learnt to keep watch on the poisonous leaks emanating from our own *desi* industries or to protest when people are killed by various acts of commission or omission of our nation's owners. It seems they do not want a strong nation. For, if they did, they would not try to weaken the hands of our government by constantly criticizing it. For, after all, a strong nation means a strong government. And who else can a government test its strength on but its own people?

I appeal to all the trouble makers, the human rights activists, the civil liberty *wallahs* and all the self-proclaimed democrats of various hues not to come in the way of our attempts to build a strong nation.

11

Beyond For or Against*

Unexplored Complexities of India's Reservation Policy

EXPLORING THE COMPLEXITIES OF RESERVATION POLICY

One of the most often repeated criticisms levelled against the V.P. Singh government for announcing the implementation of reservation policy was that this was merely a 'populist' measure for the purpose of consolidating a particular vote bank. The word 'populism' came to be used simply as a pejorative. The dictionary defines populism as 'a political philosophy directed to the needs of the common people and advocating a more equitable distribution of wealth and power.' The word owes its origin to the philosophy of the Populist Party, a US political party formed to represent agrarian interests in the Presidential election of 1892, also called the People's Party.

No democracy can function meaningfully without politicians feeling pressured to be responsive to the needs of their vote banks—or for that matter attempting to represent well-defined interests consolidated through vote banks. This is one way the vote acquires meaning and importance for ordinary people. By getting organized as vote banks, even the relatively disadvantaged can hope to have some influence on government policies.

Therefore, the pressure towards 'populist' measures (in the sense of responding to the needs of the common people and advocating a more

---

*First published in *Manushi*, Issue No. 63–4, March–June 1991

equitable distribution of wealth and power) should not be seen only in negative terms. However, populism can acquire a negative dimension when:

(i) the idea of social justice is reduced to political gimmicks and no meaningful redistribution of resources and power actually takes place;

(ii) when overblown rhetoric becomes a substitute for well-worked out policies; when measures announced are seen as temporary palliatives to garner votes at times of elections without any real intention to implement effective measures;

(iii) when the interests of even larger groups of similarly disadvantaged people are overlooked consistently and policies are devised to win over only those groups who have political clout;

(iv) when the leadership lacks the ability to give creative direction to popular sentiments. If the leadership fails to channel the aspirations of their vote banks or support base in a way that goes beyond mere symptomatic redressal of group grievances towards evolving a more viable and healthy social and political balance, populism can assume very negative overtones.

However, the critique of the urban elite who led or lent support to the anti-reservation movement was not inspired by concern for a more accountable and a more socially responsible polity. It seems to have been motivated by the fear of the growing power of organized vote banks of groups lower down the social hierarchy. For example, when certain Janata Dal leaders defended their action with the plea that they were merely implementing one of the key promises made in their election manifesto, leading editors and academics cynically argued: 'Whoever takes the election manifestos seriously?' Behind their contemptuous dismissal of 'populist' measures was a sense of outrage that, as the self-appointed arbiters of the country's destiny, they were being bypassed.

In recent years the increasing power of the media, controlled by the urban educated upper caste elite, has given newspaper writers and sundry intellectuals an exaggerated sense of their social worth and importance. They have come to believe that the business of politicians is to read newspaper editorials and articles, and implement the advice given therein, that no other social group needs to be listened to except when it gets its demands approved by and routed through academics and journalists. Their sense of outrage at being by-passed by the V.P. Singh government was so strong that they openly instigated the anti-reservation agitation encouraging the young impressionable students to believe that they were making heroic sacrifices for a noble cause even when the agitation assumed violent and suicidal forms.

CYNICAL OPPORTUNISM

However, even the most vigorous defenders of the reservation policy cannot deny that there was something very cynical about the manner and timing of its announcement, on the eve of a show of strength rally being organized by Devi Lal and company, in an obvious bid to out-manoeuvre this lobby within the Janata Dal. It had elements of gang warfare with rival gang leaders trying to enhance their clout by encouraging defections from each other's gangs by offering a bigger share of the booty. This perhaps was one reason the reservation announcement evoked the kind of violent response it did. It was widely perceived as an insincere gimmick, and not altogether without reason, for when the Janata Dal government was faced with very determined opposition, they kept diluting the Mandal Commission recommendations (for example, defence services and research establishments were exempted and state governments were allowed to decide their own policy), so much so that at the end, very few sectors were left where reservations would apply. Moreover, since most Janata Dal leaders had a history of unsavoury political deals, they were not able to convince their opponents that their commitment to social justice was genuine.

The politics of vote banks often tends to sharpen conflicts between contending social groups. This is not entirely avoidable in a democracy. Yet in a diverse and multi-ethnic society like ours, it is crucial that leaders who wish to initiate measures for the redistribution of social and economic power, possess the skills to evolve some measure of social consensus and inspire political confidence in various sections of the population, especially those who are not to be direct beneficiaries of their policies. If they are seen as merely thinking of ways to acquire or stay in power through crudely worked out populist measures, then they are much less likely to be able to evolve a measure of social consensus about the desirability of affecting redistribution of power in society. The cause of the betterment/empowerment of the relatively disadvantaged sections has to be believed to be a desirable social goal (as opposed to being a mere sectional demand) for which at least sections of the elite are won over to the extent that they are willing to make space for the rising aspirations of groups lower down the social hierarchy. If the major contending groups are mobilized as inherently and permanently hostile camps and are unable to work out a meaningful consensus, a democratic polity cannot be sustained for long.

IDEALISM OR SELF-AGGRANDIZEMENT

While a small section of the student community may have joined the anti-reservation movement out of idealism, by and large, the opposition to job reservations was based on defending narrow sectional interests. Women students shouting slogans like 'we don't want rickshaw *wallahs* or unemployed men as our husbands' gave a clear message that caste considerations remain paramount in the marriage market and that they would not consider marrying 'lower caste' men even if they had good jobs. Likewise, male students made a show of shining shoes, selling vegetables and polishing cars to drive home the message that they would be driven to performing such 'degrading' menial jobs if the reservation policy came to be implemented. They displayed open contempt for all the disadvantaged sections who do these jobs every day. Among university teachers one often heard vicious comments like: 'Now we will be compelled to marry our daughters to *churhas* and *chamars* since they will be the only ones to get jobs.' Khushwant Singh in one of his columns went as far as to say that job reservation for OBCs was acceptable as long as it was confined to the jobs of peons and drivers, at the most, clerks. But Class I and II services should not be touched by the reservation scheme. Those who romanticized and glorified the student protest by comparing it to the May 1968 student revolt in France or the recent pro-democracy protest by the Chinese students at Tianenmen Square, overlooked the fact that the anti-reservationist students were not inspired by any vision of a new, more egalitarian society. Unlike the French and Chinese students, they were not protesting against power and privilege and securing greater democratic participation. They simply wanted to retain a clear monopoly of high status jobs for the upper caste, upper class. It is sad that even when they were involved in defending nothing more noble than their narrow sectional interests the anti-reservationists self-righteously projected them as 'national interests'.

A DIVISIVE MOVE?

In order to provide respectability to their fight for self-interest, one of the main arguments used by the leaders and idealogues of the anti-reservation movement was that caste-based reservations would divide the nation into warring caste groups and undermine 'national unity'. The continuing hold of caste identities was presented as an unhealthy hangover from the so-called feudal past. It was argued that this negative legacy had to be rooted out in order for India to qualify as a unified modern society.

The opponents of caste-based reservations come predominantly from among the upper caste English educated elite and the idealogues of the Sangh Parivar. These two in recent years have become strong allies in the cause of a strong, centralized, authoritarian polity. For most of the English educated elite, national unity is synonymous with their own pan-Indian dominance. This group has emerged in the last hundred years or so as a distinct caste claiming superior rights. Even though its members are drawn from varied sections of upper castes, the non-English speaking members of those castes rarely belong to this exclusive club. The way power was transferred from the hands of the British to Indians ensured the continuance of a narrow segment of elite whose power was chiefly based on controlling the centralized, bureaucratic machinery. Near total monopoly of jobs in the IAS, IPS, central and state services and the military as well as managerial positions in key public sector institutions, gave them unrestrained power and an exaggerated sense of pre-eminence.

Their desire to control all of the country from the ministerial *bhavans* in Delhi (Krishi Bhavan, Udyog Bhavan, Nirman Bhavan *et al.*) has brought them into conflict time and again with aspirations of people excluded from power and privilege in different parts of the country. Every time they face any resistance to their imperial status, they dub the group opposing their dominance as 'anti-national', be it a regional group demanding political decentralization or a group pressing for its economic interest or for recognition of its linguistic identity. Interestingly, the Sangh Parivar's vision of a strong '*Hindu Rashtra*' fits in admirably with this imperial vision. Hence the two have been able to forge a close alliance, with many of the English educated elite actually joining the ranks of the BJP in recent years. These two groups share a common obsession. They both want to bring about 'national unity' by convincing people to disown all other competing identities based on caste, language, religion, region and other ethnic solidarities. They see these multiple loyalties as the cause of all of India's problems just as the British rulers once did, and for pretty much the same reasons. These cross-cutting identities make the people of this country difficult to govern through diktats of the Delhi *durbar*. People's own requirements and aspirations seem to move in directions contrary to those desired by the hegemonic elite, who like the British, want to remould the people of this country into becoming one mindless monolith called 'Indians', blindly obeying the rulers at the Centre, subordinating their own well-being to the leaders' commands.

INTOLERANCE OF PEOPLE'S MULTIPLE IDENTITIES

The assumption behind this homogenizing effort is that once the people become 'proper Indians' overcoming other loyalties, they will learn to put 'the nation before self', which is really a euphemism for learning to obey quietly whatever the ruling elite demand of them, be it getting oneself sterilized in order to meet the norm of 'one child families' set by the government for the poor, or willing acquiescence to the suspension of the democratic rights of people in Punjab, Kashmir, or Nagaland in the name of safeguarding 'national interests'.

The intolerance of the multiple identities held important by the people comes under the garb of progressivism, liberalism, modernism, nationalism. But at the core of it is authoritarian statism based on deep contempt for the people. It is time we asked: what is so morally superior about identifying oneself solely as an Indian as opposed to feeling a strong sense of identity as a Punjabi or a Jat or a Vokaligga? In fact, one can't be an Indian without belonging to a specific community, Maratha, Marwari, Parsi, or Kayastha. Yet we are continually being exhorted to eviscerate our other identities in the all-consuming one of being 'Indian', as though that in itself represents a higher state of evolution and moral superiority. The 'national unity' mongers wish to destroy all the cultural and social specificities of Indian society. They wish to refashion Indian society on the basis of their poorly grasped ideas of what makes western societies dominant just as the British rulers tried to do.

For the Sangh Parivar combine this obsession takes the form of trying to 'unite' the diverse people of India into unidimensional creatures called Hindu Rashtravadis. They want them to 'become one' like they imagine Germans or Japanese to be one people without realizing that whenever and wherever attempts have been made to unite people in a monolith, it has led to warfare and violence. The Leftists and liberals would like to see caste and other ethnic identities give way to a textbook version of class identity of the kind prescribed by Marx and Lenin. Both want people to worship the national flag and the

Constitution instead of worshipping this or that deity or holy book. Both are uncomfortable with the people of India as they are and have adopted theoretical models of western societies for emulation.

SAFEGUARD AGAINST AUTHORITARIANISM

While the negative aspects of ethnic identities have been over-emphasized, we have seldom recognized the positive role they have played in our society and polity giving democracy real roots and in resisting centralized, authoritarian power structures imposed by the ruling elite.

Every Indian has a multiplicity of identities that are equally dear and deep-rooted. This acts as the most effective check against the emergence of pan-Indian tyrants whose writ can run across the length and breadth of the country. All such megalomaniac politicians find their grand designs frustrated at the borders of contending identities. For example, the RSS–VHP–Shiv Sena attempts to unify all Hindus under one umbrella get automatically thwarted because every Hindu is simultaneously rooted in his or her linguistic, regional, and caste identity, in addition to a distinct identity as a member of one of the numerous sects within the Hindu fold. A Hindu is no less attached to being a Punjabi or a Tamilian and further on—a Punjabi Khatri or a Punjabi Jat—a Tamilian Brahmin or a Tamilian Mudaliar, a Punjabi from Doab or one who migrated from Lahore, a Punjabi Nirankari, Radhasoami, Arya Samaji or a Mazhabi. A Tamilian Brahmin is likely to feel a greater sense of commonality with a Tamilian non-Brahmin than with a Brahmin from Punjab or Uttar Pradesh, especially on the language issue. An Advani is unlikely to be able to convince a Mulayam Singh Yadav no less pious a Hindu than Advani that he should give up his struggle on behalf of certain caste groups in favour of building a new Ram Mandir at Ayodhya, or that Muslims constitute a threat to Yadav's Hindu identity more than Advani does to his political survival. Likewise, Bal Thackeray's gigantic ego gets deflated the moment he crosses the border of Maharashtra. Even within Maharashtra he is unlikely to ever succeed in forcing the Marathas, Kunbis, Dalits, and Brahmins to unite under one single political banner. The continuing hold of these competing loyalties is India's best guarantee against dictatorship because dictatorships are based on eliminating multi-layered loyalties.

It is not a coincidence that in 1947 India gravitated towards a democratic polity whereas Pakistan inevitably moved towards a military dictatorship as Jinnah and the Muslim League succeeded, for a while, in undermining all other identities to forge a monolithic Muslim identity, whereas the Congress Party under Mahatma Gandhi's leadership provided space for the assertion of regional, linguistic, and a host of other identities.

Despite serious setbacks, even today it is impossible for our society to be unified under a tyrant. Likewise, it is not possible for any hate-mongering politician to unite all Hindus against Muslims, as Hitler was able to unite the Christians against Jews in Germany, no matter how hard the Sangh Parivar may try.

This factor of cross-cutting identities has been crucial in defining limits for authoritarian politics in India. No one *danda* can work for all of India's people. That is what makes them 'difficult to govern' and, therefore, mistrusted by the 'national unity'-mongering elite.

PLURALITIES PROTECT DEMOCRACY

Among other pluralities, the much reviled caste system has played a very significant role in making Indian democracy vibrant and difficult to destroy as well as requiring some amount of redistribution of power through the democratic process. But the modern educated elite have a deep love–hate relationship with the institution of caste. On the one hand, they find it difficult to bypass it in most essential matters—they marry within caste, reside in caste clusters yet they continue to heap rhetorical abuses on it, treating it as a symbol of all that is evil and backward in Indian society. They keep asserting that the hateful caste system should be 'wiped out', as a necessary step towards modernization. It is a schizophrenic attitude. They are obsessed about destroying caste while at the same time clinging on to it, even enhancing its salience in many essential matters.

The English educated elite inherited its critique of Indian society from the views and writings of colonial administrators, orientalists, anthropologists, and missionaries. Since they inherited it along with the imperial ambitions of the colonial rulers, it suited their interest to stick to it with vigour even after Independence.

One of the key tasks for any alien ruling elite is to destroy the sense of self of the society it seeks to subjugate. It needs to compel the people to adopt as their own self-view the contemptuous view that alien rulers have of them. Hence, the colonial rulers had launched a vigorous, well orchestrated attack on all aspects of Indian society—its learning, its social and political institutions, its family life and organization. Everything that was different from the habits and customs, institutions of governance and beliefs of the British was targeted for attack. For instance, the much healthier vegetarian food habits followed by several Brahmin communities and many other sections of Indian society were ridiculed, and projected as the cause of the inherent inferiority of Indians justifying their political slavery. Meat eating, for example, was held up as a sign of modern, enlightened, healthful living. So powerful was this ideological attack that meat eating became a status symbol for educated Indians—a proof of their modernity. Gandhi admits in his autobiography that as a young boy he too felt compelled to try eating meat, though the very idea revolted him.

Of all the institutions, caste as a unit of social organization came under the most severe attack, not as it existed but as the British portrayed it to be.

How *Jatis* Became Castes

'Caste' was a concept alien to the people of India. The term caste, as is well-known, was first used by the Portuguese in the early decades of the sixteenth century. As pointed out by Gita Dharampal-Frick in her thesis 'Hinduism, Self-Perception and Assessment of Tradition', 'The word itself not only embraced several meanings such as "family", "stock", "kind", "strain", "clan", "tribe", or "race", but consequently was also used to designate various kinds of groups, besides Hindu ones, such as the "caste of Moors", the "caste of Christians", etcetra. Hence, the much-discussed notion of "purity of blood" deduced from the etymological derivation of the word from the Latin *castus,* meaning "chaste" or "pure", was only one among many distinct meanings. It was only later that the Dutch and then the English employed the term caste as a technical social term, in short as a one-word restricted description of the approximately 3,000 groupings within Hindu society. However, though the term caste had been coined in the initial stages of European contact with India, the fact that in most early reports various other more familiar terms, [that are] more commonly employed in the European context, were preferred, indicates that the distinctive traits perceived in Indian society were being brought in line with apparently similar European social divisions; India was thus being drawn closer to Europe, be it in the latter's own terms, and not being distinguished from it as was to be the case later on. Hence, the coeval nature of India was implicitly acknowledged, a striking contrast, indeed, to more recent Western attitudes.'

The operative units in India were *jati* and *biradari,* which still remain relevant for certain important functions.

However, caste has become a reality in post-British India due to the onset of new social and political institutions requiring new tactics for upward mobility and for acquiring socio-political power. At the operational level the social system, based as it was on kinship ties expressed through *jatis,* was characterized by fissiparous tendencies tending to break down into new endogamous sub-units, leading to a continual upward, downward, and sideward mobility of various old and new *jatis.* This system in no way resembled the 19th century European view of Indian society as being governed by the four main *varna* categories of Brahmins, Kshatriya, Vaishyas, and Sudras, placed hierarchically in that order. They built this theoretical model from a peculiar selection of ancient texts with the help of the *pundits* and *shastris* they hired. According to their text book model, Brahmins were the dominant group in society and the only ones allowed to acquire learning. This view was not reflected in political structure of India, even in eighteenth and early nineteenth century India when the British got their first foothold in the Indian subcontinent. For example, eighteenth-century India had hardly any Brahmin dynasties. Political and military power rested in the hands of other groups in society. Many of the ruling chieftains were from what are designated as the Sudra castes. Some even had their genealogies altered to successfully claim *Kshatriya* status, even though they were from *Sudra jatis.* Similarly, *Yadavas* (who came to be designated as a backward caste) were ruling chieftains in many areas of the North before the British took over. Yet, in conjuction with the destruction of institutions of Sanskrit learning, the sheer power of incremental repetition succeeded in making the colonial view of caste acquire dominance over reality.

The textual view of Indian society put together by Orientalists projected Indian society as static, timeless, and spaceless. Arbitrarily selected texts from as early as the third century were used as though they could describe the nature of society and culture in the eighteenth and nineteenth century. This picture allowed for no regional variation. It acknowledged no gap between prescriptive, normative statements derived from certain texts and the actual behaviour of individuals or groups. Indian society was seen as obeying a set of fixed rules which every Hindu followed. Texts that did not fit in with the British constructed model were bypassed and even suppressed and certain others systematically built up as the ultimate and final authority in the matter. For example, the *Manusmriti* became the favourite text of the British. Its reprinting as an authoritative text was approved by the Governors in London as late as 1815, even when the publication of most other ancient Indian literary and legal texts did not secure their approval.

While the Orientalists in the late eighteenth and early nineteenth century presented Brahmins as the source of authority and power, both sacred and temporal, and built a romantic, mythical picture of the hierarchical nature of Indian society, the colonial administrators and missionaries picked up this stereotype view for vigorous attack on the entire social system. They felt that the caste system, the legal system, institutions of governance, and above all, the despotic role of the Brahmins were the cause of the 'degraded' state of the Hindus whose only hope for progress lay in elimination of Hinduism. Here is a typical quote: 'Like all other attempts to cramp the human intellect, and forcibly to restrain men within bounds which nature scorns to keep, this system, however specious in theory, has operated like the Chinese national shoe, it has rendered the whole nation cripples. Under the fatal influence of this abominable system, the bramhuns have sunk into ingnorance, without abating an atom of their claims to superiority; the kshutriyus became almost extinct before their country fell into the hands of Musulmans; the voishyus are nowhere to be found in Bengal; almost all have fallen into the class of shoodrus, and shoodrus have sunk to the level of their own cattle.'[1]

There were occasional voices which tried to contradict this stereotype view—for example H.T. Colebrook, who on the basis of his observations rather than textbook knowledge, wrote in 1806 that 'in practice little attention was paid to the limitations' of 'hereditary prohibition on undertaking other than one's father's occupation' supposedly imposed by the caste system or the four varna theory. '...daily observation shows even Brahmins exercising the menial profession of a Sudra. We are aware that every caste forms itself into clubs or lodges, consisting of the several individuals of that caste residing within a small distance; and that these clubs or lodges, govern themselves by particular rules and customs, or by laws. But, though some restrictions and limitations, not founded on religious prejudice are found among their by-laws, it may be received as

---

[1]Ward, William, *A View of the History, Literature and Mythology of the Hindoos,* London: Kingsbury, Panbury and Allen, 1822, Vol. 2, pp. 64–5.

a general maxim that the occupation, appointed for each tribe, is entitled merely to a preference. Every profession, with few exceptions, is open to every description of persons; and the discouragement, arising from religious prejudices, is not greater than what exists in Great Britain from the effects of Municipal and corporation laws...'[2]

But the dominant view continued to project the caste system as a barbaric and hateworthy institution—the root of all evil in Hindu society. It was presented as a rigid and unchangeable hierarchy. Even though in actual practice most *jatis* were horizontally placed with regard to each other, the British were obsessed with grading of groups in a tight hierarchy, assigning high and low status resembling the medieval European theory of the Chain of Being.

The venom heaped on the caste system was deliberate and systematic. For the administrators, it was part of an ideological attack to convince the Indians that the British were here on a 'civilizing' and 'modernizing' mission. The missionaries considered it necessary to destroy what they thought was the social basis of Hinduism. Caste provided an important obstacle to large scale conversions and made cultural enslavement of Indians a more difficult and slower process. Social ostracism was a powerful weapon in the hands of caste panchayats in dealing with the few who accepted Christianity. As long as an individual who converted cut himself/herself off from the rest of society, there was little hope of the spread of Christianity. The severance of *beti roti ka rishta* and being cut off from sharing *hukka pani* among one's kin group was a potent factor in preventing large scale conversions in India, except in tribal areas which were outside the pale of the caste system. Much of the missionary anger against upper castes is related to their inability to find converts among them. They knew that they could not break down Indian society nor ideologically hegemonize it as long as only a few of the marginalized and poorest groups were available to them for conversion. And even with those they had limited success.

The Story of John Ram Singh

The following joke narrated to me by famous lyricist and film script writer Javed Akhtar, captures the resilience of the *jati* identities very poignantly:

---

[2]Colebrook, Henry Thomas, *Remarks on the Husbandry and Internal Commerce of Bengal,* London: Black and Party, 1806, p. 174.

Ram Singh was a poor and illiterate peasant. A missionary came to live in his village and after years of persuasion succeeded in converting him to Christianity. The priest wanted to give him an altogether new name which would indicate that Ram Singh had shed his caste identity and adopted a different religion. But since Ram Singh was illiterate and simple minded, the missionary thought he may not be able to adjust or even respond to an altogether English name. Therefore, he worked out a via-media and christened him John Ram Singh.

One day while the priest was walking past the house of John Ram Singh, he saw him performing the ritual of *muhcchua* with his cow. [Among the cow worshipping groups among the Hindus, members of the family eat only after the first morsel of food cooked in the house has been offered to the cow.]

The priest was very upset. All his labour would be a waste if John Ram Singh continued to observe the "superstitious" rituals and practices associated with Hinduism. The priest indignantly asked him: "John Ram Singh, why are you performing *muhcchua*, now that you have become an Isai?"

Ram Singh was surprised and puzzled at the naivety of the question and replied: *"Arre sahib, Isai ho gaye to kya hua? Dharm to nahin chhod diya hamne apna!"* (So what if I have converted to Christianity? I won't give up my *dharm* for that!)

The word *dharm* is used here in the popular sense of the term, not to mean religion, but to mean a code of conduct accepted by the concerned community, based on a notion of desirable social/individual norms of behaviour.

The colonial administrators hated the caste and other diversities because it made this society harder for them to understand and even harder to govern. For example, the verdict of a caste *panchayat* was commonly more potent than the judgements of the British law courts which could rarely exercise direct hegemonic sway over the vast population. Bernard Cohn's study of a Rajput dominated village in Uttar Pradesh points out that up until 1906 not a single case went up to British established courts from that particular *taluka*, once a final decision had been given by the panchayat of chiefs.[3] All the new fangled

---

[3]Cohn, Bernard, *An Anthropologist among the Historians and Other Essays*, Delhi: Oxford University Press, 1991, p. 269.

laws, including those meant for the 'reform' of Indian society, could be ignored with impunity if caste and *biradari* leaders decided otherwise. The British needed to destroy all rival power centres in order to become effective rulers and impose a new system of centralized governance.

At the same time, the British were great supporters of their version of the caste system, as they saw caste as one of the sociological keys to understanding the Indian people. From the first census onwards, caste became the basis of information collection. Many nationalist leaders were to later allege that this was done with a view to keep alive and exacerbate the numerous divisions already present in Indian society. The British began by placing castes (*jatis*) in the four *varnas* or in the categories of outcastes and aborigines. The next stage was to order the castes on the basis of social precedence.

There were widespread protests from various caste groups regarding their placement in the social hierarchy. Petitions galore were submitted to the government by newly formed caste *sabhas* (associations) to claim a status different from the one assigned to them. This resulted in a livening up of the caste spirit. To quote M.N. Srinivas: '...the ranks accorded to castes in census reports became the equivalent of traditional copper-plate grants declaring the status, rank and privileges of a particular caste or castes' (cited in Cohn, op.cit, p. 241). The British even added the notion of racial superiority to explain the hierarchy of castes. Since scholarship to educational institutions and government jobs were being linked to caste characteristics (for example, the notion of martial castes for recruitment in the army), it set into motion new conflicts between castes while at the same time artificially ossifying caste status though in reality *jatis* were not the static entities they were made out to be. They had a history of undergoing major changes and transformation in status over time and space.

Even though the practice of collecting caste-based information was discontinued after 1931, the emergence of new caste-based organizations changed the Indian political scene for ever. *Jati* still remained the operational unit for marriage and kinship ties, but political mobilization came to be based on a merger of several similar but dispersed *jatis* in horizontal placement to forge a new common identity over larger geographical territories to form caste-based political organizations. Thus, caste associations are a modern creation and have been both the product and agent of fusion of *jatis* within an overarching caste category. In the pursuit of political power, caste associations have spilled over all the earlier restrictive boundaries. For example, the All India Yadav Mahasabha attempts to bring a heterogeneity of *jatis* under one umbrella. The operational units of *jatis* were and continued to be much smaller. The organization of castes on such a large scale is a post-British phenomenon.

While providing legitimacy to the new caste system that the British helped evolve by their policies of governance, from the mid-nineteenth century onwards they launched a very vigorous ideological attack against it. But their hatred towards caste organization was not really based on hatred of power and privilege per se, even though they often used a radical, progressive vocabulary to critique it. Nor was it born of a zeal to make society more egalitarian. It could not be, because they came to establish the rule of a vastly privileged minority based on notions of racial superiority. (Even with regard to their own society, their notion of governance justified concentration of power and privilege in the hands of a small elite.) Writings on the caste system focused either on the abusive aspects or those aspects of the caste system that did not aid the British in their designs. Their attack was aimed especially at the Brahmins who were projected as the symbol of all that was evil in the caste system. The critique based itself on a caricatured stereotype of a Brahmin—someone arrogant, superstitious, and tyrannical—a repository of all the negative qualities. The noteworthy point is that the critique levelled at the Brahmins (claims to special privileges, tyranny based on false notions of superiority) was even more true of the British elite, not just in their role as alien rulers in India, but even as ruling elite within their own country.

A society with a long tradition of learning and sense of history, as was India, is much harder to enslave than societies without a literate tradition and written records of its past. To effect that severance with its own past, groups who acted as repositories of learning, art, and culture had to be undermined. Thus the English educated groups of Brahmins who became the super elites of Indian society had their cultural social roots severed and all their aspirations directed towards becoming part of a westernized international elite. This group adopted the British critique of Indian society lock, stock and barrel and went about heaping contempt on all the surviving traditional institutions much in the same way as did their colonial masters. Secure in their own new found super privileged status, they were extremely resentful of the elites of groups lower down and never tired of projecting those elites (calling some *kulaks,* others blood-sucking *banias,* etc.) as the exploiters of society while projecting themselves as the forces of 'progress and national unity,' just as the British did.

MORE RADICAL CRITIQUES OF CASTE

The contemporary critique of the caste system that has surfaced in a
virulent form with the announcement of caste-based reservations draws
heavily from this colonial tradition. This is not to suggest that the
division of society into *jatis* with some claiming over arching
superiority, is without problems. In fact, a much more genuine and
radical critique of such pretensions to superiority came from within
India. The *Bhakti* movements that spread in waves from the south to
the north from the sixth to the seventeenth centuries articulated, among
other things, a very strong and uncompromising voice of protest against
privileges based on particular hierarchical interpretations of *jati* or
possession of wealth. The *bhakts* asserted the equality of all souls before
God, regardless of caste and economic status, even indicating that
power and wealth were impediments to building oneness with God.
They emphasized love and good deeds as much more important than
knowledge gained from book learning, and denounced the self-
righteousness of religious and other authority figures. The brahminical
pretension to exclusive monopoly over learning and scriptures came to
be ridiculed and challenged in an enduring kind of way with the
establishment of a large number of new sects which did not recognize
brahminical authority.

What makes this critique more genuinely radical as compared to the
one initiated by the colonial rulers is that the *bhakts* did not arrogate to
themselves the role of the super elite, as did the colonial rulers and the
modern English educated Indians. Many of the *bhakts* came from so-
called lower caste groups. In challenging brahminical authority they did
not seek to set themselves up as alternative authority figures. They
challenged all claims to superiority based on birth rather than seeking to
supplant one kind with another. That is perhaps why they succeeded in
inspiring large followings of people with a relatively more egalitarian
vision of society and compelled brahminism to make space for the
aspirations of groups lower down the social hierarchy. The *Bhakti*
movements left a permanent legacy of a strong and enduring
counterview to the ideology of exclusive power and privilege propagated
by certain dominant caste groups.

In contrast, the harangues of the modern elites against caste seem to
have the contrary effect of making people cling to their caste identity
even more vigorously because their latter critique is not motivated by
the desire to do away with privilege but to maintain an exclusive

control over power and privilege. Witness the arguments of those who are upset at reservations for certain caste groups. They argue that reservations will militate against merit, implying that 'merit' consists merely in getting a certain percentage of marks. They allege that the induction of OBCs will bring 'inefficiency' into administration and professions, will condemn the children of the elite to menial jobs like shoe polishing and will encourage less privileged groups to cling to their caste identities.

The more generous among them say they are not averse to reservations on a class basis, that is, using income levels as criteria. The assumption is that class-based divisions are somehow more desirable or superior, as though exploitation based on class is necessarily less obnoxious. As proof of their 'modernizing' drive they are forever talking of wiping out the evil caste system in favour of a class-based society. But the caste system refuses to oblige. People cling on to their caste identities despite the onslaught of modernism. In fact, they have been consolidated and resurrected in many new forms and have made remarkable adjustments with modern institutions such as representative democracy. Caste associations are successful because they make good use of readymade traditional channels of mobilization. Caste (in the sense of *jati* as opposed to *varna* theory) has been the most central and enduring feature of Indian society. A popular proverb says it well: *'Jatee nahin, voh jati'* (jati is that which can never be obliterated.) It's not just the so-called upper castes which cling tenaciously to their caste identity, the so-called lower castes do not seem willing to give it up either. The latter, no doubt, want to escape the tyrannical and abusive aspects of being considered low caste, but do not seem willing to give up their caste identity altogether, especially in the area that gives continuity to it, namely marriage. Even lower caste groups are, by and large, not keen on inter-caste marriage, not even with someone of the upper caste. Even those who converted to Islam or Christianity often continue to differentiate themselves from their co-religionists on the basis of *jati*. Statements like: 'We are Rajput Muslims or Kayastha Christians' are made commonly not just by the concerned groups in India but even in Pakistan.

Undoubtedly, there are many exploitative and degrading aspects of caste-based social organization as we know it today. Among the most shameful and brutal is the stigmatizing of a number of castes as untouchables. The presumption of superiority on grounds of heredity does vitiate social relations in a serious way. The pressure to marry only within one's *biradari* often takes a deadly form, especially for women who are compelled to live very circumscribed lives so that they do not have much of an opportunity to develop relationships outside those sanctioned by the family.

CLASS VERSUS CASTE

However, some of these features are present in class and racially divided societies as well. Exploitation is no less brutal in many of the non-caste based societies. In fact, some of them put greater hurdles in the way of upward mobility for individuals than does our caste-based society. Therefore, there is nothing inherently morally superior about class-based societies. If our aim is to make society more egalitarian the so-called class divided societies do not provide an ideal role model. In fact, caste identities provide certain advantages to its group members which are not available in what are supposedly class-based societies. That may well be the reason why people cling tenaciously to these identities. Some of these advantages are:

1. A relatively more secure social life, even for the poor, and a less hazardous process of upward mobility since it usually comes as part of group mobility. Unlike class-based societies which glorify individual initiative for upward mobility and atomize human beings in the process, who owe responsibility to no one but themselves, caste and kinship ties provide a much more effective security net than anything offered by class organizations or the modern state.

2. In any crisis, be it a sudden death or any other calamity, closely connected kin from one's own caste are the ones who are supposed to help. Even loans needed to tide over crisis or set up a business often come from within this group. The responsibility for social functions is shared. It is not uncommon for poor members of a *biradari* to get financial help at the time of a daughter's wedding from the better off members. In most cases, they will ensure a decent cremation and last rites even if a particular member of the *biradari* dies penniless. Even in metropolitan centres like Bombay, caste/*biradari* associations make provision for book banks and scholarships for students from poorer families among other facilities. Setting up of student hostels in towns by well organized caste panchayats played an important role in the spread of higher education among certain rural-based groups whose children could not have made the transition to city education without this support. Establishment of community centres and *baraat ghars* and

dharamshalas at important pilgrimage centres are among other important social services provided by caste organizations.

3. Since most caste groups are not economically homogeneous, it gives the poorer members of that caste group access to economically better off people. As a consequence of *biradari* and caste connections, the rich and poor in India (barring the absolutely marginalized groups and a few at the top who have severed ties with their community in favour of being part of a national or international elite) do not live in mutually exclusive worlds. The case of Laloo Prasad Yadav, the former chief minister of Bihar, one of whose brothers is a peon and the other one an ordinary peasant, is not an exceptional one. Most of the urban upper and middle class are linked through caste/kinship connections to a whole range of people much lower down the economic hierarchy—a bus conductor who can claim a close relationship with a minister or MP, a poor peasant—one of whose nephews becomes a Superintendent of Police—are fairly common occurences in India. The solidarity of the caste group ensures that even the poor can lay some claim to sharing some of the crumbs of power and privilege that certain members of a caste group achieve. Thus caste solidarity becomes an important tool for upward mobility of the entire group, even though internal differentiation may continue to exist for a while. Even if a few members of a caste group get access to jobs which bring power and influence, it begins to slowly affect the social and economic status of the entire group.

4. When people migrate to the cities in search of jobs, it is usually their own *biradari bhais* who give them shelter and other support, including help in finding a job and a house. These *jati* and kinship connections function much more effectively in helping people find employment than the non-functioning wasteful employment exchanges set up by the government. This support system makes migration of the poor a much less traumatic experience than it would be if they come in as atomized individuals. The efficacy of this system is evident from the fact that it functions amongst Indians even in far off countries such as Canada or England. Even when the poorest of the poor migrate they do so as part of a kinship/caste group and follow others who have preceded them. When they make *jhuggis* as encroachers on public or private land, they do so as a group, almost never individually, for it gives them relatively greater power in resisting demolitions and evictions than if they were unconnected individuals.

5. For the poor this solidarity is very important in their dealings with better off and more powerful groups as well as the government machinery. Caste kinship ties spread over neighbouring villages, provide places of shelter and resistance when the lower castes face atrocities at the hands of upper castes. It is a common occurrence that in case any one member of the group is subject to abuse by his/her employer, the whole *biradari* will descend to protest and settle scores.

6. Police atrocities on the poor would be even more frequent were it not for the fact that in many cases when a slum dweller is arrested on false charges, a large number of his *biradari* people will gather at the police station and protest, with a relatively better chance of being heard than the protest of a lone individual or family, who in most cases would be too intimidated to protest without the protection that numbers give. Thus groups which have greater caste cohesiveness are relatively less vulnerable to the tyranny of the government machinery.

7. The creation of new elites (popularly referred to as the 'creamy layer') within disadvantaged caste groups should not be dismissed as a negative development. This is often part of the process of democratizing society. Groups without an integrally connected elite of their own tend to become far more vulnerable and are more exploited if they cannot claim protection from the elite of their own community. Their own might exploit them, but have to observe some semblance of restraint which an outsider elite, such as the modern IAS or IPS officer, does not have to observe. Moreover, the success stories within an oppressed caste groups become symbols of hope giving rise to new aspirations, motivating people to believe that opportunities for advancement are not shut out to them on account of their birth in a certain community.

8. Caste *panchayats* give even the poor some sense of internal control over their community affairs and opportunity for the exercise of power. Each caste has its own authority figures. An elder who is considered a respected leader of his own caste is likely to be treated with deference by members of a dominant or higher caste. This provides a space for the emergence of political leaders from even poorer castes who are able to mobilize their community for making collective efforts for upgrading their social status.

9. Caste associations provide the lower castes an opportunity to achieve, through politics, the social and political power that is inaccessible to them through other social instrumentalities. Modern democracy has strengthened not weakened caste ties because elections provide the occasion for successful organization of lower castes against

the hitherto dominant castes and give them an opportunity to develop their own leaders rather than be dependant for leadership on other dominant groups. For example, the emergence of Scheduled Caste leader Kanshi Ram's Bahujan Samaj Party reduces the dependence of lower caste groups on upper caste leaders in espousing their cause. Through caste and kinship networks the poor and socially disadvantaged groups are able to mobilize themselves into powerful vote banks. Their numerical strength gives them some bargaining power against politicians who must woo them for votes and in many cases gives a winning chance to their own candidates wherever they are or are able to put together an effective coalition. Due to the interaction of caste and the democratic process, the political leadership even at the national level is forced to make concessions to local aspirations and sentiments and learn to adjust to the claims and counter-claims of various communal groups. This has provided some measure of check against centralized authoritarian polity. For example, the *Chaubisi* (a *panchayat* of 24 villages) of Meham district in Haryana was more successful in challenging the tyranny of the Devi Lal dynasty than most of the modern institutions like the police and judiciary, the Election Commission, or even the national press.

These and many other support mechanisms provided by the kinship and caste networks have ensured their survival through creative adaptation to modern socio-political life. It is time we accepted this reality and stopped indulging in pious, radical posturing expecting caste to disappear and give way to a modern society of our fantasies. Only then can we meaningfully deal with combating some of the oppressive aspects of caste, chief among them being claims of notions of hereditary superiority coupled with concentration of economic and political power among certain dominant castes leading to a great deal of local tyranny and brutal abuse, especially when certain caste groups are economically dependant on others. Resistance to the tyrannical aspects are already underway but have had only mixed success despite instances of mobilization of various lower caste groups challenging the privileged status of upper castes. These movements in many ways further strengthen caste identities among lower caste groups. Simply because democratization of power continues to take a casteist route in our society, it need not on that ground be viewed as altogether unprogressive, as long as those organizing caste mobilizations are willing to accept the democratic ethos, both for internal functioning as well as for inter-caste relations. Unfortunately, not much attention has been paid to this aspect and caste rivalries often take deadly forms.

INDIVIDUALS VERSUS COLLECTIVES

Just as the doomsday prophesies of anti-reservationists regarding the consequences of the proposed reservations are inappropriate and exaggerated, likewise the claims of pro-reservationists that this step is a precursor to a great social revolution are also exaggerated. Both pro- and anti-reservationists have made much fuss over whether or not the implementation of the Mandal Commission recommendations will bring about social equality—the pro-reservationists insisting that this is a major step towards a great social revolution and those opposing it vehemently asserting that this will only benefit elites of certain caste groups and that benefits won't percolate down to the really poor and downtrodden. Many of them extend the argument to suggest that reservation should be on the basis of economic criteria so that it can benefit the really poor. Those who argue that there is danger of misuse of reservation on the basis of caste, ignore the fact that economic criteria are even more tricky to apply.

In an economy like ours where the majority of people are self-employed and whose wages or incomes do not come into official records, it is impossible to have a reliable measure of family income. With the use of economic criteria as a basis for job reservations, we will only give further encouragement to the industry for the manufacture of false income certificates. Dissimulation about caste identity is not altogether uncommon. But misrepresentation of income is a much more routine matter. It is harder to detect and involves no stigma. In fact, having a hidden income is considered a status symbol whereas lying about one's caste evokes genuine social disapproval.

There are distinct advantages to using caste criteria. Despite some amount of diversification there is still a good deal of continuing association of caste with certain occupational categories. If one takes into consideration regional specificities/variations one finds that members of a caste tend to share a common level of opportunities and resources. Thus, it becomes a convenient way of identifying persons with a low level of opportunity and resources as well as taking into account the negative effect of social prejudices in determining lack of access to social opportunities. There is sufficient affinity of conditions among members of a caste group irrespective of its socio-economic heterogeneity. Since communal membership is more readily ascertainable, there is relatively little slippage in distribution. The benefits do reach the group for whom they are meant, even if not to the poorest among them.

Moreover, the benefits arising from jobs given to even a small number of a particular caste group very soon have a multiplier effect within the whole community. This would not happen if such benefits are endowed on isolated individuals. Ties of kinship, loyalty and the social pressure for mutual support ensure that many more people are able to derive benefits from one single individual getting a good job. Communal groups have a greater potential capacity for political organization to counterbalance the inefficiency and sluggishness of the administrative machinery in delivering benefits to those for whom they are meant. For every one person who gets a government job from a particular community, dozens of his *jaat bhais* could benefit by way of help in getting jobs, hundreds others will be helped in getting a water connection, a licence, a loan from a bank or help in securing information from a government office which would not come to them otherwise. These individuals also act as important role models for others to emulate, thus creating new aspirations within the community. Thus even the process of creation of a job holding elite among disadvantaged groups is a welcome development from the point of view of democratization of opportunities.

The idea of compensatory discrimination does not altogether detract from the principle of equality as is often argued by anti-reservationists. It is to promote equalization by offsetting historically accumulated inequalities. To sum up Marc Gallanter: 'The poor among upper castes could be viewed as those who have failed to benefit from a favourable heritage and the better off among the deprived castes seen as those who did well despite unfavourable circumstances and heritage. Even the relatively well off individuals within lower castes may be thought of as worse off than they if they had not suffered social disabilities on account of their caste status.' (The OBCs suffered not as much due to 'social' disabilities but more due to their being part of a much neglected and exploited rural sector.)

BROADBASING THE ELITE

Many of the contemporary upper caste groups, both in the North and the South, have since the early 20th century changed the source of their power and privilege from land to acquiring a monopoly over jobs in the bureaucracy and in elite professions. They are known to have held a similar position in pre-British India, enjoying the patronage of various local dynasties, but lost this eminent position temporarily with the coming of British rule which limited avenues of their social advancement till they took to English education. This provided them with many new avenues of upward social mobility. It is noteworthy that one of the earliest demands of the Indian National Congress was that the British reserve for the Indians a reasonable proportion of jobs in the Indian Civil Service (ICS). This elite service in those days allowed entry to very few Indians.

Having cornered most of the elite jobs in urban areas, especially after Independence, the upper castes slowly dispersed far away from their villages. As a result, there has been a relative decline in the power and influence of their caste *panchayats*. At the same time the caste organizations among those termed Backward Castes (BCs) have acquired a new ferocity and power, especially those that are primarily rural-based. With some of the upper caste elite abandoning the villages in favour of urban opportunities, the BCs have emerged as the new rural elite. Hence they can easily be targeted for attack as the oppressors of the rural poor.

Till not very long ago the Indian middle class and professionals were recruited almost exclusively from among select urban upper caste groups. With reservation this can no more be the case. The recruiting base of the urban middle class and elite professions will be expanded as 'lower' caste groups acquire positions of power and influence in the bureaucracy. Already we have witnessed the emergence of a very small middle class among the Scheduled Castes (SCs) and Scheduled Tribes (STs) in most parts of the country as well as a larger group among BCs in the South, thanks to the job reservations implemented there for a few decades now. A similar development among the OBCs of the North should not be viewed as an unwelcome development. Among other things, it will help bridge the pernicious rural–urban divide in India because most of the OBCs are rural based peasant or artisanal groups. They have taken much longer than their counterparts in the South to get organized politically in such a way as to create pressure from below for demanding a certain share of power and influence. The strong adverse reaction to reservations may in part be due to the fact that being politically well organized, they are actually in a position to effectively challenge the dominance of the urban upper caste elite and ensure that unlike the SC/ST job quotas, which often lapse for lack of candidates, OBC quotas are actually utilized. Their claims need not be dismissed on account of their 'elite status' vis-à-vis other rural groups.

Historically, the power of the existing elite has always been challenged by newly-emerging elites of the groups below them, almost never by the absolutely downtrodden. That may explain why the English educated national elite are so fond of verbally championing the cause of the poor and landless in rural society. That provided them a moral legitimacy when denying the claims of newly emerging regional elites. The rural destitutes are in no position to challenge the power of the upper caste English educated elite. At the same time they provide them with a good stick to beat the OBCs and other peasant groups who are projected as the rural tyrants who need to be controlled by the upper caste national elite. But the upper caste elite who easily assume the mantle of the defenders of the rights of the rural poor against the landowning peasant groups have a dismal record of concern for the rights of the poor when it comes to their own acts of commission and ommission. The upper caste dominated bureaucracy is almost uniformly oppressive, both for the BCs and SCs, and have neglected to provide even basic amenities like water, primary health care and schools for the urban and rural poor. In fact, most of the so-called rural elite share many of the deprivations in common with the rural poor due to the absence of basic amenities in villages.

WHY THE BATTLE AROUND GOVERNMENT JOBS?

The performance of the bureaucracy since Independence is universally acknowledged to be dismal. Unfortunately, despite acute and widespread disgruntlement against the malfunctioning of the government machinery, the band of culprits who occupy positions of power are not a despised community but, on the contrary, a highly prestigious group. About two-thirds of the government's budget is eaten up by the administration. While the capacity of the civil service to do good is limited to itself and their hangers-on, its potential for harm is unlimited for the citizens as a whole.

If there is such a murderous battle over government jobs, including that of peons and clerks, it is proof that control over this monstrous machinery is indeed a matter of life and death for any group. Whichever groups control the government machinery and can influence the decision-making process, including the lower levels, come to be the powerful groups. They acquire an unmatched power to tyrannize people and indulge in self-aggrandizement. Groups that do not have access to government jobs remain vulnerable and powerless. If we had a civilized system of administration this would not be the case and being a member of this tyrannical clerkdom would not be such a sought after boon.

No matter what be one's economic status, the key to power in modern day India is the control over the bureaucracy. In the 1970s even a supposedly powerful Chief Minister like Karpoori Thakur remained helpless in many ways because he was not able to get the cooperation of the Bihari upper caste dominated bureaucracy due to his own status as a BC leader. Today, with the consolidation of BC and OBC power, Mulayam Singh Yadav or other OBC chief ministers do not face similar non-cooperation and hostility from the bureaucracy.

In recent years peasant movements have directed their wrath primarily against an organized bias against rural areas in the terms of trade and against callous neglect of rural areas combined with the tyranny of the bureaucracy. Protest is one response. The other response is a murderous battle over government jobs, including that of peons and clerks. The ferocity of battle is a proof that control over this monstrous machinery is indeed a matter of life and death for any group. Government in India is regarded, not just as another employer, but as one that affords a high degree of control over vital resources, security, prestige, and authority, not obtainable elsewhere. Therefore, it is the prime focus of ambition for the educated. In the 57 years since Independence, people have despaired of India keeping its tryst with destiny in an upsurge of collective achievement. It is each one for himself and devil take the hindmost. Since it is much harder to fend for oneself individually, people stick to their caste/community identity more ferociously than would be required if our system of administration was more responsive and civilized. Having a few relatives or kin in the government assures accessibility and a sympathetic response to one's interests. Access to government jobs is crucial for advancement, especially for the newly educated groups who have not diversified their educational skills sufficiently for them to enter other well-paying professions and private sector jobs.

This in part explains why the lower middle class students from non-elite institutions joined the anti-reservation movement with such zeal, why they felt desperate that the new reservations would completely ruin their life chances. For those among upper castes who are unable to have access to elite English medium schools, the only hope of a secure future is to get a class III or class IV government job. For it requires very little talent or skill, and assures a middle class salary with the guarantee of lifetime security involving very little work and even less accountability. In addition, a number of government jobs fetch a lot of bribes. They provide one an opportunity for reciprocal obligation so that one's area of influence extends far beyond one's own job. The poorly educated lower middle class youth are unable to enter the much more competitive and insecure private sector. Therefore, access to government jobs becomes a life and death issue for those who have few other avenues of social advancement open to them, especially those for whom *sifarish* is the chief mode of getting a job—something that works more easily in government jobs than in the private sector. If we had a functioning educational system and a more accountable system of administration, accountable in accordance with predetermined parameters which recognize legitimate interests, not of this or that powerful lobby but of the people as a whole, being a member of the inefficient and tyrannical clerkdom would not be such a sought after boon. Unless we move determinedly in that direction, the ferocious battles over government jobs will continue and assume the dimensions of a virtual civil war.

NEED TO ENFORCE ACCOUNTABILITY

Job reservation for OBCs might bring about a certain redistribution of power and patronage and democratize corruption, but it will not in itself bring about an efficient and egalitarian social order. It is no doubt important to see that government jobs are not monopolized by certain groups. But equally important is to ensure that the government machinery becomes more accountable to the people. If those in government jobs are actually made to work in a way that people can demand service of them (as against the present mode of having to grovel before them), and dismiss them if they do not perform well, it is unlikely that there will be such a scramble for government jobs.

Let me illustrate this through an example. Among the most sought after jobs is that of a policeman—not just at the IPS level but even more so at the lower levels of a constable or sub-inspector. The working conditions of policemen at the lower levels are poor and hazardous. Their duty hours are long and unpredictable. They are constantly subjected to scoldings and humiliation by their senior officers. Policemen are viewed with fear and suspicion by most people and thus lack social respect. Yet many a family would pay any price to get a son in the police force.

Firstly, there is the lure of large amounts of bribes that are expected to come with a police job. SHOs of important *thanas* are known to make several lakhs of 'extra income' every year and are known to 'buy' those postings. But no less important than this bribe money is the power to harass and intimidate that a policeman acquires. In many instances, policemen virtually get away with murder, as long as they please their bosses, who themselves are often involved in similar abuse of power. A citizen has no real redress possible unless he or she can put pressure on a more senior officer. In addition, a policeman, including an ordinary sub-inspector, has tremendous power of patronage, the ability to get work done from other government departments.

But most important of all, a policeman can avoid doing the work he is primarily meant for—namely crime control. Barring a few exceptions, policemen are among the chief patrons of crime and collect regular payoffs from all kinds of criminals.

The possession of so much arbitrary power in the hands of a policeman, makes his job a sought after privilege. Compare it with an ordinary *chowkidar,* the kind that every colony or *mohalla* association appoints on their own to guard their neighbourhoods. This *chowkidar* does a part of the job that the police should actually be doing, but do not often do—keep vigil in order to protect a neighbourhood from thieves and criminals. The *mohalla* appointed *chowkidar* has to take his rounds at night and dare not sleep during his duty hours. If residents find him cheating on his job, he is fired immediately. If there are any thefts in the neighbourhood he will likewise find his job in danger. Even a hint of suspicion about his complicity with thieves and he faces immediate dismissal.

No wonder that the job of a *mohalla chowkidar* is not at all sought after as is the job of a policeman, even though the former's 'salary' may be as much as the policeman's. Linked to this is the question, how is it that any neighbourhood association can exercise such effective control over their *chowkidar* but not over the local policeman—though the job of the two is very similar.

The difference is obvious: the community has the right to hire and fire the *chowkidar* (each household pays a small sum towards his salary and thereby everyone acquires the right to check him if found negligent), whereas the policeman is appointed by a very distant and inaccessible authority whom they cannot call to account. His job is guaranteed for life and salary ensured as long as he does not annoy some higher official. Even in cases where local residents have protested vigorously over long periods of time against particular misdeeds of the police station—for example, death in police custody—the maximum that may result after a long drawn out struggle is that one or two of the policemen may be transferred to another posting, that is, allowed to run amok elsewhere. In most cases the person is reinstated after the protest has calmed down.

What is true of the police is true of the entire government machinery in India. Its lack of accountability on the basis of established norms is the source of its tyranny and corruption.

For example, if every school were supervised by a committee of concerned residents and parents (instead of *babus* of the education ministry) who have the power to appoint and dismiss teachers on the basis of how well they teach their children, we will have more efficient teachers than the ones being presently appointed, ostensibly on merit, but without accountability to teach.

In most cases it does not matter who occupies a certain chair, what percentage of marks he or she got, whether the person is 'Forward' or 'Backward'—anyone who gets to acquire so much power without accountability will become inefficient, and tyrannically so, in many cases even deliberately so, because inefficiency of the government machinery invites bribes. Someone desperate to get a water connection will be compelled to pay a bribe if the files refuse to move without greasing palms.

The colonial rulers, who built this over centralized and authoritarian administrative machinery, like the present English educated elite, built a whole myth of efficiency around their administration. We were taught to believe that the ICS and other elite services had to be their preserve because Indians lacked the requisite talent and efficiency. We know from experience that they were indeed very efficient and talented in their techniques of exploitation and left this country's people impoverished and ravaged from their rule. Those who inherited power from the British have followed a similar pattern of 'efficiency'. Despite the trappings of democracy, the bureaucracy continues to be even more unaccountable than the politicians. At least politicians must go and seek a fresh mandate every five years; bureaucrats need not. The only legitimacy they have for their vast arbitrary powers is the need to secure a certain percentage of marks in certain examinations.

The key to a truly efficient government is accountability—and not so much the skill to pass an examination with high marks. Extending job reservations to more and more groups without a simultaneous effort to make the administrative machinery truly accountable to people will only permit additional social elites to acquire a vested interest in perpetuating this tyrannical system. The real issue, therefore is not who gets this or that government job, but how to make the government machinery really accountable to the people so that government functionaries do not operate as licensed looters and tyrants but as real servants of the people (as opposed to government servants).

Real accountability will be possible only with decentralization of power—with effective control over the administrative machinery by the local community including the power to hire and fire.

FLAWS IN THE MANDAL RECOMMENDATIONS

The ferocity of the anti-reservation movement and the blatantly elitist bias it displayed polarized the discussion with battle lines sharply drawn. One had to be either totally pro-Mandal or rabidly anti-Mandal. The political context of the announcement of the reservation policy only aggravated the polarization. The pre-reservationists were unwilling to acknowledge the serious shortcomings in the new reservation policy using the pretext that any such discussion would only add grist to the mill of anti-reservationists. On the side of anti-reservationists hysterical abuses became the standard way of expressing one's opposition. Even ordinary, mild-mannered students indulged in plain abuse and threats like 'Let any *churha* dare speak in favour of reservations and I will break his head'. Thus on both sides vituperation came to substitute dialogue with neither side willing to work out a settlement.

Among the serious flaws in the Mandal Commission recomendations are:

1. It builds a case for the OBC reservations by citing social disabilities suffered mainly by the SCs and STs. Among many others, the famous Eklavya story is used to make the point about hurdles placed by the upper castes in the way of lower castes acquiring learning and knowledge. But Eklavya would not qualify in the OBC category. He was a member of the Bhil tribe.

Only one instance is cited—that too not from history but from the epic Ramayana—the killing of Shambhuk at the hands of Ram as a punishment against a Sudra daring to perform *tapasya*. But the Commission omits to mention that such exclusive claims to knowledge and rituals status by the twice born castes were powerfully challenged by the *Bhakti* movements in India which gave birth to many important *sants* from non-Brahmanical caste groups as well. For example, Guru Nanak was from the Khatri biradari—a trading community of Punjab, Sant Kabir, a Julaha, Guru Raidas, a Chamar, Sant Tukaram from the Vani (*bania*) jati, Sant Chokhamela was a Mahar. These and many more spiritual leaders who came to play a vital role as religio-social reformers, were successful in changing the nature of religious discourse in an enduring way.

The Hinduism being practised today by ordinary people is far more influenced by the *Bhakti* tradition (despite the Sangh Parivar's attempts to destroy this legacy) than by the code of Manu or Vedic Puranic texts. But the Commission relies unnecessarily to build its case for reservations on the supposed low status prescribed in ancient texts to Sudra castes, even though these texts have no prescriptive value today. In reality, many of those designated as Sudras were politically dominant groups in different regions in pre-British India, just as today they have become strong enough to challenge the power of the national elite.

Lord Krishna, whose pronouncements on caste are cited from the Mahabharata, though born in a Kshatriya family was raised by a family belonging to Yadav community which today claims OBC status. The report admits that he 'linked an individual's caste to his karma instead of the accident of birth' ('the four-fold order was created by Me on the basis of quality and action') Statements like: 'A Brahmin is one who has the qualities of truthfulness, generosity, sympathy, a dislike for cruelty and a capacity to do *tapas*. This is a Brahmin and no one else'; 'a Kshatriya is one who protects the weak and oppressed', abound in the Mahabharata.

In short, even as far as ancient texts are concerned, there is a vast diversity of opinion and interpretation on the subject. Quotes can be selectively strung together to prove almost anything. Therefore, it is more appropriate to base our contemporary politics on the realities operating at the ground level today rather than a poorly understood past.

Given that most OBCs are drawn from peasant and artisanal castes, some of whom, despite their poor economic status, are the currently dominant social groups in the villages, the deprivation they suffer in terms of access to education and jobs is not as much due to social disabilities as the systematic exploitation of the rural sector and the failure to provide basic amenities to the villages. This is borne out by one, and perhaps the only, concrete example cited in the Mandal report from contemporary life to show the disabilities suffered by OBCs.

The report argues that it is unfair to compare the performance of a boy who comes from a well-to-do, urban educated family with easy access to books and other modern sources of information with that of a village boy whose backward class parents occupy a low social position in the village hierarchy. But then, when referring to the disabilities suffered by such a boy, there is very little mention of social, caste-based persecution. I quote from the report: 'His father owns a four-acre plot of agricultural land. Both his parents are illiterate and his family of eight lives huddled in a two-room hut. Whereas a primary school is located in his village, for his high school he had to walk a distance of nearly three kilometres both ways. Keen on pursuing higher studies, he persuaded his parents to send him to an uncle at the *tehsil* headquarters. He never received any guidance regarding the course of studies to be followed or the career to be chosen. Most of his friends did not study beyond middle-school level. He was never exposed to any stimulating cultural environment and he completed his college education without much encouragement from any quarter. Owing to his rural background, he has a rustic appearance. Despite his college education, his pronunciation is poor, his manner awkward and he lacks self-confidence.' Assuming that a boy from an educated middle-class family and this village boy 'had the same level of intelligence at the time of their birth, it is obvious that owing to vast differences in social, cultural and environmental factors, the former will beat the latter by lengths in any competitive field.' Even if the village boy is brighter 'the chances are that [he] will lag behind' the other boy 'in any competition where the selection is made on the basis of merit.'

It is noteworthy that in this entire narrative there is no mention of upper caste persecution and prejudice of the kind that is a reality for many of the SCs even today, but does not apply to most OBCs. There is also no mention that even an upper caste child living in a village would face the same disadvantages as an OBC child.

2. The disabilities suffered by the OBCs are primarily due to the bias in the modern education system and skewed economic structures. In our economic system the job market or the opportunities for self-employment do not build on or utilitize the enormous reservoir of skills and knowledge systems acquired by these groups over centuries. It puts a premium on mindless acquisition of mostly outdated, irrelevant information acquired in English and systematically downgrades and excludes those who do not have access to this deadening form of examination-oriented knowledge. The Mandal report has no answer to this more basic problem.

3. Devising a reservation policy without simultaneously working out far-reaching institutional reforms in the machinery of governance as the Mandal Commission does, will have several negative social consequences including for the OBCs whom it seeks to empower. It will make corruption and nepotism even more widespread because those among the OBCs who make it to the citadels of power, become beneficiaries of the system of non-accountability and thereby acquire a vested interest in perpetuating this tyrannical machinery. The most talented and ambitious among the BCs will thus be sucked into the system as petty tyrants and corrupt officials and lose the ability to be of help to their own community.

4. The Mandal Commission used fairly comprehensive social, educational and economic criteria for assessment of backwardness. But data was treated on the basis of caste divisions. An objective treatment of the information would have revealed clusters of backwardness correlated to other considerations, for example, women, peasantry in arid regions, families with low per capita land holdings, artisans particularly adversely affected since colonial days. Neither Article 15(4) of the Constitution nor the mandate of the Commission imposed the obligation to treat caste as units for assessment of backwardness, but the Commission had a clear ideological bias which pre-empted it exploring other routes.

5. While reservations for the SCs and STs is an easier affair because there is a greater affinity of life conditions among members of Scheduled Castes, the same cannot be as easily assumed for other castes, including those termed as OBCs. They are far less homogeneous as a group and vast variations exist in the life conditions of castes with the same nomenclature across regions, sometimes even within the same state. Therefore, some blatant absurdities have cropped up in the way the Mandal Commission drew up its list of beneficiary castes. For example, Yadavs in North India, or Malis in Maharashtra have already a good proportion of members doing well in all fields, economic, social, educational, and political. Even more absurd is the inclusion of all Bengalis in Madhya Pradesh as OBCs. Likewise all Marwaris in Tamil Nadu and Bengali Kayasthas in Assam are termed Backward by it.

6. While the creation of a caste-based elite has some potential of benefiting other members of the same caste group, the Mandal Commission recommendations do not take into consideration the vast enormity of differentiation between and within various castes to be benefited as OBCs. Unless remedial measures are worked out carefully, it

is likely that the benefits will be cornered by the economically and politically more powerful among the OBCs, for example, upper layer of Yadavs and Ahirs, at the cost of poorer and less organized caste groups who will not even have the benefit of downward percolation effect.

7. The most serious flaw in the currently proposed reservation scheme is that there is no exit principle in-built into the scheme. There are no review procedures for determining at what point a caste group must move out of the reservation scheme and how the progress of beneficiaries will be monitored. This despite the experience of states like Karnataka and Andhra where OBC reservations have brought new elite groups into dominance who refuse to give way to others. For example, the Vokaliggas and Lingayats in Karnataka have consolidated their hold over the political and administrative machinery in a big way and have successfully resisted all attempts to take them off the reservation list and include the groups lower down the economic and caste hierarchy. Since they are the ruling elite at the state level, wresting these concessions out of their hands is proving to be as difficult as it is from the traditional upper caste elite in the North. Had this exit principle been carefully worked out, the opposition to reservations in the North may have been less hysterical.

8. The Mandal report is curiously silent on how the benefits of reservations are to be reached to women of the OBCs. In any disadvantaged group, women are among the most oppressed. The hurdles that operate against the social advancement for OBC men are far more intense in the case of OBC women. For example, the literacy rate among OBC women is far lower than among OBC men.

Moreover, the culture of most North Indian OBC groups is far more oppressive for women than among their southern counterparts. Among the dominant peasant groups of North India, women are compelled to live under crippling restrictions on their mobility and social interactions and kept in virtual *purdah* among many castes. As things stand there are deep prejudices against women's education and employment within these communities. The literacy rate among OBC women is much lower than among OBC men and this gap is growing. These castes systematically exclude women from all decision-making processes. Women are not allowed to be even present in the *biradari panchayats,* leave alone take part in the deliberations.

This bias of viewing the culture of restrictions as a proof of high social status comes through even in the Mandal Commission Report. A high rate of women's labour participation is used as evidence of social backwardness of any group. Thus, the ability to withdraw women from labour outside the home compound and making them housebound is seen as a positive indicator of a community's well-being. Given that women have to bear the brunt of drudgery with the dual burden of house-work and field labour, it is likely that many women themselves may view their withdrawal from labour outside the house as a welcome relief.

However, the Commission has not paid attention to the fact that this withdrawal will result in a life of much greater demeaning dependence for women and has not acknowledged the need to redress the social, economic, and political power imbalance between OBC men and women.

Women are the real Dalits among these castes and have not benefited from the clout these castes have acquired through their political mobilization because they are disallowed any role in the social, political arena. Therefore, reaching these benefits to women is crucially important as it will help to democratize the internal functioning of caste organizations and encourage women's participation in it.

For OBC reservations to be meaningful, there should be a 50 per cent quota for women within the OBC quota at all levels of job recruitment. Otherwise women's status within these communities will be further downgraded as their men become increasingly powerful.

TOWARDS A NEW CONSENSUS

However, much more harmful than all the 'flaws' in the proposed reservation policy was the manner in which most anti-reservationists expressed their opposition. This movement was viciously elitist and showed callous disregard for the sentiments and aspirations of the vast majority of this country's people. It is not just over reservations that this insensitivity is being made manifest. In other matters too the Indian elite is no longer ashamed or guilty about the appalling conditions under which large sections of our population live.

During the freedom movement leaders like Gandhi had been fairly successful in inculcating a healthy sense of social obligation among the Indian elite. Instead of crudely seeking to protect and enhance their power and privileges, they were encouraged to think that they had to take some responsibility for bettering the life of the poor and disadvantaged sections of our society. Thus in the years following Independence, the elite continued to express, at least in words, a sense of responsibility in removing poverty and social injustice.

However, in the recent decades the Indian elite seems to have determinedly made a break with that legacy. They have come to treat India's poor as liabilities to be dispensed with. Instead of *'garibi hatao'* the dominant sentiment seems to be *'garib hatao'*. They are impatient with any measures that divert resources towards the poor, who are perceived as impediments in the elite's grand designs for themselves. They talk of dismantling the licence-permit-petition *raj* only to the extent that it affects them adversely. There is little care and concern to free the poor from the clutches of the bureaucracy or devising effective means to protect the poor from the rapacity of the rich.

When the elite in any society get to be brutally self-seeking and altogether lose sense of social obligation, their lawless unrestrained self-seeking begins to be emulated as a social norm by all other groups as well. Such a social atmosphere is least conducive to bringing about a more egalitarian, just, and humane social order. Therefore, winning over sections of the elite in the struggle for social justice needs to be undertaken seriously.

12

Marks, Merit, and Competence*
Are Reservations Inherently Anti-Efficiency?

The entire debate after the implementation of the Mandal Commission's recommendations centred around the fear that if the OBCs are not required to enter into an open competition with other candidates for government jobs, they will bring inefficiency and incompetence into those jobs because they got the jobs on account of the marks criteria being lower for them. It is argued that if these OBCs become engineers and doctors, the bridges they build would supposedly fall down and their patients die due to their incompetence. Some even went to the extent of saying that the 'security of state will be threatened' if OBCs are recruited into key services, especially the defence forces. Why do we deliberately forget that all the defence related scandals, illegal kickbacks, purchase of substandard weaponry and rampant corruption have so far mostly involved the upper castes who dominate the top layers of the defence establishment?

Are marks the only criteria for measuring merit, and that too with discerning precision? Is a candidate with 80 per cent marks really superior to the one with 79.5 per cent? Creating merit lists only on the basis of marks scored in a written exam amounts to placing an incongruous premium on its consequences. The argument that reservations necessarily generate incompetence is neither logical nor borne out by experience. We need to make a distinction between merit and competence. Reservations may sacrifice merit as defined by marks. But no well worked out

*First published in *Manushi* Issue Nos. 63–4 March–June 1991.

programme of reservations should abandon the required level of competence as a necessary qualification for job selection.

Those who harp on the stereotype of incompetent OBC doctors, engineers, civil servants and the like, willfully and maliciously invent a false version of reservations to mobilize bias.

Incompetence is indeed too high a price for a society to pay to bring about social justice. But competence and social justice need not be mutually exclusive. Compensatory discrimination makes provision for preferences where people fall within a zone of competence. Even if they may not appear at the top of the merit list, the candidates concerned should be expected to have an adequate level of competence for that particular job. Reservations are meant to compensate for social disadvantage. They are not meant to be a charity being doled out to the unemployable or those who are hopelessly unable. Contrary to popular prejudice that those who get in through the reserved quota are inherently incompetent, the experience in the Southern states, where reservations have been implemented for decades now, shows that the gap between the cut off points of the general, OBC and SC/ST groups is narrowing. In fact, reservations, by providing strong motivations, seem to have stimulated the spirit of competition and spurred the BC–SC/ST students to perform better, as is demonstrated by the table prepared by Era Chezhiyan and published in the *Hindu* of October 1990. Thus for example, in the MBBS course, the cut off point for open competition was 95.22 per cent. It was 93.18 per cent for Backwards, 89.2 per cent for the Most Backward, and 83.98 per cent for SCs. In using the above example, one is not attempting to strengthen the common understanding that marks obtained in examinations, either solely or even primarily, measure merit or even competence. In fact, the reliance on using the marks obtained criteria in admissions or jobs is more for the purpose of weeding out rather than selecting, thereby reducing the number of candidates from amongst whom final choice is to be made. It is important to keep in mind that most employers or institutions today carry their own selection tests rather than depend upon marks obtained in examinations. Thus marks obtained may be a worthwhile initial screening criteria, but should not be seen as the final validation of merit/competence.

It is neither being demanded nor required that incompetent people be recruited for jobs simply because they carry a certain caste certificate. In fact, our country's enduring problem lies precisely in the inability of the present job controlling elite to enforce even minimum levels of competence and efficiency standards in educational institutions and the running of the government machinery, even when they themselves dominate it.

From about 1920, when Indians began to replace the British, we have had certain upper caste groups increasingly monopolizing jobs in the government, in the universities, in medical institutions, in the legal profession and everywhere else. Not even the most ardent apologists of the status quo dare assert that the administrative machinery and other government-controlled institutions have functioned well. Their functioning is unanimously considered as intolerably inefficient and corrupt. The bureaucracy seems to respond only when approached through *sifarish* (string pulling) or with bribes. Be it the poor or rich, upper caste or low caste, these are the only two available routes for getting even the most simple work done through the government machinery. So hopelessly rotten is the system of administration that it does not function efficiently even for the elite groups, leave alone the poor. Even the privileged, whether they need a water or an electricity connection, a trading or a driving licence, a cooking gas cylinder or a phone connection, a transport or an industrial permit are faced with only two options—grease the palms of a government functionary or get a higher-up to put in a strong word of *sifarish* and the work gets done. Those unlucky enough not to have the money or the right connections just wait and wait and give up. Virtually nothing comes via standard public procedures or as a right. The system is deliberately designed in a way that only a kick from above or a bribe from below makes the machinery move. Those who do not have the power to get help via intervention from above have to grovel and humiliate themselves and are compelled to offer bribes to government officials to get their work done.

Anti-reservationists have indulged in much tear shedding over the woes of all those who will have to be treated by all those doctors who do not possess requisite 'merit' and will therefore pose a grave risk to the lives of their patients. With all the upper caste domination of the medical profession, we have one of the poorest health delivery systems resulting in one of the highest infant mortality and maternal mortality rates in the world. Even the most elementary health care is not available to the vast majority of India's people, especially in rural areas more than four decades after Independence. Even where trained doctors with fancy degrees are available, many function as licensed killers, for there is no system of accountability in the medical profession. They may kill you in a combination of different ways— including neglect, wrong medication and badly performed surgery. Yet, there is virtually no redress possible.

Every one of us is familiar with nightmarish stories of the brutality of the medical profession. Most public hospitals are so filthy and unhygienic that even a healthy person is likely to come back sick with infections from a few days of stay there. The use of sub-substandard medicines, wrong medication, unsterilized instruments are all routine affairs. This despite the fact that the medical profession, like most other money making elite professions, is dominated by the upper castes.

The great believers in meritocracy have never protested against the mushrooming of capitation fee colleges which routinely give admissions to the children of the rich who perform poorly in exams. Why are they not afraid of being treated by doctors who get into medical colleges not on the basis of their marks but the hefty donations their parents give to the college to purchase a seat for their sons?

There is very little merit evident in the way our educational institutions function from the school to the university level. Barring a few elite institutions, most of our schools are not even imparting basic reading and writing skills to the students. This is true not only of our rural schools, about whom the less said the better, but even urban schools run in metropolitan cities.

The following report reveals the real state of affairs in a majority of schools, especially those in rural areas.

'All the 74 students of class X of the government school in Channa village of Sangrur district failed in the matriculation exams held in March 1990'. The reason? Just a fortnight before the exams the Punjab militants placed an announcement in the local newspapers banning cheating on exams and threatened 'dire consequences' to those who violated their order. In nearby Bhalwan village only two per cent of the students cleared the exam. It was not very different in other schools of the districts. One of the teachers explained the high failure rate thus: 'Students were previously promoted up to class 10 as a matter of course. All one needed was a *sifarish*. Only in class 10 do they face Board exams. There was rampant copying here as well.' As the militants forbade cheating, the students failed enmasse (*Sunday Observer*, 30 December 1990, p.12).

Year after year as a college teacher I have had to deal with students the majority of whom cannot write ten correct sentences in any language, including their mother tongue. In three years of college we compound the damage already done to them after 12 years of similar schooling. I have as little accountability as a teacher as the doctors who have the licence to kill without suffering any consequences. Our universities are mass producing degree holding semi-literates. The teachers, educationists, and bureaucrats responsible for this continuing crime against students are mostly upper-caste 'merit-*wallas*'.

The press tried to systematically romanticize the participation of students in the anti-reservation movement as proof of their idealism in wanting to restore the primacy of merit in academic institutions and in the job market. As a teacher I fervently wish this was true. There have hardly been any serious attempts by the students in India to protest against the absurd and irrelevant curriculum, poor quality teaching or inadequate library and related facilities. Students unions have so far confined themselves to protesting against bus fare hikes, fees enhancement, admission quotas, removal of this or that principal or vice-chancellor, and indulged in gang warfare on behalf of various political parties.

Among the teachers the situation is even more dismal. The teachers' unions have almost never taken up the issue of improving teaching standards. They have focused exclusively on their economic demands— hikes in pay and allowances, increase in medical benefits, housing and car loans, etcetra.

A large number of Delhi teachers who went on strike three times in the last eight years to oppose, among other things, the introduction of the principle of 'merit' in their promotion scheme, suddenly become champions of meritworthiness for jobs. Those who talk of merit in obtaining jobs or education are deliberately overlooking the fact that in our present education system, merit is judged by the percentage one secures in examinations, which requires no more than the ability to memorize and reproduce answers to five questions from among one dozen one has mugged from guidebooks or class notes.

The hollowness of the argument about primacy of merit comes out clearly if one considers that as far as the English educated elite are concerned, almost 100 per cent of them manage to get admitted to the best of institutions for their education and almost none among them ever remain unemployed. The curriculae are set to their convenience. In fact, they are alienated from people's needs, people's knowledge and their environment. And through the system of education that they devised to suit their needs and imposed on others, they systematically destroyed much of the valuable skills and knowledge possessed by groups which were unable to acquire 'modern' English education.

Kancha Ilaiah provides a good example of this process: '...till 1920 in districts like Nizamabad and Karimnagar, wootz steel was being manufactured out of iron ore available in that region. The steel that was being made there was being exported to Persia only to be converted into beautiful swords to be sold in the entire European maket... Who after all were these steel-makers? They hailed from a caste called "Yanadees"... they had developed a remarkable knowledge of the metal ores available in these areas as well as of the physical and geological characteristics of the region. They had developed crucibles of such shape and quality that they could withstand the 1000°c heat required for smelting the steel for 24 hours. Several extremely sophisticated engineering calculations had gone into converting the clay into a crucible wall. A lot of skills had gone into preparing the charcoal and the furnaces in order to heat the ore-stones and separate the steel from the ore. Yet all these people were called "Yanadees" (ignorant people).' Without a doubt the children of these people would make much better engineers and technologists if allowed the opportunity to enter IITs and engineering colleges. But the way our curriculum is devised, none of these children will ever qualify using the 'merit' criteria. And most of them are likely to be pushed towards menial, unskilled occupations, as is happening with a whole range of peasant and artisan groups with the decline of rural industry and economy, and condemned to live as the 'backwards' of our society.

It is no coincidence that the upper caste elite who are deadly opposed to reservations are as threatened by moves to use the regional languages as the language of administration in place of English. For example, the reaction against Mulayam Singh Yadav's move to introduce Hindi as the language of administration in UP, replacing English, was as hostile and virulent as it was to the Mandal Commission recommendations. Much of the supposedly superior merit flaunted by the national elite would disappear into thin air the day knowledge of English ceased to be the unfailing passport to exclusive power and privilege. When they have to begin operating in a language that even ordinary people can understand and use with ease, the gap will narrow down easily, as has been happening in the Southern states. And if we go further and reform the curriculum in a way that knowledge and skills actually required for the efficient functioning of our economy, polity, and civic life are being generated and updated in our schools and universities, those who are condemned as backward today may even acquire a distinct advantage over some others.

If we had built an education system based on the upgradation of local skills of the peasant and artisanal groups in our society, children of ironsmiths, weavers, and peasants would by a gradual transition have gone on to become much better metallurgists and textile engineers and botanists. They would not then have been compelled to work as rickshaw-pullers and domestic servants in urban centres after the systematic distruction of rural crafts and industry, and then thrown a few grudging crumbs by way of job reservations. The negative aspects of the caste system could have been more effectively countered if the principle of hereditary division of labour had been taken to its logical conclusion and seats in engineering, science, and technology institutions were reserved for the children of artisans, and in medical institutions for traditional *vaids, dais,* and *hakims.* They would have advantages in certain areas over those from upper castes who have no other skills except book learning. Instead, we are directing too many people's aspirations into becoming inefficient peons, clerks and petty bureaucrats, jobs which are parasitic for the entire society and encourage petty tyranny.

Taking into account caste-based social division of labour would in fact destroy the pernicious aspects of the caste system sooner than all the laws and constitutional provisions banning discrimination on the basis of caste. It would also have improved the quality of skills in all concerned professions. If entry into modern elite professions could not be the monopoly of the upper caste English educated elite, they would lose their pre-eminent position very soon.

13

Majoritarianism vs Minoritarianism*
Hindu–Muslim Relations in Post-Independence India

*In this essay I focus almost exclusively on Majoritarianism and
Minoritarianism as it is reflected in Hindu–Muslim relations in India. The
continuing conflicts between these two communities threaten to jeopardize
the entire society and seriously endanger our otherwise resilient democracy.
This is not to suggest that this is the only form of ethnic conflict India needs
to confront. However, I believe that if we can find a workable solution to
Hindu–Muslim relations in India, we would find it easier to deal with all
our other ethnic problems.*

For thousands of years, aside from limited and brief exceptions such as
in Periclean Athens, the idea that the State needed to demonstrate
support of a majority of its people to claim legitimacy of its rule in
society would seem so ridiculous that no one would ever suggest it. Use
of majorities in decision-making probably arose historically out of the
need for deciding on special issues in small elite groups such as the
Senate of Rome or the Council in Venice. These elite bodies had
stringent rules for determining qualifications for membership, including
aristocratic birth. The idea of 'majority' thus had emerged in the
context of decision-making within a homogenous group, as a mode of
clinching persistent differences in a group of individuals of more or less

---

*'Majoritarianism vs Minoritarianism' paper presented at a conference at the
Indian Institute of Advanced Studies in 1997. The essay was revised in 2003.
© Madhu Purnima Kishwar.

equal status and similar backgrounds. The preferred mode was, however, to reach a consensus rather than to force a 'division of votes' that would divide the group into identifiable subgroups as a 'majority' and a 'minority'—'we' and 'they'.

The assembly of armed male citizens, that might have been one of the progenitors of later political institutions, made important choices in many societies at crisis points. However, to be effective they would usually have to come to something close to a consensus on an issue that would have been chewed over and carefully prepared long before it was put to them. Then they would ordinarily shout 'hurrah' as their betters asked of them, or display such vehement opposition as to frighten leaders who were afraid of their rising up and taking direct and immediate action against their rulers if their wishes were not heard. In urban areas, even as late as in medieval Rome, it was amazing how often vehement rejection by the ordinary people of Rome could and would overturn rulers as powerful as the Pope and force them to flee the city, even during a period when Papal power could humble many of the mightiest monarchs of Europe.

In traditional micro-societies seeking consensus rather than divisions, leaders who could display patience and conciliatory or manipulative capacities to elicit consensus, or something as close to it as possible, were the most prized lot. A decision by majority would not be useful, since the participation and agreement of significant minorities was essential to keep the community from internal conflicts that could seriously affect their viability and even their survival.

It would probably have seemed impossible to pre-modern peoples that a majority drawn from an amalgam of warriors, shamans, priests, women, farmers, slaves, craftsmen, lineage family members, recent settlers and landless serfs, debtors, and all the other categories, some crosscutting, into which people were divided, could have conceptual or political significance. It would seem more logical that different groups or individuals would make decisions about different matters using different rules, and that on almost all matters majorities, even within the family, would be irrelevant. Decisions would not be made by society on a territory-wise basis as often as on a sectoral and status basis (for more dispersed areas for the ruling status groups and on a very local level for the ordinary folk).

Most decisions were made on the basis of custom. Custom, though a most powerful force, was not always so decisive as it might look to someone on the inside of a mainly pre-literate society where selective recollection could smooth over many awkward problems. For custom was interpretatively used; in effect lending itself to different interpretations and uses. Here, also, consensus, rather than division, was a preferred mode of overcoming differences. Nevertheless, even powerful rulers who wished to be seen as legitimate hesitated before overturning custom.

Few could have realized that over the millennia the model for majority rule by the people of a society would evolve out of the assemblies of representatives of the most powerful estates (status groupings) in the society. At these meetings both religious and secular decisions were made establishing doctrine, legitimating the rule of a religious or secular monarch or dynasty, and considering the ruler's requests for funds.

However, as more powerful states arose in the last couple of hundred years, some rulers saw that in order to compete with other growing political powers it was becoming more and more vital to mobilize as much as possible of the large relatively passive general population under their control, to get the rural and urban folk to participate actively in the development of the polity under the direction of their rulers. At first ordinary people's participation was seen primarily as a device useful, among other things, for raising the proportion of population taken into the army through the practice of some form of conscription. Later it was considered advantageous to national or ruler power to widen participation in assemblies and to reduce the limitations on eligibility for entry into these assemblies.

These representative assemblies took over the rules used in elite assemblies, and by adding additional precedents evolved, as a consequence of their own ever-increasing experience, further developed rules of procedure for deciding issues brought before them. One of the most useful decision-making rules was to decide issues on the basis of a single vote per representative. Some issues required more than a majority for approval. But as time went by more and more issues began to be decided based on majorities, and sometimes even on pluralities among those voting on an issue. However, at almost all times the system worked more effectively when the issues brought before these assemblies for decision were not such as necessitated abrupt major adjustments in the power relations within the society, or that endangered important components of the political body. The notion of counting the votes of eligible individuals in deciding who these representatives to the assemblies were to be slowly became accepted, and limitations on eligibility to vote for these representatives decreased in many states.

However, in today's world, rule by majority vote of all adults—males and females, poor and rich—has come to be considered the hallmark of democracy. The western nations, which first developed present-day democracies, are seen as role models for building democracy in the rest of the world. The idea of rule by majority vote became distorted in the twentieth century, the pre-eminent age of nationalism, as it almost deified head counting, and thus tended to move towards majoritarianism—that is, almost total control over the fate of the minority by the majority. In some countries, census counts become an instrument for a group to claim supremacy through attempting to demonstrate it is a majority in a particular area. This has escalated ethnic tensions to unprecedented levels of conflict and bloody slaughters.

If we look around the world today we find that the original idea of democracy by majority vote is working well only in those societies that have:

(i)   either small, homogeneous populations where there is a broad consensus regarding the basic organizational principles of that society as, for example, in Sweden and Denmark; or

(ii) some multicultural, multi-ethnic populations where over long periods of time the common acceptance of certain workable political rules of decision-making have more or less allowed for their evolution into functioning polities (e.g., Switzerland, Canada, USA).

But even in the most well functioning western democracies a certain equilibrium between the majority and minority populations has been arrived at by setting definite limits to minority rights. To begin with the ethnicity principle has been secularized whereby minorities are assured rights of political participation and of sharing public resources but the right of political separation is not on the agenda at all. The minorities in these societies are now being given special spaces for cultural expression and identity assertion in the context of highly homogenized societies, but not the right to challenge or veto the basic principles of governance such as questioning individual freedom or seeking parallel governance by subjugating individual members of their group in ways that conflict with their citizenship rights. In other words, they can live as distinct communities but do not have the right to declare themselves as separate nationalities. Since their right to life, to liberty and freedom to pursue occupations is guaranteed by the nation-state, minorities in these democracies are not permitted the right to challenge the nation-state itself.

Even so, it is important to note that Europe began to have a stable political context in which to have majority rule on just a few mutually agreed upon areas of political functioning only after tens of millions of Europeans were killed in total wars or were exterminated or were forced to migrate. Democracies of European settlers such as those in the US, Canada and Australia, were built only after the indigenous populations were either wiped out or confined to reservations and peripheral areas.

And now that Europe is once again forced to confront non-European peoples on its soil who were originally asked to come to provide temporary 'guest workers' as cheap labour, there is a fresh resurgence of violent forms of racism. The breakout of a genocidal conflict in the former Yugoslavia after the collapse of communism and the ethnic conflicts that have broken out in other areas of Eastern Europe show that most parts of Europe have not learned even yet how to evolve genuine democracies within a framework of ethnic diversity.

THE INDIAN EXPERIENCE

By contrast, '...India is a striking example of a state maintaining a reasonable democracy despite its plural structure and profound internal dissension.'[1] But much of our political mess has arisen out of our uncritical acceptance of many of the continental European national ideologies that make the mechanical equivalency of ethnic and national identities the keystone of nation building and head counts of ethnic majorities a license to carry out all sorts of genocidal acts.

Thus, while the principle of majority vote may have proved facilitative in areas where there has been basic agreement about the ruling principles of state functioning, it has created disastrous consequences when it is applied to making fundamental choices regarding the character and guiding principles of the nation-state, especially regarding the critical choice of who is to have what rights and who is not to have certain rights. Significant populations of many countries have been 'constitutionally' disenfranchised, expelled, annihilated, or sub-humanized by the application of this 'democratic' principle.

In the twentieth century it became more and more vital to belong in some sense to one or the other of the nation-states that have divided up the whole world, leaving no significant areas out of its all-

---

[1]Smith, Anthony D. (ed.), *Ethnicity and Nationalism*, New York: E.J. Brill, 1992, p. 44.

encompassing system, leaving no security for those not under the protection of one or the other of these powers. And the 'nations' to whom all the states belong are implicitly, but inevitably, articulated permanent and fixed ethnic 'majorities'. Nationalist ideologies in these newly growing or forming states failed to distinguish clearly between the use of majority votes as a decision-making rule on subordinate issues within a society that had achieved over time a degree of general agreement on principles, and majority rule as a device to decide survival issues in a society where some of its subgroups had not come to an agreement about guiding principles, basic ground rules, or what is up for reconsideration and what should continue to be decided by previous customs or agreements.

In our modern age of nationalism we have thus come to confuse a simplified and primitive notion of majority vote with the deadly notion of majority rule based not on decisions on issues but rather on 'objective' characteristics of a majority of individuals in the nation, such as skin colour, language, cultural traits, ancestry, religion, and other markers that have little to do with issues the people living in a territory need to decide among themselves. This has allowed a large-scale political mobilization of populations around these characteristics producing almost permanent categories of 'majority' and 'minorities' with certain leaders claiming that they both represent and control these as undifferentiated entities, constituting primary units of the polity as a whole. At least this is how the majority–minority concept seems to have developed in India over the years as a criterion of separation and division of population rather than a principle of decision-making. This peculiar patterning of difference in our polity emerged with the formation of the colonial state. As in so many other aspects of the development of our national consciousness, British administrative devices contributed to the way it was shaped. They created an awareness of there being one overriding majority–minority division, that between the Muslims and the Hindus, from the very early censuses, starting in the late nineteenth century. As Van der Veer puts it: 'This is not to say that there was no division of Hindu and Muslim communities in the precolonial period. There was: the division was not a colonial invention. But to count these communities and to have leaders represent them was a colonial novelty, and it was fundamental to the emergence of religious nationalism.'[2]

---

[2]Van der Veer, Peter, *Religious Nationalism: Hindus and Muslims in India*, Berkeley: University of California Press, 1994, pp. 19–20.

He goes on to point out 'the odd effect of the census was that it simultaneously cut the society up into infinitesimal units and yet created a huge "Hindu majority," together with several "minorities," of which the most significant was the Muslim' (Ibid., p. 26).

The notion that an arbitrarily defined internal majority could claim sovereign rights over parts of the newly emerging and yet undefined nation-state where they were in a majority led to the disastrous Partition in 1947. The breakaway of Pakistan was justified on the ground that the sole spokesman for a majority of those resident in certain provinces could claim sovereignty for those who had been born into the same faith. This sovereignty, in turn, was supposed to give him the right to push out from their homes many millions of people merely because they were not of the same faith despite the fact that the two communities had lived together for centuries sharing common territory, languages and culture.

Sadat Hasan Manto's powerful story *Toba Tek Singh* describes the bewilderment of the 'mad' hero who resists being forcibly moved to a new state of which he is a 'national' while he has no right to live where his family had lived for centuries. He finally collapses on the imaginary line called the 'Indo–Pakistan border'. This ending brings out the tragedy and the absurdity behind the notion of carving out nation-states on the basis of a politically manipulated majority vote.

The dominant political leadership of India was determined not to go the way of Pakistan and identify the state with any particular religion; they publicly committed themselves instead to maintaining a secular state within which religious minorities would have the same rights and responsibilities as citizens. Several additional measures were included that were aimed at protecting the sensibilities of religious minorities against certain violations of their internal customs and religious practices. But, despite all this, Muslim relations with Hindus and Sikhs in India have come to be very heavily influenced by the continuing volatile relations between the two states that have resulted in numerous Indo–Pakistan conflicts since 1947.

THE LIMITS OF HINDU MAJORITARIANISM

Hindu–Muslim relations in post-Independence India are increasingly becoming hostage to a similar ideology to the one that provided the political legitimacy for the breakaway of the Muslim majority areas in 1947. This ideology is now used by the Sangh Parivar combine to consolidate the Hindus into a large vote bank so that they can gain power. They claim that because there are more Hindus than there are any other religious groupings in post-Partition India, they therefore ought to have the right to do what was done in Pakistan, namely implement a policy of the majority ethnic domination over the polity as a whole, and in the process, establish a complete equivalence between the ethnic majority and the nation. After coming to power at the centre, in 1999, important BJP leaders changed considerably on this issue and made significant moves towards building bridges, not only with the Muslim community in India but also with the peoples and government of Pakistan.

The task of extremist Hindu nationalists who wish to follow the Jinnah path is made unachievable because in actual fact, India is a country of minorities. The term Hindu encompasses many crosscutting identities. No one is merely a Hindu. To be a Hindu you have to belong to one of the many sects or groups—Shaivite, Vaishnavite, Arya Samaji, Sanatani, Radhasoami, Ramnami, Satnami. The list is endless. Furthermore, you have to be a member of a particular *jati* in order to qualify as a Hindu-Brahmin, Kayastha, Rajput, Jat, Vokkaligga, Lingayat, Julaha, Mahar, Yadav, Kurmi, Musahar, Reddy, Kamma. The list is still more endless. At the *jati* level, there are only two all-India communities within the Hindu fold—the Brahmins and the Vishwakarmas. Like all others they too are as much rooted in their linguistic and regional identity as they are in their *jati* or caste identity. For instance, it is not enough to say you are a Brahmin. For all operative purposes it matters as much whether you are a Kashmiri Brahmin, Punjabi, Tamil or Gujarati Brahmin. If you take into account all these functional identities, the idea of a monolithic Hindu majority becomes absurd. These identities are functional not only at the ritual, or cultural level, not just in deciding marriage alliances but also political alliances and voting behaviour. This is precisely why attempts by the Sangh Parivar to unite the Hindu community into a solid monolith have proved not just slippery but led to a powerful backlash of caste assertion.

In fact, at one level Sangh Parivar politics is achieving the very opposite of what they intended to accomplish. The more they insist on Hindus being 'one' the more their political ambition for hegemony is challenged by a variety of leaders of the lower and peasant castes. It has led to their political isolation because this 'majority making' is interpreted by others not just as an anti-Muslim enterprise but also an attempt to strengthen the hegemony of upper castes.

There are indeed serious limitations on the construction of a Hindu political majority. This is an important reason that parties of religious nationalists remain nervous and confused, and find themselves unable to push their agenda as far and as fast as they would like. In certain ways the Sangh Parivar leadership perceive themselves not as the representatives of the overwhelming majority their rhetoric would indicate, but rather as a besieged political minority trying to consolidate a recalcitrant vote bank of an incredibly heterogeneous group of ethnic and religious identities into a united vote bank. At some more fundamental level these leaders recognize that Hindus can only be a 'conditional majority': that is, only if various communities that come within the Hindu fold are willing to submerge their other identities to facilitate the Sangh Parivar's aspiration of homogenizing the almost unhomogenizable Hindu communities. They are also nervous about the fact that the SCs and STs who together constitute 20 per cent of the population have proved soft targets for conversion to Christianity, Islam, and Buddhism. Even without conversion they have very little stake in upholding 'Hindu unity' under an upper caste leadership.

In fact these self-proclaimed leaders of a Hindu majority find it difficult to maintain their hegemony even among those castes who see themselves as firmly within the Hindu fold but are unwilling to incorporate themselves politically in the Hindutva movement of the BJP and the Sangh Parivar. For all the efforts of the BJP leaders, their use of the concept of Hindutva to rally support among the rural peasant castes has had very limited appeal. Leaders like Mulayam Singh Yadav, Laloo Prasad Yadav, and the leaders of the numerous regional and caste-based parties, all of whom have a widespread regional support base among a variety of peasant castes, diminish the likelihood that the Sangh Parivar will be able to unify all Hindus under their banner. Linguistic and regional diversity among the Hindus acts as another serious check on the majoritarian aspirations of the Sangh Parivar. These internal doubts about the feasibility of uniting all Hindus into a single community under their leadership makes them paranoid and drives their perception of Muslims as a community with a monolithic solidarity.

The failure of the Sangh Parivar to construct and communicate a meaningful political programme to unite the Hindus makes them appear as attempting to mobilize large segments of the Hindu communities on one single issue—anti-Muslim sentiment. By presenting Muslims as an untrustworthy anti-national community who are acting as a cohesive and united power threatening the security of the Hindu majority, the Sangh

Parivar can portray itself as the vehicle for uniting a divided Hindu community in its own defence. Paradoxically, however, every effort the Sangh Parivar makes to unite all Hindus in its 'hate Muslim' campaign also results in promoting greater unity in a disparate Muslim community than has ever existed heretofore. It prods Muslims into forging a single-issue political programme and strategy to defeat the BJP and its anti-Muslim confederates.

In reality, Muslims are far from being a monolithic community. Muslims of Kerala, for instance, share much more in common with Malayali Hindus than they do with Muslims of Rajasthan. The caste system is pretty much intact within the Muslims—the Qureshis, the Gujjars, the Jats among Muslim peasants, the Kasais, Ansaris and various other occupational groups reflect a great deal of cultural diversity. However, the anti-Muslim thrust of Sangh Parivar politics is ironically ending up unifying the Muslims on select issues far more than it has unified the Hindus.

Thus, the political polarization in actual terms works out to be not so much Hindus versus Muslims but the BJP versus the Muslims, with the BJP trying to project itself as the sole representative and most legitimate voice of all Hindus, despite their failure to gather all major groupings under their banner, and the Muslims willing to put their weight in favour of whoever is capable of defeating the BJP.

In my interviews in Meerut during the 1993 election campaign, a recurring theme in the responses of Muslims—men, women and children alike—was the all-out opposition to the BJP as the promoters of anti-Muslim rioting. I quote from one such typical interview with one Sarfaraz Alam who lives in one of the outlying villages of Meerut but comes to work in the city everyday:

> No matter how good the BJP candidate, we cannot ever support him under any circumstances because the party is really bad. The main problem we have with the BJP is that even if there is a minor scuffle or quarrel between little kids, they all gang up and make a big fuss out of it. For instance, the neighbourhood in which I live has always been peaceful. It has no history of Hindu–Muslim fights. Even during the 1987 riots not a single policeman was required to be posted there because the Hindus and the Muslims have such good relations with each other. But in 1991, during the *rathyatra* days, young BJP kids got into a minor fight with some Muslim kids while playing cricket. This was all in fun. But in no time the entire

lot of BJP leaders descended on our neighbourhood and created so much tension that we began to fear the administration might have to call in the army. They are forever looking for opportunities to convert even kids' fights into a communal clash.

Interestingly, this same man, Sarfaraz Alam, also told me that, even though for him the personal honesty of the candidate was an important criterion in deciding who to vote for, and even though he and other Muslims recognized that the local BJP candidate for that particular election was not a corrupt man, there was no possibility they would vote for him, simply because he belonged to the BJP. And the BJP did indeed lose this seat primarily because Muslims ended up voting more as a bloc while the Hindu votes could not be similarly consolidated, despite the organizational finesse of the BJP and the relatively clean image of their candidate.[3]

In each constituency that I was able to monitor, Muslims appeared to wait as long as possible during the campaign to pick out the candidate who showed the best potential to defeat the BJP and did not have a track record of fomenting communal hatred—whatever his other limitations—and vote for him *en bloc* so as to forestall as much as possible the victory of those candidates who saw communal riots as a political opportunity. The careful calculations of this single issue minority played an important role in preventing the BJP from coming to power in UP in the 1993 election and marginalized the Congress party altogether.

The failure of the BJP and its political allies to unite the Hindu castes and linguistic groups into a political community is not only due to their inability to cope with the diversity among Hindus, but also to their failure to evolve a meaningful and comprehensive political programme. For instance, none of the BJP supporters I interviewed could explain why they considered the BJP pro-Hindu even while that was its most important qualification in the eyes of its supporters. The following conversation with a young man in his twenties is typical of many others. He proudly admitted to being an enthusiastic supporter of the BJP 'because they are very forthright and do not mince words'. The most he could tell me was that 'They speak of Hindu *hita* because they want us to unite against the Muslims.' How will that increase Hindu welfare? He had no answer.

---

[3]Author interview during 1993 elections in Meerut, Uttar Pradesh.

The BJP is aware of the vagueness of its societal goals. This vagueness keeps the party desperately looking for issues that have the potential of becoming emotive symbols—Ram Mandir yesterday, the Idgah Maidan in Hubli or the Bhojshala in Bhopal another day.[4] It is a party always itching for a fight with the Muslims but also perpetually nervous because it can never be sure that it has picked issues that will not antagonize in some unforeseen way some parts of its own constructed constituency as has happened in various assembly elections since the demolition of the Babri Masjid.

Thus, the rich and vibrant diversity within Hindu society is one of the most important factors that makes it impossible for Hindus to be brought together for murderous purposes on a very large scale for long periods of time as, for instance, Germans could be united for the purpose of exterminating the Jews. The brazen demolition of one mosque, something of relatively minor significance when compared to genocide, produced widespread dismay and rejection among large sections of the Hindu community, whereas the Nazis' campaigns against the Jews in Europe did not produce any comparable condemnation of the Nazis in Europe while they were proceeding through the early stages of carrying out their deadly project. The internal diversity of the Hindu community is its best guarantee against politicians with Hitlerian ambitions and against deadly forms of majoritarianism. This is what explains the compulsion of the BJP to give up many of its divisive agendas and move towards a consensual polity, if it has to be in power. The Indian voter has made it very clear that they do not trust it to hold power on their own and that they need the restraining influence of their coalition partners, most of whom represent constituencies that do not endorse the anti-Muslim thrust of *Hindutvavadis*. This perhaps explains why post-1999 Advani has transformed himself from being just a leader of *Hindutvavad* to being a national leader who is working to build bridges with elements of the Muslim community in India, including those like the Hurriyat who have pursued secessionist politics.[5]

---

[4]Author interview during 1993 election in Meerut.

[5]There has been a steady change in the BJP's attitude, at least at the national level ever since Vajpayee assumed Prime Ministership of India with the BJP in power at the Centre as a leading partner of the NDA alliance. However, the severe drubbing the BJP got in the 2004 elections was in part due to the shameful handling of the Gujarat riots by the BJP.

REASONS FOR SANGH PARIVAR'S WIDENING APPEAL

Yet there is no denying that in recent years the Sangh Parivar has had a remarkable degree of success in consolidating a large vote bank among the Hindus who are beginning to assert majoritarian tendencies in an unprecedented way, especially towards the Muslims. In fact, this is the only issue on which a large section of the Hindus are capable of thinking and behaving like a monolith and lose their sense of balance and proportion. However, the success of the Sangh Parivar derives from their appealing to very deep-seated fears, resentments, and anxieties of the Hindu community that go beyond the narrow electoral success or setbacks of the BJP and allied outfits and find echoes among Hindus across the political spectrum from the Congress to the Communist Party cadres, Janata Dal rank and file and even the educated among the Dalits.

A peculiar feature of the Hindu community in India vis-à-vis the Muslims in particular is that despite being a preponderant majority of 80 per cent with Muslims constituting 12 per cent of the population, the educated Hindus have actually developed phobias and fears characteristic of minorities. Many 'secularists' attribute it mainly to the machinations of the Sangh Parivar, and underplay the depth of this sentiment among the general population. It is important to recognize the factors that give rise to these fears rather than be dismissive about them.

After Independence the Muslims left behind in India were largely poor and illiterate, and urban Muslims were largely confined to ghettos. However, the wary Hindu majority in the North remained fearful of Muslim minoritarianism because of the pattern of issues the post-Independence Muslim leadership chose to highlight for uniting Muslims, as well as the manner in which this Muslim leadership has tried to join all Muslims into a mindless monolith keeping the memories of Partition alive.

The modern, educated Hindus have internalized a deep sense of inferiority complex and insecurity over the fact that small armies of invaders were able to conquer large parts of the Indian subcontinent with relative ease starting with Mahmud Ghazni and Mohammad Ghauri in the eleventh and twelfth centuries. Even though the Mughals who came later, settled down here and adopted this country as their own, unlike previous invaders and subsequent British rulers, most Hindus see their history as one of more than a 1000-year-long subjugation to alien rulers. At the same time they are taught to believe that theirs was one of the great ancient civilizations. Why then were they so powerless to face foreign invaders? Colonial historians have been successful in convincing most educated Indians that their political defeat was due to theirs being an internally divided society on the basis of caste, region, religion, sect, language and so on, whereas the invaders came from relatively more cohesive societies which gave them a common sense of purpose. This has made most educated Hindus come to perceive religious and cultural diversity among the Hindus as the prime source of their 'weakness' even while they themselves are unable to overcome their own multilayered ethnic identities. They have also been told that the tolerance inherent in the polytheistic, non-Semitic faiths leads to their inability to unite and resist foreign aggression. So many among the educated have come to associate tolerance with 'weakness'. The Hindus have thus by and large not only lost the confidence and habit to rule but are prone to believing that they could be conquered and enslaved again by the Muslims or any other determined foreign power. The presence of some hostile and some powerful Muslim countries all around India makes it easy to feed their fantasy and fears of another round of subjugation. In this context, even the continuing large inflow of illegal Bangladeshi migrants many of who come as destitutes in search of menial forms of livelihood, gets to be interpreted as part of a well-planned Islamic invasion. Many Hindus have come to seriously believe that the Muslims plan to render Hindus into a minority by a combination of over-breeding, illegal migration, and invasion from neighbouring Islamic countries. The demographic changes in some of the border areas are being viewed with great anxiety.[6]

In this context, when a leader like Shahabuddin insists on calling the magazine he edits *Muslim India* rather than *Indian Muslims* or even *Muslim Indians*, people begin to have phobias that the hidden agenda behind Muslim politics is to Islamicize India in alliance with the surrounding Muslim nations. Or, at the very least it is a statement of separation like the Partition. That only strengthens the votaries of a 'Hindu India', even though Shahabuddin himself denies this interpretation.

Moreover, when they see that in all the Muslim countries, not just Pakistan and Bangladesh, minorities live very vulnerable lives as third

---

[6]See for example, Joshi, A.P., M.D. Srinivas and J.K Bajaj, *Religious Demography of India*, Chennai: Cenre for Policy Studies, 2003.

class citizens and have to accept many restraints the majority imposes on them, they feel Hindus are being 'weak' in not being able to impose their writ on the Muslim minority. In this scenario the Gandhian, Nehruvian, and the supposedly secularist approach in handling Hindu–Muslim equations are seen as betrayals of the Hindu interests. They have come to believe that their leaders helplessly succumbed to the Partition of the country because they were not as firm and determined as the Muslim leadership. That a minority could succeed in forcing its will on the majority in such a cataclysmic way has left a very deep scar among some Hindus.

Very few understand that leaders like Gandhi opposed ethnic cleansing in India not only on moral grounds but also because their notions of self-interest were enlightened. Mahatma Gandhi took the stand he did against Hindu nationalist movements in part because he saw the evil behind the notion of majoritarianism. He also refused to accept the idea that Muslims were a separate nationality. He insisted that they were one among many diverse communities of the subcontinent who had for centuries before the coming of the age of nationalism, co-existed with various Hindu communities, evolving workable norms of mutual accommodation through a process of give and take. And history has proved that Gandhi was more right than Jinnah.

Muslim nationalism may have succeeded in creating Pakistan, based on the majority rule principle, but Pakistan in turn came to be challenged by Bangladeshi nationalism based on the same rule but on account of linguistic and cultural differences, despite their religion being common. Even after the breakaway of Bangladesh, Pakistan remains faced with acute internal dissensions on account of Sindhi, Baluchi, Pakhtooni, Mohajir, and Punjabi assertions of their right to separate national identities based on their being ethnic majorities in certain areas, even though all are Muslims.

If we accept the logic that, within the territory of the nation-state, every majority has unlimited rights to subjugate, eliminate or push out as a minority one after the other all the heterogeneous amalgam of peoples that make up the Indian nation-state, we will likely be forced to live through an unending series of tragedy after tragedy of ethnic cleansing, murderous riots, and political chaos.

CONFLICTING NATIONALISMS, NOT A RELIGIOUS CONFLICT

The Hindu–Muslim conflict whether in Kashmir or in the rest of India is not a religious or theological conflict between two contrary religions, as is often assumed but a conflict between two differing and opposing versions of nationalism.

According to Balraj Puri: 'For the Hindus, the difference between Hinduism and Indian nationalism, Indian history and Hindu mythology, national and mythical heroes is altogether blurred. In fact, Indian mythology became the basis for Indian nationalism. Hinduism in fact, is a religionized version of nationalism because the Hindu mind turned revivalist in response to the Western onslaught.'[7] For instance, Swami Dayanand, Aurobindo, Mahatma Gandhi, and Tilak turned towards the Vedas, the Gita, and the Ramayana to seek intellectual sustenance for their nationalism. They all attempted in various ways to go back to the 'roots' of our civilization. However, these 'roots' were discovered for the Hindus by British administrators and Orientalist scholars.

The Hindus were never governed by Shastric or Vedic tenets in their day-to-day living. It was the British who revived these 'scriptures' for the Hindus and convinced them that these ancient texts defined their civilization and provided a framework of do's and don'ts. Modern Hindus can not distinguish between the secular and the religious because there is no well-defined religious boundary or scriptural authority to demarcate the two realms. By contrast, the Muslims can more easily draw a line between the two realms even while they are more prone to theocratic politics. Jinnah seldom quoted the Quran to press his claims for Muslim nationalism but Gandhi did imagine that there would be adequate safeguards for Muslims in his *Ramrajya* if they could have recitations from the Quran and Gita in the same prayer meeting.

The choice of Hindu 'national' heroes shows this confusion clearly. For instance, Shivaji and Maharana Pratap were at one time idolized as regional heroes who fought for their respective kingdom. However, they have slowly been transformed into national heroes who fought against 'foreign domination'. Ram who is a mythological figure, has been formally adopted by the Sangh Parivar as a national hero.

The success of the Sangh Parivar on the Ram Mandir issue lies in precisely this fusion. It is not presented as a fight between two religious communities over a religious monument but as a fight between nationalist and anti-national forces. A foreign invader, Babar, is alleged to have destroyed the Ram Mandir, believed to be the birthplace of

---

[7]Puri, Balraj, 'Communalism v Pluralism', *Frontline*, February 2003.

Ram, who they project as a national hero, not a Hindu religious figure. In this scenario, Babri Masjid becomes a symbol of national humiliation at the hands of a foreigner. Thus, all those Muslims who sought to defend the mosque as a symbol of their religious identity came to be projected as anti-national.

The Sangh Parivar's demand that in order to prove their patriotism, Muslim communities should accept the arbitrarily chosen figures of Hindu mythology as not only common national heroes but put national loyalty above religious commitment, makes for a stalemate. For Muslims this is theoretically not possible, even though in day-to-day living and in actual politics various ethnic identities do come to play a more overwhelming role than their religious identity. For Muslims, the Quran is a symbol of their distinct identity within India; it also links them to a pan-national identity. Most Hindus have no problem in respecting the Quran as a religious text. But they probably are concerned with the way it apparently unites Muslims across national borders, and especially how it ties Indian Muslims with those of Pakistan.

The Hindu counterpart of the Quran is not the Ramayana or the Gita because these texts do not command universal allegiance among the Hindus. Therefore, many Hindus would project the national flag and the Constitution of India as their most sacred symbols, Bharat *Mata* as their most sacred deity, and *Vande Mataram* or the National Anthem as their most sacred hymns. The Muslims' insistence on having separate personal laws thus becomes a 'proof' of their disloyalty to the nation-state because many Hindus see them as going against the Constitution and creating their own separate universe. This also explains why a Congress Muslim leader, Salman Khurshid, could easily become a celebrated hero for the Sangh Parivar simply because he defended India's standpoint with ability and conviction in the United Nations when Pakistan challenged India's right to Kashmir and pressed for a plebiscite. In their eyes, by that one act he proved himself a loyal son of Bharat *Mata*, no matter what their other political differences are with him.

LOYALTY TESTS AND DRAMATIC SWINGS IN MOOD

The issues that are picked up by the *Hindutvavadis* are all proxies set out as traps to test the 'nationalist' credentials of the Muslims. The Sangh Parivar's insistence on building a Ram Mandir at the site of the demolished Masjid, their insistence on imposing a common civil code on the Muslims or wanting to hoist the national flag at a disputed Idgah Maidan in Hubli or reclaim the Bhojshala in Bhopal are all symbolic of the majority community's desire to subject Muslims to a loyalty test to prove that they are not 'anti-national'.

It is the same with the recurring irritant in Hindu–Muslim relations over occasional celebration by some Muslims if Pakistan wins a cricket match against India. Many of us have argued in defence of Muslims pointing to how Indians in Britain often behave likewise and rejoice when India wins a match against England, even though they may be British citizens. But it is not convincing to most Hindus beyond a point because it confirms their fears about Muslims being pro-Pakistan and, therefore, by definition anti-Indian. As trivial and phony as these issues seem to be, they have become major irritants in Hindu–Muslim relations even while they take attention away from some more genuine irritants and grievances of the two communities.

The Kashmiri Muslim demand for secession in recent years further deepened this anxiety and fear that Muslims are inherently disloyal to India and will not hesitate to break it up further, pushing Hindus out of territories in which they are a majority. However, the much-discredited Farooq Abdullah overnight became a national hero when, after leading his party to victory in the last elections to the Kashmir assembly, he declared that Jammu and Kashmir would stay an integral part of India and that he would take on and marginalize all those leaders who were playing pro-Pakistani politics. But within no time he became a hated man because he failed to give a sense of belonging to Kashmiri Hindus who were driven out of their own home state following targeted attacks by Islamic *jehadis*. Similarly, Mufti Mohammad Sayeed was seen as a threat to the Indian nation when as Home Minister in the V.P. Singh government, he allowed four arrested terrorists to be released in return for the release of his abducted daughter. However, the same man quickly won the confidence and respect of educated Hindus and the entire spectrum of political leadership of India, including *Hindutvavadis* after his assuming the Chief Minister's office in October 2002 because he made genuine and concrete gestures to restore people's faith in Indian democracy and is effectively combating the secessionist movement in Kashmir.

A moving example of a dramatic swing in Hindu–Muslim relations was narrated to me by several people in Meerut (a city with a long history of communal rift) after the Kargil war that led to a new high in anti-Pak feelings, which easily translate into anti-Muslim sentiments in

India. The first few bodies of Kargil martyrs that came to Meerut were those of Hindu soldiers. With a view to whipping up anti-Muslim hysteria, some Hindu nationalists decided to take the dead bodies in a procession through the city. When they reached the Muslim majority areas, they began raising provocative slogans like: *Musalmaan, Musalmaan, Pakistan ya Kabristan*. (Muslims belong either to Pakistan or graveyard). They expected the Muslim youth to react with anger, shout counter slogans or throw stones at the procession.

However, they were completely stumped to see that as their procession passed through the Muslim neighbourhoods, people in thousands stood in the balconies and verandahs of their homes and shops showering flower petals on the dead bodies of Kargil war heroes. To top it all, they were greeted with slogans like: '*Hindutstan Zindabad, Hindu-Muslim Ekta Zindabad*' *and some anti-Pakistan slogans.*' This totally disarmed even the diehard among *Hindutvavadis*. They not only joined the Muslims in shouting slogans of Hindu-Muslim unity, but also when the bodies of Muslim soldiers killed in the Kargil war began coming to Meerut, members of the Sangh Parivar are reported to have assumed an active role in the processions taken out to honour Muslim war heroes of Kargil. I was told by members of both communities that the astute handling of the situation by experienced Muslim leaders in Meerut led to an unprecedented show of warmth and solidarity between the Hindus and Muslims in the otherwise communally charged city.

ONENESS VS SEPARATENESS AS THE HALLMARK OF IDENTITY

In most parts of the world, the majority's insistence on the 'otherness' of the minority and their own 'superiority' sours majority–minority relations. In India, the situation is the reverse. Here the problem is created by the insistence of the Hindu intellectuals that the Muslims are not really different from Hindus, that the term Hindu includes all the people of Hindustan and is not a religious marker. They bolster this argument by pointing out that an overwhelming majority of Muslims are converts from various Hindu sects and that the term Hindu was used to denote people living in the land of the Sindhu River.

Muslims fear this assimilative tendency of Hinduism perhaps more than its aggressive attacks. The thrust of twentieth century Muslim politics has been to stress the separate identity of the Muslim community and differences between Islamic and Hindu civilizations and cultures. Their political demands are not simply for equal rights on the basis of common citizenship. An essential component is the recognition of their separate identity and concessions or special rights based on that separateness.

Muslim politics moved through distinct phases depending on the emphasis the leadership placed on both separateness and commonality. It started with Sir Syed Ahmed Khan describing the Hindus and Muslims as the 'two eyes of *Bharat Mata*'. From there it moved on to recognition of certain power imbalances between the two but within the framework of a sibling relationship—the two being compared to the elder and younger brother. It required the genius of Iqbal and Jinnah to convince themselves and their followers that 'the two eyes of *Bharat Mata*' were actually two distinct, separate and irreconcilable nationalities and, therefore, requiring a partition of the country so that each could claim a separate territory as homeland.

Iqbal, the leading brain behind the idea of Pakistan, had in his early years composed many a beautiful verse to the composite culture of Hindustan. His famous poem, '*Sare jahan se acchha Hindustan hamara / hum bulbulein hain iski, yeh gulsitan hamara*,' evokes the sentimental image of both Hindus and Muslims singing joyously together as *bulbuls* and belonging to the same *gulsitan* (garden). However, he outgrew and rejected Indian nationalism after he returned from Europe in 1908 and became obsessed with safeguarding and strengthening Muslim solidarity because he felt they were a 'distinct' cultural community. His demand for Pakistan was based on the headcounting majoritarian principle that he imbibed from Europe. He advised Jinnah to 'ignore Muslims of minority provinces and concentrate on the North West' where Muslims were in a majority.[8]

Jinnah developed the idea of Pakistan in such a muddle-headed political direction because he was faced with a practical limitation. In the Muslim majority provinces of the North-West, he found hardly any support for the idea of Pakistan because his phobias about Hindu domination did not evoke much response since Muslims felt they could wield power and hold their own through the democratic process. In the Muslim majority areas it was the Hindus who lived under the cultural hegemony of the Muslims. However, in the Muslim minority provinces, notably among the educated Muslims of Uttar Pradesh, Jinnah found a

---

[8]Letters to *Quaid-e-Azam Mohd Ali Jinnah, Ruh-I-Makatib Iqbal, Mohd Abdullah Qureshi*, Lahore: Iqbal Academy, p. 638. Quoted in Balraj Puri, 'Azad and Iqbal: A Comparative Study', *Economic and Political Weekly*. XXXI (10), 9 March, 1996, p. 592.

responsive chord to his campaign that in independent India, Muslims would end up having to live under Hindu domination.

As opposed to the majoritarian vision of Iqbal, Jinnah's was a minoritarian campaign whereby he was not willing to settle for safeguards for the minority within the framework of democracy. If the one person-one vote principle was applied, the Hindus would be, at the all-India level, at a permanent advantage on account of being the majority community. Therefore, he came up with the bizarre idea of Pakistan as a homeland for all Muslims. His success in mobilizing Muslim masses at a critical point of time in favour of the demand for Partition was not a triumph of religious appeal over secular politics, as is often believed, but because he could convince them that he alone could safeguard their economic, political, and cultural interests and protect the Muslim community from the assimilative tendencies and domination of both the Congress Party as well as Hindu culture.

EMPHASIS ON SEPARATENESS

The emphasis on separateness, and on irreconcilable differences kept growing as the Hindu leadership responded with emphasis on the essential oneness of the two. For instance, the more Gandhi harped on his Hindu-Muslim *bhai-bhai* theme, the more he used the Ram–Rahim approach of the *Bhakti–Sufi* tradition to bring the two communities together, the shriller became Jinnah's insistence on Muslims being irreconcilably different from the Hindus. The more Gandhi worked to include Muslims in the Congress, the more hysterical Jinnah became about claiming that he was the sole spokesman and his Muslim League the sole representative of all Indian Muslims and that no Hindu could claim to represent or include the political interests of the Muslims. It is noteworthy that this insistence on radical separateness and the idea of partition originated with Iqbal and Jinnah, both of whom were products of western education, more British than the British. Both their families were recent converts to Islam. Iqbal, in fact, boasted of his Brahmin ancestry and Kashmiri origin. Jinnah's Gujarati family had also taken to Islam only a generation ago.

By contrast Maulana Azad, who stood steadfast in his commitment to India, was born in Mecca where he spent his childhood in a very orthodox Muslim family. He traced his ancestry to Maulana Jamaluddin who refused to sign the infallibility decree of Akbar. He was often hailed as 'Imam-ul-Hind'. Even after the Partition, Azad remained firm in his commitment to Indian nationalism while remaining an orthodox Muslim to the end of his days. He carried a large number of Muslim *ulema* with him whereas the non religious Muslim leadership and the western-educated elite among the Muslims came to be more enamoured with Jinnah and Iqbal. Thus, the theory of Muslim separateness does not owe its inspiration as much to Islamic history, tradition or faith requirements of the Muslim community, as it does to the idea of national ethnic identity as it developed in Europe and came to play an important role in shaping the aspirations of many western-educated Muslims.

GANDHI'S *BHAI-BHAI* APPROACH FAILS TO WORK

There were indeed serious flaws in the Gandhian approach to Hindu–Muslim relations. Mahatma Gandhi tried to forge Hindu–Muslim unity by:

  (i) Insisting on the oneness of all religions. His Ram-Rahim approach was drawn from the *Bhakti–Sufi* traditions;

  (ii) Insisting on the shared common heritage and bonds of co-living;

  (iii) Expecting Hindus to play the role of indulgent, large-hearted elder brothers willing to make unilateral gestures of generosity towards their Muslim 'younger brothers'.

While Gandhi made numerous attempts to placate Jinnah through moral appeals and by unilaterally offering him the prime ministership of free India, he did not try to arrive at a political settlement by working out a concrete formula for power sharing among the Hindus and the Muslims. Nor did he confront Jinnah with the logic of his own demand for Partition. He stayed rooted in the Hindu–Muslim *bhai-bhai* world-view and expected the Hindus to play the patronizing role of a generous elder brother dealing with a rather difficult younger brother. This patronizing attitude became a major irritant for leaders whose goal was to acquire power. It continues to be an irritant in India-Pakistan relations even today. The Muslim elite of Pakistan feel that Indians treat them like errant brothers who will one day realize the 'mistake' they made in demanding the break-up of India.[9]

---

[9]Even while Pakistanis resent the 'big brotherly' attitude of Indians, they themselves slip into the same sentimental mode no less easily. For example, a big trade delegation from Pakistan that came to India in 2003, concluded their negotiations with a press conference in which they advised that 'as an elder brother' Indians should be more generous in making concessions to Pakistani business interests!

As the failure of the *bhai-bhai* approach became obvious, Gandhi and other Congress leaders moved from one pendulum swing to another—from 'partition over my dead body' and total refusal to make that the basis of negotiations to supinely accepting the Partition as a *fait accompli* when the Muslim League leadership forced the transfer of population. It is this image of a hapless Hindu majority meekly accepting the will of the minority with millions being forcibly uprooted from their homes that has given the Hindus a deep sense of fear of the supposed power of the Muslims and mistrust of secular Hindu leadership. The memories of small armies of Muslim invaders coming and building their empires in India along with the Muslim minority forcing its wishes down the unwilling throats of the Hindu majority adds to the sinister image of the Muslim community in the minds of even educated Hindus.

LIMITS TO MUSLIM MINORITARIANISM

Just as there are serious limitations in the emergence of Hindu majoritarianism in India despite the desperate attempts by the Sangh Parivar, there are equally serious limits to the growth of Muslim minoritarianism in India after the Partition. I define minoritarianism as the tendency of a minority to want an unconditional veto on all issues it considers important. The minority does not just demand reasonable safeguards before agreeing to a deal, they also demand more than parity in the settlement for themselves; in the process they lose the positive aspects of democracy based on majority vote, while undermining some of the major incentives among the majority community for making a compact. Jinnah represented that trend.

Jinnah's political rise as the sole spokesman, which resulted in the Partition of India, was a symptom of the failure of the nationalist politicians to work out a satisfactory arrangement for guaranteeing basic security and cultural protections for both Muslims and Hindus within the framework of a nation-state whose powers could be appropriately circumscribed by both formal written agreements and personal commitments. Jinnah could not stomach the idea of accepting a secondary status as sole spokesman merely because Muslims were a minority within India on an all-India basis. For some years he tried extracting a deal from the Congress whereby Muslim leaders could have a permanent veto on matters he defined as of major significance despite their being in the minority. When this deal was rejected he began to play for larger stakes, threatening to partition the country and seek an independent state for Muslim-majority provinces.

However, after the Partition Muslims are economically too vulnerable and politically too dispersed (except in a few constituencies) and numerically a poor match for the Hindus to get away with demanding that they have an unconditional veto on all issues considered important by their community leaders. Yet the Jinnah legacy continues to haunt post-Independence Muslim politics and has influenced many of its important leaders, making Muslims appear as a very difficult and unreasonable minority in the eyes of many Hindus. This, despite the fact that at the level of everyday living, the two communities show a remarkable capacity to make mutual adjustments and work out functional norms for co-living as long as political parties and politicians of the two communities are out of the picture.

Just as the Hindu majority is rather confused about its goals and weightage and therefore prone to jingoism, the Muslims too are very confused about their aims, especially with relationship to Indian democracy because of their peculiar history, their present position in Indian society as also due to the inclinations of their leadership.

Unlike the Hindu majority who see their history in terms of having to adjust to an endless stream of foreign conquests, living under alien rulers, adapting to their culture, language and social norms, many among the Muslim minority, especially the elites, relate to their past in terms of glorious conquests and setting up of huge empires. Their memories of being part of the ruling race are kept alive because monuments and historical records of this period of history are relatively better known and preserved whereas the history of India prior to Muslim conquests and rule is far more hazy in the minds of most people. Many Muslims associate their religion with victories and conquests, with the powerful sweep of Islam in the wake of those conquests. Even in today's world, many Indian Muslims see themselves as part of a worldwide wealthy Muslim community with Dubai, Saudi Arabia, Kuwait and now even Malaysia and Indonesia, exercising a great pull for their aspirations.

Indian Muslims are mostly considered converts from the supposedly lower caste groups of Indian society. Therefore, many Hindus have a casteist prejudice against the Muslims but they cover it up saying that the Muslims who converted betrayed their *dharma*.

Modernization and tremendous advancement in communication technology has brought greater awareness of the Muslim communities outside India and thus makes it that much harder for Indian Muslims to accept a 'second-class status' in India, especially for the Muslim elite. Their aspirations of a good life are linked to migrating to one of the wealthy Muslim countries because India offers relatively few opportunities for advancement for Muslims today. The Gulf connection has also brought in its wake a new fervour for the Middle Eastern version of Islam. The flow of Gulf money for mosques and other Islamic institutions has strengthened the fundamentalists among the Muslim leadership who are trying to wean the Muslims away from the Indic Islam towards a more Middle Eastern version of the faith, removing from it practices which built close cultural bonds with the neighbouring Hindus. Even the Urdu they advocate is heavily Arabicized. Having internalized the stereotype that Muslims are a brave martial community whereas the Hindus are mealy mouthed cowards, Muslims do frequently behave like aggressive bullies contrary to the behaviour of most minorities the world over. In recent decades, due to widespread unemployment, poverty and poor education many young Muslims have taken to crime as a way of life. They are quick to pick fights and retaliate violently, leading to riotous situations even over flimsy conflicts. Most important of all, the emergence of powerful underworld Muslim dons as 'cultfigures' who have been using their economic and political clout for supporting terrorist operations in India strengthens the worst of negative stereotypes prevalent among influential sections of Hindus.

The fact that the desperation of the riot-ravaged Muslim communities occasionally finds expression in lending some legitimacy to such 'cult figures' makes for increased mistrust. The fascination for the outlaw as a hero is a worldwide phenomenon among communities that feel endangered—rightly or wrongly. But many Hindus have come to believe that they alone are endangered.

After the Partition, the Muslim leadership in India felt so rudderless that it quietly latched onto the Congress party, expecting it to provide the Muslims protection and security. As long as there were credible leaders like Rafi Ahmed Kidwai and Maulana Azad representing the Muslims in the Congress, it gave the community hope and confidence. These leaders could also act as an effective communication bridge with the Hindu community because the latter respected them no less for their leading role in the freedom movement and for standing steadfastly against the Partition. The inspiring speech of Maulana Azad at the Delhi Muslim Convention on 4 November, 1947, calling upon the

Indian Muslims 'to take the pledge that this country is ours, that we belong to it and that fundamental decisions of its destiny will remain incomplete till we participate in them' provided a beacon of light not only to the demoralized Muslims but acted as balm on the hurt Hindu psyche.[10] However, after the death of these tall figures and the estrangement with Sheikh Abdullah, the Congress party did not let any credible leaders emerge among the Muslims in order to keep them a captive vote bank. Nehru in his lifetime ensured that there were no serious Hindu–Muslim riots so that memories of Partition could slowly fade away. After his death, Muslims were kept tied to the apron strings of the Congress as a vote bank in the most cynical fashion by encouraging them to get addicted to crumb gathering in the name of special concessions to the community. The Nehruvian brand of secularism misled the Muslim community into believing that as long as they had a certain clout with the government and the latter mouthed secular slogans, their interests were safe. Just as Jinnah had bargained on the British government providing for the safety of the Muslims against the Hindus, post-Independence Muslim leadership focused exclusively on extracting 'concessions' from the government (mostly phoney ones at that) while allowing themselves to be continually estranged from the Hindu majority and other communities.

The Congress party encouraged this estrangement in order to cultivate them as a vote bank too frightened to look elsewhere. After they were thoroughly disappointed with the Congress party they latched on to the Janata Dal–Samajwadi party bandwagon. However, these parties are acting not much differently than the Congress party in giving token concessions to Muslim vote banks in ways that further estrange them from the Hindus. For example, among the first measures of V.P. Singh's Janata Dal government was to declare Prophet Mohammad's birthday a holiday. His party refused to consider steps like disbanding a paramilitary force like the Provincial Armed Constabulary (PAC) with its alleged track record of anti-Muslim massacres. The Janata Dal's choice of 'history-sheeter' Muslim leaders for allocating election tickets or the 'secular' Laloo Yadav's dependence on some Muslim mafia dons shows that they too are not interested in promoting genuine and responsible leadership among the Muslims.

---

[10]Quoted in Puri, Balraj, 'Indian Muslims Since Partition, *Economic and Political Weekly,* 2 October 1993.

Dubious concessions, such as the enactment of the Muslim Women's Protection Act, and the banning of Salman Rushdie's book have strengthened the stereotype of Muslims as an intolerant community that is supposedly being pampered by the 'pseudo-secular' politics of the Congress Party. Many Hindus have today seriously begun to feel that Muslims have an unfair advantage over them, and will cite instances such as the Congress forcibly imposing personal law reform on the Hindus much against the wishes of the majority but succumbing to the pressure of Muslim leaders and letting them continue with their personal laws. The hysterical manner in which Muslim leaders responded to the Shah Bano judgement and insisted that a patently unconstitutional law be passed to put Muslim community laws altogether out of the purview of the civil laws of the land, making Muslim women among the most discriminated against women in India in terms of family laws, makes Hindus fear that Muslims want to be treated as 'above the laws of the land'.

The excessive emphasis the leaders have placed on their special rights as Muslims, even while consistently failing to claim many of their more important rights as citizens, has contributed a great deal to the growing divide between the two communities. Riot after riot, the Muslim leadership has focussed its ire on the government for failure to provide it protection, making demands such as proportional representation of Muslims in the police force, but has paid scant attention to the growing communication gap between the Muslim community and the rest of the people, so that its demands, such as proportional representation, get to be viewed with mistrust and hostility.

Just as the Sangh Parivar ideology poses a great danger to the well-being of the Hindus because of their wanting to destroy the internal heterogeneity of the Hindu community, the Muslim leadership's attempts to make the equally heterogeneous Muslim communities of India behave like a mindless monolith poses a great danger to the well-being of the Muslims themselves as well as to the rest of society. The short-sighted politics of the Congress party, especially after Indira Gandhi's rise to power, has played a very important role in encouraging the irresponsible among Muslim leaders to gain ascendancy and the increasing appeal of the Sangh Parivar. The cynical manner in which the Congress leadership cultivated Muslims as a vote bank through controlling some of those Muslim leaders who were willing to barter away their community's interests for personal crumbs has left the Muslim community rudderless and consequently easy to manipulate.

Muslim politicians who do not want to act as spokesmen just for other Muslims and have tried to take responsible and thoughtful positions on various issues have been systematically bypassed by the Congress party in favour of the more obscurantist leaders. At the time of the Shah Bano controversy, for instance, certain prominent leaders within the Congress opposed the Muslim Women's Protection Bill. Nevertheless the party yielded to pressures from the Shahi Imam, Shahabuddin, and leaders of the Muslim League, thereby making it seem as if these were more genuine Muslim leaders than those who were in favour of reforming discriminatory aspects of Muslim law. Similarly, the deliberate sidelining of men like M.J. Akbar (who had given a decisive electoral defeat to Shahabuddin without using communal rhetoric to win the Muslim vote) while simultaneously giving excessive importance to leaders of the Muslim League who mostly draw a blank even in Muslim-dominated constituencies creates the mistaken impression that it is the latter who represent the true sentiments of the Muslims.

In their attempt to become the sole spokesmen for the Muslim community, many leaders have tended to articulate the grievances of the community in an exclusivist and minoritarianist way. This is one reason they tend to evoke nearly hysterical responses from the Hindus, who fear further partitions of the country if the Muslims are allowed to have greater influence on national politics. Many Hindus have become concerned that the Muslim minority will veto everything that the majority wants to do. Consequently, these Hindus fear the Muslim vote and see an urgent need to 'put the Muslims in their place.'

Similarly, the manner in which the demand for recognition for Urdu is being framed is likely to produce backlashes of the Bangalore variety when an innocuous ten-minute news bulletin in Urdu became the excuse for widespread anti-Muslim riots. Urdu can only be legitimately promoted as one of the languages of Uttar Pradesh, Bihar and of some sections of Hyderabad. Instead, Muslim leaders project it as the language of the all-India Muslim community, and attempt to get all of Indian Muslims to use it as an identity marker when there is no basis for it in most of the southern, eastern, and western states of India, or for that matter even in Kashmir.

The matter is made more complicated by the fact that some Muslim leaders are not very tolerant of dissenting voices within the community and some have even gotten into the habit of issuing Khomeini-like *fatwas* as happened in the case of Mushirul Hasan. He was beaten up and banned entry into Jamia Milia despite being its pro-Vice-Chancellor simply because he did not think banning Rushdie's book was appropriate. Similarly, the aggression and violent indignation over the Salman Rushdie book, getting it banned in India even before any Islamic country learned of it, created the stereotype of an aggressively intolerant community. This strengthens and legitimizes the voices of intolerance within the Hindu community and weakens the position of those who wish to see the Muslims enjoy secure citizenship rights in India.

The rise of Taliban and Al-Qaeda like forces practicing very murderous forms of politics in the name of Islam has given greater legitimacy to the prejudice against Muslims and their negative stereotyping as a violent and aggressive community that imposes very obscurantist beliefs and social norms through terror and oppression. Now that even western nations led by the US are seen as battling Islamic fundamentalism (as in Afghanistan) through strong arm methods, including war, many educated Hindus have come to believe that India's interests lie in joining the western powers 'against' the Islamic world.

The overall effect of such minoritarian politics is to strengthen majoritarian tendencies even further, giving undue legitimacy to the politics of exclusion being propagated by outfits like the Bajrang Dal. The only redeeming feature is that after the restoration of democracy in Jammu and Kashmir, the national level BJP leaders, especially Atal Bihari Vajpayee and L.K. Advani, seem to have decided that their battle against Pakistan supported *jehadi* terror will be more effective, if they succeed in winning the confidence of Indian Muslims, including those in Kashmir. Therefore, after the Gujarat riots and its negative international fallout, they tried hard to keep the VHP–Bajrang Dal leadership under some checks and control. However, their perceived failure to question Narendra Modi, after the anti-muslim riots in Gujarat took the sheen away from their position initiatives and played a significant role in the defeat of the NDA in 2004.

CHECK ON MINORITARIANISM

However, minoritarianism of the Muslims is kept in check for the same reason that defines the limit of Hindu majoritarianism. The Muslims are not a monolith. Like the Hindus, the Muslims of the subcontinent have a great deal of internal diversity based on language, region, class, occupational category and even caste. As long as they feel secure about their secular interests, it is not easy for their leaders to unify them into a monolithic community for even limited political purposes. In recent decades, election after election has demonstrated that, despite all the talk about a unified Muslim vote bank, their vote is as influenced by regional and other considerations as that of the Hindu majority except in phases when they have been under attack as happened after the demolition of the Babri Masjid. But then too they got consolidated as an anti-BJP vote and anti-Congress block, voting for whoever seemed most capable of defeating these two. As soon as they feel a measure of security, their internal diversity begins to assert itself. Once again I cite from the Meerut example because, as a riot-prone city, it gives one important glimpses into the working of the Muslim mind. In the 1993 assembly election, they helped the Janata Dal candidate, Haji Akhlaq, win with a comfortable margin as Muslims of all shades and hues (social and political) decided to vote for him, as he alone seemed to be able to take on the BJP and defeat it (the top priority then). By 1996, the communal divide had healed considerably and with even the BJP communicating its desire to make peace, a section of the Muslim community ended up voting the BJP, helping Lakshmi Kant Vajpayi to win the Meerut seat even though the Hindus were not any more as enamoured with the BJP as they were in 1993. The swing in the Muslim vote was influenced by the following factors:

  (i) Muslims began to feel relatively secure and, therefore, not so desperate for 'protection' from their own;

 (ii) After the elections, the traditional rivalry and conflict between the Ansaris and Qureshis, the two dominant groups among the Muslims in Meerut reappeared because of the alleged anti-social behaviour of Haji Akhlaq's family and followers. Haji Akhlaq had succeeded in getting the Ansari role in 1993 using the anti-BJP sentiment as a unifier. But by 1996, the occupational and caste rivalries resurfaced and ensured that most Ansaris did not vote for the Haji;

(iii) Some educated Muslims felt distanced on account of their prejudice against the Kasi community considered *jahil* (uneducated) and began to respond well to the friendly overtures of the BJP on account of them representing a 'more educated and cultured class of people';

(iv) Lacklustre performance of alternatives to the Congress and the BJP (including Janata Dal and the Samajwadi party) as ruling parties on all other issues except their commitment to protecting the Muslim minority from riots apparently helped tilt a section of the Muslim vote in favour of the BJP;

(v) Their assessment that if the BJP became beholden to them for votes, that party may develop a real stake in allowing the Muslims a sense of security and not use riots as a method of consolidating Hindu votes;

(vi) Lakshmi Kant Vajpayi proved exceptional in that he served his constituency well even after losing the election and demonstrated that he would be sensitive to the grievances of Muslims and act in a relatively non-partisan manner.

However, in the rest of UP, the BJP did not manage a similar swing in its favour and Muslims seem to have voted depending on the ground-level realities in each constituency, contributing to a hung assembly. Thus the Muslim community's one-point programme of the early 1990s of defeating the BJP at whatever cost seemed to have lost its urgency even in a communally polarized city like Meerut. By contrast, at about the same time, Muslim electoral behaviour in Mumbai was dramatically different even in the 1993 election. There they decided that it was the Congress party that needed an electoral snub for taking their vote for granted. Therefore, they ended up voting the BJP–Shiv Sena combine, which alone seemed capable of defeating the Congress. With the Shiv Sena realising what was required to win the elections and come out of the shadow of the Congress party, they along with the BJP made a peace offering to the Muslims. As a result a section of Muslim leaders are believed to have worked out a deal with the Sena–BJP leadership that the 1991 variety of riots would not be repeated in the city. Since on this one issue the combine seems to have kept its word, the Muslim vote did not revert back to the Congress even in the 1996 election.

Today, many more Muslims realize that their minoritarian politics strengthens the forces of majoritarianism, which endangers their very being because those claiming to speak on behalf of majorities try and capture state power and can make the enforcement machinery of the state serve their own majoritarian purposes, by fair means or foul. For instance, even before the BJP came to power in Uttar Pradesh, the party, along with the RSS, is reported to have inducted a lot of their committed cadres into the PAC in order to organize this force as an instrument for carrying out anti-Muslim pogroms in the name of maintaining law and order during riots. The PAC has acquired a notorious reputation on this count and its role during the riots has been blatantly partisan with PAC jawans playing a lead role in murderous attacks on Muslim *bastis*.[11] Similarly, during the 1992-93 Mumbai riots it became obvious that the Shiv Sena had allegedly infiltrated the police force on a large scale and succeeded in using the Mumbai police for that period as its private army. This was made especially easy since most Congressmen were apparently in alliance with the Shiv Sena in fomenting anti-Muslim violence in the city. The Congressmen in power have often used the police and paramilitary forces for wreaking vengeance on minorities who oppose them, as happened during the anti-Sikh riots in November 1984 in North India. This may have emboldened BJP leaders like Narendra Modi to do the same when they came to power in different states. The anti-Muslim violence in Gujarat carried forward the terrible example set by the anti-Sikh massacre in Delhi and the many massacres of Muslims in North India during Congress rule in the 1980s.

Today, Muslims seem ready to break away from the clutches of those leaders who pursue the minoritarian brand of politics because they seem to have realized that in the long run it works against their overall interests by producing a backlash among the majority community and estranges them from the Hindu community at large. They understand that the kind of clout Jinnah acquired in pre-Independence India is out of question in post-1947 India. Therefore, the community is actually pressurizing its leaders to play a more responsible role so that the Hindus as a community do not move towards majoritarian politics.

THE APPARENT LET DOWN BY THE CONGRESS

In the post-Independence years Nehru became a hero of the Muslim communities because they saw him as keeping the Hindu chauvinist organizations who wanted to implement the Jinnah formula of majoritarian rule in India at bay. The Congress party won the support of Muslims in election after election as long as Muslims continued to feel that Congress leaders like Nehru remained committed to protecting them from major outbreaks of religious riots, as well as to respecting their cultural and religious sensibilities. In addition, Nehru encouraged a certain amount of participation of nationalist Muslims in positions with high visibility in the central and northern state governments.

---

[11] Engineer, Ashgar Ali (ed.), *Communal Riots in Post-independence India*, Hyderabad: Sangam Books, 1984

However, these Congress party deals were worked out on rather arbitrary considerations and were limited to positions at high levels; these same accommodationist principles did not percolate down to the level of everyday life for ordinary Muslims. In general, in the politically important and relatively more advanced sectors of the society and economy, Muslims have lived under the burden of a great deal of mistrust. They are often discriminated against in jobs and housing and have been ghettoized more than ever before.

Thus, in post-Partition India, the question of majority–minority relations never got seriously addressed, nor were there any clear rules laid out for determining what Muslims could count on as their legitimate due. Instead, Muslim political leaders ended up being forced to petition each time in the hope of receiving occasional favours for cooperating with the dominant political and administrative forces in the new nation. The ease with which Nehru was able to electorally marginalize parties like the Jan Sangh and the Hindu Mahasabha made him overlook the fact that substantial sections of the Hindu community, especially the educated groups and those who were victims of Partition, had not fully reached any new way of coming to terms with living within the same polity with their Muslim neighbours, especially in the North, where the trauma of Partition remained severe.

Many Hindus could not understand why millions of Muslims were continuing to stay on in India even after the Muslim League claimed that Muslims are a separate nationality and on that basis had driven out millions of Hindus from Muslim majority areas. This question never got explained adequately in political terms. The appeal was always at the level of pious, goody-goody slogans: 'Hindu Muslim *bhai-bhai*' even after the *bhaichara* of the centuries-old bonds had been effectively destroyed by the Partition in large parts of India.

In fact, Muslims became a deeply mistrusted minority not just at the level of ordinary people but even among the slogan-givers. Nehru's treatment of Sheikh Abdullah shows that Nehru himself was as prone to mistrusting even close Muslim friends and colleagues if he thought or suspected that they harboured pro-Pakistani sentiments. The same Sheikh Abdullah, who was a close personal friend of Nehru and who played a crucial role in bringing about the accession of Jammu and Kashmir to the Indian Union at a time when the Hindu Maharaja was unwilling to merge the state with India while Pakistan was trying to occupy it by force, was imprisoned by Nehru for the better part of his later life on suspicion of hobnobbing with Pakistan and for allegedly trying to veer the state towards secession. Muslim leaders even today are expected to prove their loyalty to India by being more anti-Pakistan than Hindus themselves.

But the real damage to Hindu–Muslim relations occurred after Indira Gandhi assumed leadership. Repeated use of the trump card of nationalist rhetoric to put down democratic demands during Indira Gandhi's regime resulted in the Congress party veering more and more towards chauvinist nationalism. This was especially true in dealings with movements in border regions such as Kashmir, Nagaland, and Punjab, where a majority of the population is not Hindu and their demands could easily be targeted as being anti-Indian. As the nationalism of the Congress party got increasingly divorced from social justice and democracy and came to rely more and more on 'nation in danger' gimmicks, it has provided tremendous legitimacy to the chauvinist nationalism of the Sangh Parivar whose politics rely on cultivating a siege mentality among the Hindus.

THE FAILURE OF 'SECULARIST' POLITICS

The Nehruvian approach at its idealistic best attempted to solve the problem by detaching ethno-religious identities on the assumption that if the state professed neutrality in religious matters, but left space for religious and cultural identity assertion by the minorities, in the political and public realm a whole new generation of 'modern' citizens would emerge rising above religious divides, united by secular nationalism. Hindus and Muslims were thus expected to become 'Indians' first and foremost, with other identities playing an increasingly small role in public affairs.

There were many flaws in this framework. But the tragic form that Hindu–Muslim relations have assumed in recent decades (as the example of the Gujarat massacre in 2002 and similar riots in the 1980s and 1990s demonstrates) is largely due to the gap between the pious platitudes mouthed by the post-Independence political leadership and the cynical political games it actually played. Even in Gujarat, Congress workers are alleged to have actively participated in the killing of Muslims hand in hand with members of the Sangh Parivar. So also during the Bombay riots of 1993, Hindu Nationalist cadres apparently got full cooperation from Congress workers in attacking Muslims. The Congress professed belief in separating religion from politics but in actual fact it has apparently injected party politics into several religious institutions in its bid to become politically hegemonic. This includes attempts to wrest controls of the *gurudwara* network in Punjab from the Akali party, and its takeover of Waqf Boards and its moves to convert the Imams into employees of the government by offering them monthly salaries, all with an eye perhaps to use these religious functionaries as vote mobilizers for the party during elections. Many prominent Hindu temples like the shrine of Vaishnodevi, the Meenakshi temple in Madurai, the shrine at Tirupati have been taken over directly by the government and run by bureaucrats and their nominees. This goes against its oft-repeated claim to be the leading secular force in India.

It is the same story with the supposed autonomy of minority-controlled educational and cultural institutions. To an extent, there has been subversion of the whole idea of minorities having the freedom to run their own institutions by making them dependent on government grants. Be it the Aligarh Muslim University or the Urdu Academy in Delhi, they all survive on government patronage. From there it is a small step towards assuming control over appointments and other administrative functions whether it be done directly through legislation as in the case of Aligarh Muslim University or through other bureaucratic strings that come with government grants. Thus it is not religion intruding into the political sphere which is causing communal tensions in India but the takeover of religious spaces and minority institutions by political parties for secular ends which has pitched different religious communities into hostility and conflict.

RAM–RAHIM APPROACH AND REVIVAL OF FAILED FORMULA

Ironically, the failure of Nehruvian secularism in creating harmonious relations between the Hindus and the Muslims is bringing about a revival of the Gandhian *bhai-bhai* approach to sorting out Hindu–Muslim relations, even though Gandhi's Ram-Rahim approach was a tragic failure. Even the Marxists who used to call Gandhi derogatory names and condemned the religious overtones in his politics, among other things, have taken to organizing festivals of *Sufi-Bhakti* songs to combat the Hindu–Muslim divide following the demolition of the Babri Masjid. Similarly an important thrust of the BJP–RSS campaign is that the Muslims ought not to consider themselves different from the Hindus. Late RSS leader K.R. Malkani's thesis, for all his anti-Muslim prejudice, essentially argues that the Hindus and Muslims were inseparable till the British came and divided them. RSS leader Sudershan takes this view to its logical conclusion by asserting that Indian Muslims and Christians (unlike Parsis and Bahais who came from outside) cannot be considered different from the Hindus and ought not to be treated as minorities because they are all of local origin and were converted from various Hindu sects.

It is time we recognized that this emphasis on 'oneness' cannot be the basis of solving the Hindu–Muslim conflict in India. Even to the extent that Gandhi succeeded in his life-long endeavour to forge emotional and political unity among the Hindus and Muslims, we would do well to remember that the *Bhakti-Sufi* approach works only if those who preach it are genuinely inspired by the love of humanity emanating from their love of God—rather than by political considerations, as is the case with today's politicians who use this issue to expand their own base among the Muslim 'vote bank'. Gandhi could inspire millions of Hindus and Muslims to resist divisive politics because his life was his message and he sacrificed his all, including his very life for this cause. For him it was an article of faith, not a political convenience or tactic, as it is for many of today's secularists.

The *Ram-Rahim* approach historically evolved in the process of resolving theological conflicts between Islam and Hindu faiths in medieval times. It is not appropriate for solving political conflicts today. We have wasted too much time insisting on oneness. However, when a group has come to a point when its primary urge is recognition of its 'separate' identity with a view to demanding a share in political and economic power as a distinct cultural entity, emphasis on oneness can only act as an irritant. In fact, the more similarities there are between two groups, the more their emotional bonding, the more violent is the assertion for a separate identity when differences arise over sharing of power and resources, as the recent experience of ethnic genocide in eastern Europe shows. Failure of a polity to provide a legitimate space for identity assertion of various types along with well worked-out norms of power sharing between different groups can lead to deadly breakdown of the social compact and a civil war type situation, or give rise to strong secessionist movements as has already happened in many regions of India. The Hindu–Sikh conflict of the 1980s and early 1990s provides a good example of how over-insistence on 'oneness' on the one hand and absence of institutions for conflict resolution can tear asunder even those who were actually inseparable.

Fallout of Over Emphasis on 'Oneness'

Till a few decades ago, Punjabi Hindus and Sikhs were indeed indistinguishable in most respects, especially since keeping a beard and long hair was not an integral part of Sikh identity as it has come to be in recent decades. The Sikhs, in fact, projected themselves as brave defenders of the Hindu faith from the onslaughts of Muslim rulers. The first assertion of their identity came in response to the gratuitous attack by the overzealous Hindu reformer, Swami Dayanand, who responded to Christian proselytization of Hindus by introducing *Shuddhi* campaigns to reconvert and purify not just the Christian converts but also those who had converted to Islam or become Sikhs. He also attacked the Sikh *gurus* emulating the Christian missionary attacks on the Hindu religion. The more the Arya Samajis argued that Sikhs were essentially 'impure' or 'corrupted' Hindus and tried to bring them back into the Hindu fold, the more vehemently the Sikh leadership responded with counter-tracts such as '*Hum Hindu Nahin Hain* (We are not Hindus)'. The Singh Sabha worked to consolidate this sentiment of Sikhs being distinct from the Hindus, claiming to purify Sikhs of Hindu influences, even though in many Punjabi families it was common to find one son given to the *guru* and another remaining Hindu. Many Punjabis prayed in *gurudwaras* and considered those institutions as their own at the turn of the century.

The next major wave of Sikh assertion came in the 1950s with the demand for 'Punjabi *Suba*'. The Sikhs made a case that they were being discriminated against as a linguistic group since the principle of carving out states around linguistic boundaries was not applied to Punjabi-speaking regions. Therefore, they demanded a separate state for Punjabi speaking people. In most other parts of the country, linguistic reorganization of states strengthened regional identities, which proved an effective safety valve for ethnic identities. In Punjab, the Arya Samaj influence had weakened the regional, linguistic identity of the urban educated Hindus who began to identify more with Hindi and with 'nationalist' politics as against regional politics. This left the field open for the Akalis to imagine themselves as the sole guardians of Punjab and the Punjabi language. The Punjabi Hindus, egged on by the Congress and Jan Sangh, felt threatened by the Akali demand for Punjabi *Suba* for if the Hindu majority areas of Himachal and Haryana (which were till then part of Punjab) were cut off, that would reduce the Punjabi Hindus to a permanent minority in Punjab. Therefore, to contain the

Sikhs, they went as far as disowning their own linguistic identity and declaring Hindi as their mother tongue because they felt the Punjabi *Suba* would result in a Sikh majority state. The Akali party, being gurudwara-based, could not provide space for the political aspirations of non-Sikhs and, therefore, could not mobilize them in favour of a regional, linguistic demand. The result was that the Sikhs got a truncated state of Punjab with several Punjabi speaking areas going to Haryana and Himachal Pradesh. In the process, the Hindu community too has been permanently marginalized in Punjab politics despite being nearly 40 per cent of the population.

Therefore, the Hindus began to look more and more towards 'national' parties like the Jan Sangh (now BJP) and the Congress to safeguard their political interests. This has further eroded the regional identity of Punjabi Hindus, who are easy prey to chauvinist nationalism, because they suffered greatly during the Partition. Yet, for the purpose of power sharing, the BJP (Jan Sangh) representing the Hindus and Akalis representing the Sikhs ran effective coalition governments in Punjab in the 1960s. In its bid to capture power in Punjab, the Congress party successfully smashed this coalition not just by dismissing state governments but also by instigating Hindu–Sikh estrangement. In response to the repeated dismissal of duly elected state governments by the centre, the Akalis launched a movement in the early 1970s demanding a reorganization of centre–state relations and providing for decentralization of political and economic power. This was an assertion of their regional identity as Punjabis. They were articulating the economic interests of Jat farmers who constituted their political base. The Jat peasantry provided the thrust for decentralization because since the 1960s, the central government began to force the Punjab peasantry to sell its wheat at artificially depressed government-controlled prices by imposing draconian restrictions on the movement or sale of foodgrains to curb private trade. The freedom to trade across Punjab's borders, including the export of farm produce was the key demand of the Bharatiya Kisan Union (BKU) movement as well as in the Anandpur Sahib resolution of the Akali party. This demand served the economic interests of the Hindu trading class as well because government procurement drives were accompanied by ban on private trade and all manner of restrictions on inter-district and inter-state movement of grain. The Hindus of Punjab not only undermined their economic interests as a trading community but also their regional identity as Punjabis and opposed the demand for regional autonomy because they felt the Akali party would gain more political power in Punjab. The inability of the gurudwara-based Akali party to carry along the Hindus who constitute 40 per cent of the Punjab population in their struggle for the much-needed decentralization of power made it easy for Mrs Gandhi to dub the whole movement as 'communal' and 'anti-national'. She could then easily take the path of repression in dealing with the Punjab peasantry and Akali Party culminating in Operation Blue Star.

Punjabi Hindus who have held the Granth Sahib and the Golden Temple in high reverence ended up supporting and legitimizing the desecration of the Golden Temple because by then the Congress party had succeeded in convincing large sections among the Hindus that the Akali movement was anti-Hindu. The assassination of Mrs Gandhi by her two Sikh guards was also interpreted in communal terms rather than seen for what it was—an anti-Congress wave among the Sikhs. Consequently, when Congress supporters and leaders in apparent connivance with the police allegedly massacred thousands of Sikhs, most Hindus justified this criminality on the ground that Sikhs needed to be 'taught a lesson'. This caused an unprecedented schism between the Hindus and Sikhs all over the country.

Sikh militants pushed the movement for decentralization of power in the direction of a demand for Khalistan with the help of the Congress, which had propped up Bhindranwale to destroy the influence of the Sant Longowal's Akali Dal. Even though it was well known that Bhindranwale began as a Congress Party agent, many Sikhs began to identify with his demand for Khalistan after the Sikhs got targeted as a community following Operation Blue Star. They began to declare themselves to be a separate *qaum* or nation, in the same way that some Muslim leaders came to do in the 1930s and the 1940s, leading to the disastrous Partition in 1947. Fortunately, ever since coalition governments started being formed at the centre with the help of regional parties leading to far greater devolution of power to the states, the Khalistani movement has died a natural death.

COMMUNITIES VERSUS NATIONALITIES

Communal differences or conflicts can be easily resolved by the communities concerned at the local level on the basis of their several shared interests as co-habitants of a common region. However, the moment one or the other community decides to purify itself and declares itself as a separate nationality, their interests appear almost irreconcilable and the conflict assumes the shape of a civil war. In the 1950s and the 1960s, the Jan Sangh, the party representing urban Hindu interests, had no difficulty in forming coalition governments with the Akali party, their political, religious, and other differences notwithstanding. But the moment a section of the Sikhs began purifying the Sikh religion of Hindu influences, and declared Sikhs to be a separate nationality, Hindus even of Punjab, not to speak of distantly situated ones, became willing to condone the worst atrocities against the Sikhs, even though culturally and ethnically the Sikhs are inseparable from the Punjabi Hindus. Similarly, militant Khalistanis felt no compunction about selectively killing Hindus in order to force them to move out of Punjab so that Punjab would become a Sikh state.

As long as the Sikh urge for identity came in the form of asserting regional identity with linguistic, economic, political dimensions included in it, it had the potential of uniting them with Punjabi Hindus. But once this urge seeks majoritarian assertion—that is, demand for a Sikh homeland, it became a recipe for ethnic cleansing. Similarly, Hindus harmed their own interests by disowning their regional, linguistic identity in their attempt to feel part of an all-India Hindu majority rather than accept the role of a substantial minority in Punjab working out concrete arrangements for power sharing with fellow Sikhs.

If the Sikhs, who have historically played the role of defenders of Hinduism and despite being a minority at an all-India level displayed the natural confidence and assertiveness typical of self-assured majorities, could begin to feel a persecuted minority and declare themselves as being inherently different from the Hindus, we need to understand that old historical ties and *bhaichara* can easily break down if new consensual compacts are not arrived at for power sharing within the framework of electoral democracy.

The logic of majoritarianism, of identifying a group by certain objective characteristics, and then claiming the right to drive them out of the area because they are a hated minority is inherently arbitrary. It can easily move its focus from group to group depending on the advantages the leaders of the majority perceive will come from such an act, balanced against the perceived risk of undertaking such a campaign. For instance, during the terrorist campaign in Punjab, absence of turban and beard became a marker for targeting Hindus even though these are recent symbols of Sikh identity. Similarly, during the massacre of Sikhs in 1984 in North India, anyone with a turban or beard became a target of murderous attack. The demand for Khalistan had come from a section of the Jat Sikh peasantry of Punjab but most of those killed in Delhi were non-Jat urban Sikhs, many of them lower castes such as Labhanas from areas other than Punjab. They had no interest in Punjab politics but got targeted simply because of some external markers and because they were vulnerable as a minority in Delhi. Thus majoritarianism has an inevitable tendency towards fascism and ethnic cleansing just as minoritarianism can lead to endless splits and secessions.

DEMAND FOR PLEBISCITE IN KASHMIR

The enormous bloodshed caused by the secessionist movement in Jammu and Kashmir provides yet another example of how deadly can be the logic of majoritarianism. The section of Kashmiri Muslims who have been fighting for secession to Pakistan base their claim on the premise that as a Muslim majority state Jammu and Kashmir should necessarily have become part of Pakistan. They call it 'the unfinished agenda of the Partition'. They joined the Pakistani rulers in using the rhetoric of democracy and 'people's right to self determination' as a stick to beat India with, even though Pakistan itself has never been serious about holding the plebiscite on the terms and conditions agreed upon in 1948.

The promised plebiscite was to be held in both Pakistan Occupied Kashmir (POK) as well as in the areas that voluntarily opted to be with the Indian Union. Interestingly, Pakistan studiously avoids talking of plebiscite in POK and has done its best to confine the issue of plebiscite only to the Kashmir Valley where the Muslims are a preponderant numerical majority. There is hardly ever a mention of plebiscite by Pakistani politicians in Jammu or Ladakh regions of Jammu and Kashmir where Hindus and Buddhists constitute numerical majorities in the respective regions.

An essential pre-condition set by the UN resolution for holding a plebiscite was that Pakistan should withdraw its army and armed civilian invaders from parts of Kashmir it had illegally occupied. However, total withdrawal of the Army from POK has always been seen as a high-risk game that the military establishment of Pakistan was never willing to play. This is not to deny that even Jawaharlal Nehru lost the nerve to honour his commitment to hold a plebiscite because another secession by Muslims would have emboldened the hitherto marginalized militant Hindu organizations to demand that the Partition be carried to its logical conclusion by driving all the Muslims out of India in much the same way that the Pakistanis carried out a near total ousting of Hindus and Sikhs in the newly created Islamic Republic. Thus both India and Pakistan, for their own different reasons, let the issue of plebiscite be buried for nearly three decades until a series of allegedly rigged elections in the state led to massive resentment in the Valley.

Nevertheless, even at the height of estrangement of Kashmiri Muslims from the Indian government, pro-Pakistani sentiment has remained confined to a minority, even in the Valley, while it is negligible among the Muslims of the Jammu and Ladakh regions. Even those among Kashmiri Muslims who are determinedly 'anti-India' demand *azadi* or independence for not only the Kashmir that once opted to be with India but also for POK. It is noteworthy that even when Kashmiri Muslims boycotted elections, alleging fraud and manipulation, the economically mobile segments of the people showed which side they align themselves with for their own economic self-interest. Those who needed guns went over to Pakistan. However, all those Kashmiri Muslims engaged in business shifted their base from Kashmir to cities in the heartland of India such as Delhi and Bombay. Thus they could be said to have voted with their feet. Their choice clearly demonstrated that they saw at least their economic interest better protected in the heartland of India than in Pakistan. And yet there is no denying that a large section of population are deeply estranged by the many acts of commission and omission of the Government of India and feel badly let down that the promise of plebiscite which would have respected their right to 'self determination' was never honoured.

When the average Kashmiri Muslim demands that the Kashmiri people be given the promised right to self-determination, he or she sees it primarily as a way to win *azadi* for Kashmir, rather than be forced to opt for either Pakistan or India. However, the terms set for a plebiscite in 1948 do not make this third choice available. As per that covenant, people can only opt for either India or Pakistan. At that time, if the Maharaja of Jammu and Kashmir had opted for Pakistan or India, they were likely to have passively gone along with him, as did people of other states. When Sheikh Abdullah made the tilt in favour of India, Kashmiri Muslims went along with him. Today, citizens insist on their sovereignty and want the right to decide Kashmir's future. They have become far more important as political players and stakeholders. Over the years

Kashmiris have opened up many new options. For example, the Simla Accord between Mrs Gandhi and Bhutto committed the two sides to treat Kashmir as a bilateral problem and move towards accepting the present Line of Control (LoC) as the international border. This was at that time widely welcomed by the people of Kashmir. The National Conference, which even in its battered condition won 28 out of 87 seats and got 29 per cent of the vote share and still commands the status of the single largest party in Jammu and Kashmir after the October 2002 election, has publicly committed itself to this position.

Similarly, there has been a consistent demand from a section of the Kashmiris for the last decade and a half that the border between POK and Jammu and Kashmir be made porous to allow for a natural process of social integration of the two Kashmirs, uniting divided families, de-escalating tension as necessary steps towards preparing for a plebiscite. All these new options being put on the agenda by the Kashmiri people themselves cannot be dismissed in favour of the old plebiscite formula, which becomes irrelevant because it was put in deep freeze and allowed to ossify, whereas the political situation at the ground level became more and more dynamic and open ended.

PLEBISCITE VS ELECTION AS AN INSTRUMENT OF PEOPLE'S WILL

Those who insist on a plebiscite as the definite way to determine the will of Kashmiri people forget that there is more than one democratic method, and some more democratic than a plebiscite, of ascertaining people's will. Election is one of them. The very fact that the people of Kashmir have enthusiastically participated in at least four elections after 1947 and disowned or boycotted only a few, shows that they did take elections as an instrument of self assertion seriously.

As Elie Kedourie in his discussion of plebiscites points out: 'There is really nothing conclusive about plebiscites except that a certain population subject to conflicting propaganda or pressures or inducements voted on a given day in one manner and not in another. The result, if accepted once and for all, has the same element of arbitrariness as any other, which may come about by reason of conquest or bargaining'.[12]

Kedourie also argues that: 'If plebiscites are justified by the same reason as elections, why should plebiscites not be held regularly like elections, and

---

[12]Kedourie, Elie, *Nationalism*, Oxford: Blackwell, 1993, p. 126.

why should a population not be able to change its allegiance periodically, as it is able to change its government?'[13]

To illustrate the point: if a plebiscite were held now not just in Indian-held Kashmir but in Pakistan-occupied Kashmir, as well as in other parts of India and Pakistan on the issue of Partition, the results might be very different from the political boundaries that emerged from the Partition of 1947.

We have yet to develop political systems, which provide for effective mechanisms for broad based participation of the people in decision-making without the use of a one-dimensional majority vote as the single decisive criterion in decision-making on particular issues. But at the same time we must recognize the limitations of the use of the principle of majority rule when its leaders disregard minority rights that must be clearly stated and carefully observed if we seek to create acceptable, just and stable polities. Too often political leaders identify their self-defined majority not as a temporary group that has decided to vote together on a particular issue, but rather as an unfettered and unchallengeable permanent rule maker for all.

In unstable societies with deep divisions and little agreement about basic principles there must be implicit or explicit agreement on what issues may be amenable to being decided by majority vote and what issues require limitations on the will of the majority and its representatives over certain basic human rights of the minorities. These need to be sorted out on some other basis than majority rule. For instance, voting on how much society should be spending on health, education or transportation should under ordinary circumstances be handled through the rule of the majority by voting. However, we should not entertain the possibility of a majority of any kind assuming the right to exterminate the minority groups, or to confine them to prisons or reserved areas, or to disenfranchise them, through the instrument of a majority vote.

A plebiscite is not the best instrument of democracy because the decision of a plebiscite is irreversible whereas in elections the voters can change their choice and verdict with every round of elections. Whether the Chief Minister of Jammu and Kashmir is from the National Conference or the Congress party does not have the same kind of bearing on people's lives, as the decision about whether Jammu and Kashmir becomes part of India or Pakistan. For example, many of those

---

[13]Kedourie, *Nationalism,* p. 126.

who voted for the National Conference in 1951 turned against it in subsequent elections. Likewise, many of those who boycotted the 1996 elections, at the call of secessionist leaders, snubbed the very same leaders in the 2002 elections by turning out to vote despite great risk to their lives. Elections involve less fundamental issues and allow people to respond to new options, choices and issues thrown up by a polity at different points of time. In some elections, the majority vote in the Jammu region went to the BJP, while at other times the Congress managed to win a majority vote in its favour. The victory of the BJP or Congress involves relatively small shifts in the state's politics because both the parties have to operate under the framework laid down by the Indian Constitution and Indian jurisprudence.

However, a vote in favour of Pakistan or *azadi* for Jammu and Kashmir drawn through a plebiscite means even those citizens who did not opt for either of those two choices have to end up living under a radically different dispensation—to be ruled the way that Pakistan is ruled. Therefore, a plebiscite must operate within a democratic framework that maintains strong and significant safeguards against the tyranny of the majority on the minority. It should, as far as possible, be carried out when tempers are not running high and when people are in a position to carefully weigh the pros and cons of their decision. A hallmark of democracy is how well it safeguards the rights of its minorities. Therefore, important safeguards must be built in and enforced before any plebiscite is held in Jammu and Kashmir keeping in view all the varied choices and options which different sections of Kashmiri opinion have articulated in varied ways—ranging from democratic politics to support for a certain kind of militancy and rejection of the imported variety.

Broadly speaking, even if we do not take account of the opinion and desires of the diverse communities that inhabit the state of Jammu and Kashmir and take into account only the inclinations of Kashmiri Muslims, there are currently three main streams of opinion among the Muslims of the Valley:

(1) A small fringe led by the likes of Geelani and leaders of the Hizbul Mujaheddin who would like to secede. (2) A somewhat larger section among Kashmiri Muslims who want *azadi* or independence from both India and Pakistan and reunification of the two divided parts of Kashmir. (3) The most substantial section of opinion is in favour of greater regional autonomy within the Indian Union. The followers of the People's Democratic Party (PDP), the National Conference, the

Congress party and a host of other national parties, like the Janata Dal and the Communist parties are in varying degrees supporters of greater devolution of powers and rejuvenation of democratic institutions in the state.

It is noteworthy that the percentage of those who opt for any one of these three choices is very fluid. Some of those who were strongly 'pro-India' through the 1950s and 1960s turned 'anti-India' during the 1980s and 1990s. Many of the secessionist leaders of today have fought and some even won elections to the Jammu and Kashmir assembly. Similarly, many who looked over the border for a saviour during the 1990s have been disillusioned and turned back to Indian democracy and several of them even took part in the October 2002 election. While a substantial number might vote for independence for Kashmir today because there are many who still feel estranged by repeated assaults on their citizenship rights, many more are likely to opt for greater autonomy within the Indian Union after the major breakthroughs made by Mufti Mohammad Sayeed's PDP in restoring people's faith in democracy by providing more responsive governance. The central government's recent peace initiatives and willingness to have a genuine dialogue with almost all estranged sections of Kashmiri opinion, including pro-Pakistani groups, have considerably reduced the support base of the secessionist leaders. This loss of appeal for secession is likely to grow, especially considering that pro-*azadi* leaders of Kashmir have never taken the trouble to spell out the exact contours and content of *azadi*. Moreover, the cataclysmic changes in the international scenario after the military invasions of Afghanistan and Iraq by America has also made Kashmiri Muslims realize that the politics of *jehadi* and separatist leaders is full of dangers since they counted over much on American and Pakistani support to achieve their political ends.

Azadi is no doubt a very powerful and emotive slogan but it has remained precisely that: a mere slogan. Whenever I have personally tried to engage even some of the Hurriyat leaders to spell out their political vision in a concrete way or asked them to explain what is it that they would do differently if they actually got *azadi*, I have been met either with silence or with evasive replies like: 'We will figure that out once we get *azadi*.'

This is very similar to how Jinnah kept building a frenzied movement in favour of Pakistan, without spelling out even in vague outline what it would actually entail (Ayesha Jalal, *The Sole Spokesman: Jinnah, the Muslim League, and the demand for Pakistan*, Cambridge

University Press, 1994). For example, under the *azadi* dispensation, what will be the fate of the Kashmiri Pandits who have been forced out of the Valley with many still living in the refugee camps of Jammu because life became too dangerous for them in Kashmir? What about the nearly 70 per cent Hindu and Sikh population of Jammu region who will not hear of secession from India or for that matter the Muslims among the Gujjars, Punjabis and other diverse ethnic communities of the Jammu region who do not share the aspirations of their coreligionists in the Valley? What about the right to self-determination of the 52 per cent Buddhists of Ladakh who have often demanded that their part of Jammu and Kashmir be made into a Union territory because they resent the domination of Kashmiri Muslims over the politics of the state? Many Ladakhi Muslims too would rather go along with their Buddhist counterparts rather than make common cause with Kashmiri Muslims. The Mufti Mohammad Sayeed government has been able to assuage the sentiments of Ladakh and Jammu regions by giving them an effective share in power. However, before PDP's 'healing touch' policy of bridging divides between the various estranged groups of Jammu and Kashmir began, the Ladakhis were as keen to break away from Srinagar as are the Hurriyat leaders to snap ties with India.

According to the 1981 census of Jammu and Kashmir (the religious and language statistics of 2001 are not yet available and there was no census in 1991), the population of Kashmir valley was 52 per cent of the total population of Jammu and Kashmir. Out of it 10 per cent people do not speak Kashmiri and 5 percent are non-Muslims. Though the Kashmiri speaking Muslims of the Valley are in many respects the most important single community of the state, they are overall a minority. In fact J&K is a classic land of minorities.

However, the pro-secessionist leadership has so far shown no sensitivity towards the rights and aspirations of all these regional groups and minorities. If theirs is indeed a movement of regional independence, why then are non-Kashmiri Muslims and non-Muslim Kashmiris not being included in their vision of an independent Kashmir? The people of both these regions have felt as aggrieved against the domination of Srinagar in the state's polity as does Srinagar against New Delhi and have by and large stayed aloof from the secessionist movement.

Just as a plebiscite that only offers two choices to the people of Jammu and Kashmir—join India or join Pakistan—is altogether meaningless in a context where an overwhelming majority of those seeking self-determination want the third option of *azadi*, so also a plebiscite which ignores the security concerns and political aspirations of a very substantial proportion of people of the state simply because they are at a numerical disadvantage, is a mockery of the very concept of self-determination. Therefore, today's situation demands re-framing the terms of a plebiscite or referendum to make it meet the essential requirements of democracy by giving the minorities an important voice in the decision because it affects each person's very survival.

The civilized world cannot allow repetition of the murderous solution of 1947. The Partition of the subcontinent in 1947 proved to be a political disaster, not just because it divided people on the basis of religion, but because it also forced through terror and violence millions of panic-stricken people to abandon their homes and hearths, neighbourhoods and all they owned. Pakistan came into existence via mass murder and ethnic cleansing.

If we accept the logic that, within the territory of each arbitrarily carved out nation-state, every ethnic majority of its region is entitled to unlimited rights to subjugate, eliminate or push out a minority, we will be pushed to tragedy after tragedy of ethnic cleansing, murderous riots, and political chaos.

New Plebiscite Deal

Despite the principled reservations regarding the jurisdiction and value of plebiscites, I would still argue that the only way for India to get out of the current stalemate on this issue is to actively work towards a carefully redefined plebiscite on the following lines: The New Plebiscite Deal should require the winning of at least a two-third majority rather than a simple majority vote, as is required in ordinary elections, since a plebiscite involves a permanent and momentous decision with serious consequences for every single person living in that State.

In order to settle the issue once and for all, we should demand that both India and Pakistan prepare for a genuine three-phase referendum. However, a first necessary step would be to initiate serious discussion, public debate, and participative consultations regarding what range of choices should become available to the people through a referendum. The exercise should be concluded within a specified time frame, of about two years.

The unit for plebiscite would have to consist of the entire state of Jammu and Kashmir (including Jammu and Ladakh) that is presently within the Indian Union as well all of the POK. It is likely that at least the following four options would emerge out of the two-year process of public hearings and dialogue:

1. *Azadi* or Independence from both Pakistan and India for the entire and unified state of Jammu and Kashmir.
2. Secession of Indian Kashmir to Pakistan.
3. Secession of POK to India with that region joining the existing territory of Jammu and Kashmir as part of the Indian Union.
4. Both India and Pakistan agreeing to accept the existing LOC as the permanent international border between the two countries.

A likely scenario is that even if a referendum were to be held tomorrow around these four choices, a substantial number of Kashmiri Muslims would opt for *azadi* even if they were not clear about the exact implications and content of this choice. An equal number are likely to vote in favour of India. However, no more than 5 to 10 per cent would vote for Pakistan as their first choice. But if a referendum is held in the Valley about a decade from now, after two or three successful free and fair elections and meaningful devolution of powers to the state, the proportion of those opting in favour of India would shoot up and those in favour of *azadi* or secession from India will go down, while Pakistan is not likely to improve its tally. Thus, Pakistan is likely to lose its claim to Kashmir in the first round itself. However, if the Indian government fails to deliver genuine autonomy and continues with its ham-handed ways, it could lose whatever little moral and political legitimacy it has today for resisting secession.

In the second phase, the international community should offer to the Kashmiri leaders who stand for an independent Kashmir that they will facilitate Jammu and Kashmir's secession from India under the following conditions:

1. The decision for secession be endorsed by a two-third vote of the Muslim population of the State and at least 51 per cent vote among the Hindus and Buddhists of Jammu and Kashmir.
2. The rest of those who are not yet won over to the cause of secession will need to be given concrete assurance through the UN that their rights as a dissenting minority will be firmly protected and an effective formula for power sharing with minorities will be evolved under the new dispensation of '*Azad* Kashmir'.
3. The UN would retain the right to intervene in case the guarantees given to minority communities are not honoured. Thus, an

independent Kashmir, if it ever came into existence would have to agree to limited and conditional sovereignty vis-à-vis the UN with regard to the rights of minorities and institutionalizing democracy. This would include a provision that if the UN monitors find that the promises made at the time of *azadi* have not been respected the UN would have the right to enforce a new democratic mandate in the state. The Kashmiri Muslims are not likely to have problems with the enhanced role of the UN because they have been vociferously demanding the active involvement of the UN in the affairs of Kashmir.

Other necessary steps involved in the plebiscite would be as follows:

(1) India and Pakistan would withdraw their respective armies from both sides of Kashmir for five years at the end of which a plebiscite would be held under UN auspices.

(2) Both sides should allow free access of people across the LoC during the plebiscite campaigning, including the right to campaign and propagate their view point through television, cinema and other media, provided no hate speech or violence is used in the process.

Minus the above mentioned safeguards, it is likely that a Muslim-dominated independent Kashmir might simply exterminate or drive out the non-Muslim population of the Jammu and Kashmir State as happened in Pakistan where the few thousand surviving Hindus, Sikhs, and Christians live under terror facing brutal forms of discrimination in every walk of life. Therefore, pre-emptive measures are needed right at the start of the plebiscite process to place firm limits on what the winners of the plebiscite can do and not do in the area of human, democratic, and citizenship rights. The international community is not likely to object to these safeguards for minorities since a key litmus test of a democracy is what institutional mechanisms exist for the protection of the interests of minorities. These arrangements proposed for Kashmir would set a healthy new precedent for working out democratic solutions for minority–majority relations and an effective formula for power sharing which might well become a model for many other countries where ethnic minorities find themselves trapped in similar vulnerabilities.

ADVANTAGES AND LIMITS OF MAJORITY RULE

All this is not to deny that there are many advantages to the rule of the majority principle in votes on many issues in clearly defined political structures. We have yet to develop political systems which provide for broad-based participation of the people in decision-making without the use of majority vote in decision-making on many issues.

But at the same time we must recognize the limitations of the use of the principle of majority rule when its leaders neglect to consider the ground rules that must be clarified and observed in order to move towards the creation of a better ordered, more humane and stable polity. Too often these leaders identify their majority not as a temporary group that has decided to vote together on a particular issue, but rather as a majority with unlimited rights on the territory of the nation-state. Such leaders try to get their majority group to delude themselves into believing that a people who share certain 'objective' characteristics must have identical views on all important political issues.

In multi-ethnic societies there must be implicit and explicit agreement on issues that will only be decided through broad-based consensus rather than majority vote and what issues can be determined through the ballot with the majority carrying the day. For instance, it is fine to allow a political party which secures a majority vote to form the government because governments can be changed every five years. But any change in the country's Constitution which defines the rights of various groups cannot be done through a simple majority vote. Similarly, a majority decision to disenfranchise a portion of the population or confine it to reserved ghettos should be out of order. The minorities in such a case need to have an important voice in the decision if democracy is to be meaningful because it affects their very survival.

The only effective way to counter the majoritarian and minoritarian tendencies to go out of hand is to pre-empt the emergence of monolithic identities involving deadly 'purifying and cleansing' campaigns by various communities. For instance, it is only when political leaders try to insist that all Hindus or all Muslims have an identical set of interests—no matter whether they are from Kerala or Maharashtra, whether peasants or artisans, Urdu-speaking or Tamil-speaking, rich or poor, Sunni or Shia, Qureshis or Ansaris, lower caste or higher caste—that they can be pitched against each other as permanently hostile monoliths. But as long as Muslim and Hindu peasants can come together to safeguard their interests as farmers, come together as Gujaratis or Kashmiris to assert their linguistic or regional identity or acknowledge bonds of commonality on account of their being from the same village or neighbourhood, they cannot easily be pitched against each other as hostile warring groups on an all-

India basis by letting their religious identity overwhelm all other identities.

WORKABLE POWER SHARING ARRANGEMENTS

The simmering conflicts between the Hindus and Muslims are essentially due to our failure to work out decent workable norms for power sharing between the majority and minorities. All over the world, majorities tend to turn tyrannical in the absence of decent procedures for resolving conflicts. So far we have relied only on pious sermons on communal harmony, on appealing to their common heritage and bonds, on the oneness of all religions and the virtue of religious tolerance. The Hindu–Muslim *bhai-bhai* approach has long outlived its utility not only because the modern economy and politics has in basic ways destroyed the old *bhaichara* bonds, but also because modern states demand a new kind of pact. A workable pact would be one in which, no matter which party comes to power, the basic ground rules remain the same and are implemented with a measure of integrity on both sides.

For example, in Malaysia, after going through prolonged instability and riots against the Chinese minority, the majority Muslim leadership has worked out a deal with the Chinese minority, including their prosperous business leaders, whereby the Chinese are allowed to do business and provided security from violence or confiscation of property; in return the Chinese keep away from involvement with Malaysian power politics, including the distribution of government largesse and offices. This compact may not put citizenship rights of the two communities at par but has major advantages for averting ethnic pogroms as long as the terms are mutually acceptable and lead to a more stable society.

Similarly, as long as the dominant Christian group and the various Muslim and other groups in Lebanon worked according to the norms established in their pre-World War II political pact about power sharing in the offices of the State, Lebanon was a thriving city with a world class economy. However, it exploded into unimaginable violence as soon as the deal broke down due to the perception among Muslim groups that they had through population growth become a majority, though they were formerly a minority within Lebanon.

In India we do not need to have such unfair pacts between different communities because of some inherent advantages of our society. Given

India's heterogeneity, it is actually a country of numerous minorities and not exactly a Hindu majority country as some politicians would like us to believe. For example, Hindus are a minority in Jammu and Kashmir, Punjab, Mizoram and Nagaland. Muslims are a minority everywhere but in Kashmir. The Sikhs are a minority everywhere but in Punjab. The Christians are a tiny minority everywhere but in Nagaland, Mizoram, and Meghalaya. The list does not stop there. Yadavs as a caste may be a majority in certain rural pockets of Uttar Pradesh and Bihar, but an overall minority in the state. Jat Sikhs may be a majority in Punjab villages but are a minority in most Punjab cities, and if Mazhabi Sikhs and other non-Jat Sikhs of Punjab were added to the non-Jat figures, Jat Sikhs would be a minority even within Punjab. Kannadigas living in Tamil Nadu, Gujaratis in Maharashtra, and Marwaris in Calcutta are minorities outside their own states.

If India has escaped going the way of Hitler's Germany or becoming another Yugoslavia, even though some politicians are trying hard to take that route, it is because India's heterogeneity makes it far more difficult for Hitlerian attempts to unify all the people at the same time for a murderous purpose. Our rich civilization's diversity is our best guarantee against a tyrannical dictatorship. If we allow politicians to destroy it, it would amount to destroying the very soul of India. Excessive homogenization of meaningful group identities in favour of an all-powerful national state requiring sacrifices from all and benefits only to a small elite will inevitably promote more civil strife, as has happened in the erstwhile communist bloc. Chanting the *mantra* of national unity will have no effect if the nation-state is viewed as incapable of providing security of life for diverse groups and citizens.

Given that most communities in India are a minority in some places but a majority elsewhere, it is in everyone's interest to work out some agreements; not to do so is in no one's interest. This essentially means defining workable principles for power sharing that apply to every group consistently in areas where a mechanical use of majority rule would make minorities feel marginalized or endangered—be it the Hindu minority in Kashmir or Punjab, the Muslims in Uttar Pradesh, the Christians in Kerala or the Brahmins in Tamil Nadu.

However, a precondition for such a strategy to work is that people feel safe from physical and other attacks affecting their survival and the government machinery actually works to ensure physical safety and security on an equal basis to all citizens and, more important, does not get used by one community as a weapon against the others. People should not feel their only recourse for attaining personal security of life, limb and property is to join in their community's gangs or to seek protection of shady politicions and muffia dons.

Unless we succeed in making the law and order machinery behave lawfully so that individuals do not have to gang up as groups and groups do not have to seek the protection of mafias, we will continue to have more and more violence, on one pretent or another.[14]

---

[14]Note: This essay was written in mid-1997 before the BJP came to power and began to distance itself from some of the core issues of the Sangh Parivar ideology. While the main substance of the essay remains the same, I revised the essay before publication of this book and included changes at appropriate points to indicate the change in BJP politics on the issue of minority rights.

14

An Agenda for India*

The Speech We Deserved to Hear on August 15

The 50th year of India's Independence was celebrated through a host of sarkari functions presided over by netas who harangued us with pious platitudes about our supposed great achievement and the tasks before the nation. However, there has been very little sign of celebration and rejoicing among the people—rich or poor, urban or rural, young or old, male or female. There was a general consensus that we were in a deep mess primarily due to the doings and misdoings of our political leaders, policy-makers and bureaucrats. The continuing widespread poverty in India and the increasing criminalization of our economy and polity has demoralized the Indian people. We are all let down beyond words.

Our political leaders don't offer us anything more than knee jerk reactions. The historic speech delivered on the 50th anniversary of our Independence made a mockery of the ruling party's resolve to fight the all pervasive corruption in public life by announcing the setting up of a special anti-corruption cell in the Prime Minister's Office in typical imperial style as though something that has gotten into the very fabric of governmental functioning can be dealt with in one special cell. Not surprisingly the year's Independence Day speech did not evoke much enthusiasm or hope. It was filled with the usual platitudes and naïve policy announcements like banning the already banned sex determination tests, launching ambitious sounding but unimplementable schemes for the welfare of the girl child, and so on as proof of commitment to improving the life of ordinary citizens.

---

*First published in *Manushi*, Issue No. 101, July–August 1997.

What kind of speech would I have liked to hear on that historic day? What kind of an agenda of reform would make sense in today's context? Though no prime minister is ever likely to ask me to be his ghost speech writer, I did the exercise anyway to delineate and clarify for myself some of the most urgent tasks our political leadership would have to undertake and commitments they would have to make in order to bring about responsible governance and help restore the health of our society.

'My fellow countrymen and women. This is the 50th anniversary of India's Independence and yet we have very little to celebrate and a lot to feel ashamed about. I would be failing in my task if I gave you a pious hypocritical speech about our supposed great achievements in these five decades of Independence. Anyone who holds an important public office has no right to lie to the people, to deliberately misinform them about the state of affairs.

No amount of sophistry, ideological rhetoric or jingoism can help us hide the fact that we have made this country a living hell on earth for the vast majority of our people. Millions of children continue to die every year of malnutrition and easily preventable diseases. Our track record in the health sector is abysmal. We have not been able to provide functioning primary health centres in our villages. The few hospitals that exist in urban areas may be spreading more disease than helping to cure people. We have one of the highest female mortality rates in the world, pointing to the abysmally low status of women. We have destroyed people's ability to fend for themselves and made the procurement of even basic survival needs—water, food, and fuel—a grim struggle.

The majority of our people are still illiterate. Barring a tiny elite which receives expensive education in exclusive schools, the quality of education *sarkari* schools provide is so poor as to render the whole exercise a tragic waste. Millions of children never reach a school and, of those who do, a large percentage have the good sense to reject the farce that goes by the name of *sarkari* education.

The income gap between rural and urban areas has widened rapidly after Independence, pointing to neglect and stepmotherly treatment of the farm sector. The continuing stranglehold of the licence-permit *raj* despite the rhetoric of liberalization has crippled our economy and made our industrial class inefficient and corrupt.

I say all this not with a view to demoralize us all further but to tell you that we cannot afford to let things continue like this. We, the political leaders, have created a gigantic mess and failed the people of India by following suicidal policies.

The rot starts from the top and, therefore, has to be stemmed from the very top. It is with this realization that I would like to make some solemn commitments to you on this day and plead for your cooperation in helping me honour these promises.

As a person holding the highest office in the land, I promise you that I will never wilfully lie to you. I will try my best to ensure that telling the truth becomes the rule in this government. You help your leaders become corrupt by putting very low demands on them—you have come to expect them to lie and cheat routinely. You get upset only when their falsehoods get totally out of control. You have to stop being so generous and must stop making such allowances for those in positions of power and influence. If a person occupying a public office knowingly misinforms and misleads the people, such a person should be considered unfit for that position. Let us not think that truth-telling ought to be reserved for Mahatmas. It ought to be the first qualification for a person holding public office. As an ordinary citizen, I can be forgiven such failings, but not so when I am given an office of trust on behalf of millions of people.

THINGS WE SHOULD BE ASHAMED OF

The Human Development Report on South Asia (1997) tells us we have much to be ashamed of. Between 1998 and 1992 India was ranked first in arms imports but 147th in per capita income; 44 per cent of India's total population lives in absolute poverty today. Fifty-three per cent of children (60 million) under age four are underweight and undernourished; nearly one-third of the world's poor live in India, in mega cities 57 per cent of the population lives in slums; nearly one-third of India's children under 16 are forced into child labour; 88 per cent of all pregnant women between ages 15–49 are anaemic and malnourished; 291 million adults are still illiterate; every year there are 2.2 million infant deaths in India; 640 million people have to do without basic sanitation.

While taking office, I felt very distressed at having to take the oath routinely given to ministers whereby we all swear not to disclose official information. That, in my view, reflects mistrust of the people and a typically colonial mentality. A democracy cannot function effectively without citizens having the right to honest and accurate information.

My first task as prime minister will be to introduce a law to replace the pernicious Official Secrets Act with a Duty to Provide Accurate Information Act which will lay down detailed guidelines regarding how information at the disposal of official agencies has to be routinely shared with citizens.[1]

I cannot imagine any department of the government which benefits either itself or the interests of the nation by keeping its affairs secret. That includes the holiest of the holy cows—the Defence Ministry. Defence preparedness needs to be a secret affair only for those countries which have designs on others. But India, committed as it is to a policy of peaceful existence with our neighbours, need not hide from them the level of preparedness we are maintaining purely for self-defence. Excessive secrecy in our defence affairs has allowed for widespread corruption, inefficiency, and incompetence even in our armed forces, with kickbacks and commissions becoming the determining factor for all defence purchases and deals. These arrangements should be as open and transparent as the affairs of the local corporation ought to be—but are not.

The new law will provide that any official found to be providing wrong information to the public would automatically be suspended from his job and face an enquiry. The burden of proof will lie with the official and, if found guilty, he/she will be disqualified from further government service.

I am convinced that once the veil of secrecy is lifted, much of the corruption and incompetence that has come to be the hallmark of government functioning will start to disappear.

The root cause of our problem is that the system of governance we are saddled with was devised by our erstwhile colonial rulers for running an exploitative, tyrannical empire. It is totally unsuited for running a democracy. But we have so far lacked the courage to change the rules and rationale of governance through radical institutional reform. We are still governed by antiquated laws the British left behind giving vast arbitrary powers to those who hold government office.

The people of this country have continued to be treated like colonial subjects even after we got political independence. Those in power, those

---

[1]The Right to Information Act was passed by Parliament in 2002 but it gives very little clout to citizens, has exempted too many categories of information and provides no effective punitive measures against those who withhold or give misleading information.

manning the government machinery—from the minister to his *chaprasi*—continue to trample upon people's self-respect, make them grovel as though before a feudal lord. This has destroyed the collective self-confidence of Indians as a people. This relationship has to change if India is to make progress. The nuisance value of the government has to be reduced by effective controls exercised by the people over government functionaries. I mean it not just as an empty slogan—the likes of which we have heard enough—but as the guiding philosophy of a well worked-out programme for institutional reform.

Much of the mess in this country is due to overcentralization of power. The Prime Minister's Office and various ministries ought not to be allowed to function like imperial *durbars*. I vow to systematically dismantle the many vicious controls that the central government exercises as well as those that in turn allow the state governments to function in the same imperial tradition. For that purpose, my party and government stand committed to abolishing some of the imperial, all-powerful elitist services like the IAS whose bureaucratic stranglehold is responsible for most of the mess in this country. As the key instruments of centralized power and decision-making, they have imposed disastrous policies on the nation. They have too much power, but very poor skills and expertise to handle the enormous power they wield and almost no accountability. Consequently, too many of them have converted their offices into extortion centres. Without their cooperation even ministers or MPs cannot get away with corruption and shady deals. The thievery and mismanagement at the top makes it impossible to impose any discipline and accountability at lower levels. Therefore, we will begin by getting rid of all those services which have become a dead weight for the entire society.

Apart from altogether abolishing certain services, we commit ourselves to cutting down the size of the bureaucracy to one-tenth the present level within our first three years in office. Government jobs and promotions will be performance-related—not allowed to be treated as a lifelong licence to loot the public.

I also reaffirm our commitment to abolishing the four-tier services at all levels of our government which are more vicious than the much-reviled *chaturvarna* system. There will only be one entry point for all the services—only one class of government employees. The army of peons, clerks, and section heads provided to every official will be abolished through new legislation ready to be introduced before the Parliament in this session. It is time our officers learn to carry their own files, type their own letters, answer their own phone calls, drive their own cars. That would be the first lesson in teaching them to work efficiently.

The police reform will follow a similar pattern. There will be only one entry point into the service and every officer shall be expected to do field duty. We will aim to recruit the most talented and well-educated young people into the police force who will be trained in the most sophisticated methods of crime control so that they do not resort to torture and other crude methods to enforce law and order. The police force will be reorganized so that the power to hire and fire officers shall rest with the elected representatives of each community or neighbourhood that the thana is supposed to serve. This will help curb the vast arbitrary powers that the police have accumulated. The same principle will be applied to all government departments which are meant to provide public services.

Disciplining government employees and making them behave lawfully is a vital priority task before the administration. Today the proportion of crooks in our society is highest in and around government offices. The government has become the prime instrument for spreading crime in our society. This has to change if we want to move out of the political and economic mess we find our country in.

It is a sign of a corrupt polity and a stagnant economy that competition over seemingly low paying government jobs has become a do or die matter for so many of our poorly trained young men. Today, government jobs provide the safest avenue for getting rich without doing any work or possessing any worthwhile skills. That has to change. In order to encourage people's economic initiative, we will work hard to systematically remove all the needless statist controls that have made it impossible for citizens to earn an honest living without grovelling and obtaining the permission of the sarkar though bribes. This culture has wrecked our economy. A thorough dismantling of needless controls will encourage entrepreneurial skills and open up many new avenues of employment. It is time we ended farces such as the Jawahar Rozgar Yojna, which pretend to throw a few crumbs to an insignificantly small number of people while actually providing opportunities to our *netas* and *babus* to siphon off vast amounts of our scarce public funds.

Even the agenda of economic reforms has been reduced to a joke by limiting public discussion of economic reforms primarily to issues such as the entry of foreign capital and MNCs, and to dismantling some controls that impinge on the topmost economic players in our country.

It is important to remember that less than 10 per cent of the people earn their living from jobs in the government or the organized sector of the economy. More than 90 per cent are dependent on agriculture, or are self-employed in a range of occupations or work in the unorganized sector of our economy. It is time we asked what the economic reforms have to offer the ordinary citizens of the country apart from viewing them as hungry consumers of new brand products.

My government's agenda for economic reforms will focus on the hitherto neglected farm sector, for agriculture provides a livelihood to about 70 per cent of our population. We have squeezed our farmers through vicious interventionism designed to keep the prices of farm products far lower than the urban industrial goods. In the last few decades we have allowed the gap between rural and urban incomes to widen manifold which has encouraged the flight of capital and skills from rural areas. In addition we have followed policies that prevented the emergence of agro-based rural industries.

These, in my view, are the prime causes for India's grinding poverty. Our farmers and others dependent on the agricultural economy need no subsidies, no 'development programmes', no *rozgar yojnas*. All they need is that this corrupt, bloated, and obstructionist government machinery get off their backs! The government will no longer compel the farmers to sell their produce at arbitrarily fixed *sarkari* prices. We will remove all zonal restrictions on trade of farm produce, encourage agricultural exports and undertake massive investments in providing infrastructure in rural areas—electricity, water, irrigation, good roads, and telecom linkages for every village. We will do this work literally on a war footing and employ India's large standing army for this purpose so that this task can be achieved within the next five years.

I am confident that freeing the farm sector from the *sarkari* clutches will unleash unprecedented economic initiative in our own villages and we will need no foreign aid or food imports to bring down prices. In fact, our farmers have demonstrated their ability to compete successfully in the international market despite the government's obstructionist policies. By encouraging the farmers to enhance their incomes through exports, we will also be giving a major boost to production. In addition, the government will remove all the restrictions on agro-based industries so that new avenues of employment are created in rural areas by the people's own investment and initiative. India can move out of the poverty trap only when its villages become prosperous.

We boast that we are a nuclear power and have all kinds of deadly missiles for national defence. At the same time we have to admit that we have failed to defend our people against ill-health and the deadly curse of illiteracy in today's world. A country is primarily its people. If millions of Indians are illiterate, malnourished, sick and dying of easily preventable diseases, of what use are big armies and weaponry standing at the border?

To honour my government's commitment to making basic public health and primary education the highest priorities for our country, we commit to spending on these two areas double the amount we at present spend on our armed forces. We will aim for high-quality schools with enthusiastic, well-paid, conscientious teachers, and the best possible primary health centres for every single village in the country. However, these institutions will no longer be controlled by distant bureaucrats sitting in Delhi and the state capitals but by local *panchayats* who will evaluate how well the schools and health care centres function in achieving basic education and good public health; these *panchayats* will have the power to hire and fire those who do not perform well.

Decent health care is impossible if people don't have clean and adequate water for drinking and other basic needs. This has to become available in every home within the next few years, or else the government has no right to exist.

I am convinced that we cannot improve the quality of our education without doing away with the use of English for elite education and the use of regional languages for the rest. This has created a vast unbridgeable communication gap between the English-educated and the rest of society. The former can talk to and understand people in New York far better than they understand their own non-English-speaking grandmothers. The educated elites in a functioning society are supposed to provide intellectual leadership to their people. In our case, the colonial intelligentsia we are producing through English education is incapable of identifying with the aspirations of their own people. Instead, it aspires to simply mimic the lifestyles and value system of the western elites, fantasizing it can transform New Delhi into a New York for the powerful few. This dependence on the English language has crippled us intellectually and enslaved us emotionally and mentally.

We will continue to study and use the English language for communicating with foreigners, but it ought not to be the language of administration and business within the country; it ought not to invade our private lives or become the language of nursery rhymes and even be used for communicating with our pets!

People alienated from their mother tongue, their own language, cannot escape being culturally and emotionally uprooted. Through the dominance of English the collective wisdom of centuries is being lost to us and has become an important reason for our lack of self-confidence and self-respect as a people. It has taught us to view ourselves, our failings and strengths through the eyes of others who make us feel inferior, and has given us a sense of inadequacy. A people lacking in self-respect not only turn to self-hatred but also become self-destructive. That has been the all-pervasive mood for too long. I feel sad to see us grumble, criticize, complain endlessly—but without showing any initiative for collective determined action.

We can develop the confidence that we can solve these problems, no matter how overwhelming they appear today, only if we learn to act purposefully, devise institutions that function, promote team work, follow sensible, well-established norms, and learn to evaluate government performance not by its pompous claims and populist slogans but by actual results. We have wasted too much time already. We cannot afford to waste a minute more.

There is so much that needs doing in this country to make it a place where people can live peacefully in dignity and without being haunted by hunger and ill-health. However, at the same time, a sensible government ought to know the limits of its power and responsibilities. It has no business to be running hotels, airlines, steel factories or even telecom services. Useless government and public sector undertakings have become parasites sucking out the vitality of the rest of the economy. Our government will no longer allow basic industries and essential services to be kept in the government clutches and rationed out just to provide patronage for our *netas* and *naukris* for a few lakh employees. The affected working people will be provided adequate compensation so that they can employ themselves productively.

The government's primary job ought to be to ensure law and order, give people a sense of security that their human rights and citizenship cannot be trampled upon with impunity, and provide an honest, non-partisan and effective legal and judicial machinery. This is the most basic requirement of a well-functioning democracy.

We need to get rid of the vast plethora of cumbersome and useless legislations and establish very few meaningful and effective laws which allow people to live in security and carry on economic and social activities without fear. The law courts will be rehauled thoroughly. They will not function in a language foreign to most people and laws will be written in simple language. Cases will have to be argued in the language understood by the litigant. The use of English will be replaced by regional languages so that hiring trained lawyers is not a necessity for fighting one's own case. We are legislating a fixed time frame for disposal of cases. Judges will be called to account if they fail to deliver judgements within a maximum of 11 months of a case being admitted in court. In addition, the new law provides for heavy fines to be imposed on whichever of the litigants causes needless delays by seeking frivolous adjournments. Lying on oath will be treated as a serious offence in order to curb the practice of pressing false claims and trumped-up charges. The present overload on the courts will be lightened by creating *nyaya panchayats* with juridical powers in every village. The next layer of courts will be provided at the block level so as to make the judicial system more accessible, efficient, and inexpensive.

One of our greatest strengths as a society is its great diversity. Our people had over the centuries evolved very humane and sophisticated norms for living together peacefully. Pre-British India had no history of communal riots and killings. Where else in the world do you see religious shrines where people of different faiths, Hindus, Sikhs, Muslims, Christians, Buddhists join together at numerous places for common worship and even celebrate each other's religious festivals?

However, the colonial legacy of divide and rule which led to the disastrous Partition of 1947 was further perfected in post-Independence India by unscrupulous politicians who made instigation of ethnic conflict into a lucrative electoral business. The legacy of the Partition in which millions were massacred and many more millions uprooted from their homes and made refugees in their own land still haunts us because we failed to learn the right lessons from that holocaust.

The periodic eruptions of inter-community riots and massacres in post-Independence India are a matter of great shame for us as a society. Today, on this 50th anniversary of that suicidal Partition, we must resolve never to let such divisive politics succeed in this country again. I give you my sincere promise that our government will do its best to ensure that the law and order machinery functions in a non-partisan way, that the police do not join in carrying out massacres and loot, that those who commit such crimes against society are speedily brought to trial and punished. I am convinced that if the state machinery refuses to provide support and protection to such murderers, our politicians will not dare to instigate people into organizing riots and pogroms.

However, the real test of our democracy is to work out decent, workable norms for majority–minority relations and give the minorities a sense of security and a real stake in the system. This is an easy task because it will in reality benefit every community equally. Given India's heterogeneity, every community is a minority in some place or situation and a majority elsewhere. For example, the Hindus are a minority in Kashmir, Ladakh, Punjab, and Nagaland. The Muslims are a minority in every other state but not in Kashmir. The Sikhs are a majority in Punjab but a minority everywhere else. The Christians are a minority in every region but not in Nagaland, Mizoram, and Meghalaya. Caste and linguistic groups are also complexly interspersed.

Therefore, evolving decent, workable norms for power sharing and safeguards for minorities is in everyone's interest—be it the Hindu minority in Kashmir or the Muslim minority in Madhya Pradesh. So far we have been content with making gimmicky gestures to appease minorities, such as declaring Prophet Mohammad's birthday as a public holiday or giving endless coverage to various religious festivals on Doordarshan. Chanting mindless *mantras* of national unity cannot dissolve hostilities. Giving every community secure citizenship rights, equality of opportunity, a share in power, as well as enforcing lawful non-partisan behaviour by the government machinery alone can create the basis for bringing together India's diverse communities into a vibrant democracy.

In recent years, much controversy and passion has come to centre around the Women's Reservation Bill to secure one-third of seats for women in Parliament and in state legislatures. The pro-reservationists see this measure as the most necessary step for women's empowerment.

My party instead proposes a 100 per cent reservation for women at the *gram panchayat* level and 50 per cent at the *zila parishad* level with no reservation in Parliament or state legislatures. If women learn to take complete charge of public affairs at the village level without the over-bearing and corrupting presence of men, they have a better chance of evolving a better, cleaner political culture than when they come into politics as junior partners.

This massive non-controlled participation of women at the village and district level will provide a rich training ground for them so that they will need no reservations at the upper levels. It is the exclusion of women from politics at the village and community level that leads to their marginalization at the top. Therefore, my party proposes a thorough overhaul from the bottom-up.

However, women can become effective participants in the political process only if we decriminalize our polity and our political parties provide a conducive atmosphere for women's involvement. Our party has committed itself to reserving 50 per cent of all posts for women of all levels within the party. We will also ensure that 50 per cent of those contesting on our party tickets are women and also screen membership of the party to make certain that anti-social elements don't get a foothold in it.

However, the selection for both men and women candidates will be done through primary elections at the local level. The party bosses will not have the right to arbitrarily bestow tickets for elections on their favoured ones. Without practising genuine democracy within our own party, we cannot hope to provide democratic governance.

As we promised in our manifesto, I and my ministerial colleagues, as well as our party's MPs, will follow clear, simple, open and appropriate criteria in making government appointments; we will remove the excessive discretionary powers previous governments have used to unfairly allocate benefits like sundry quotas, permits, licences, and land grants which encourage ever greater corruption. Instead, we will concentrate on making policy, and ensure it is honestly and efficiently implemented.

We also intend to surrender all special perks; we are going to legislate decent salaries for the much smaller government that will be required after we cut down the over bloated bureaucracy. There will no longer be any need thereafter for free housing for government officials, MPs, MLAs, and ministers. We will expect all government officials, ministers, MPs to take care of all their needs out of their salaries just as we expect ordinary citizens to do—no more government cars, no special quotas in trains, planes, no free telephones, or subsidized land through VIP housing societies.

Each one of us has already released a detailed list of our personal assets to the press and will continue doing so every year. Along with it, we give you this solemn assurance—if any one of us is found to lie about his/her assets or is found trying to acquire additional assets through fraudulent means, the party constitution provides for immediate suspension from membership of that person and for dismissal from office if the person is found guilty after an expeditious enquiry. Our party will provide a full public account of party funds and expenditures. We have made it a policy that even the smallest contributions to our party fund have to be duly receipted. Any contribution above Rs 500 will be accepted only via cheque—all contributions will be public information, and will only be accepted if all the criteria of our new Political Contributions Act are complied with in full.

I know we have no magic wand with which to transform our country overnight into a place we can be proud to live in. But as I promised at the outset, we will not resort to misleading lies nor to jingoistic rhetoric to cover up for our failures and misdeeds.

I appeal to you to watch our conduct vigilantly, subject our actions to thorough scrutiny and keep us on a tight rein. I want us as a people to aspire high, to show the world that governments do not have to be crowded with crooks, that public life and politics do not have to be so vulnerable to power hungry maniacs. We are capable of building a system of incentives that reward honesty and do not persecute those who want to live decent, honest lives.

You may well say that all this is too romantic, too impractical. I am aware that the tasks we have are not easy to achieve. We may not succeed in doing much good as we hope to, but I assure you of one thing: we will as a team try to ensure at the minimum that we refrain from causing further harm to this wronged country and its people. *Jai-Jan, Jai Hind*.'